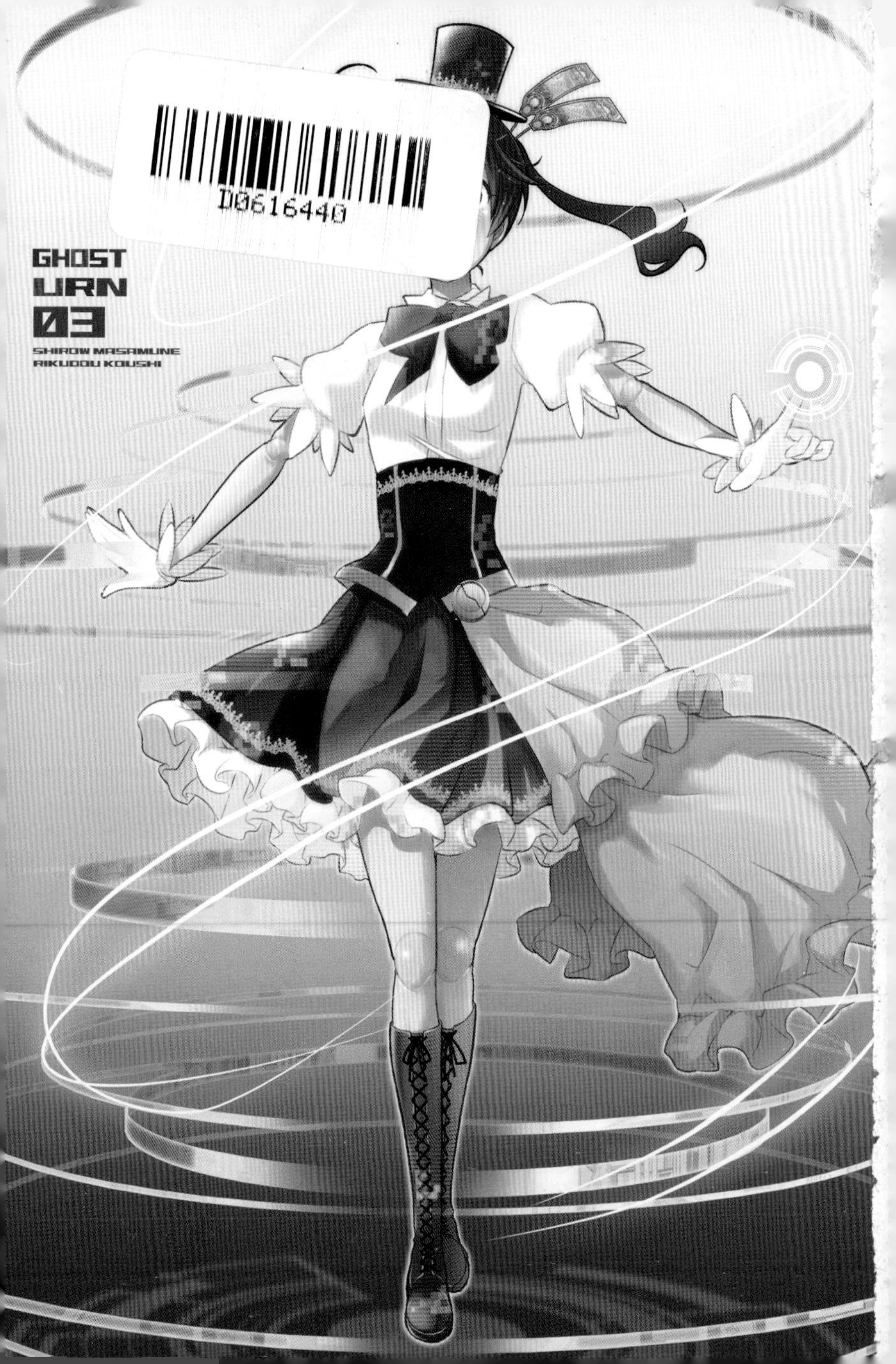
GHOST
URN
03
SHIROW MASAMUNE
RIKUDOU KOUSHI

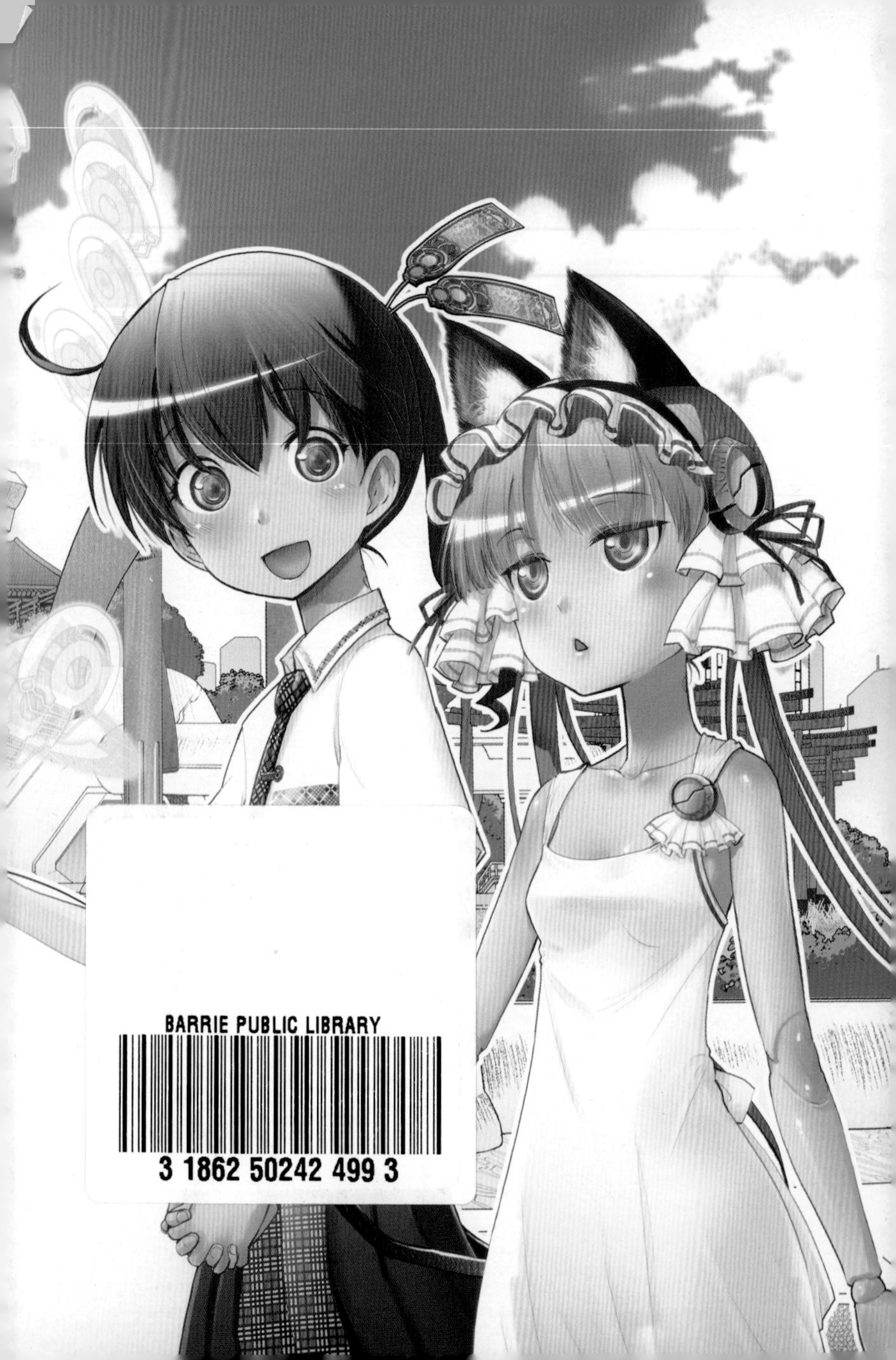

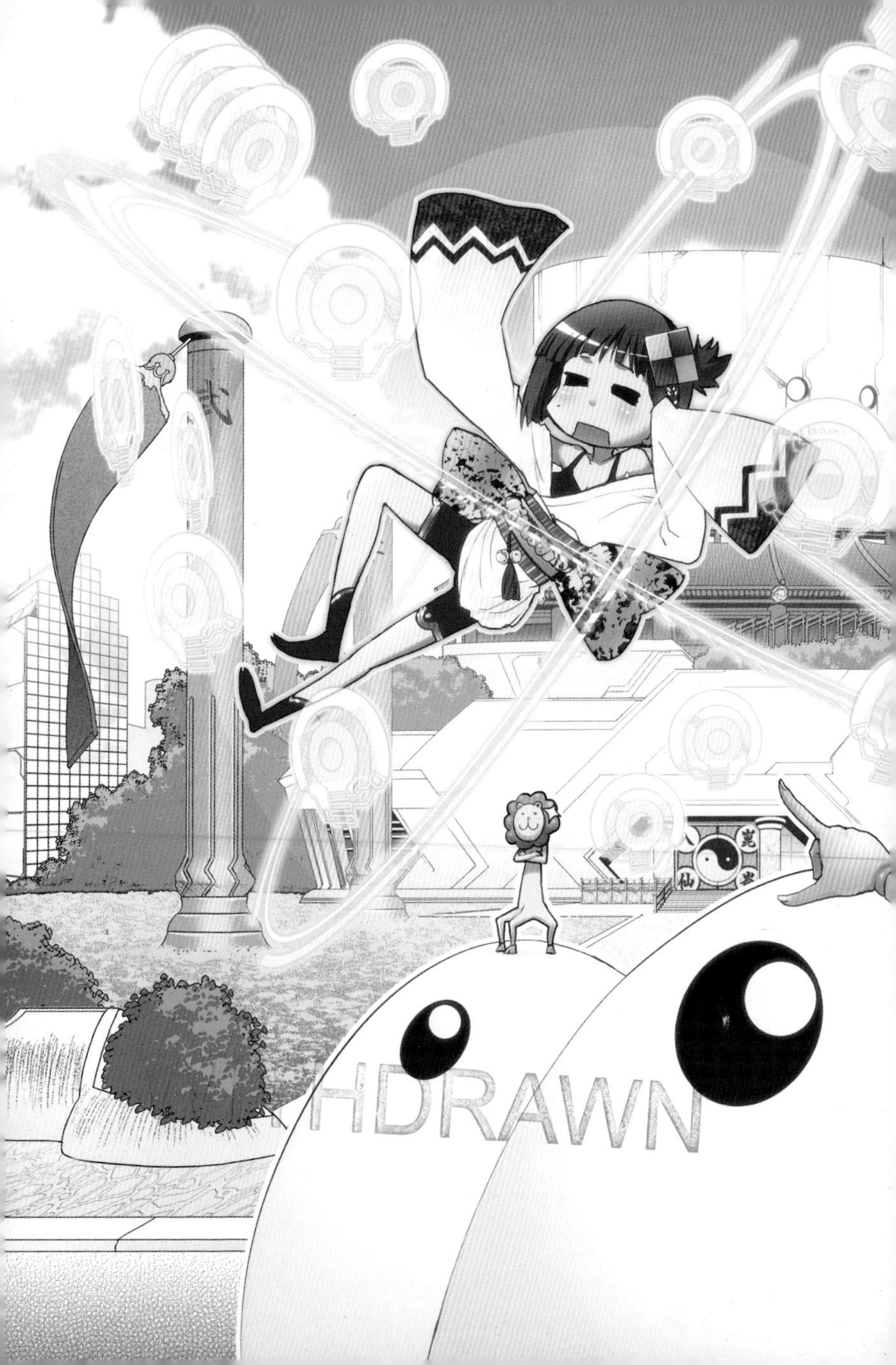

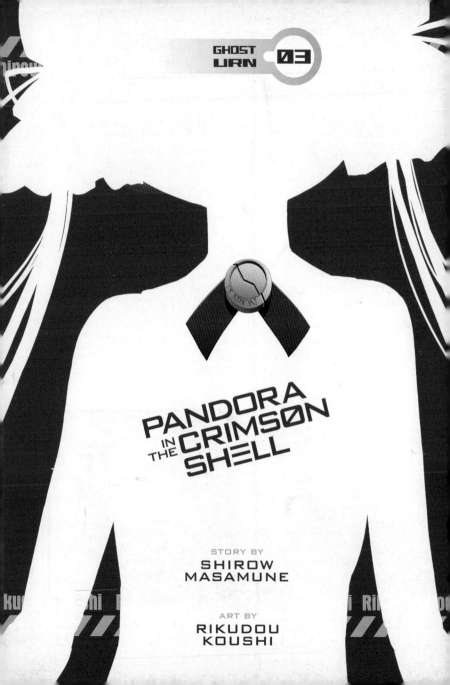

GHOST
URN 03

PANDORA
IN THE CRIMSON
SHELL

STORY BY
SHIROW
MASAMUNE

ART BY
RIKUDOU
KOUSHI

rOW Masamune Shirow Masamune Shirow Masamune Shirow Masa

GHOST URN-EPISODE.log —— The story so far!

In the not-so-distant future, humanity has entered a politically and economically tumultuous era. Wars and giant natural disasters occur frequently all over the world, while advanced information networks begin to cover the globe.

In the wake of the terrorist activity threatening the artificial resort island of Cenancle, peace and quiet have returned... at least for now. Nanakorobi Nene and Clarion begin their new life as wards of Korobase Takumi, but trouble looms just ahead: shadowy forces have set their sights on Buer, the massive boring machine left behind by Uzal...

udou Koushi Rikudou Koushi Rikudou Koushi Rikudou Koushi Rikudo

GHOST URN-CHARACTERS —— Main Characters

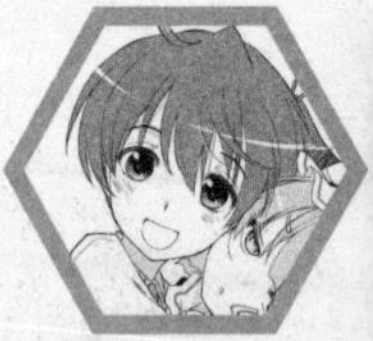

Nanakorobi Nene

A girl whose brain was implanted into an entirely artificial body after an accident when she was young. Nene has one of the few full-body prosthetics in the world!

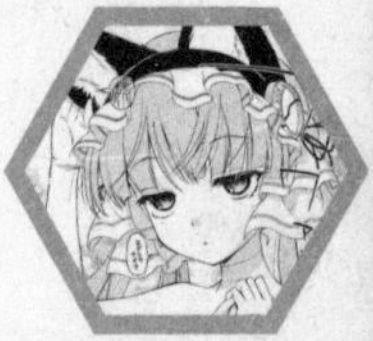

Clarion

A combat android owned by Uzal. Clarion has many top-secret, illegal programs tucked away inside her.

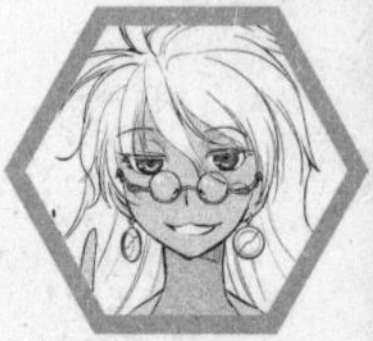

Uzal Delilah

The mysterious Uzal, also known as Sahar Schehera, is a well-known international businesswoman, but she has plenty of secrets. She's responsible for the current uproar on the island.

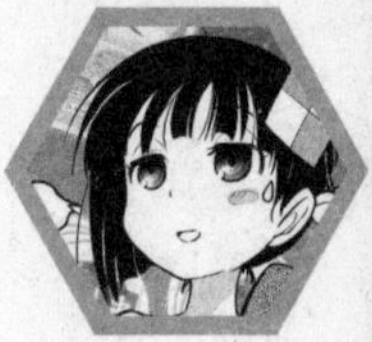

Korobase Takumi

Age unknown. She heads up the Korobase Foundation, which controls cybrain marketing, but has a pathological fear of people.

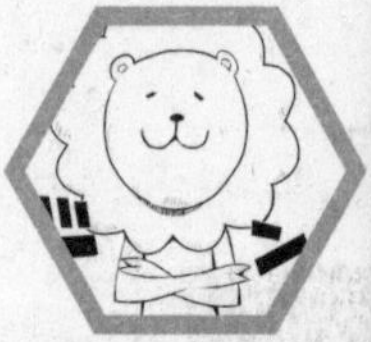

Massive boring machine Buer: Central Nervous Unit

The central control unit for the large multi-legged boring machine, Buer. The unit speaks pompously, and is often subjected to abuse from Clarion. Buer's actual body is currently dormant and hidden deep underground.

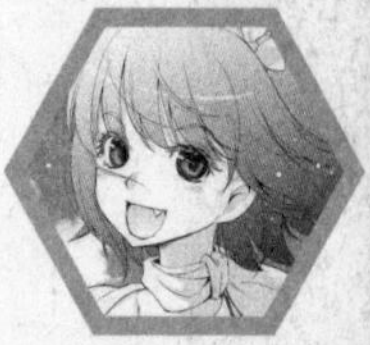

Vlind

A perky, enthusiastic new Titan TV reporter who happened to be on the scene when the terrorist incident occurred. She miraculously survived!

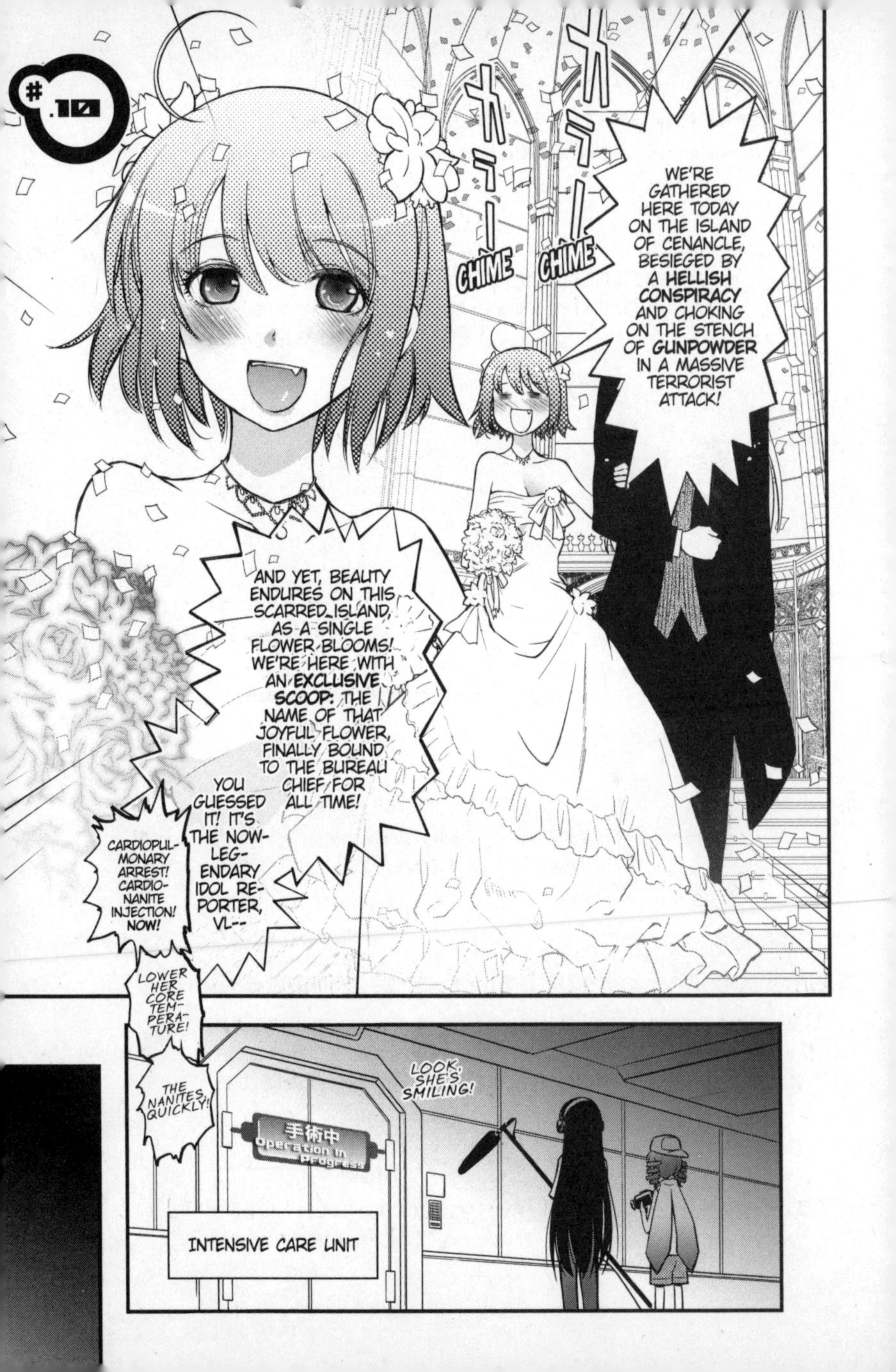
#.10
カラー CHIME
カラー CHIME
WE'RE GATHERED HERE TODAY ON THE ISLAND OF CENANCLE, BESIEGED BY A **HELLISH CONSPIRACY** AND CHOKING ON THE STENCH OF **GUNPOWDER** IN A MASSIVE TERRORIST ATTACK!
AND YET, BEAUTY ENDURES ON THIS SCARRED ISLAND, AS A SINGLE FLOWER BLOOMS! WE'RE HERE WITH AN **EXCLUSIVE SCOOP:** THE NAME OF THAT JOYFUL FLOWER, FINALLY BOUND TO THE BUREAU CHIEF FOR ALL TIME!
YOU GUESSED IT! IT'S THE NOW-LEGENDARY IDOL REPORTER, VL--
CARDIOPULMONARY ARREST! CARDIO-NANITE INJECTION! NOW!
LOWER HER CORE TEMPERATURE!
THE NANITES, QUICKLY!
LOOK, SHE'S SMILING!
手術中 Operation in Progress
INTENSIVE CARE UNIT

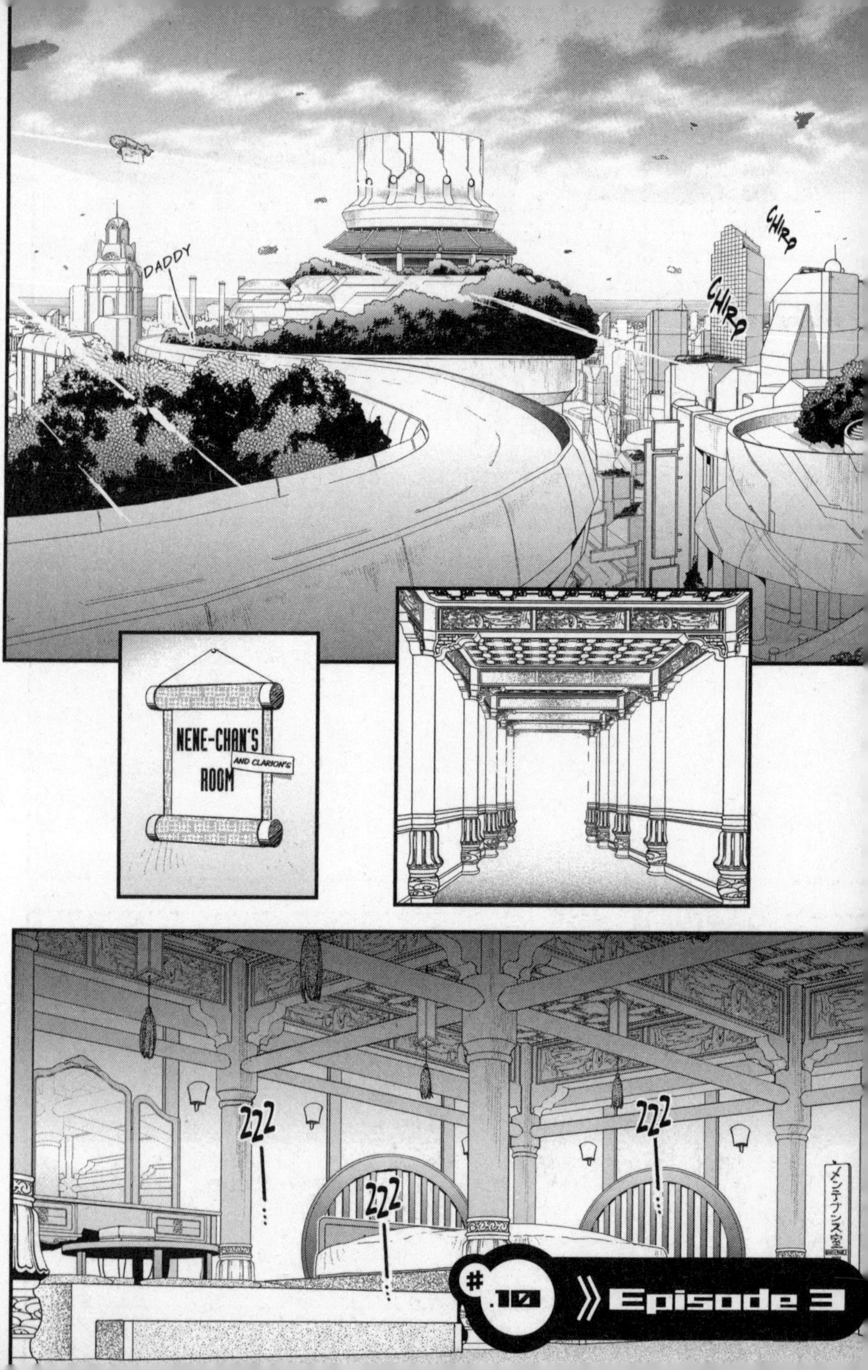
CHIRP
CHIRP
DADDY
NENE-CHAN'S AND CLARION'S ROOM
メンテナンス室
ZZZ...
ZZZ...
ZZZ...
#.10
Episode 3

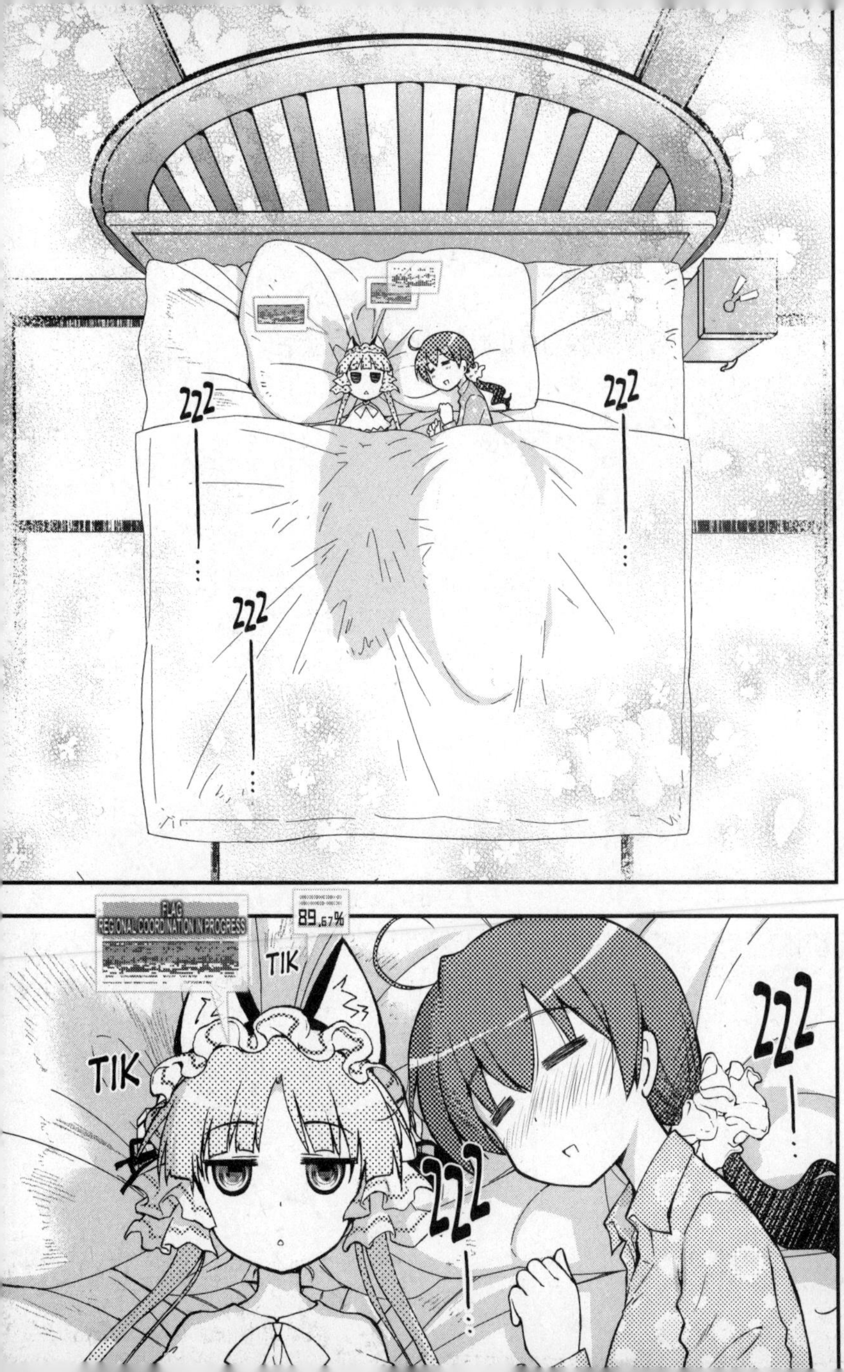
ZZZ—…
ZZZ—…
ZZZ—…
ZZZ—…
89.67%
FLAG
REGIONAL COORDINATION IN PROGRESS
TIK
TIK
ZZZ—…

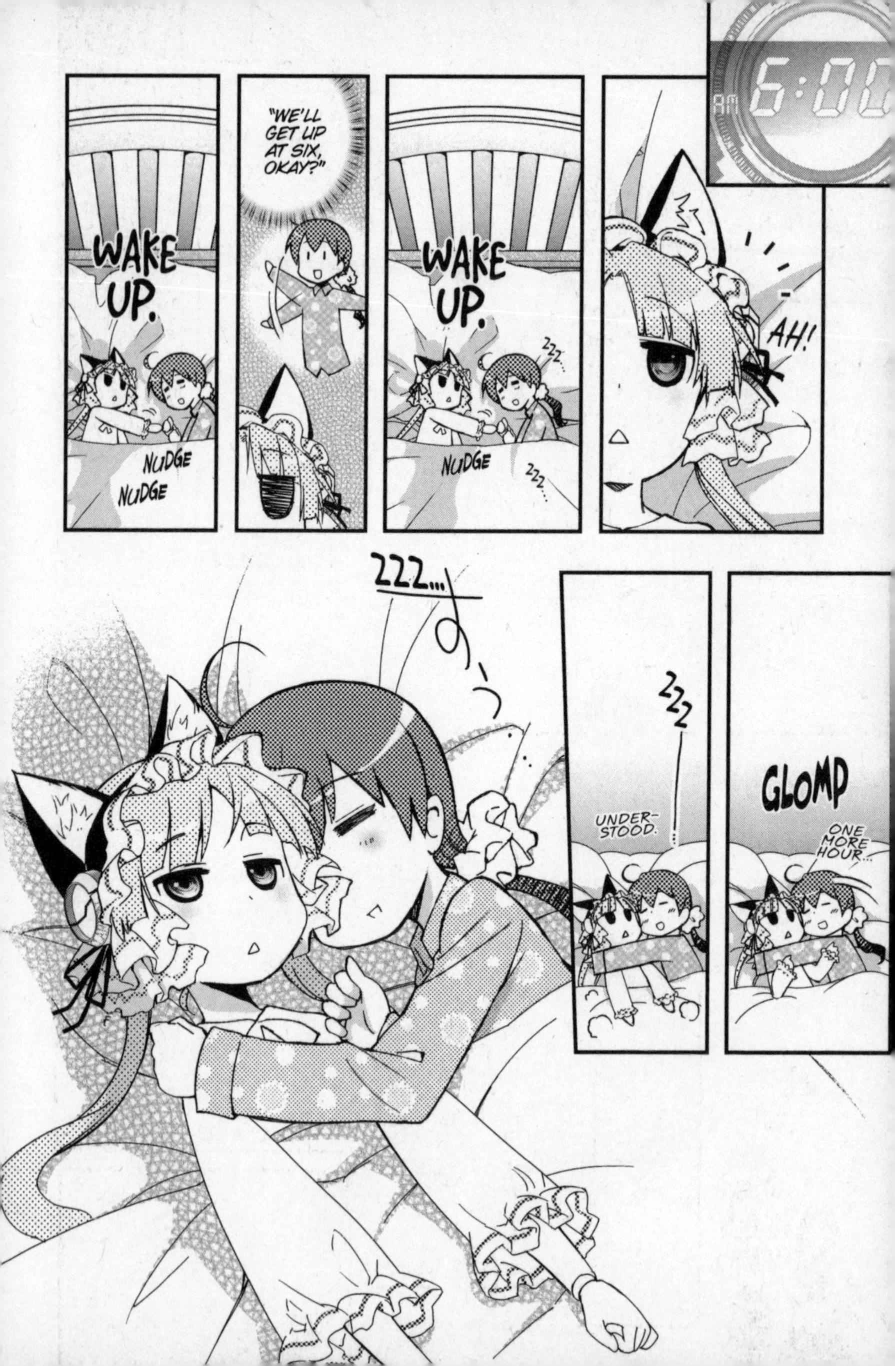
AM 6:00
AH!
WAKE UP.
ZZZ...
NUDGE
ZZZ...
"WE'LL GET UP AT SIX, OKAY?"
WAKE UP.
NUDGE
NUDGE
GLOMP
ONE MORE HOUR...
ZZZ
UNDER-STOOD.
ZZZ...

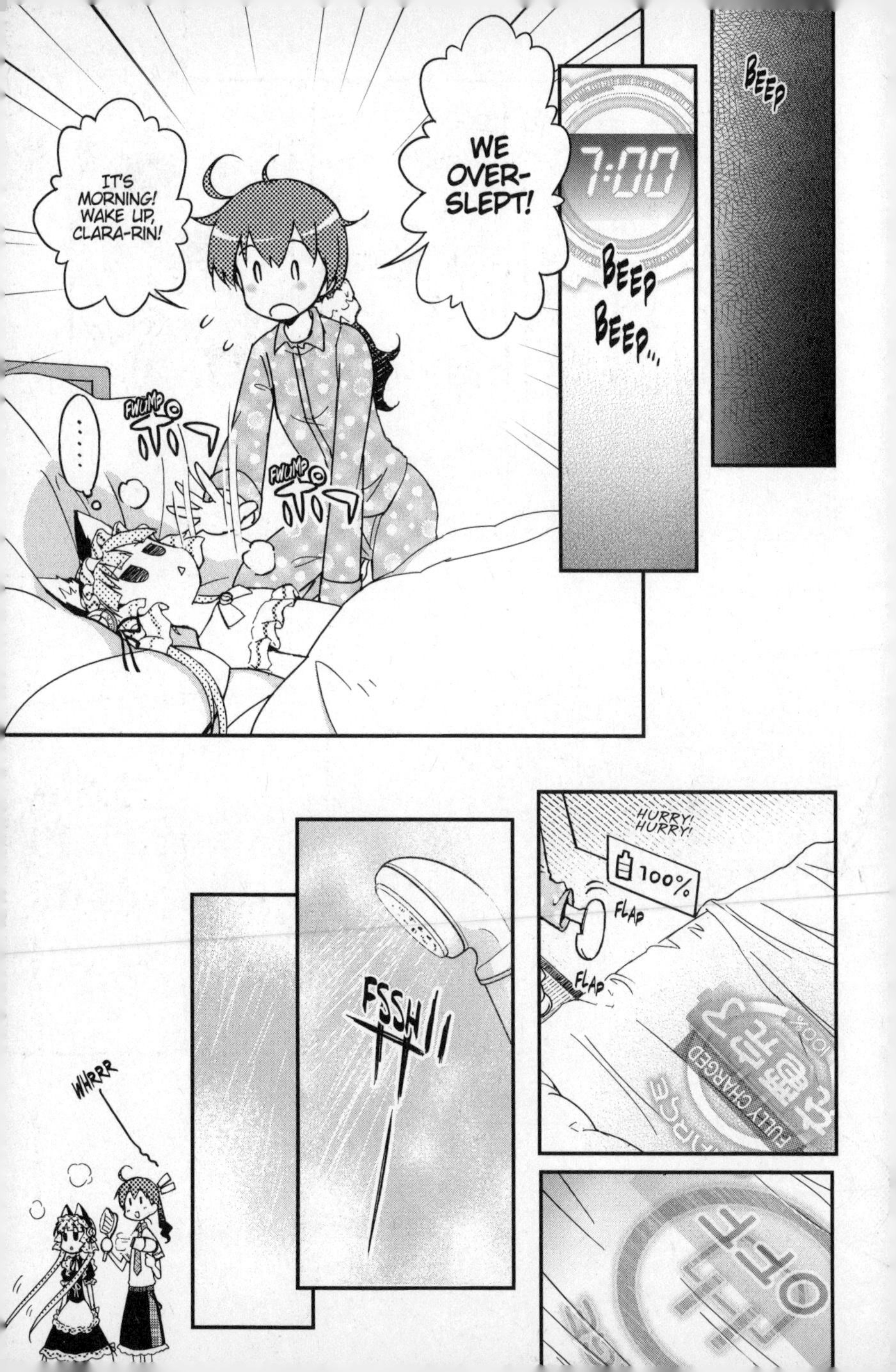
BEEP
7:00
BEEP
BEEP...
WE OVER-SLEPT!
IT'S MORNING! WAKE UP, CLARA-RIN!
......
FWUMP
FWUMP
HURRY! HURRY!
100%
FLAP
FLAP
FULLY CHARGED
FSSH
WHRRR

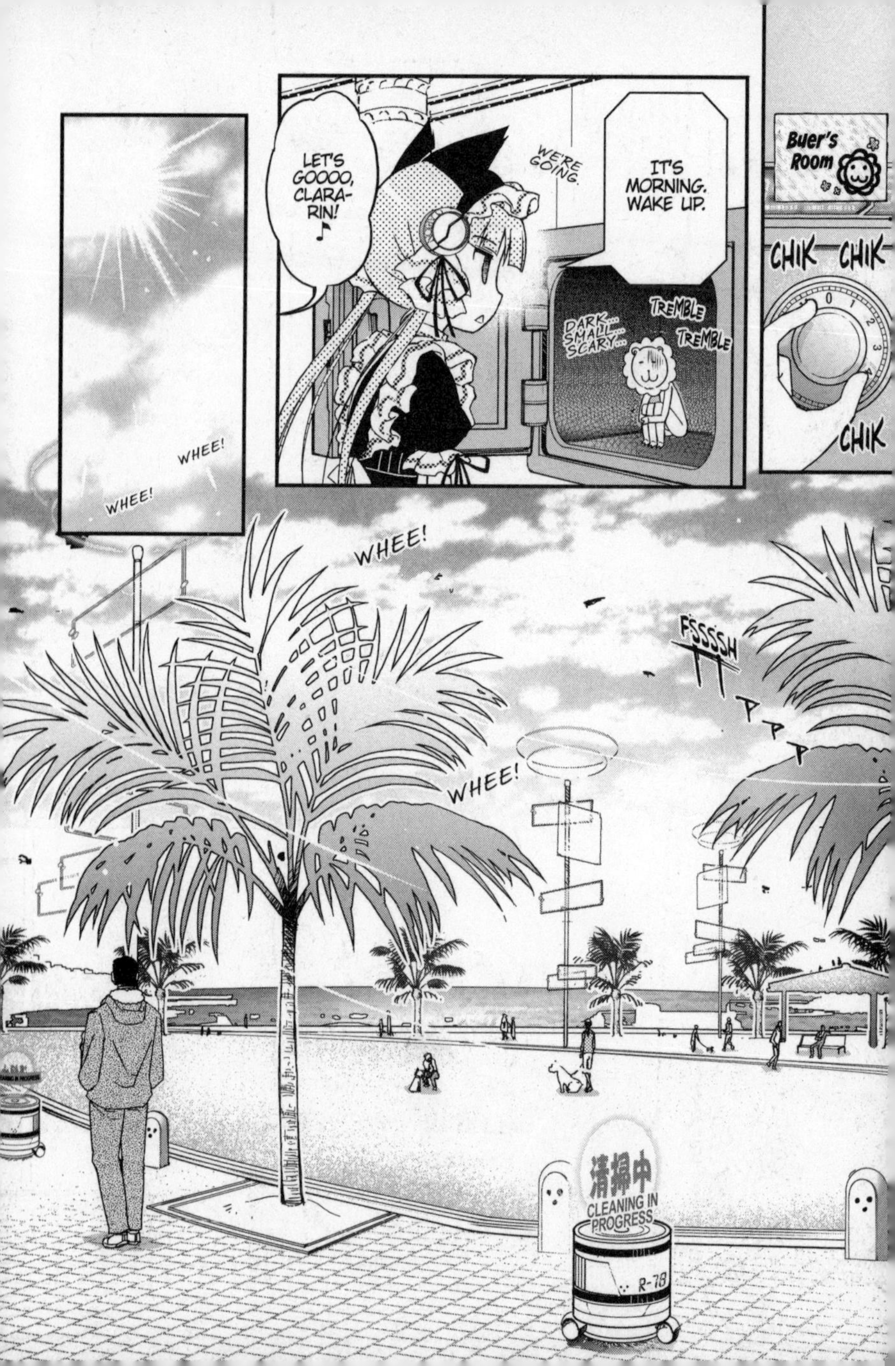
Buer's Room
CHIK CHIK
CHIK
IT'S MORNING. WAKE UP.
WE'RE GOING.
LET'S GOOOO, CLARA-RIN! ♪
TREMBLE
DARK... SMALL... SCARY...
TREMBLE
WHEE!
WHEE!
WHEE!
FSSSSH
WHEE!
清掃中
CLEANING IN PROGRESS
R-78

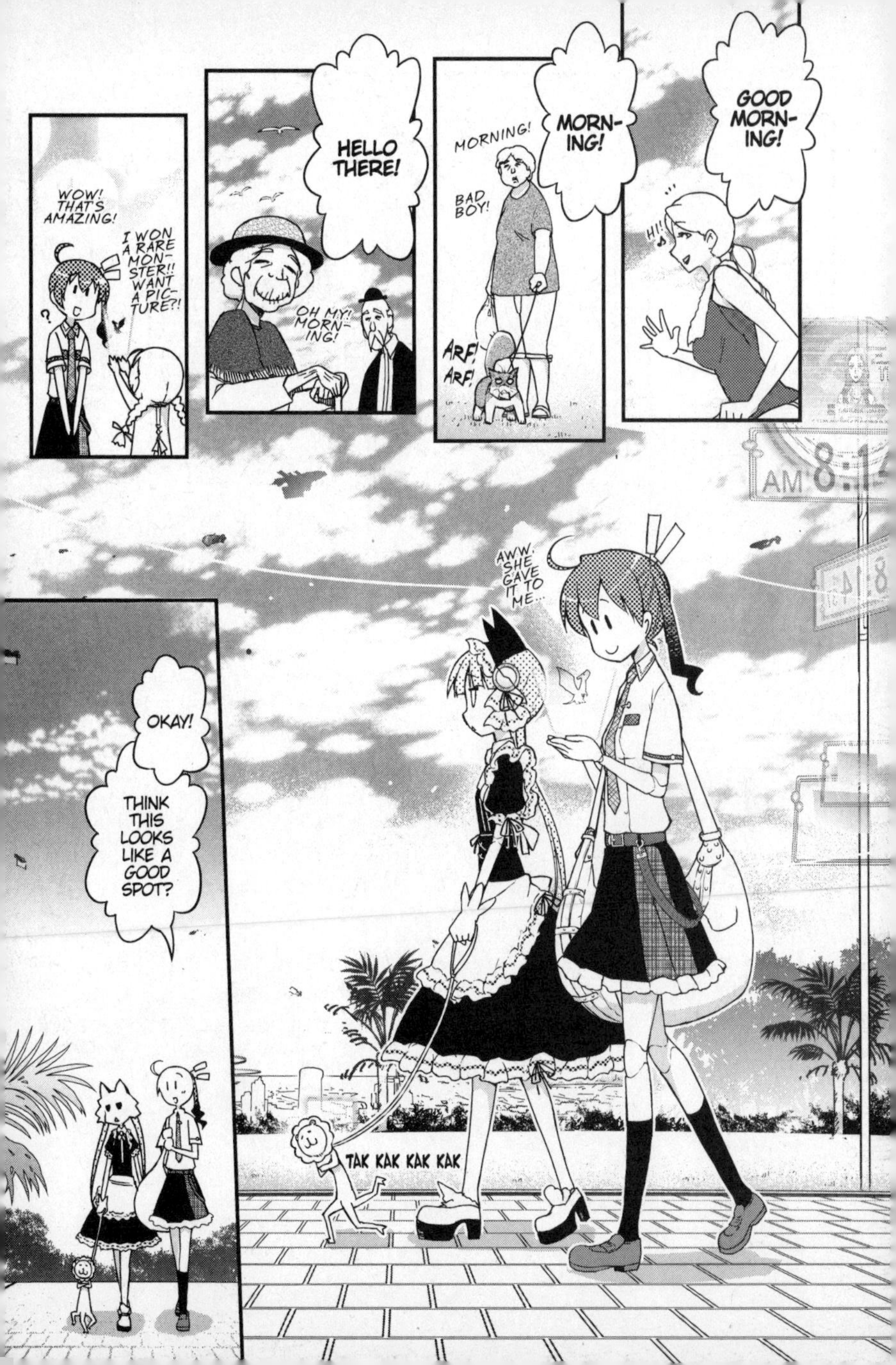

GOOD MORNING!
HI!!
MORNING!
MORNING!
BAD BOY!
ARF! ARF!
HELLO THERE!
OH MY! MORNING!
I WON A RARE MONSTER!! WANT A PICTURE?!
WOW! THAT'S AMAZING!
AM 8:1
AWW. SHE GAVE IT TO ME...
TAK KAK KAK KAK
OKAY!
THINK THIS LOOKS LIKE A GOOD SPOT?

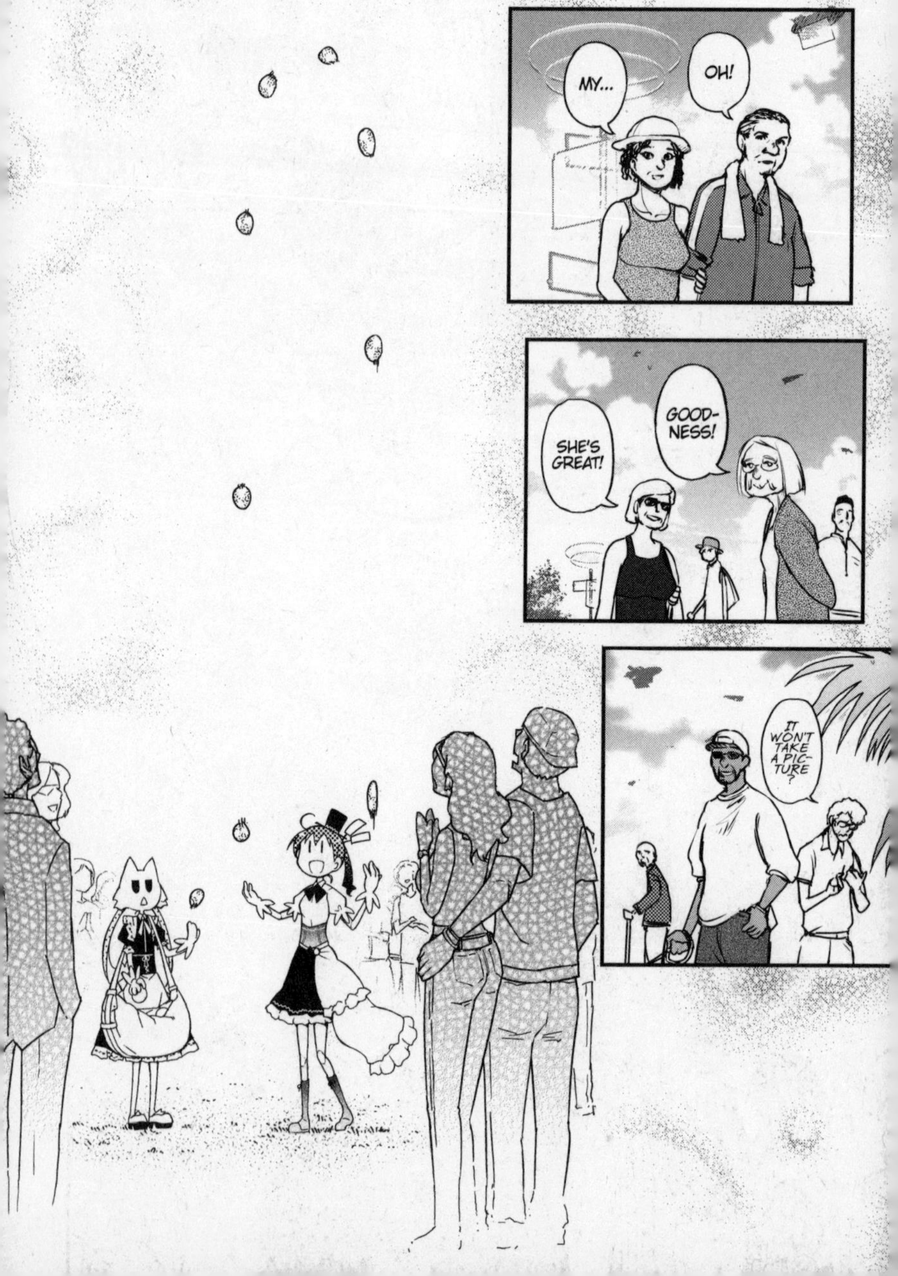
OH!
MY...
GOODNESS!
SHE'S GREAT!
IT WON'T TAKE A PICTURE?

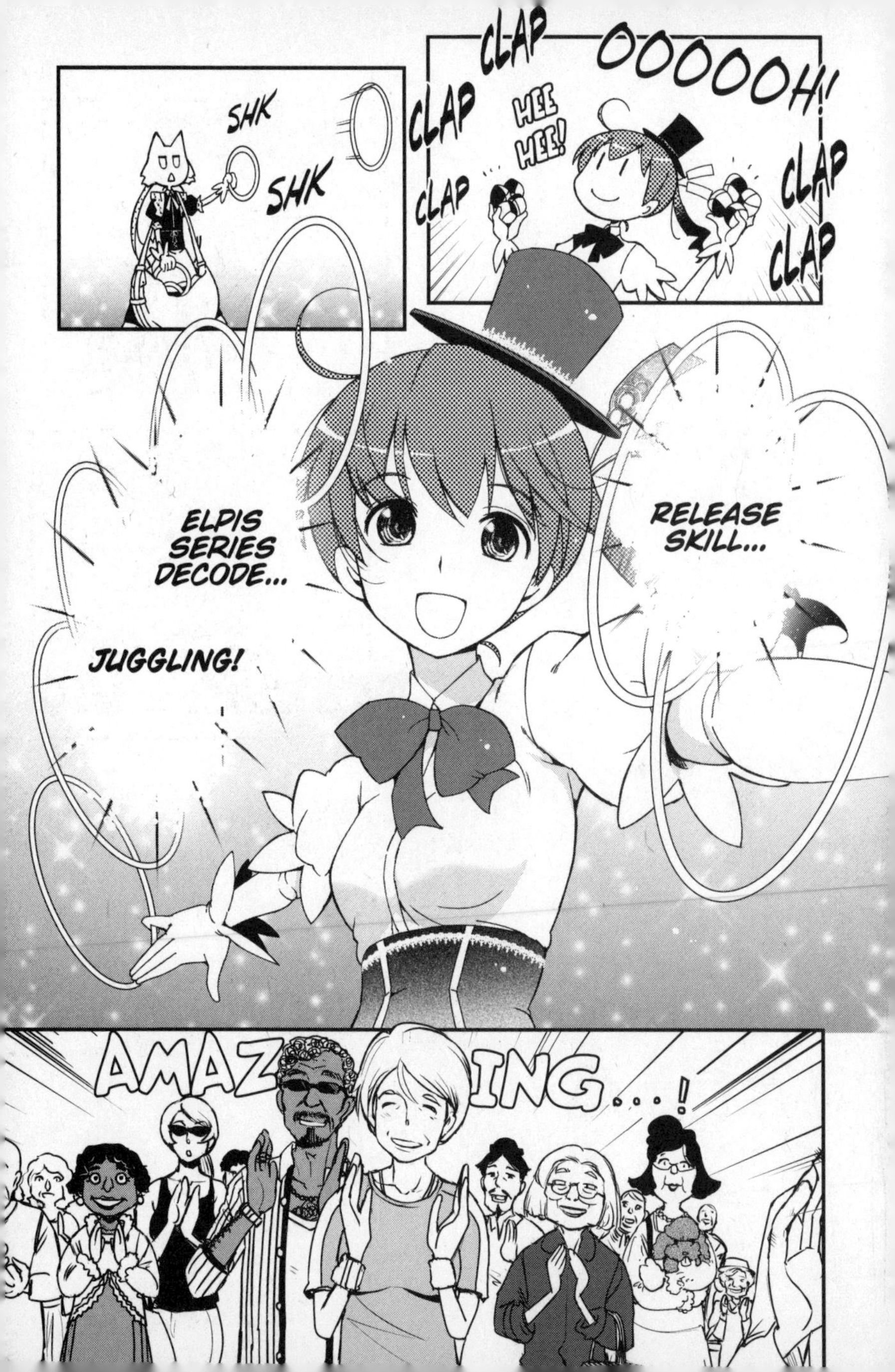
CLAP
OOOOOH!
CLAP
HEE HEE!
CLAP
CLAP
CLAP
SHK
SHK
ELPIS SERIES DECODE...
RELEASE SKILL...
JUGGLING!
AMAZING...!

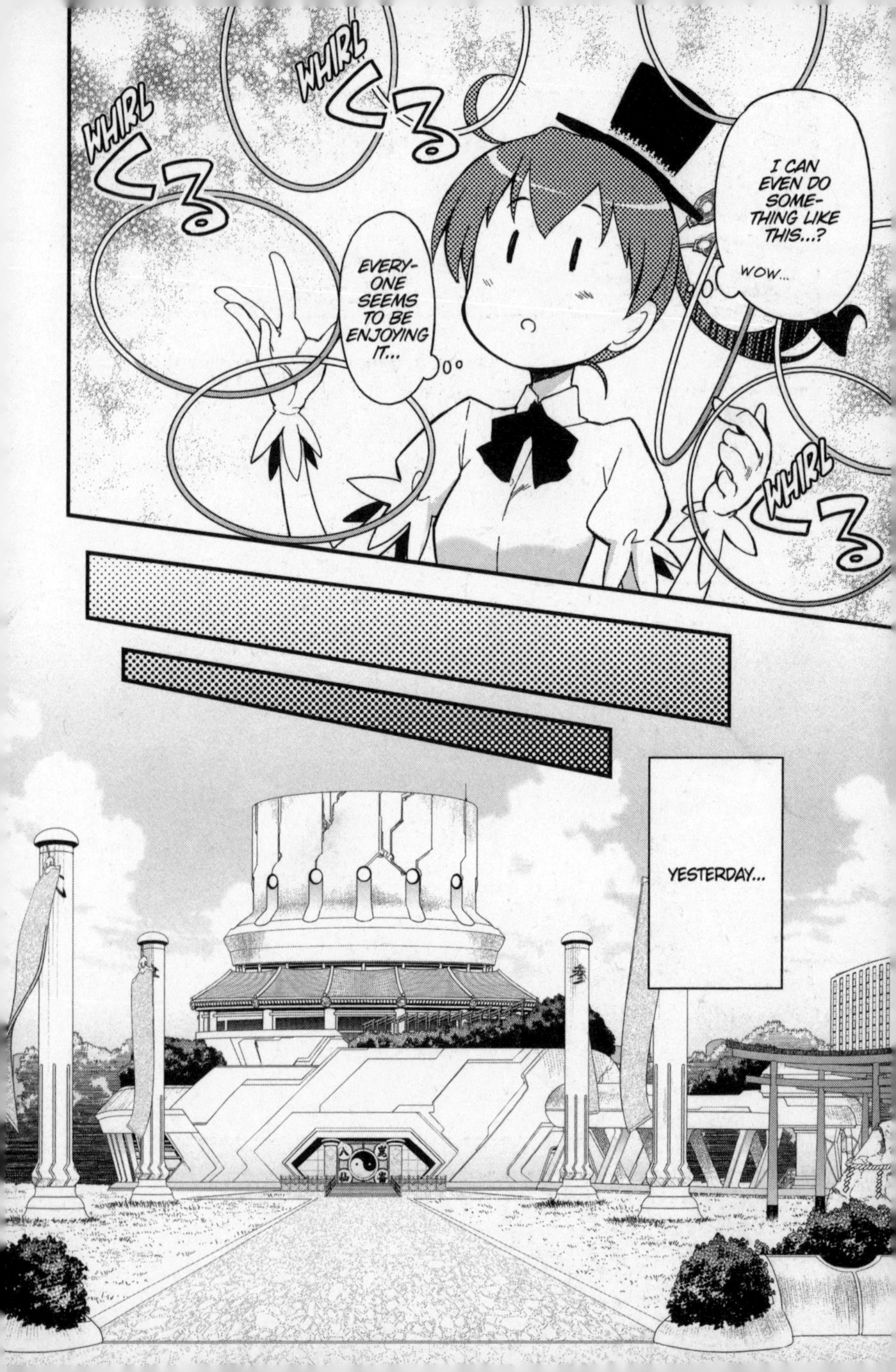
I CAN EVEN DO SOME-THING LIKE THIS...?
WOW...
WHIRL くる
WHIRL くる
EVERY-ONE SEEMS TO BE ENJOYING IT...
WHIRL くる
YESTERDAY...

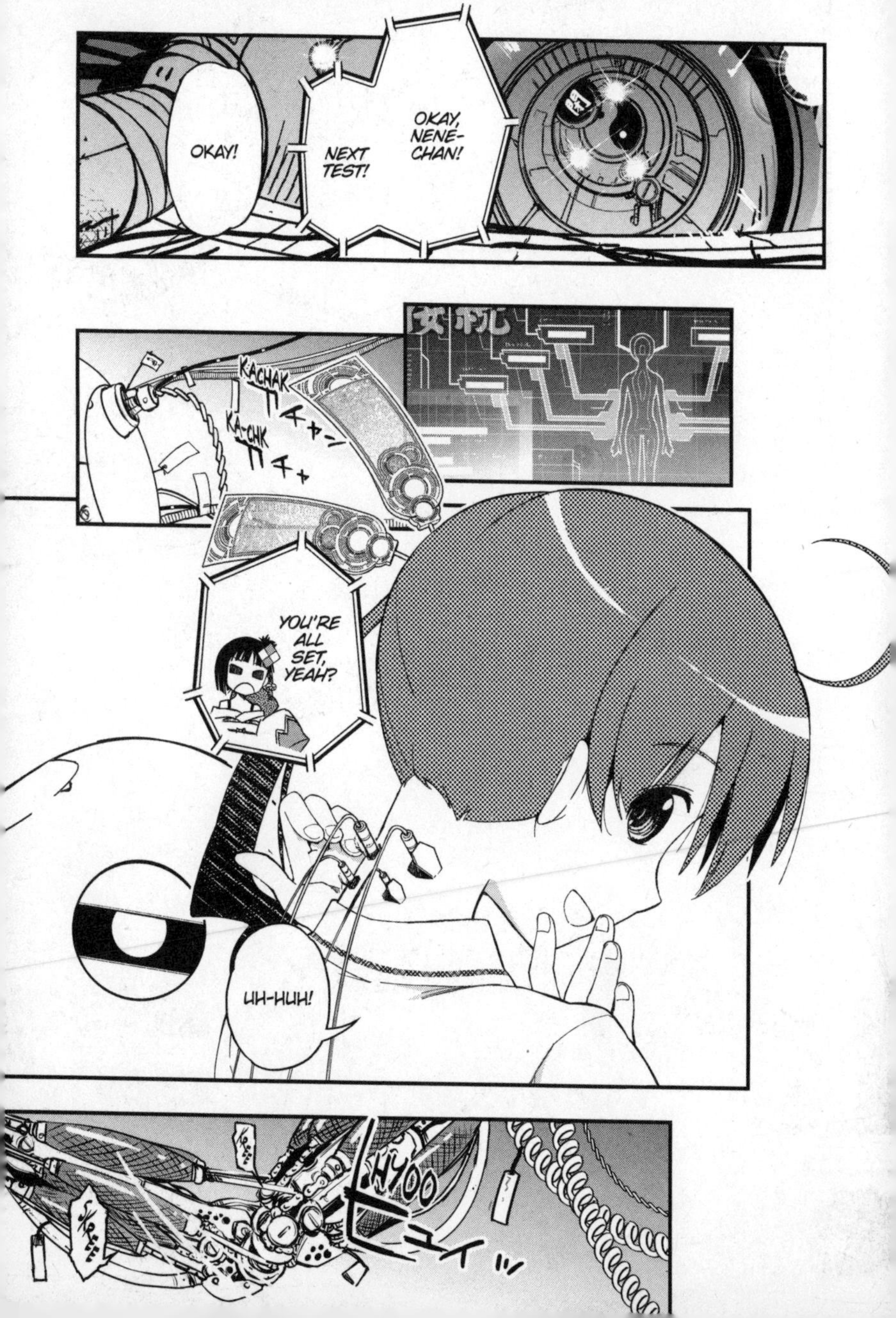
OKAY, NENE-CHAN!
NEXT TEST!
OKAY!
KACHAK
KA-CHK
YOU'RE ALL SET, YEAH?
UH-HUH!
HYOO
KREEE
SKREEE

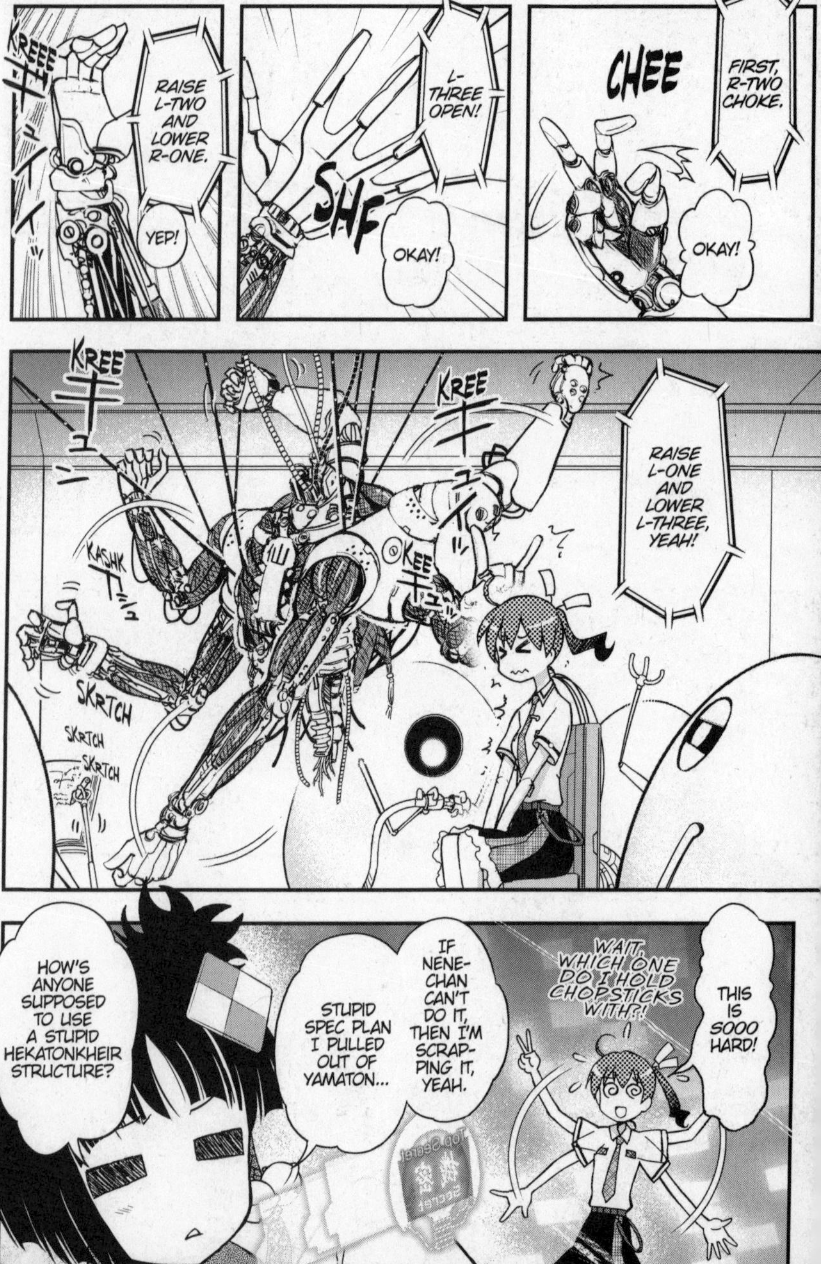
FIRST, R-TWO CHOKE.
CHEE
OKAY!
L-THREE OPEN!
SHF
OKAY!
RAISE L-TWO AND LOWER R-ONE.
KREEE
YEP!
RAISE L-ONE AND LOWER L-THREE, YEAH!
KREE
KREE
KEE
KASHK
SKRTCH
SKRTCH
SKRTCH
THIS IS SOOO HARD!
WAIT, WHICH ONE DO I HOLD CHOPSTICKS WITH?!
IF NENE-CHAN CAN'T DO IT, THEN I'M SCRAP-PING IT, YEAH.
STUPID SPEC PLAN I PULLED OUT OF YAMATON...
HOW'S ANYONE SUPPOSED TO USE A STUPID HEKATONKHEIR STRUCTURE?
Top Secret
SECRET

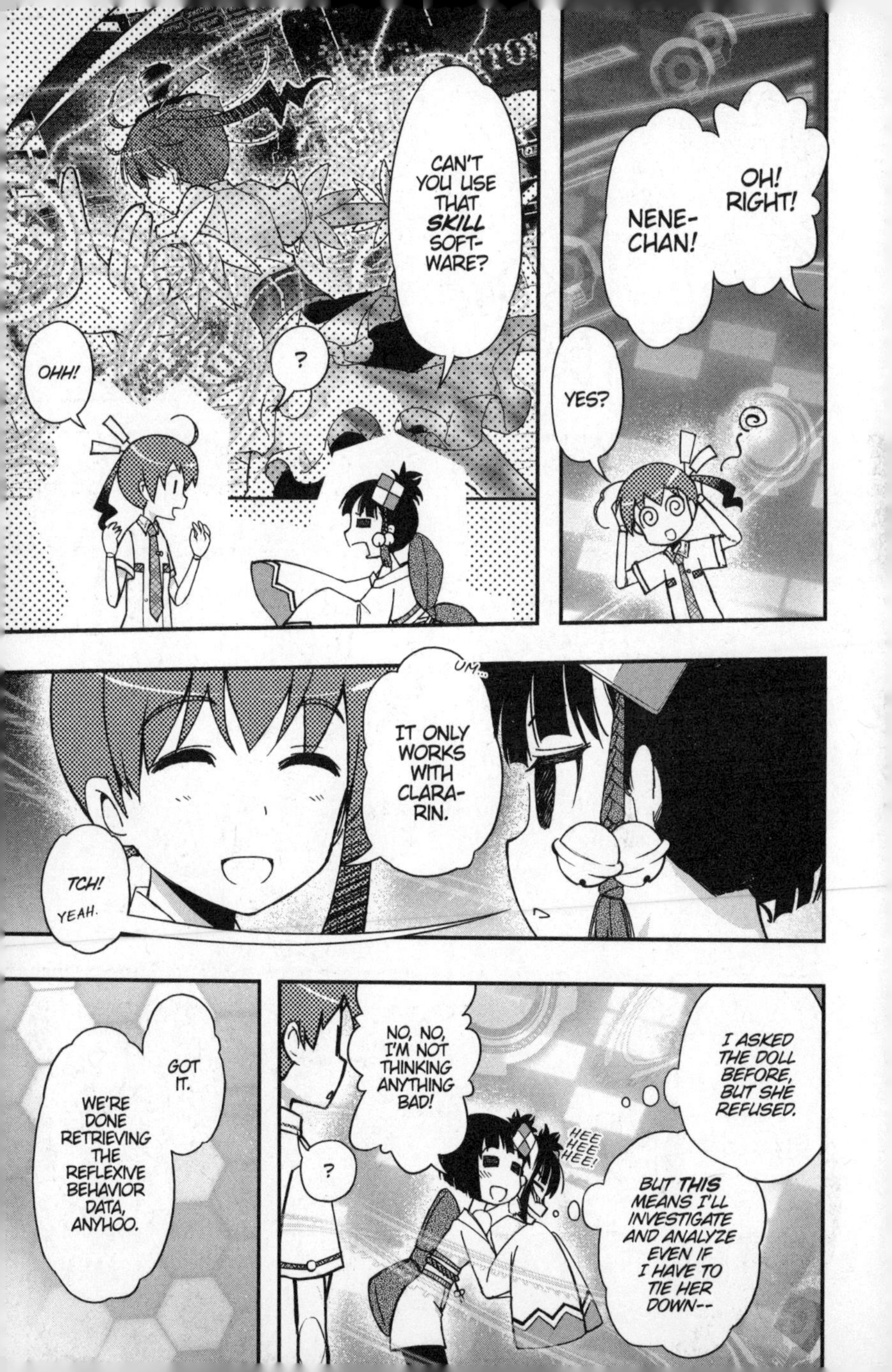
OH! RIGHT!
NENE-CHAN!
YES?
CAN'T YOU USE THAT SKILL SOFTWARE?
?
OHH!
UM...
IT ONLY WORKS WITH CLARA-RIN.
TCH!
YEAH.
I ASKED THE DOLL BEFORE, BUT SHE REFUSED.
BUT THIS MEANS I'LL INVESTIGATE AND ANALYZE EVEN IF I HAVE TO TIE HER DOWN--
HEE HEE HEE!
NO, NO, I'M NOT THINKING ANYTHING BAD!
?
GOT IT.
WE'RE DONE RETRIEVING THE REFLEXIVE BEHAVIOR DATA, ANYHOO.

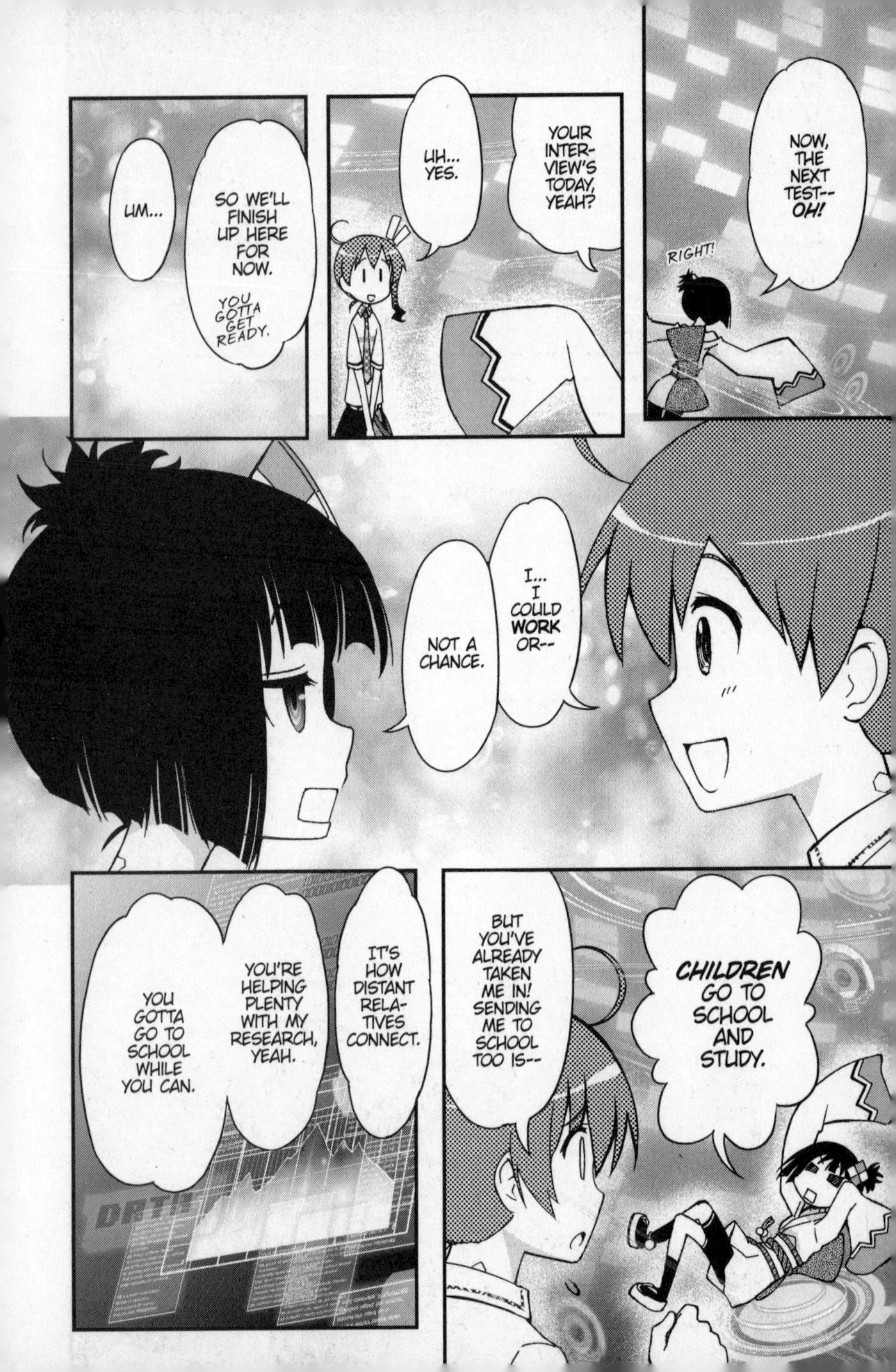
NOW, THE NEXT TEST-- OH!
RIGHT!
YOUR INTER-VIEW'S TODAY, YEAH?
UH... YES.
SO WE'LL FINISH UP HERE FOR NOW.
YOU GOTTA GET READY.
UM...
I... I COULD WORK OR--
NOT A CHANCE.
CHILDREN GO TO SCHOOL AND STUDY.
BUT YOU'VE ALREADY TAKEN ME IN! SENDING ME TO SCHOOL TOO IS--
IT'S HOW DISTANT RELA-TIVES CONNECT.
YOU'RE HELPING PLENTY WITH MY RESEARCH, YEAH.
YOU GOTTA GO TO SCHOOL WHILE YOU CAN.

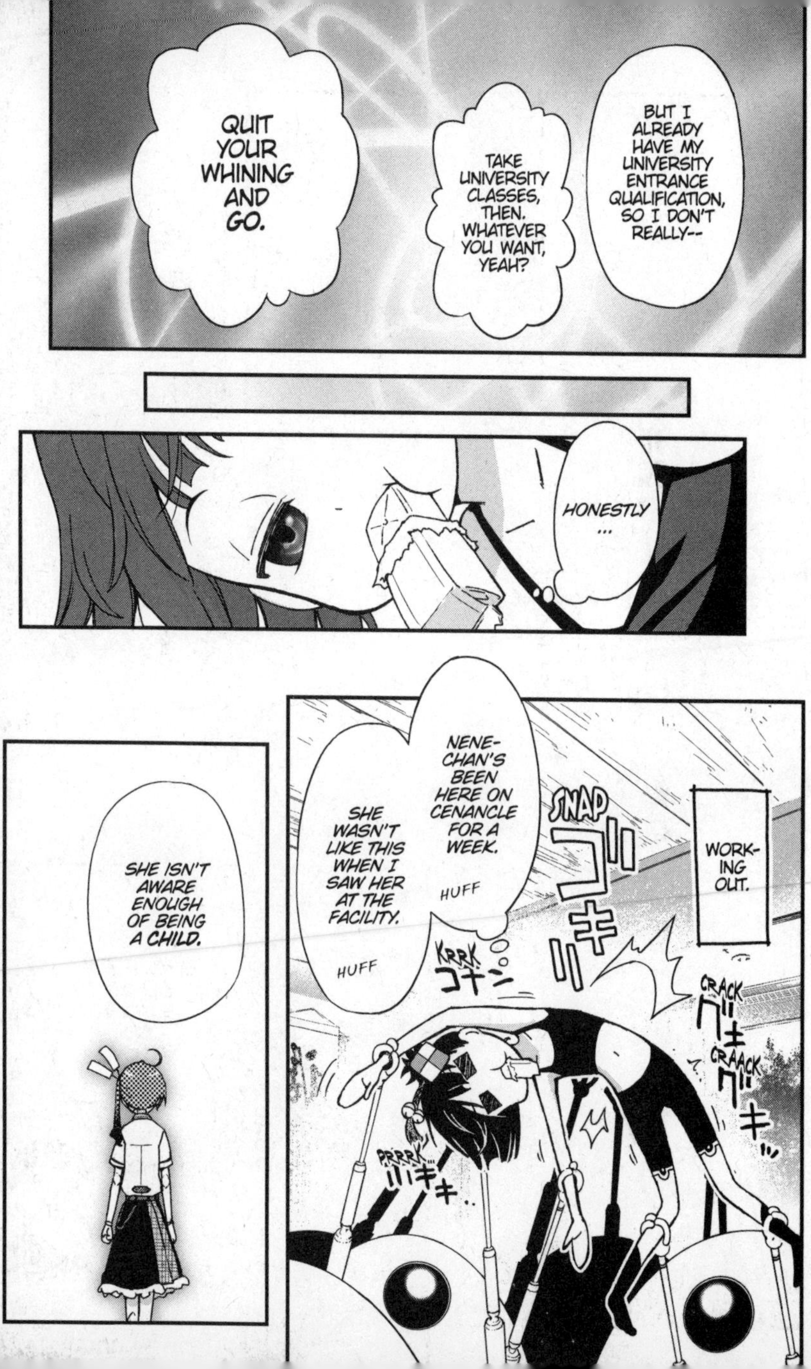
BUT I ALREADY HAVE MY UNIVERSITY ENTRANCE QUALIFICATION, SO I DON'T REALLY--
TAKE UNIVERSITY CLASSES, THEN. WHATEVER YOU WANT, YEAH?
QUIT YOUR WHINING AND GO.
HONESTLY ...
WORKING OUT.
SNAP
NENE-CHAN'S BEEN HERE ON CENANCLE FOR A WEEK.
SHE WASN'T LIKE THIS WHEN I SAW HER AT THE FACILITY.
HUFF
HUFF
KRRK
CRACK
CRAACK
PRRRK...
SHE ISN'T AWARE ENOUGH OF BEING A CHILD.

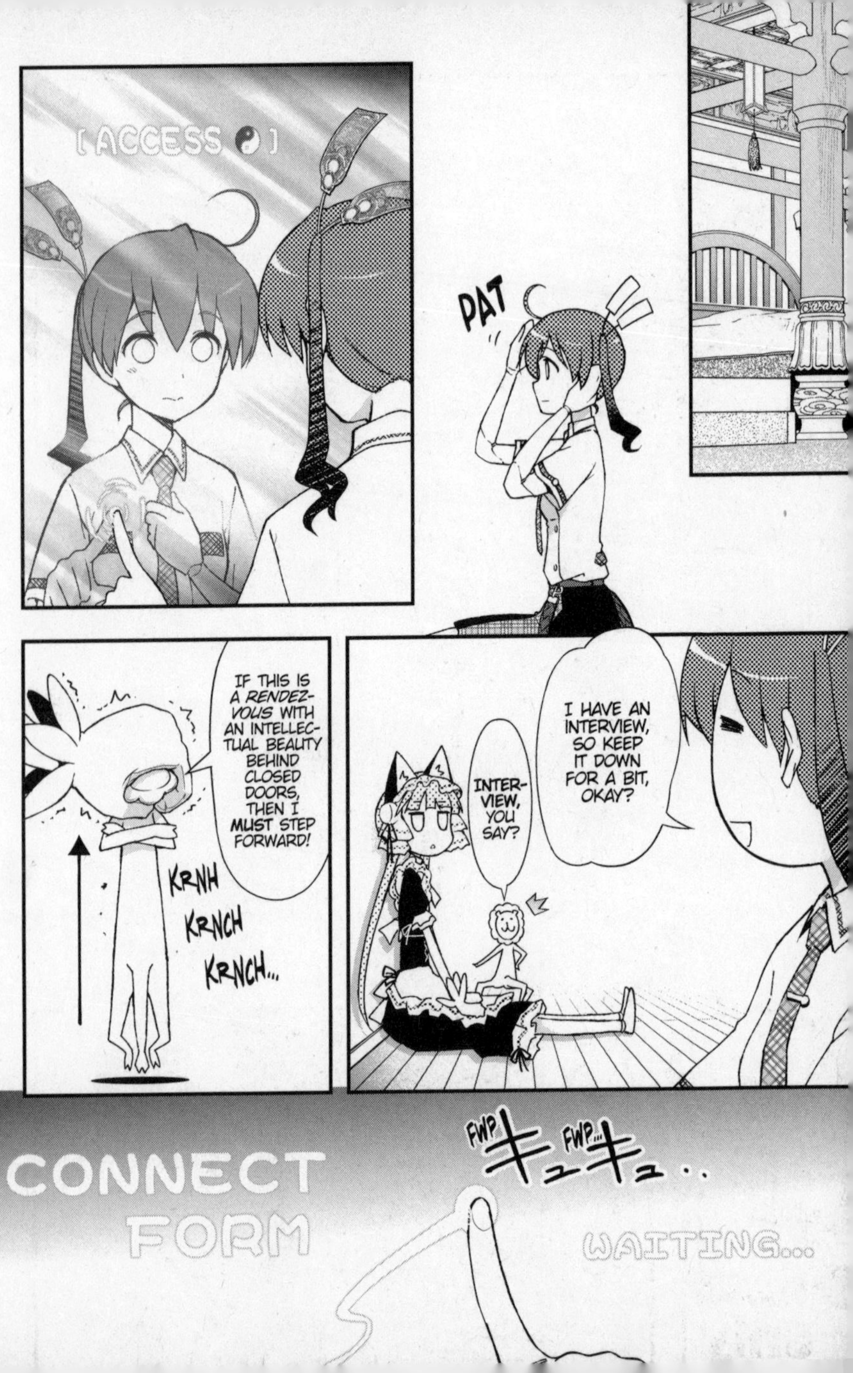
PAT
[ACCESS ☯]
I HAVE AN INTERVIEW, SO KEEP IT DOWN FOR A BIT, OKAY?
INTERVIEW, YOU SAY?
IF THIS IS A *RENDEZVOUS* WITH AN INTELLECTUAL BEAUTY BEHIND CLOSED DOORS, THEN I MUST STEP FORWARD!
KRNH KRNCH KRNCH...
FWP FWP...
CONNECT FORM
WAITING...

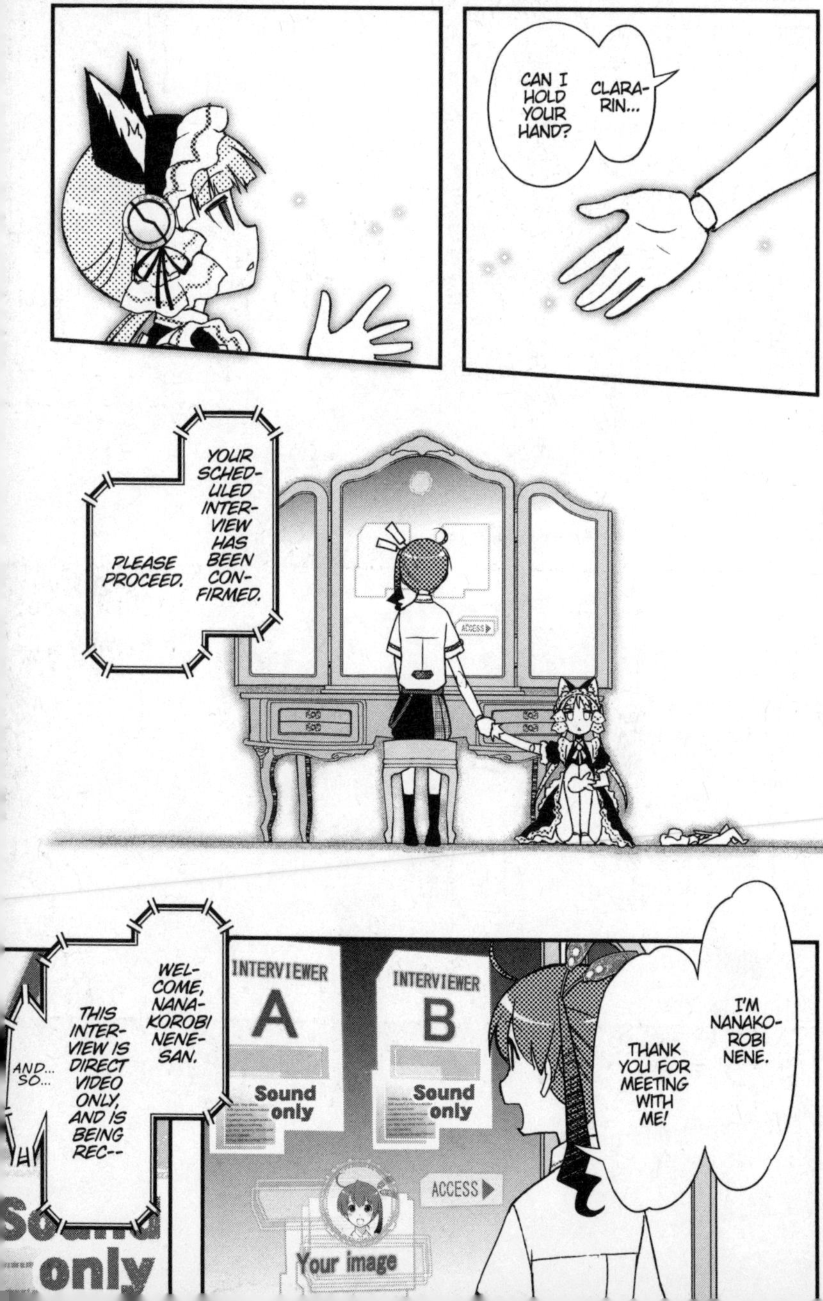
CLARA-RIN...
CAN I HOLD YOUR HAND?
YOUR SCHEDULED INTERVIEW HAS BEEN CONFIRMED.
PLEASE PROCEED.
ACCESS
I'M NANAKOROBI NENE.
THANK YOU FOR MEETING WITH ME!
INTERVIEWER B
Sound only
ACCESS
INTERVIEWER A
Sound only
Your image
WELCOME, NANAKOROBI NENE-SAN.
THIS INTERVIEW IS DIRECT VIDEO ONLY, AND IS BEING REC--
AND... SO...
Sound only

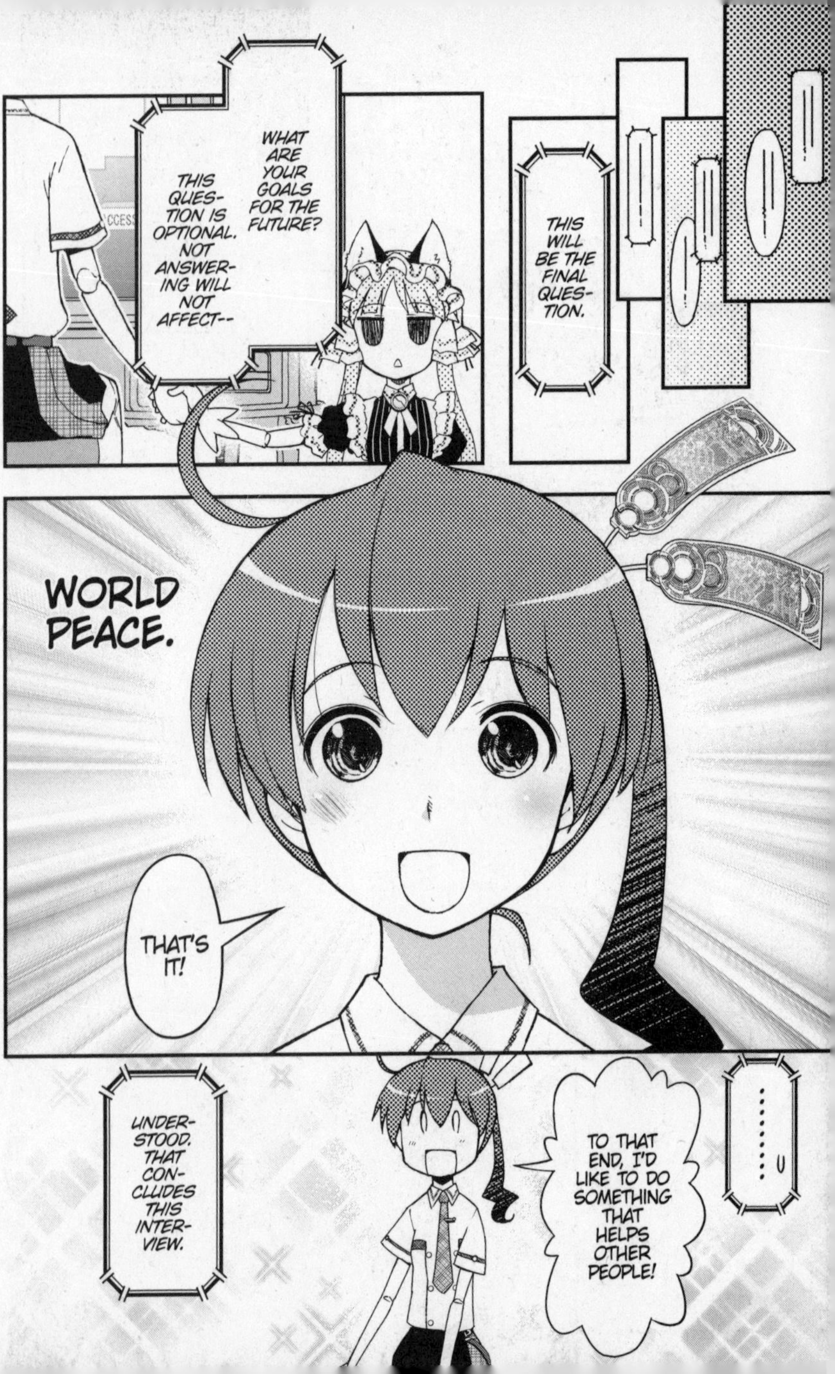
THIS WILL BE THE FINAL QUESTION.
WHAT ARE YOUR GOALS FOR THE FUTURE?
THIS QUESTION IS OPTIONAL. NOT ANSWERING WILL NOT AFFECT--
WORLD PEACE.
THAT'S IT!
......
TO THAT END, I'D LIKE TO DO SOMETHING THAT HELPS OTHER PEOPLE!
UNDERSTOOD. THAT CONCLUDES THIS INTERVIEW.

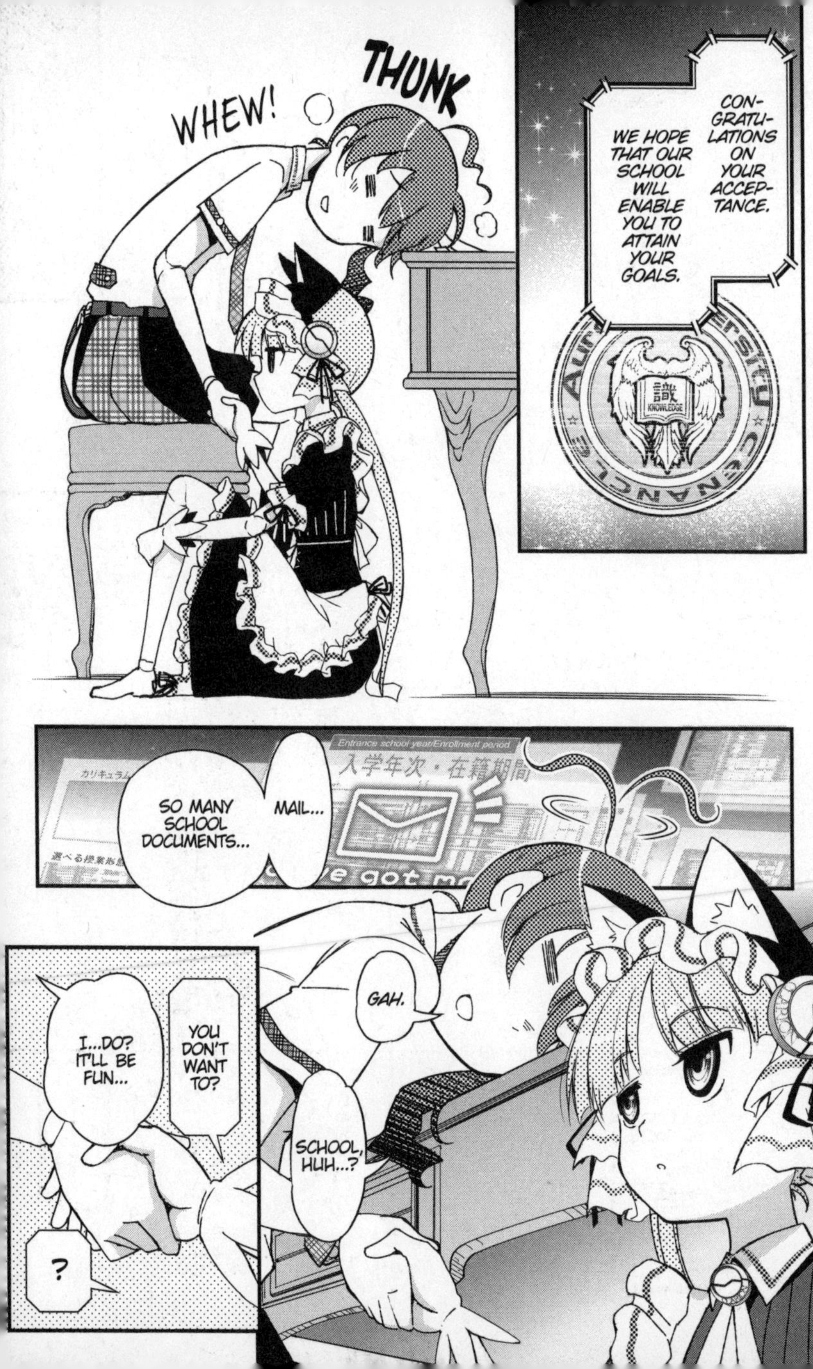
CONGRATULATIONS ON YOUR ACCEPTANCE.
WE HOPE THAT OUR SCHOOL WILL ENABLE YOU TO ATTAIN YOUR GOALS.
識
KNOWLEDGE
THUNK
WHEW!
Entrance school year/Enrollment period
入学年次・在籍期間
MAIL...
SO MANY SCHOOL DOCUMENTS...
GAH.
SCHOOL, HUH...?
YOU DON'T WANT TO?
I...DO? IT'LL BE FUN...
?

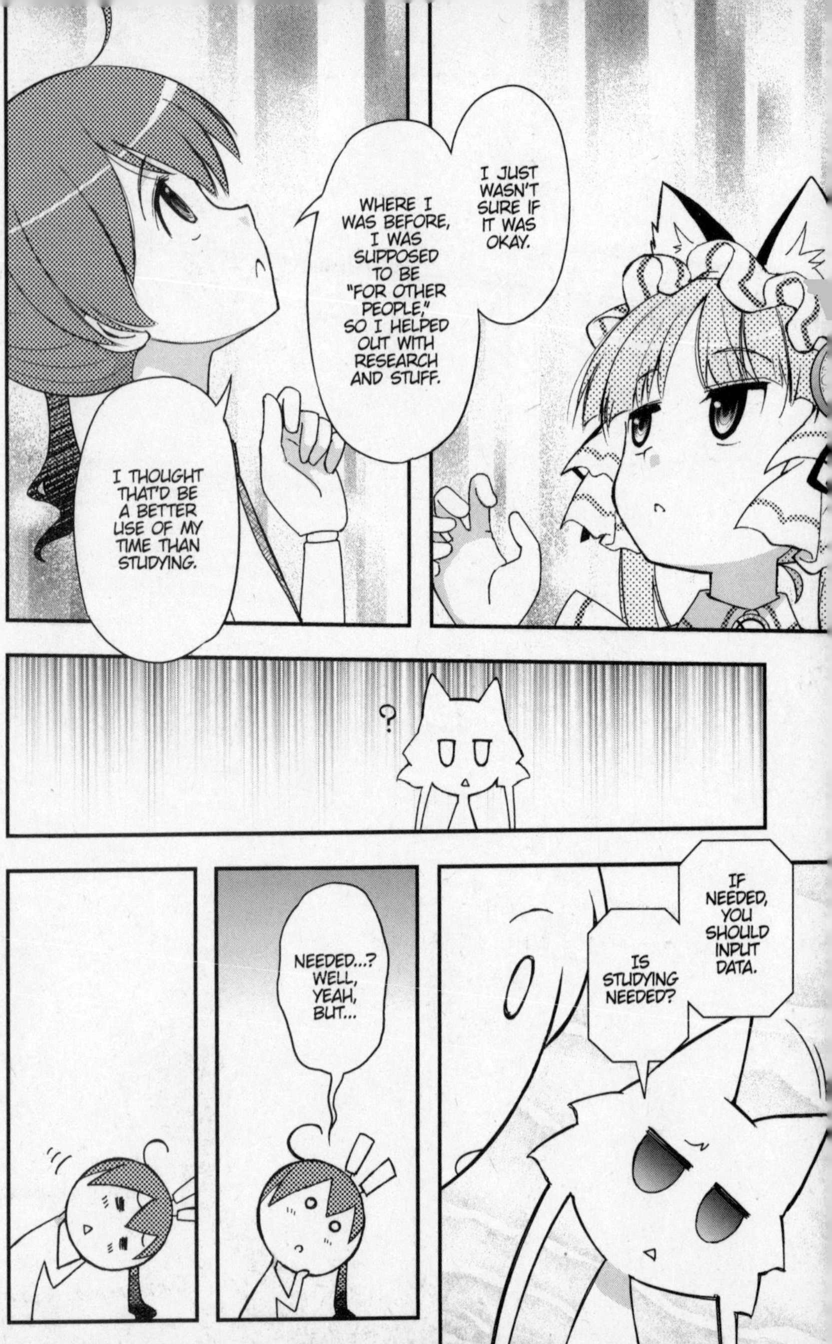
I JUST WASN'T SURE IF IT WAS OKAY.
WHERE I WAS BEFORE, I WAS SUPPOSED TO BE "FOR OTHER PEOPLE," SO I HELPED OUT WITH RESEARCH AND STUFF.
I THOUGHT THAT'D BE A BETTER USE OF MY TIME THAN STUDYING.
?
IS STUDYING NEEDED?
IF NEEDED, YOU SHOULD INPUT DATA.
NEEDED...? WELL, YEAH, BUT...

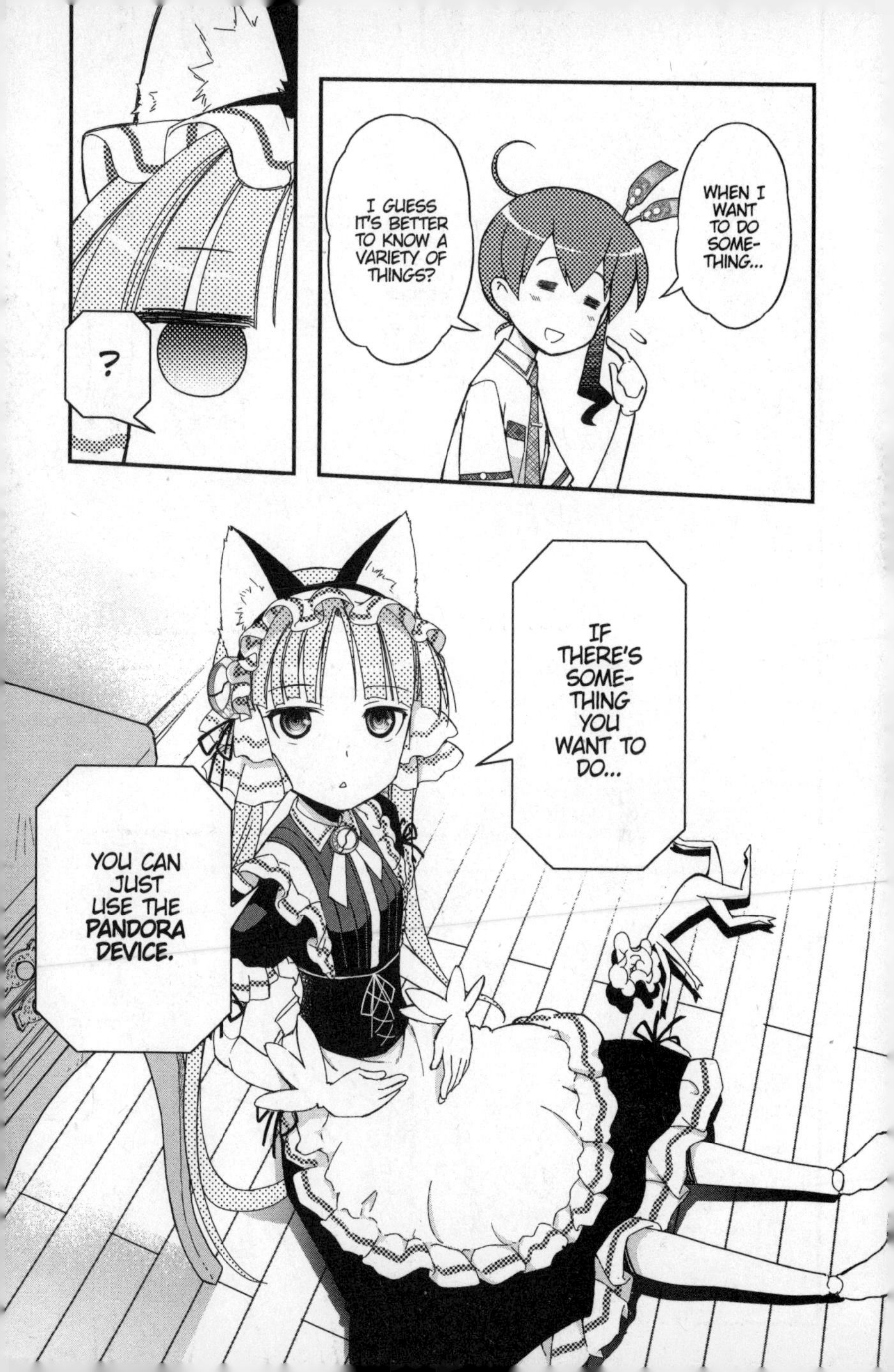
WHEN I WANT TO DO SOME-THING...
I GUESS IT'S BETTER TO KNOW A VARIETY OF THINGS?
?
IF THERE'S SOME-THING YOU WANT TO DO...
YOU CAN JUST USE THE PANDORA DEVICE.

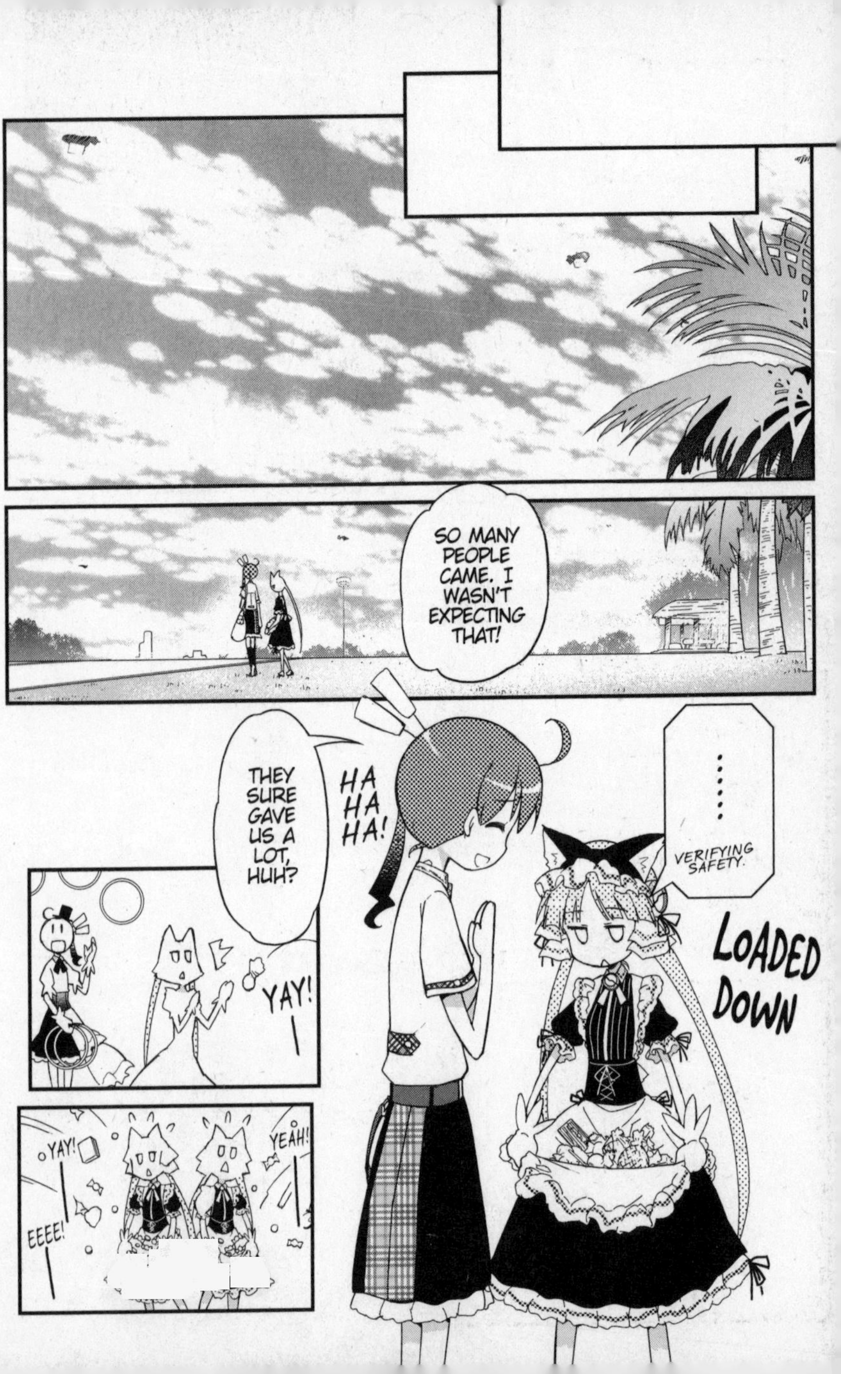
SO MANY PEOPLE CAME. I WASN'T EXPECTING THAT!
......
VERIFYING SAFETY.
HA HA HA!
THEY SURE GAVE US A LOT, HUH?
LOADED DOWN
YAY!
YEAH!
YAY!
EEEE!

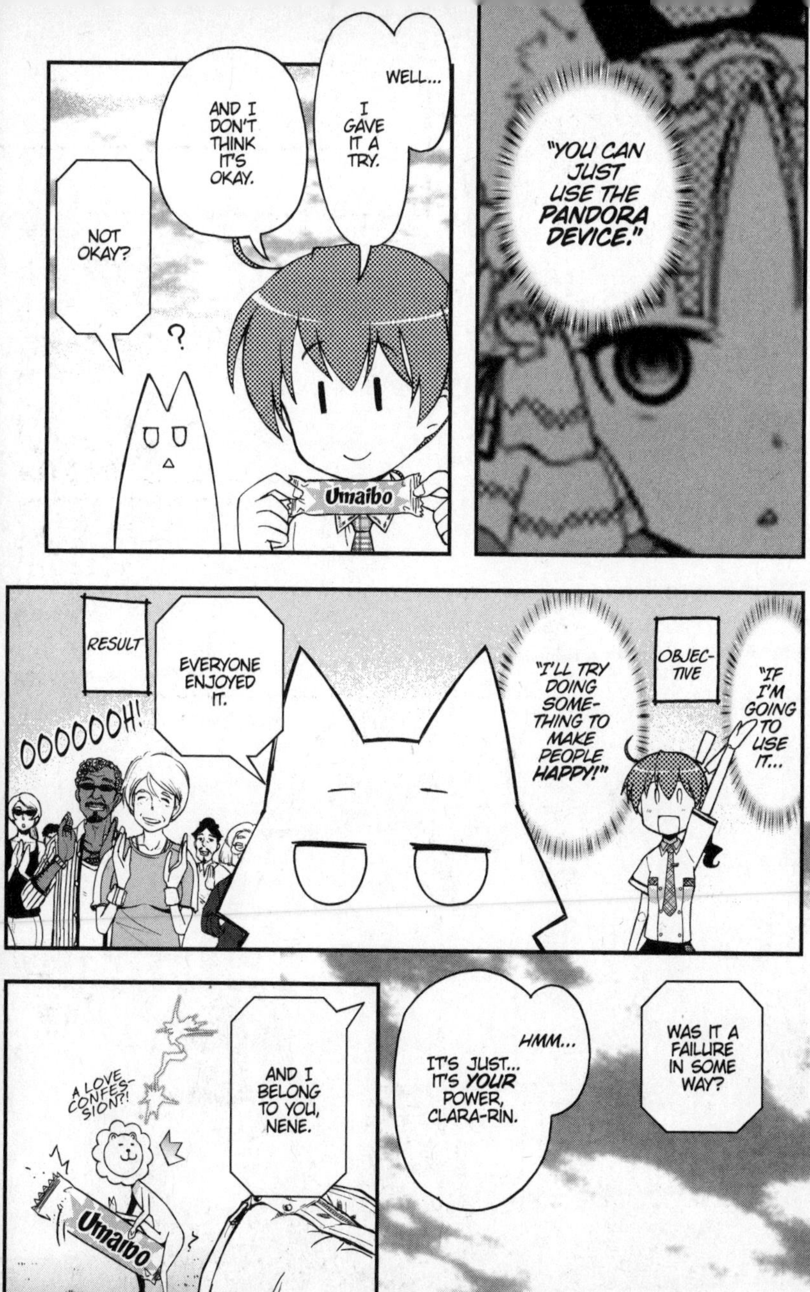

"YOU CAN JUST USE THE PANDORA DEVICE."
WELL... I GAVE IT A TRY.
AND I DON'T THINK IT'S OKAY.
NOT OKAY?
?
Umaibo
"IF I'M GOING TO USE IT...
OBJECTIVE
"I'LL TRY DOING SOMETHING TO MAKE PEOPLE HAPPY!"
EVERYONE ENJOYED IT.
RESULT
OOOOOOH!
WAS IT A FAILURE IN SOME WAY?
HMM... IT'S JUST... IT'S YOUR POWER, CLARA-RIN.
AND I BELONG TO YOU, NENE.
A LOVE CONFESSION?!
Umaibo

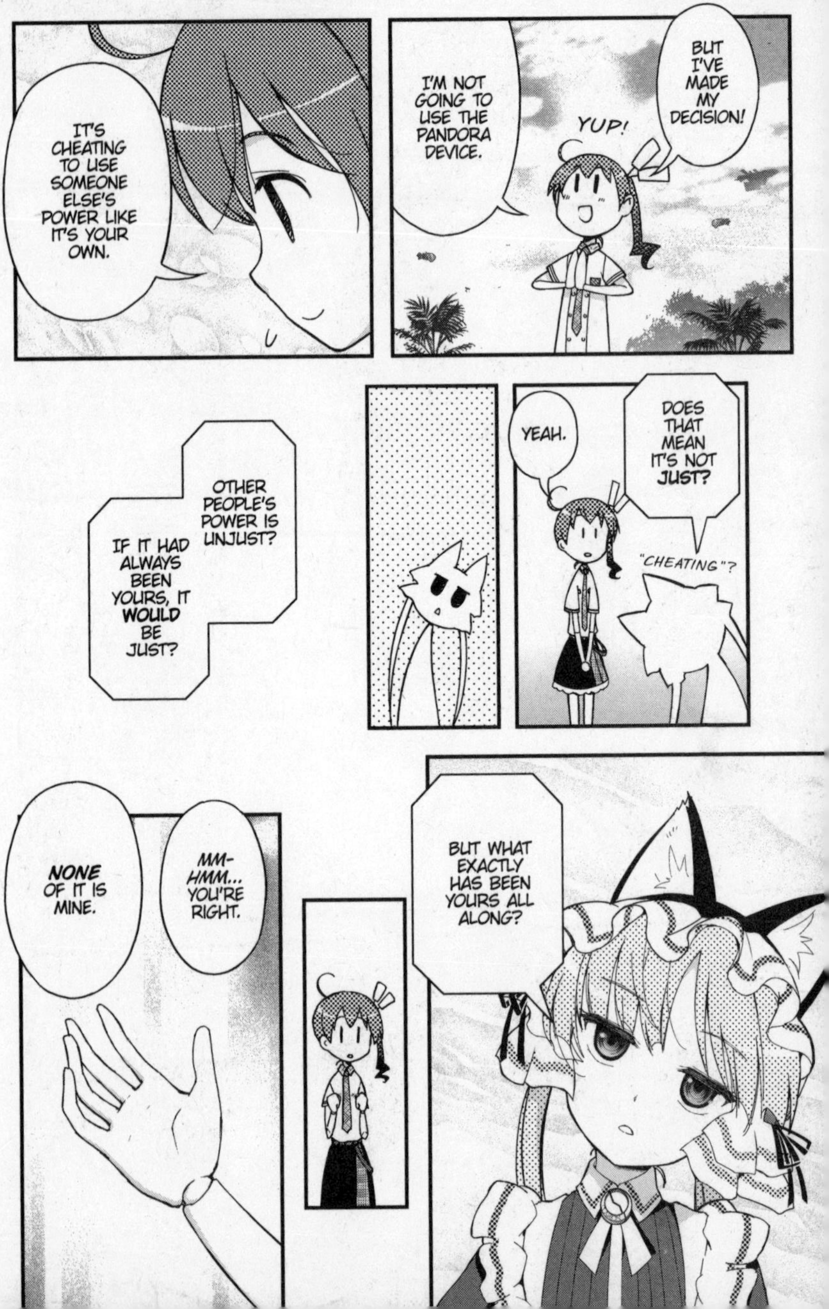
BUT I'VE MADE MY DECISION!
YUP!
I'M NOT GOING TO USE THE PANDORA DEVICE.
IT'S CHEATING TO USE SOMEONE ELSE'S POWER LIKE IT'S YOUR OWN.
DOES THAT MEAN IT'S NOT **JUST**?
"CHEATING"?
YEAH.
OTHER PEOPLE'S POWER IS UNJUST?
IF IT HAD ALWAYS BEEN YOURS, IT **WOULD** BE JUST?
BUT WHAT EXACTLY HAS BEEN YOURS ALL ALONG?
MM-HMM... YOU'RE RIGHT.
NONE OF IT IS MINE.

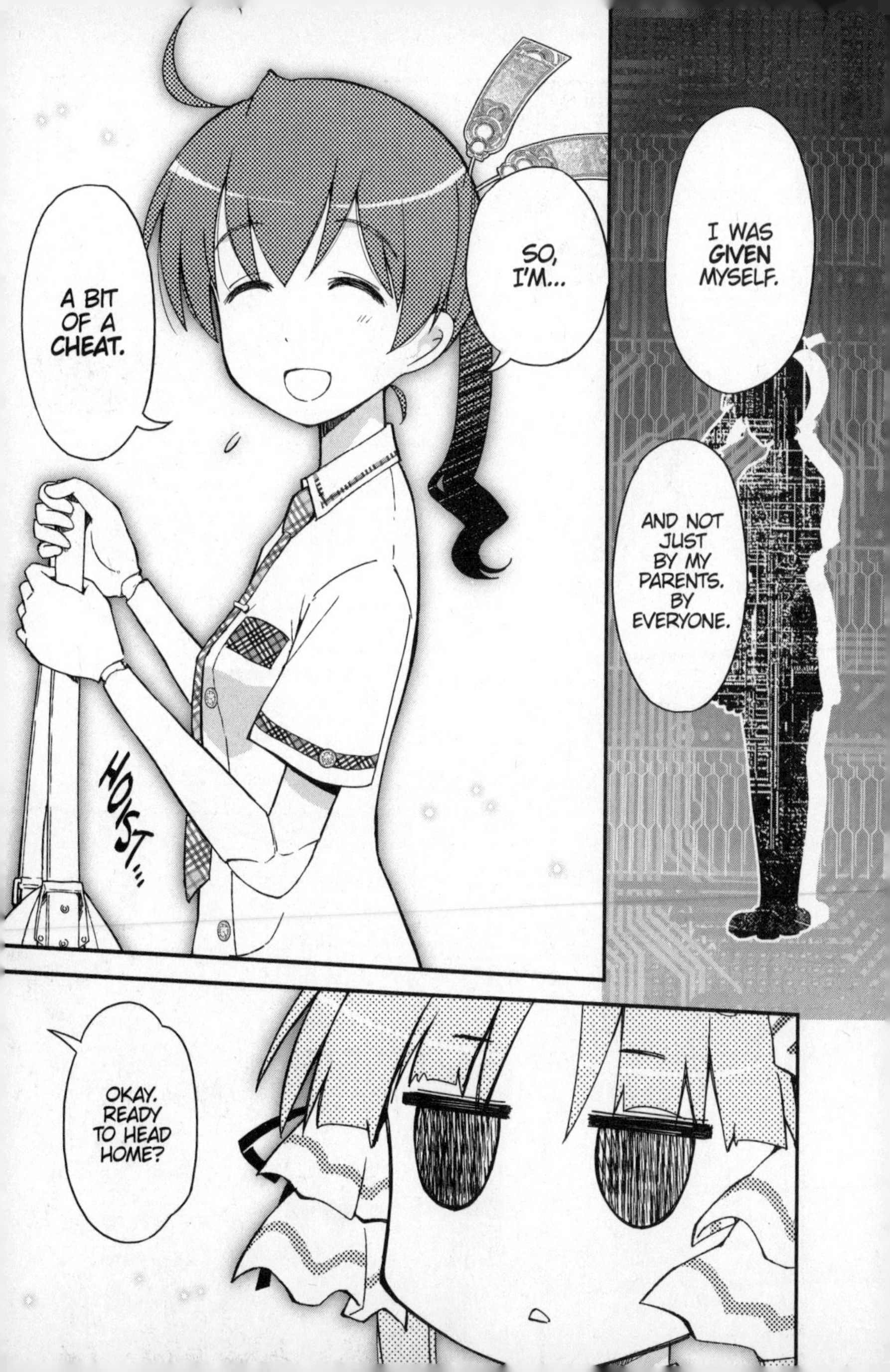
I WAS GIVEN MYSELF.
AND NOT JUST BY MY PARENTS. BY EVERYONE.
SO, I'M...
A BIT OF A CHEAT.
HOIST...
OKAY. READY TO HEAD HOME?

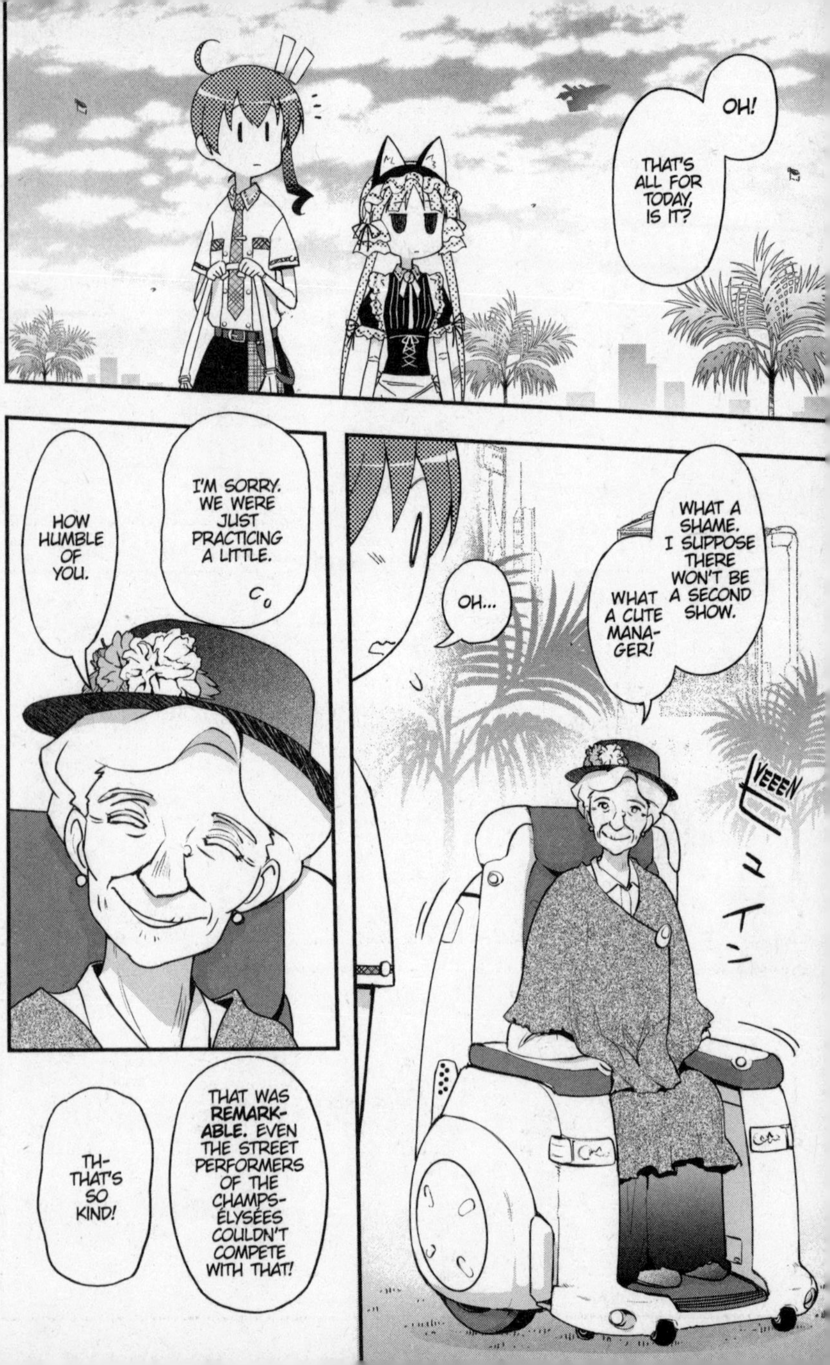
OH!
THAT'S ALL FOR TODAY, IS IT?
WHAT A SHAME. I SUPPOSE THERE WON'T BE A SECOND SHOW.
WHAT A CUTE MANAGER!
VEEEN
OH...
I'M SORRY. WE WERE JUST PRACTICING A LITTLE.
HOW HUMBLE OF YOU.
THAT WAS **REMARKABLE.** EVEN THE STREET PERFORMERS OF THE CHAMPS-ÉLYSÉES COULDN'T COMPETE WITH THAT!
TH-THAT'S SO KIND!

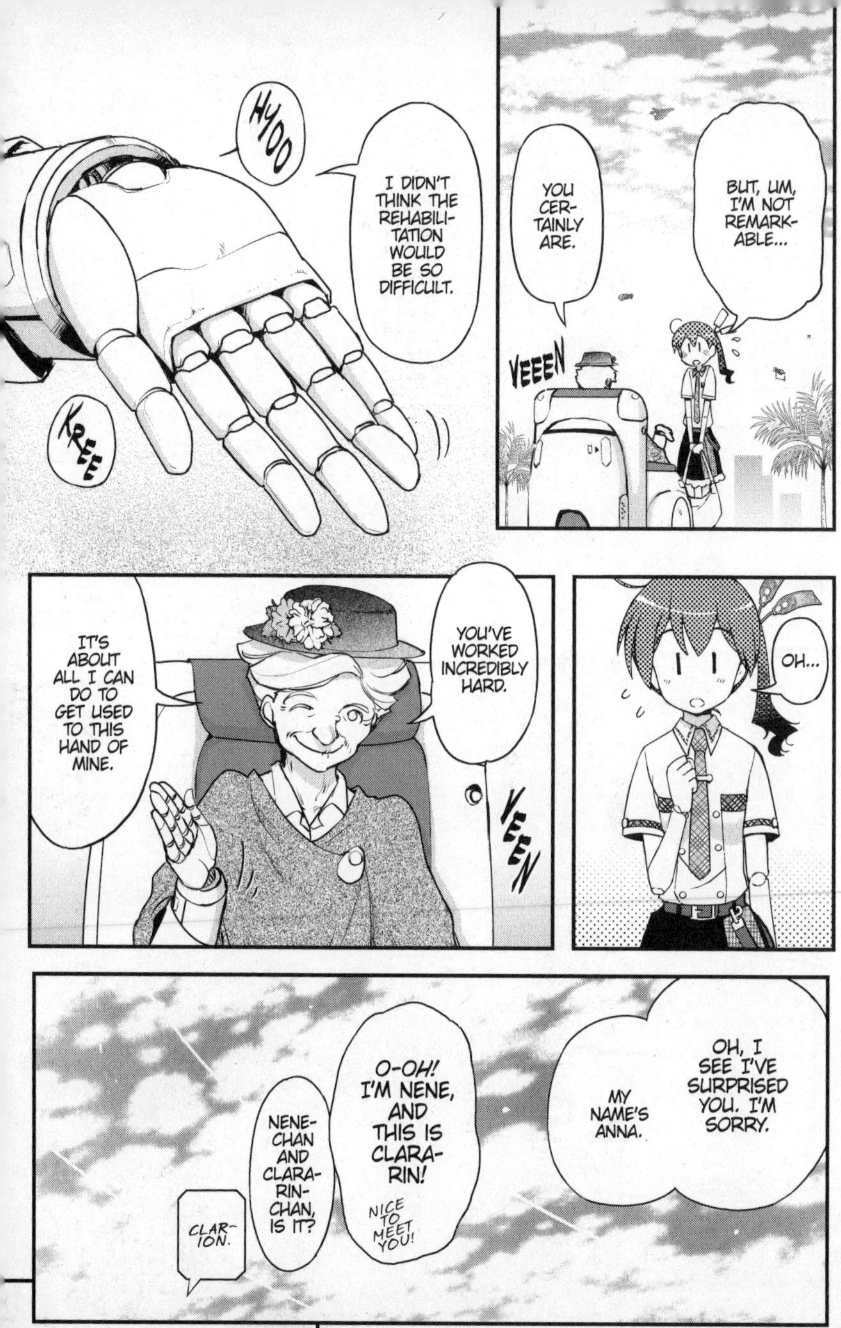
BUT, UM, I'M NOT REMARKABLE...
YOU CERTAINLY ARE.
VEEEN
I DIDN'T THINK THE REHABILITATION WOULD BE SO DIFFICULT.
HYOO
KREE
OH...
YOU'VE WORKED INCREDIBLY HARD.
IT'S ABOUT ALL I CAN DO TO GET USED TO THIS HAND OF MINE.
VEEN
OH, I SEE I'VE SURPRISED YOU. I'M SORRY.
MY NAME'S ANNA.
O-OH! I'M NENE, AND THIS IS CLARARIN!
NICE TO MEET YOU!
NENE-CHAN AND CLARARIN-CHAN, IS IT?
CLARION.

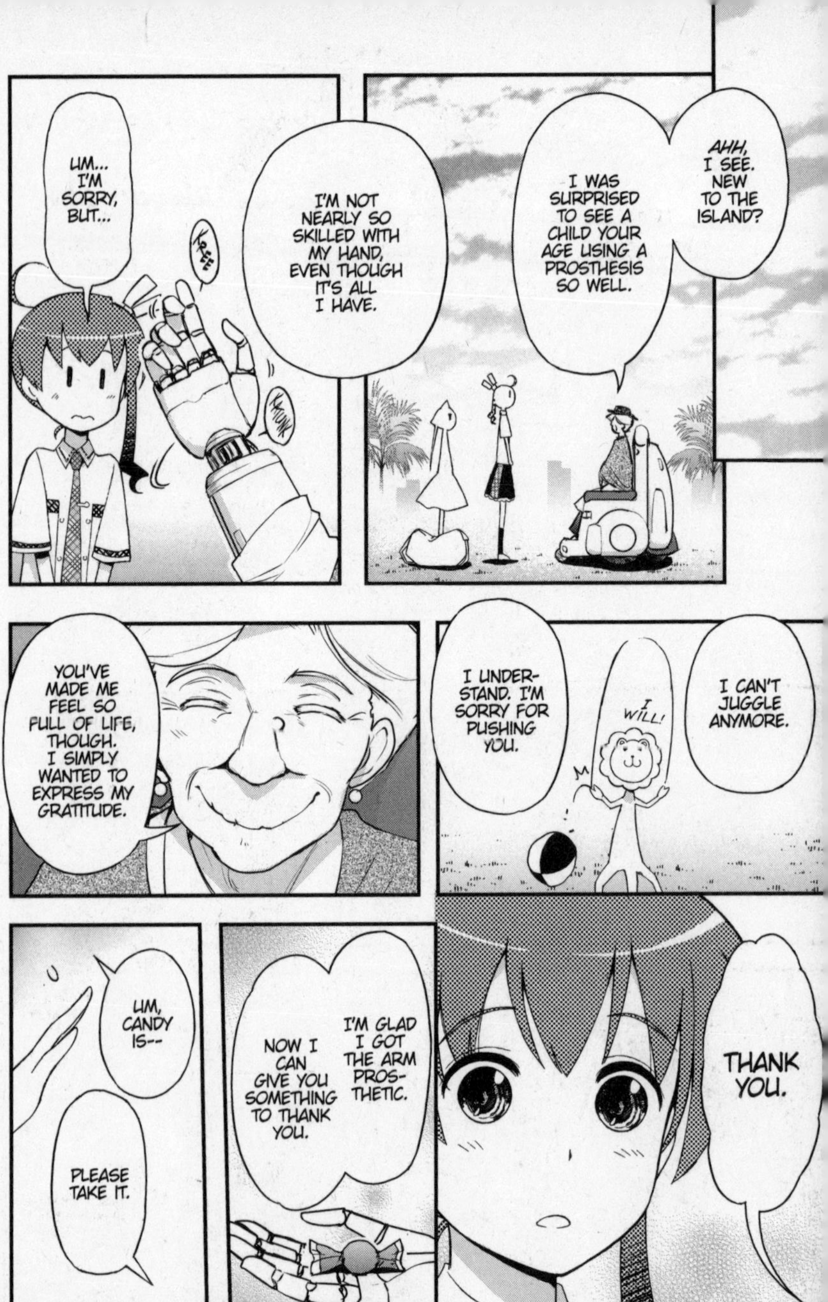
AHH, I SEE. NEW TO THE ISLAND?
I WAS SURPRISED TO SEE A CHILD YOUR AGE USING A PROSTHESIS SO WELL.
I'M NOT NEARLY SO SKILLED WITH MY HAND, EVEN THOUGH IT'S ALL I HAVE.
UM... I'M SORRY, BUT...
I CAN'T JUGGLE ANYMORE.
I WILL!
I UNDER-STAND. I'M SORRY FOR PUSHING YOU.
YOU'VE MADE ME FEEL SO FULL OF LIFE, THOUGH. I SIMPLY WANTED TO EXPRESS MY GRATITUDE.
THANK YOU.
I'M GLAD I GOT THE ARM PROS-THETIC.
NOW I CAN GIVE YOU SOMETHING TO THANK YOU.
UM, CANDY IS--
PLEASE TAKE IT.

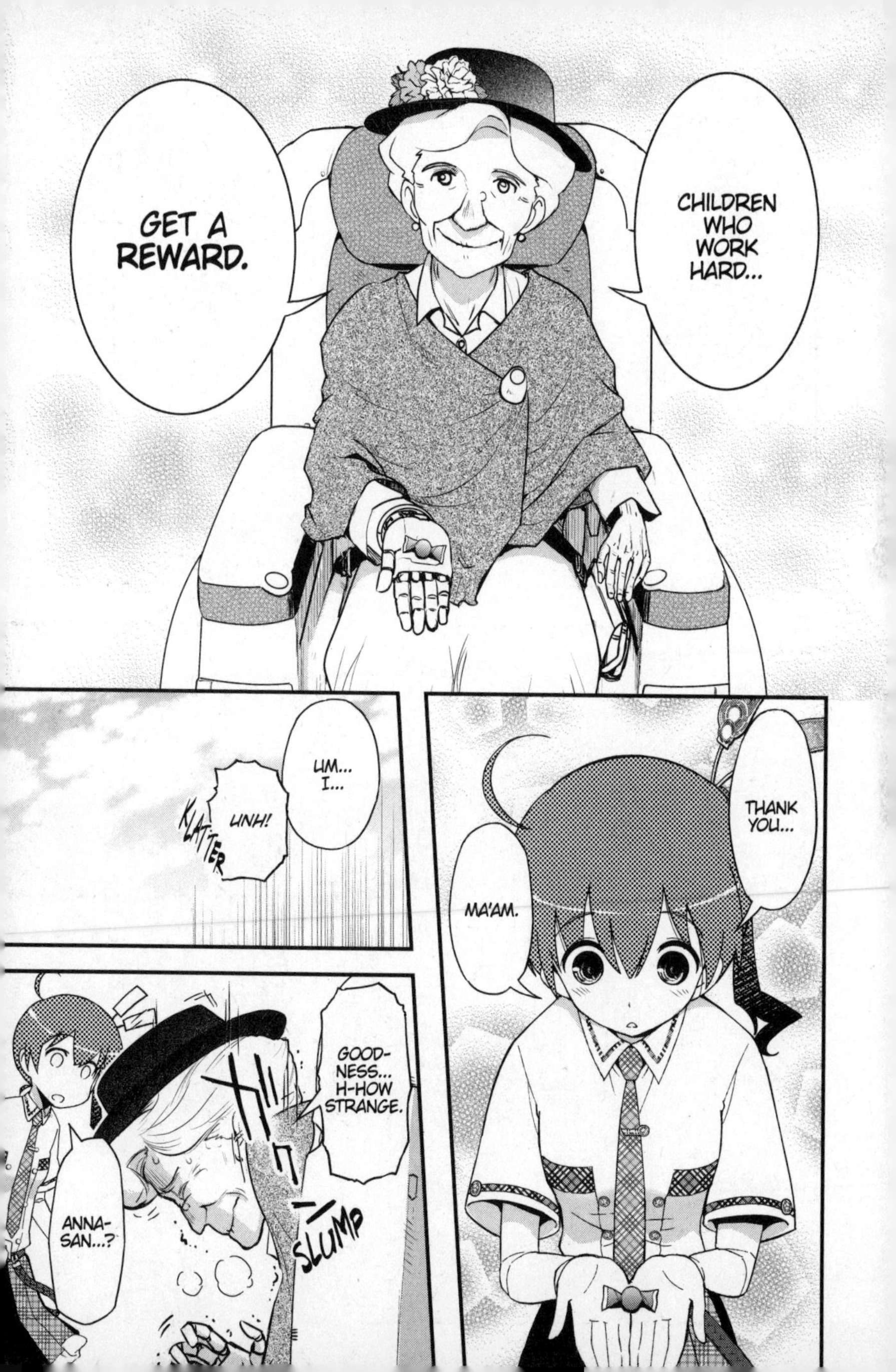
CHILDREN WHO WORK HARD...
GET A REWARD.
THANK YOU...
MA'AM.
UM... I...
UNH!
KLATTER
GOOD-NESS... H-HOW STRANGE.
SLUMP
ANNA-SAN...?

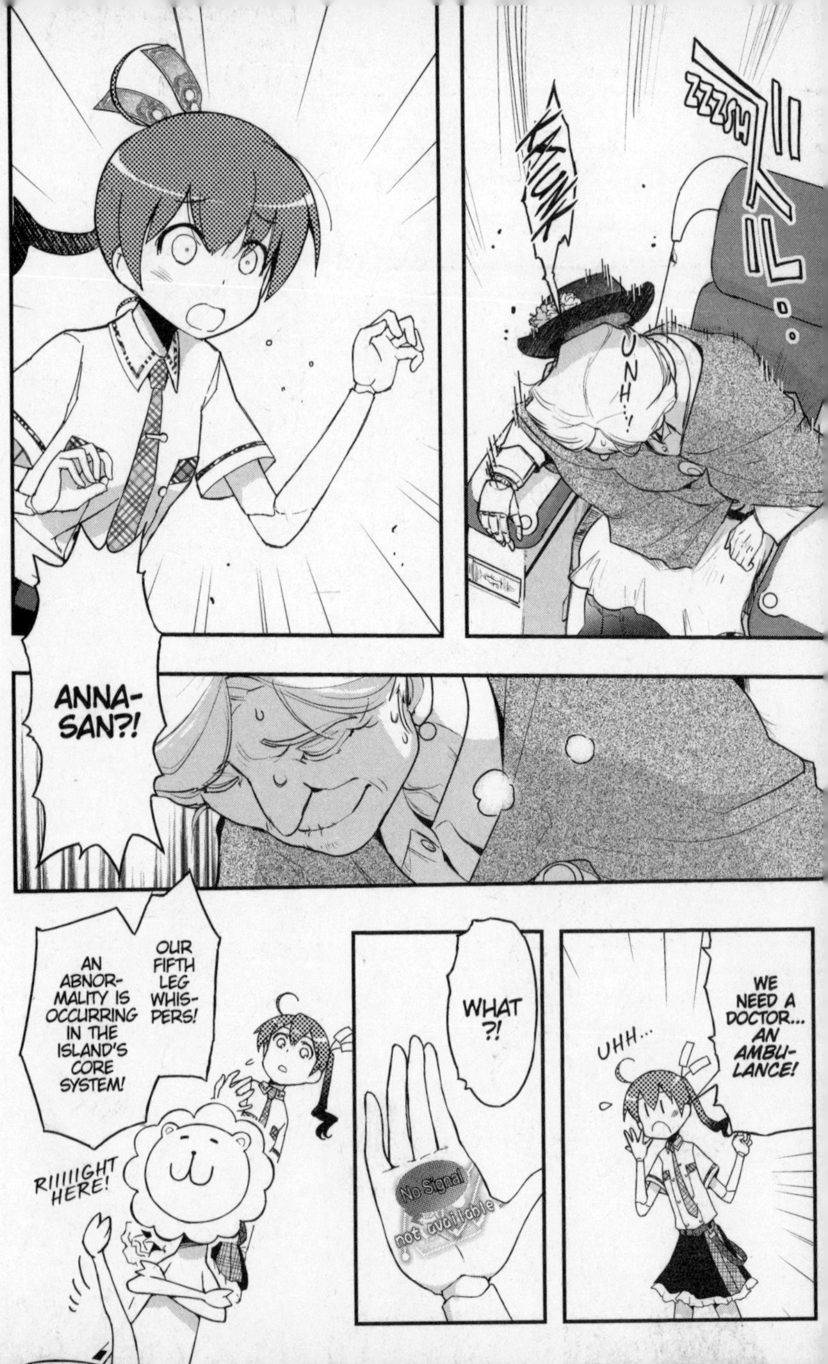
ZZZSH
ズ
ル
KATUNK
UNH...!
ANNA-SAN?!
UHH...
WE NEED A DOCTOR... AN AMBULANCE!
WHAT?!
No Signal
not available
OUR FIFTH LEG WHISPERS!
AN ABNORMALITY IS OCCURRING IN THE ISLAND'S CORE SYSTEM!
RIIIIIGHT HERE!

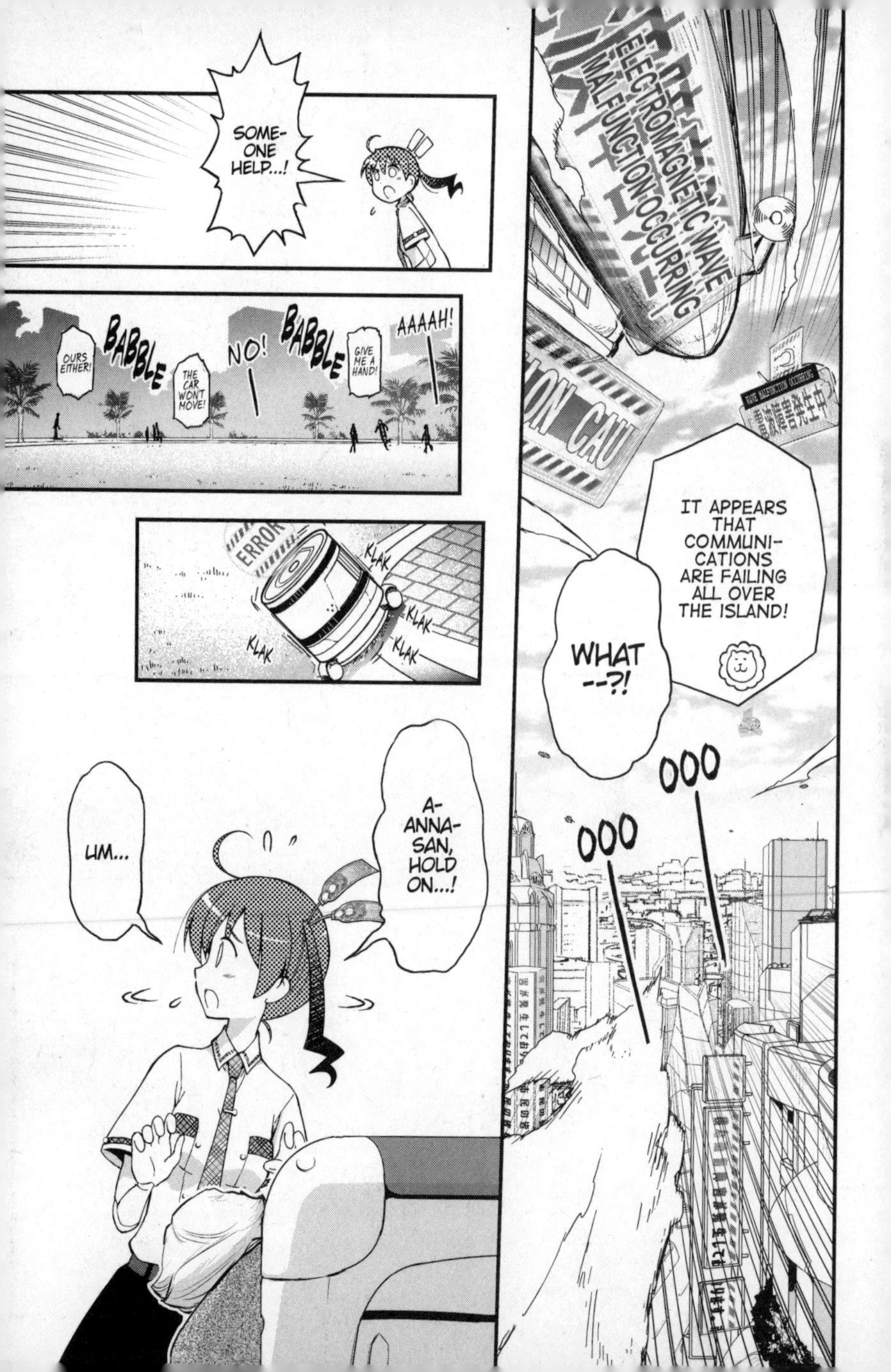
ELECTROMAGNETIC WAVE MALFUNCTION OCCURRING
WAVE MALFUNCTION OCCURRING
CAU
IT APPEARS THAT COMMUNICATIONS ARE FAILING ALL OVER THE ISLAND!
WHAT--?!
OOO
OOO
SOME-ONE HELP...!
AAAAH!
GIVE ME A HAND!
BABBLE
NO!
THE CAR WON'T MOVE!
BABBLE
OURS EITHER!
ERROR
KLAK
KLAK
KLAK
KLAK
A-ANNA-SAN, HOLD ON...!
UM...

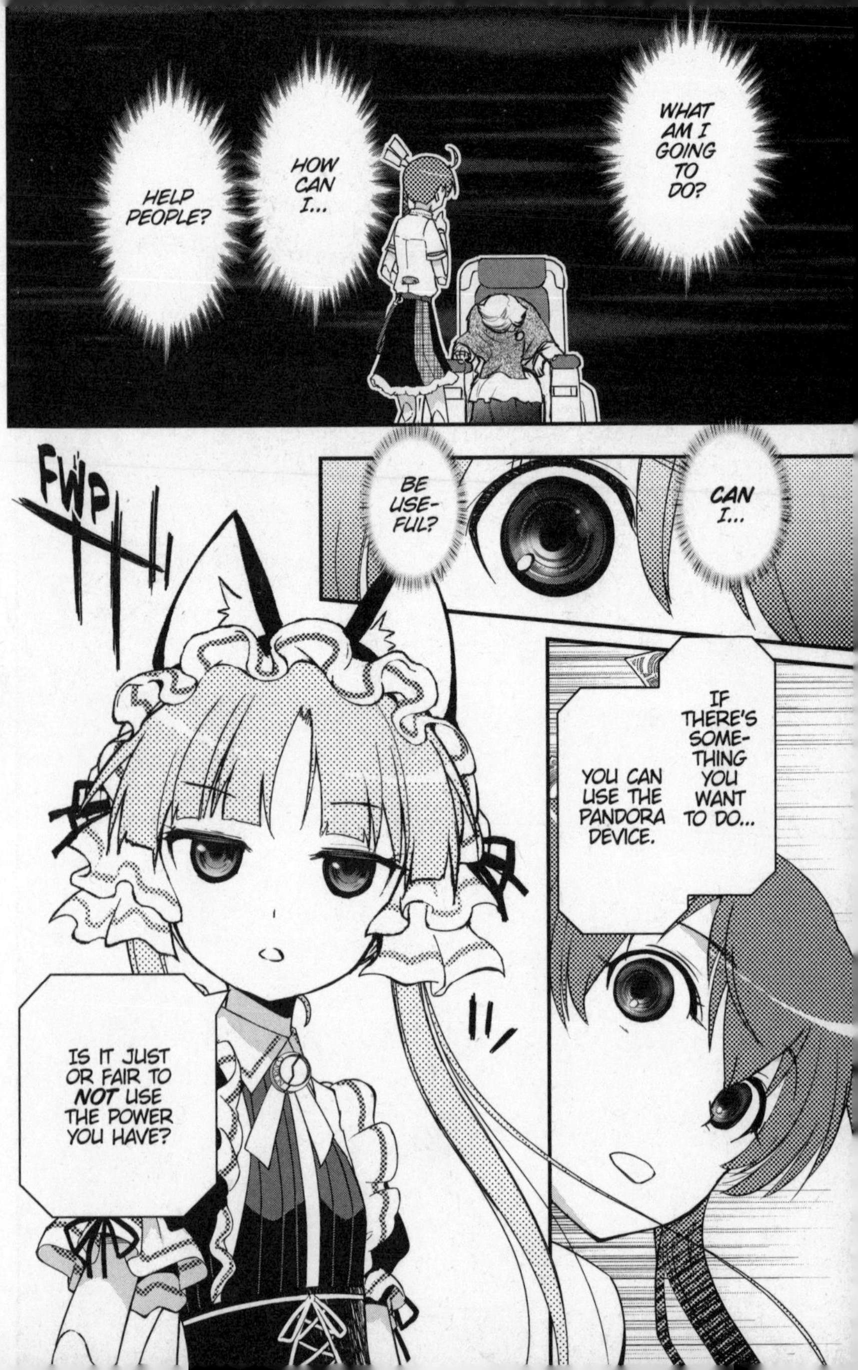
WHAT AM I GOING TO DO?
HOW CAN I...
HELP PEOPLE?
CAN I...
BE USE-FUL?
IF THERE'S SOME-THING YOU WANT TO DO...
YOU CAN USE THE PANDORA DEVICE.
FWP
IS IT JUST OR FAIR TO NOT USE THE POWER YOU HAVE?

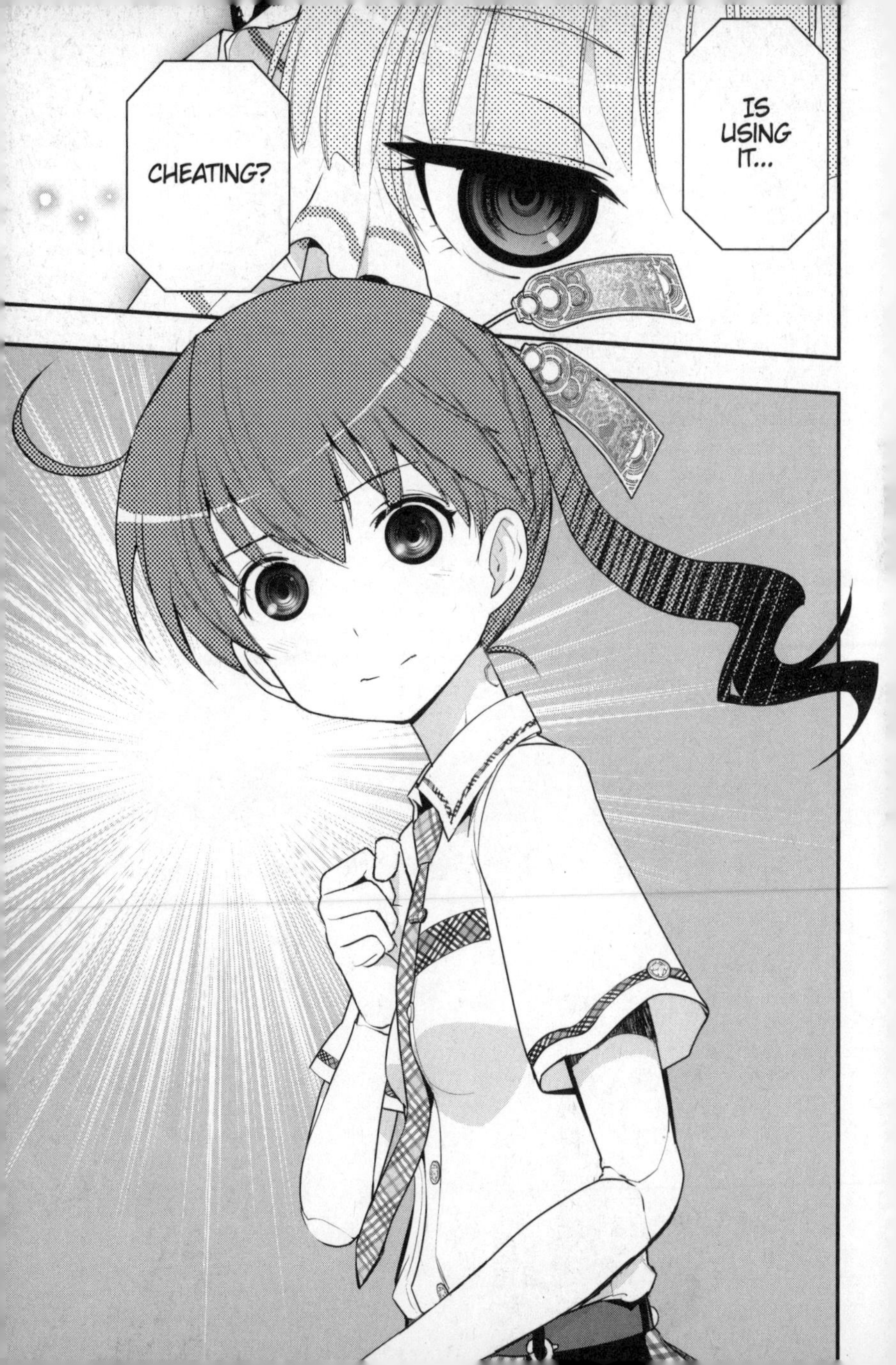
IS USING IT...
CHEATING?

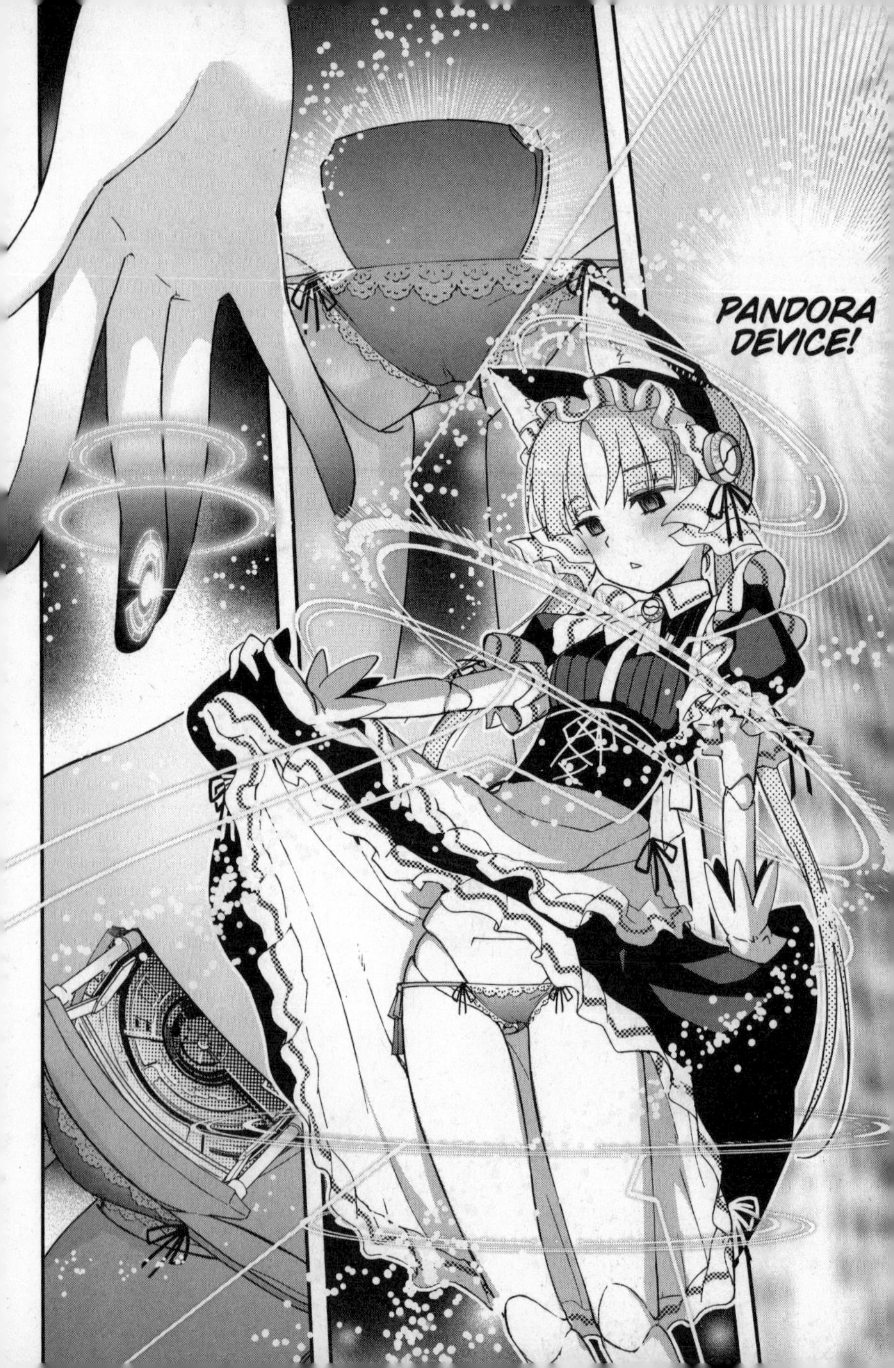
PANDORA DEVICE!

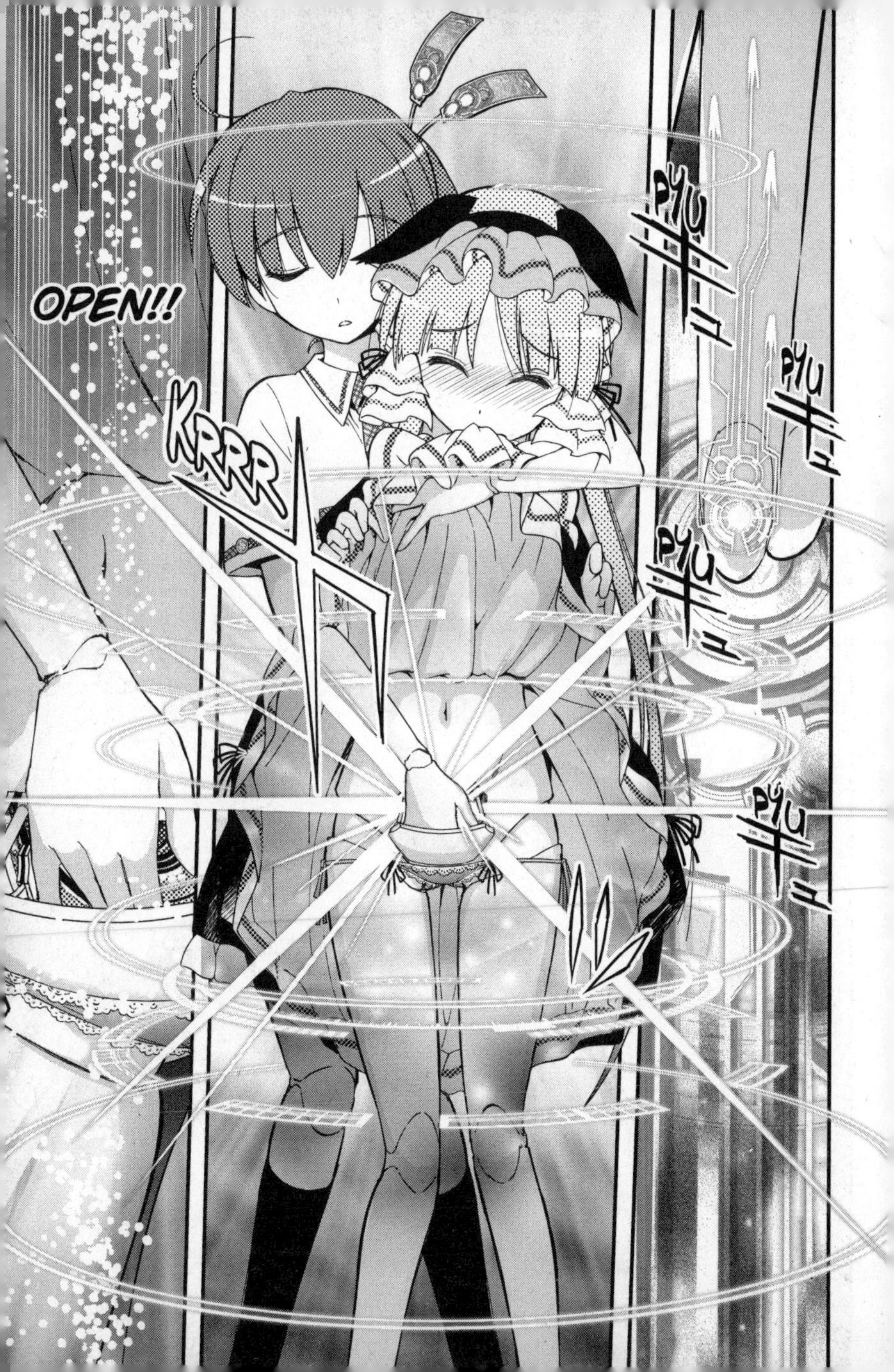
PYU
OPEN!!
PYU
KRRR
PYU
PYU

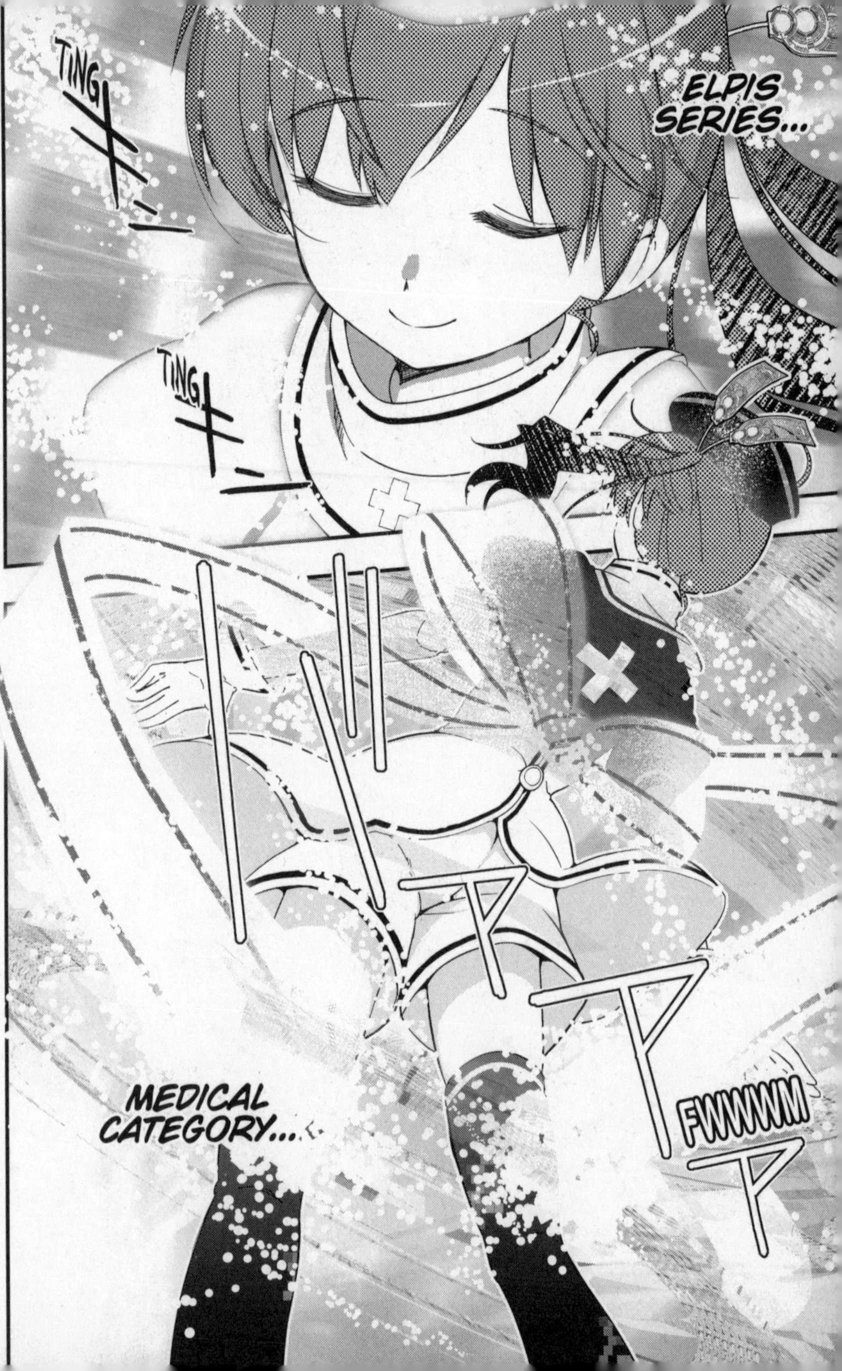
ELPIS SERIES...
TING
TING
FWWWM
MEDICAL CATEGORY...

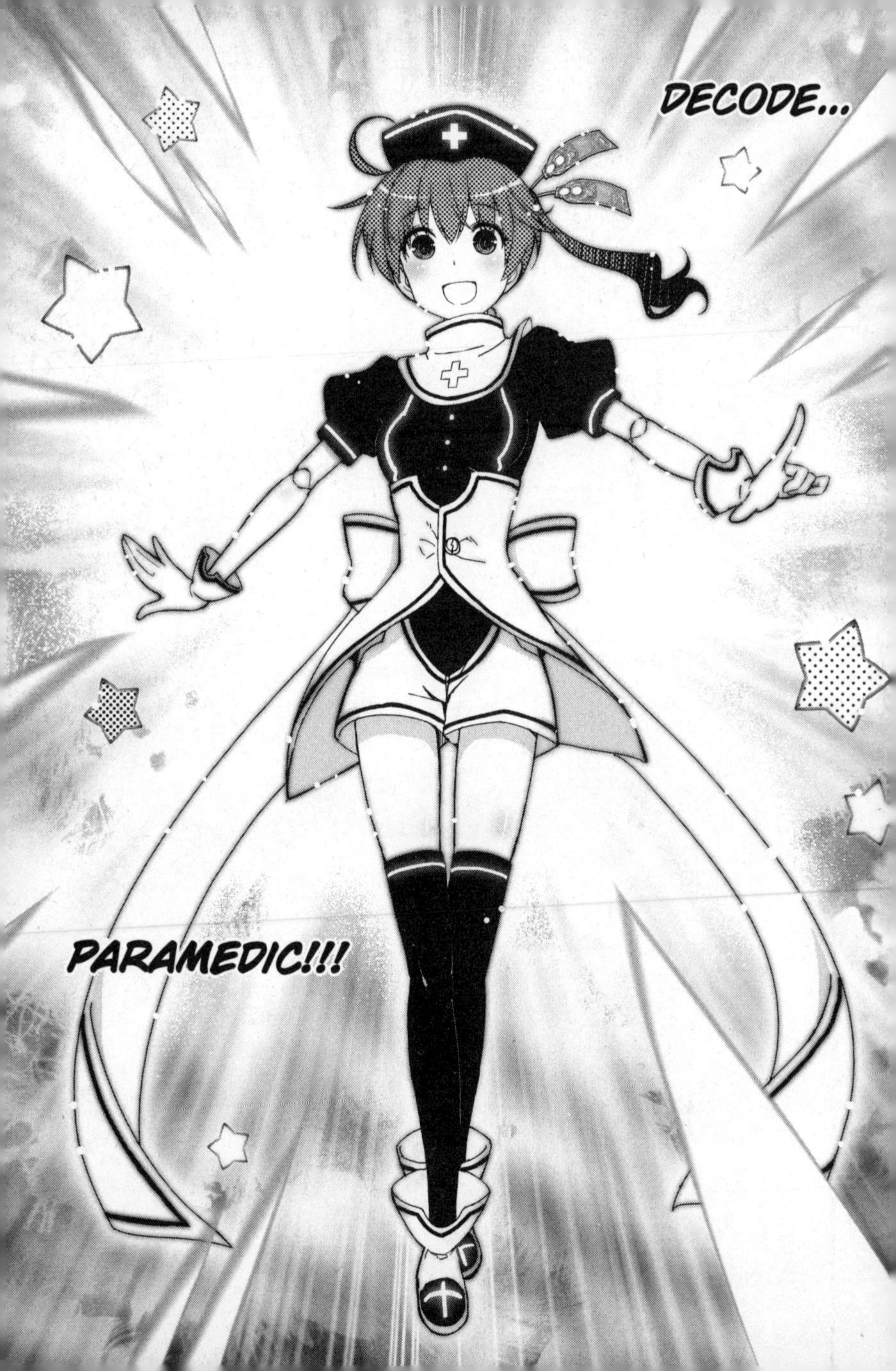
DECODE...
PARAMEDIC!!!

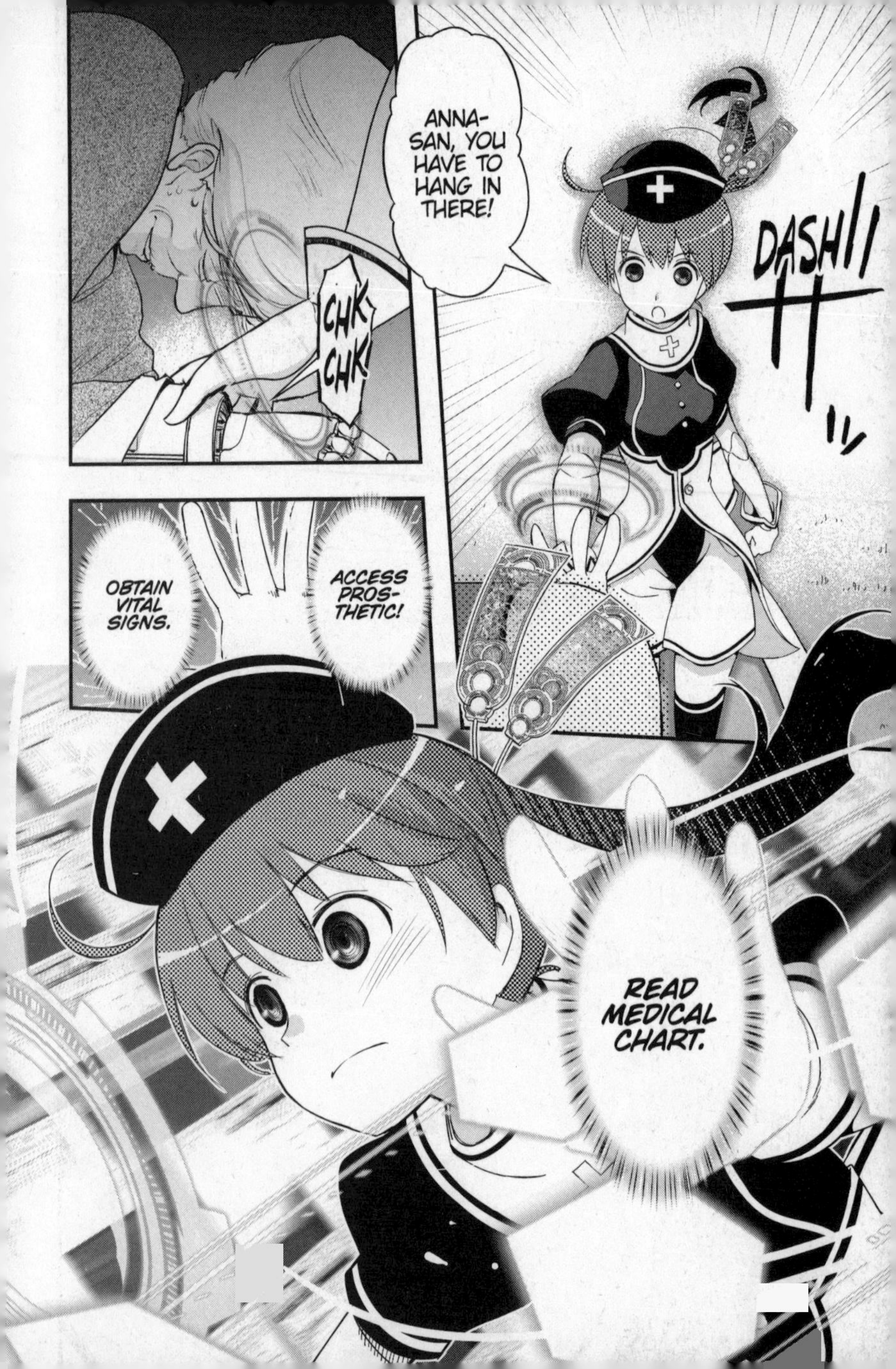
ANNA-SAN, YOU HAVE TO HANG IN THERE!
DASH!!
CHK CHK
ACCESS PROSTHETIC!
OBTAIN VITAL SIGNS.
READ MEDICAL CHART.

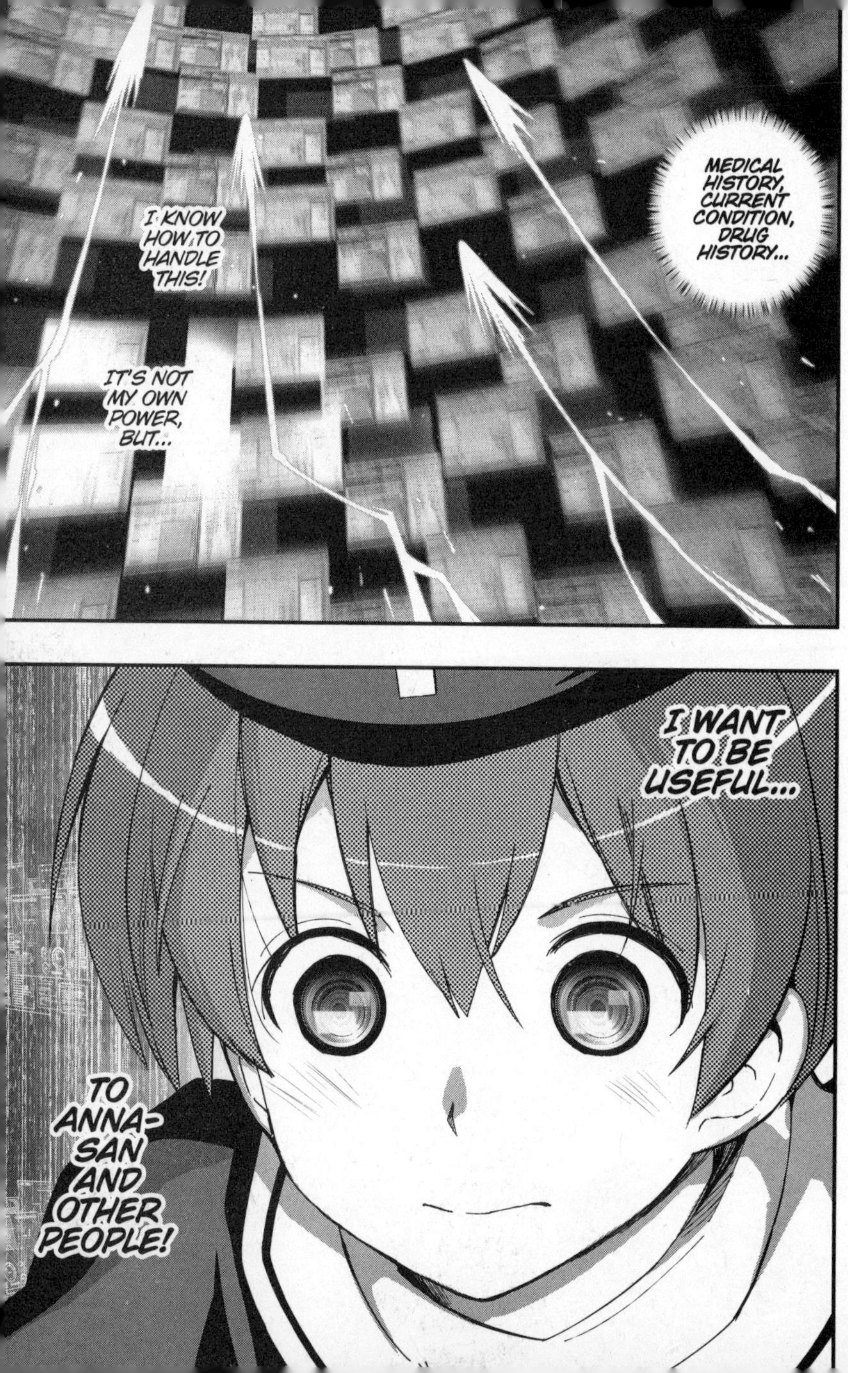
MEDICAL HISTORY, CURRENT CONDITION, DRUG HISTORY...
I KNOW HOW TO HANDLE THIS!
IT'S NOT MY OWN POWER, BUT...
I WANT TO BE USEFUL...
TO ANNA-SAN AND OTHER PEOPLE!

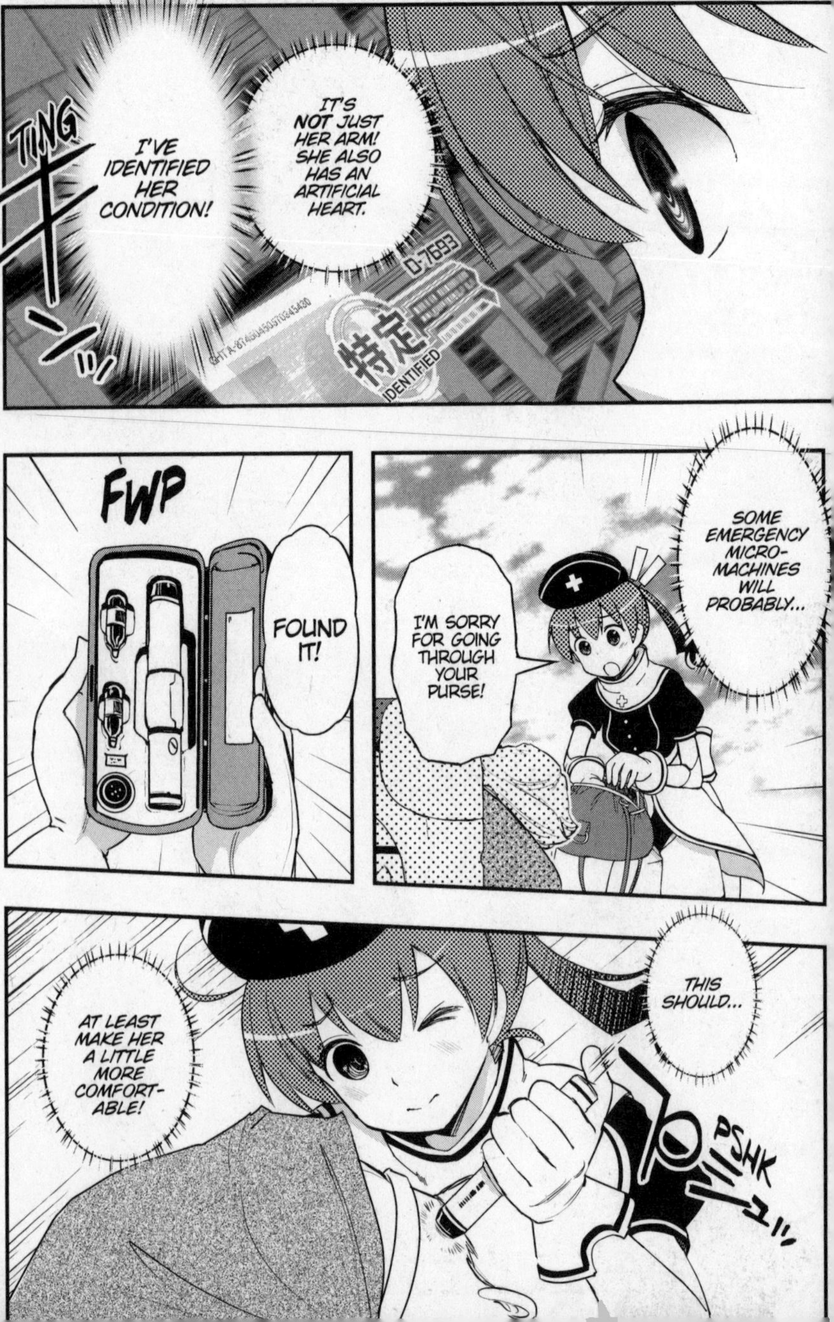
TING
IT'S NOT JUST HER ARM! SHE ALSO HAS AN ARTIFICIAL HEART.
I'VE IDENTIFIED HER CONDITION!
D-7693
特定
IDENTIFIED
SOME EMERGENCY MICRO-MACHINES WILL PROBABLY...
I'M SORRY FOR GOING THROUGH YOUR PURSE!
FWP
FOUND IT!
THIS SHOULD...
AT LEAST MAKE HER A LITTLE MORE COMFORT-ABLE!
PSHK

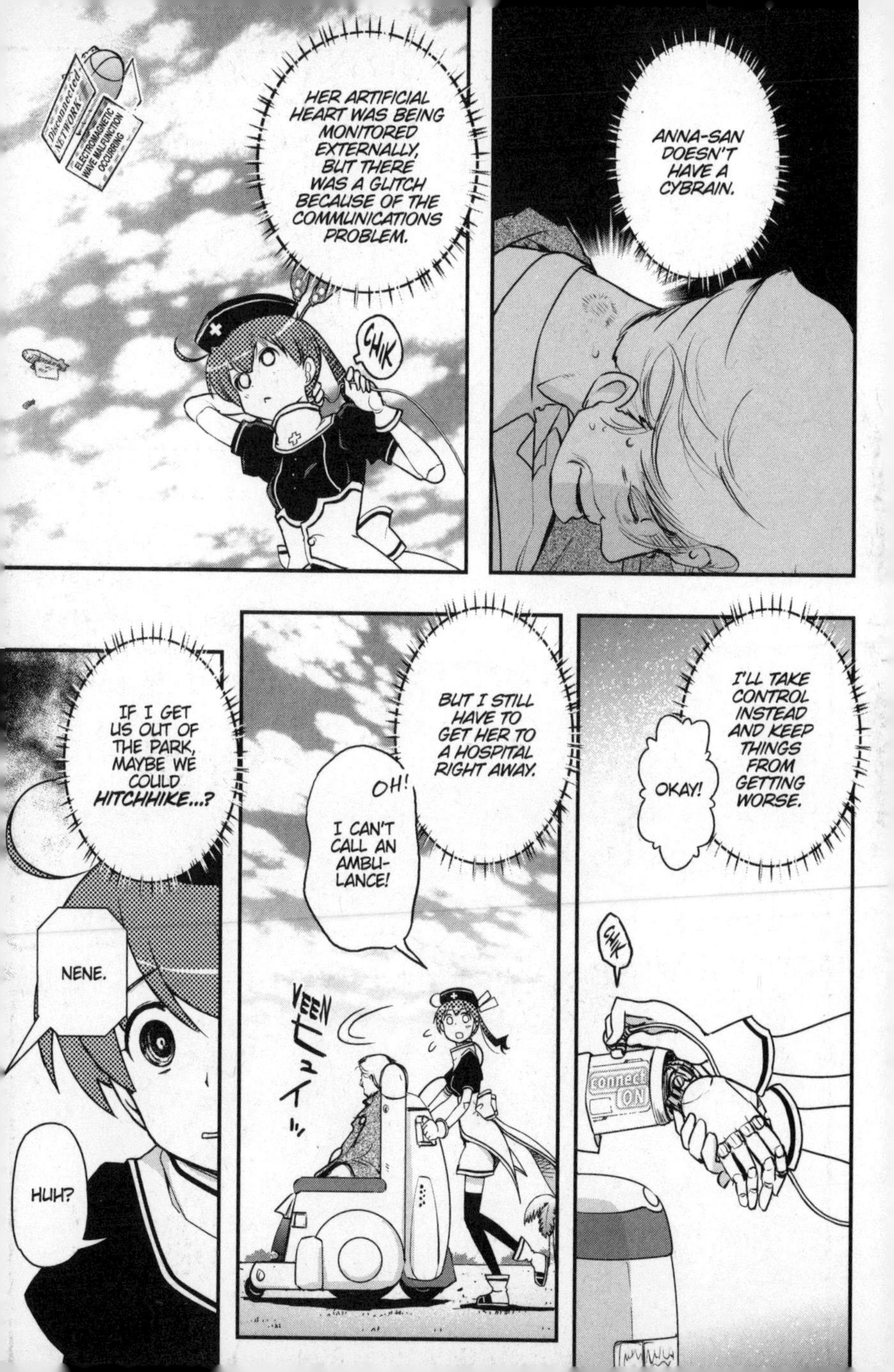
ANNA-SAN DOESN'T HAVE A CYBRAIN.
Disconnected NETWORK
ELECTROMAGNETIC WAVE MALFUNCTION OCCURRING
HER ARTIFICIAL HEART WAS BEING MONITORED EXTERNALLY, BUT THERE WAS A GLITCH BECAUSE OF THE COMMUNICATIONS PROBLEM.
CHIK
I'LL TAKE CONTROL INSTEAD AND KEEP THINGS FROM GETTING WORSE.
OKAY!
CHIK
connect ON
BUT I STILL HAVE TO GET HER TO A HOSPITAL RIGHT AWAY.
OH! I CAN'T CALL AN AMBULANCE!
VEEN
IF I GET US OUT OF THE PARK, MAYBE WE COULD HITCHHIKE...?
NENE.
HUH?

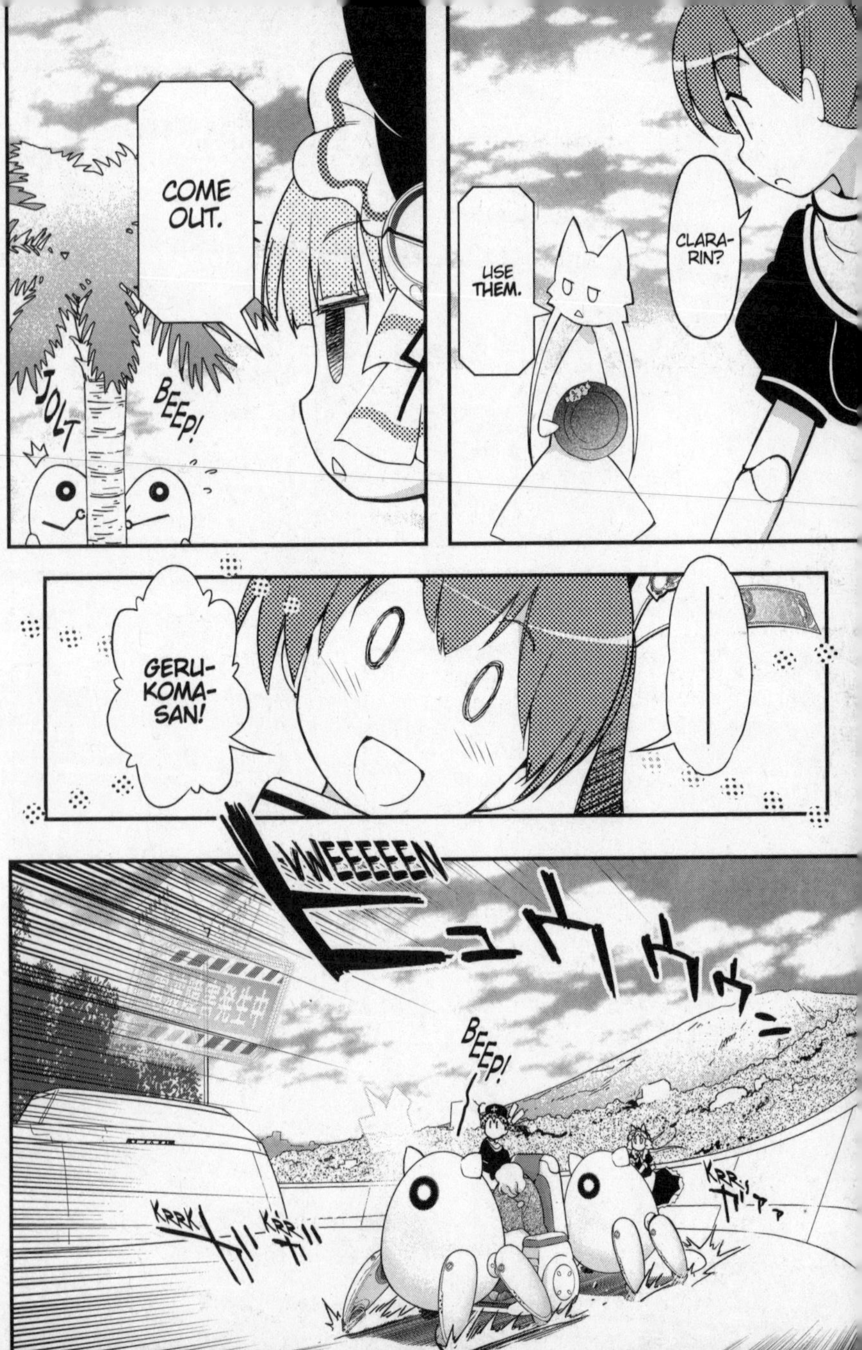
CLARA-RIN?
USE THEM.
COME OUT.
BEEP!
JOLT
GERU-KOMA-SAN!
VWEEEEEN
BEEP!
KRR
KRRK
KRR

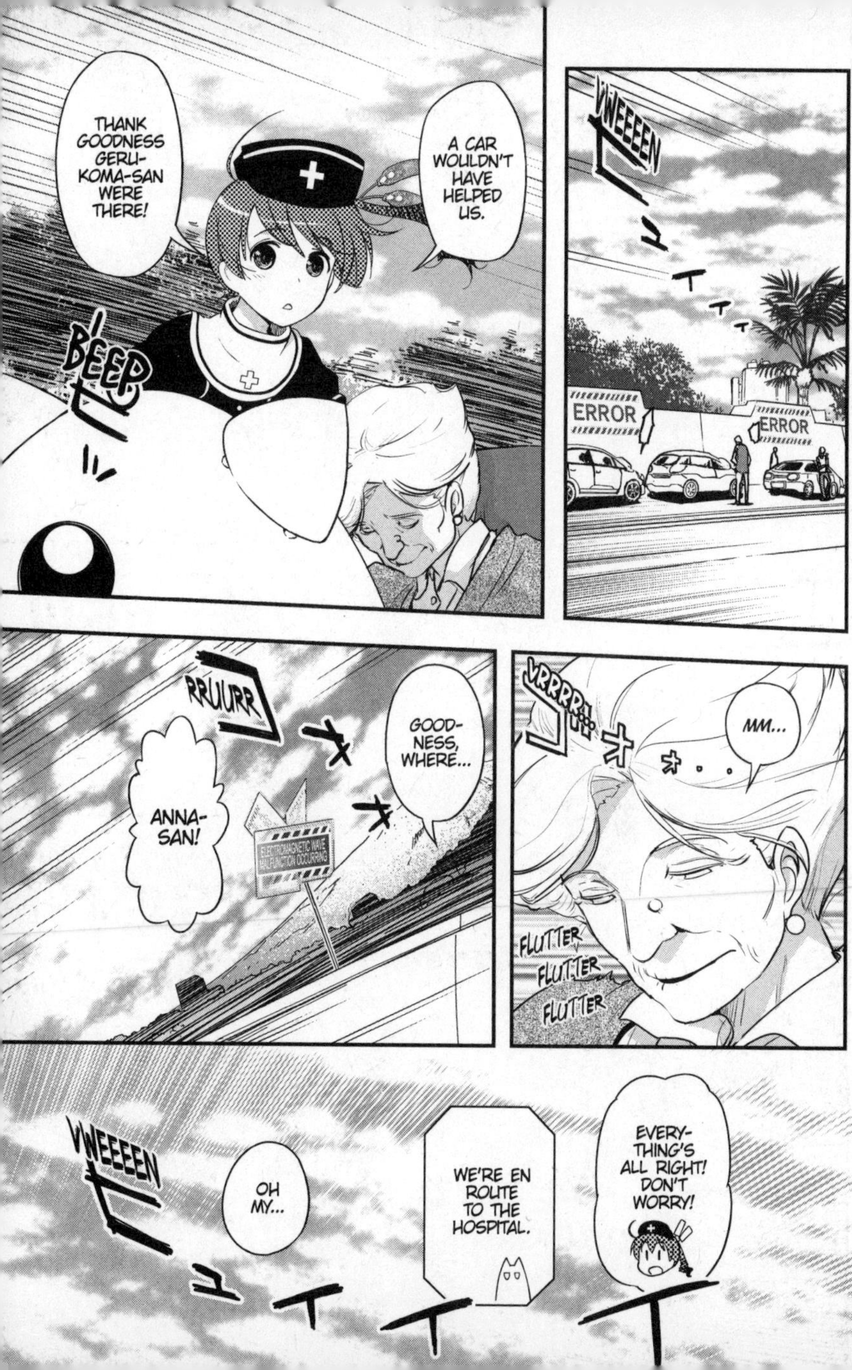
VWEEEEN
ERROR
ERROR
A CAR WOULDN'T HAVE HELPED US.
THANK GOODNESS GERU-KOMA-SAN WERE THERE!
BEEP
VRRRR...
MM...
FLUTTER
FLUTTER
FLUTTER
GOODNESS, WHERE...
RRUURR
ANNA-SAN!
ELECTROMAGNETIC WAVE MALFUNCTION OCCURRING
EVERYTHING'S ALL RIGHT! DON'T WORRY!
WE'RE EN ROUTE TO THE HOSPITAL.
OH MY...
VWEEEEN

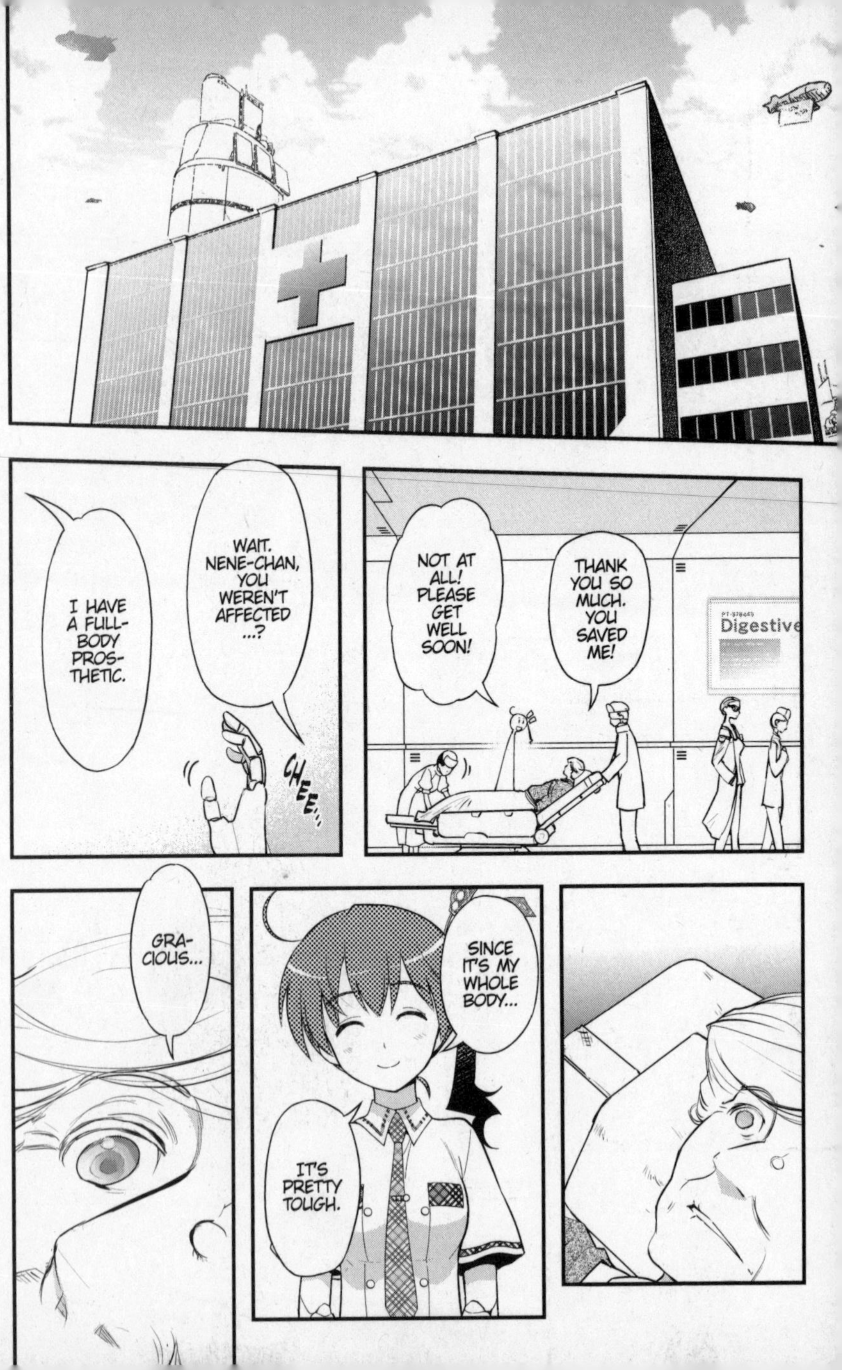
THANK YOU SO MUCH. YOU SAVED ME!
NOT AT ALL! PLEASE GET WELL SOON!
Digestive
WAIT. NENE-CHAN, YOU WEREN'T AFFECTED ...?
I HAVE A FULL-BODY PROSTHETIC.
CHEE...
SINCE IT'S MY WHOLE BODY...
IT'S PRETTY TOUGH.
GRACIOUS...

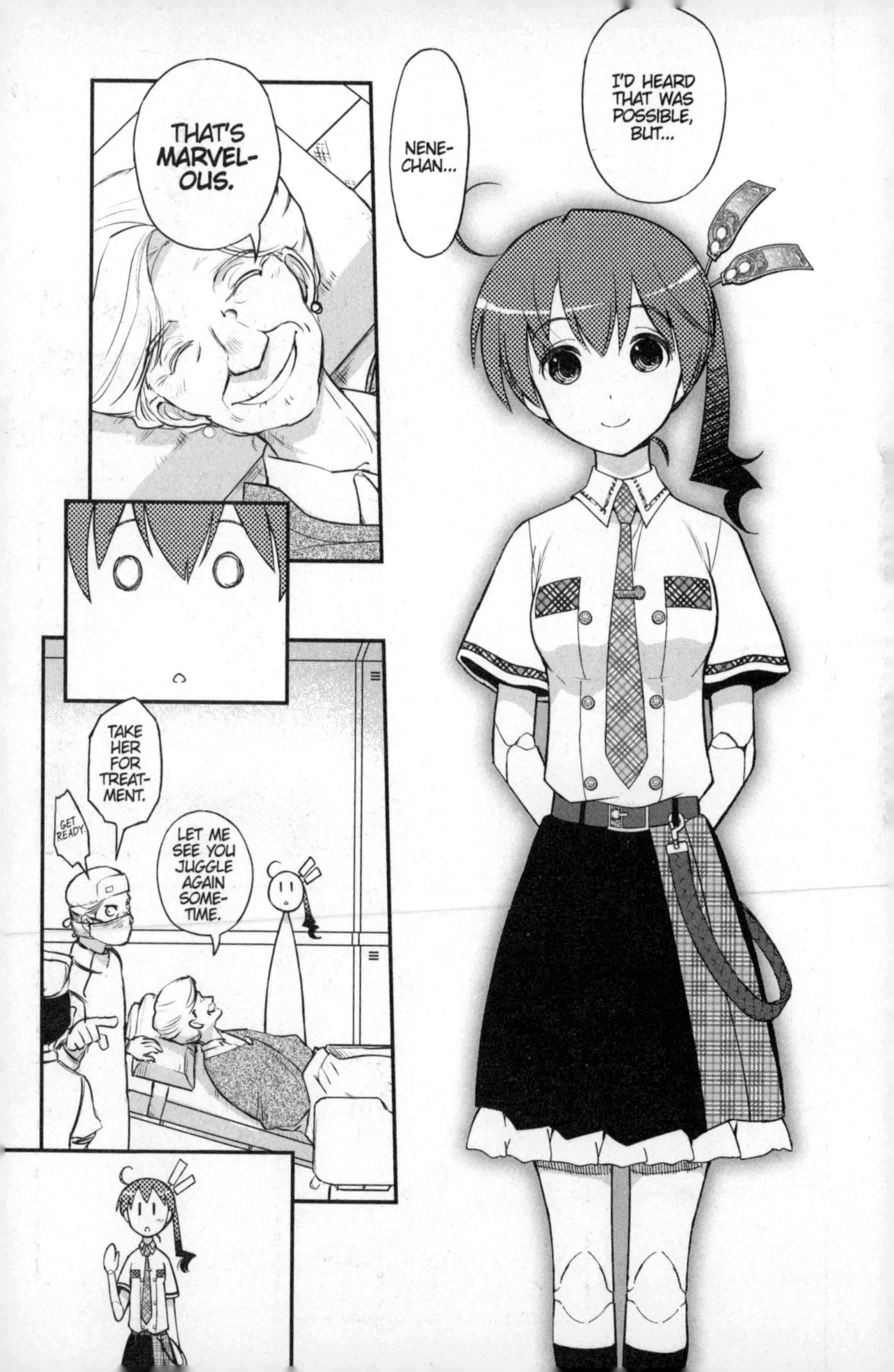

I'D HEARD THAT WAS POSSIBLE, BUT...
NENE-CHAN...
THAT'S MARVEL-OUS.
LET ME SEE YOU JUGGLE AGAIN SOME-TIME.
TAKE HER FOR TREAT-MENT.
GET READY.

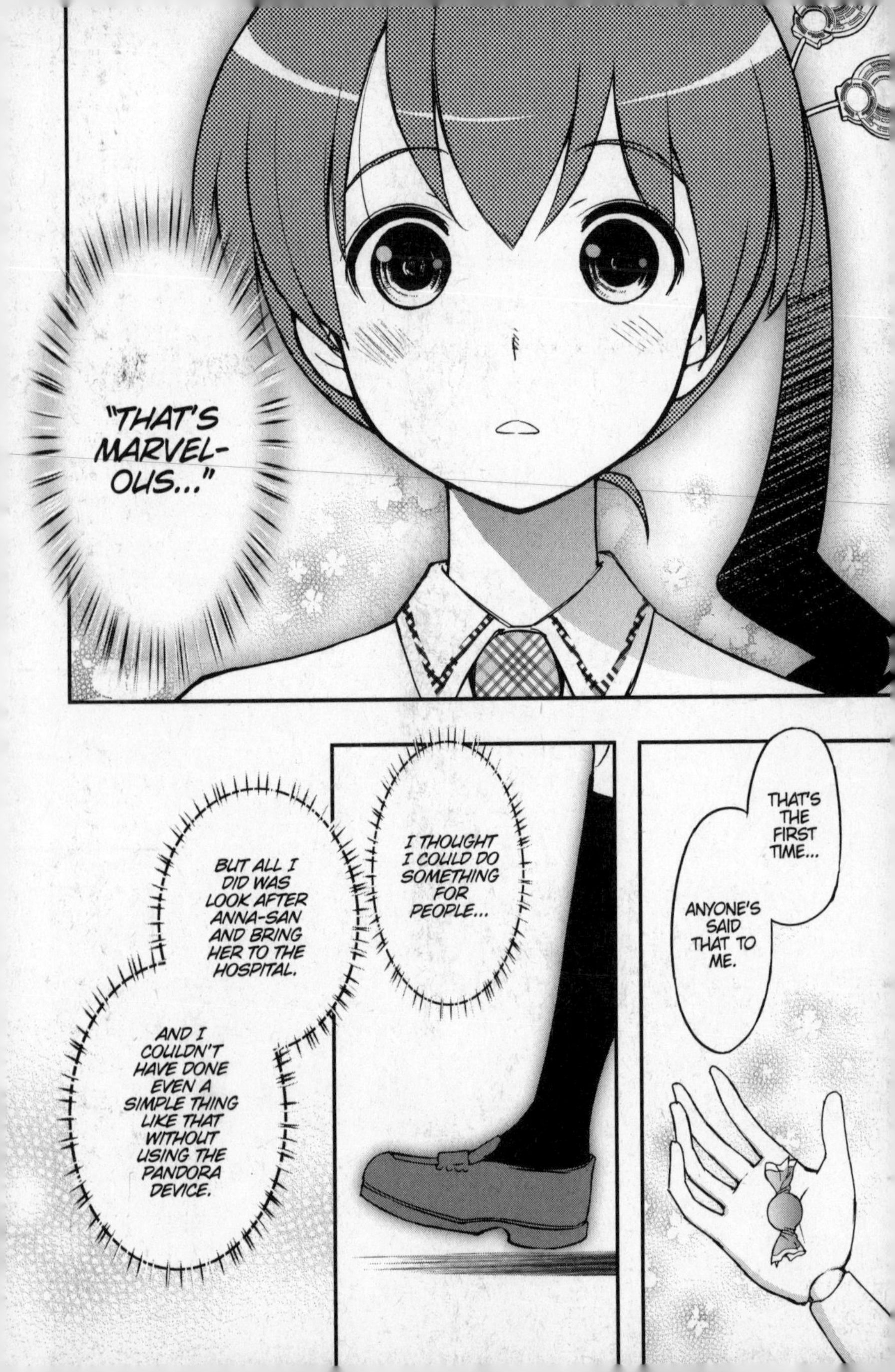
"THAT'S MARVEL-OUS..."
THAT'S THE FIRST TIME...
ANYONE'S SAID THAT TO ME.
I THOUGHT I COULD DO SOMETHING FOR PEOPLE...
BUT ALL I DID WAS LOOK AFTER ANNA-SAN AND BRING HER TO THE HOSPITAL.
AND I COULDN'T HAVE DONE EVEN A SIMPLE THING LIKE THAT WITHOUT USING THE PANDORA DEVICE.

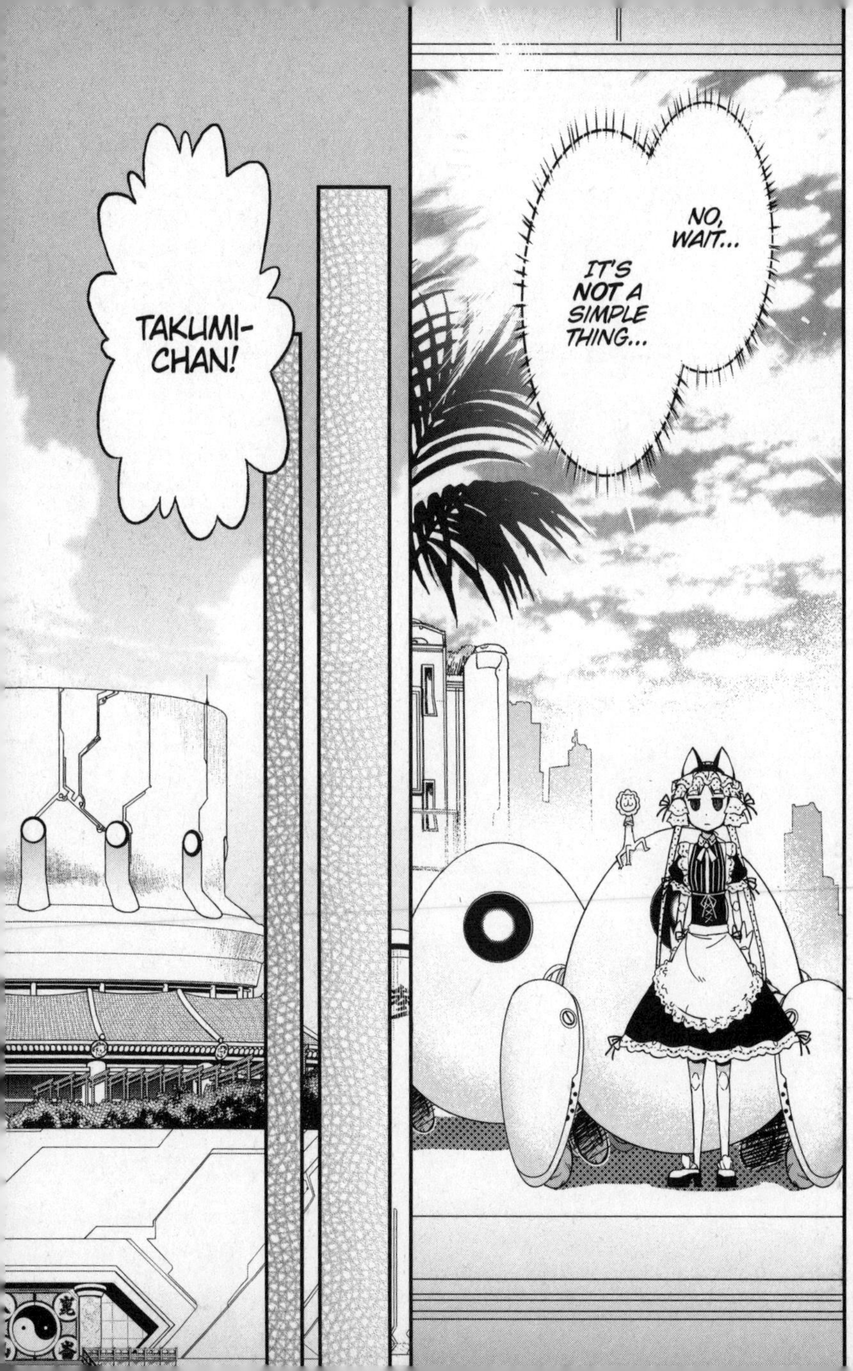
NO, WAIT...
IT'S NOT A SIMPLE THING...
TAKUMI-CHAN!

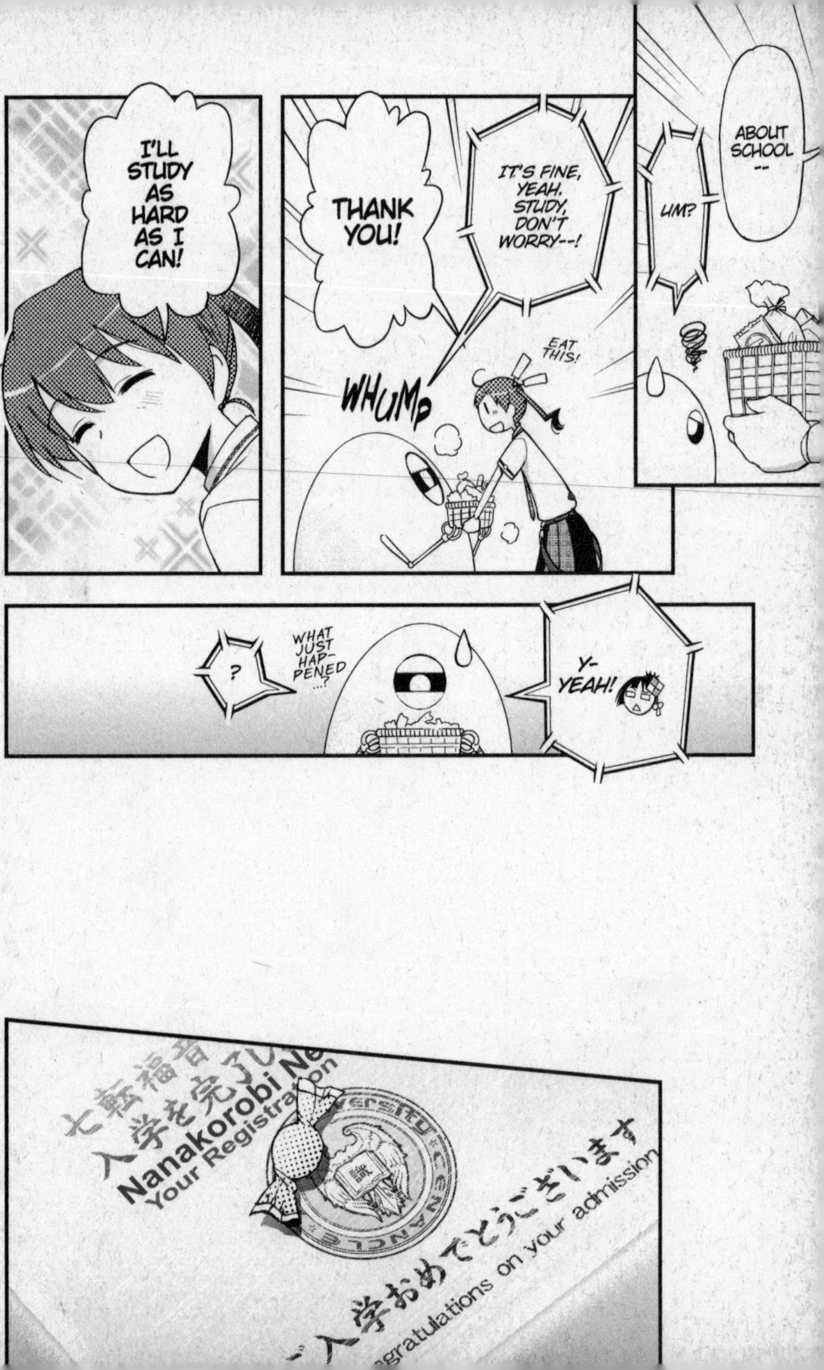
ABOUT SCHOOL --
UM?
IT'S FINE, YEAH. STUDY, DON'T WORRY--!
THANK YOU!
EAT THIS!
WHUMP
I'LL STUDY AS HARD AS I CAN!
Y-YEAH!
WHAT JUST HAPPENED ...?
?
入学を完了し
Nanakorobi Ne
Your Registration
入学おめでとうございます
gratulations on your admission

GHOST URN

GHOST URN

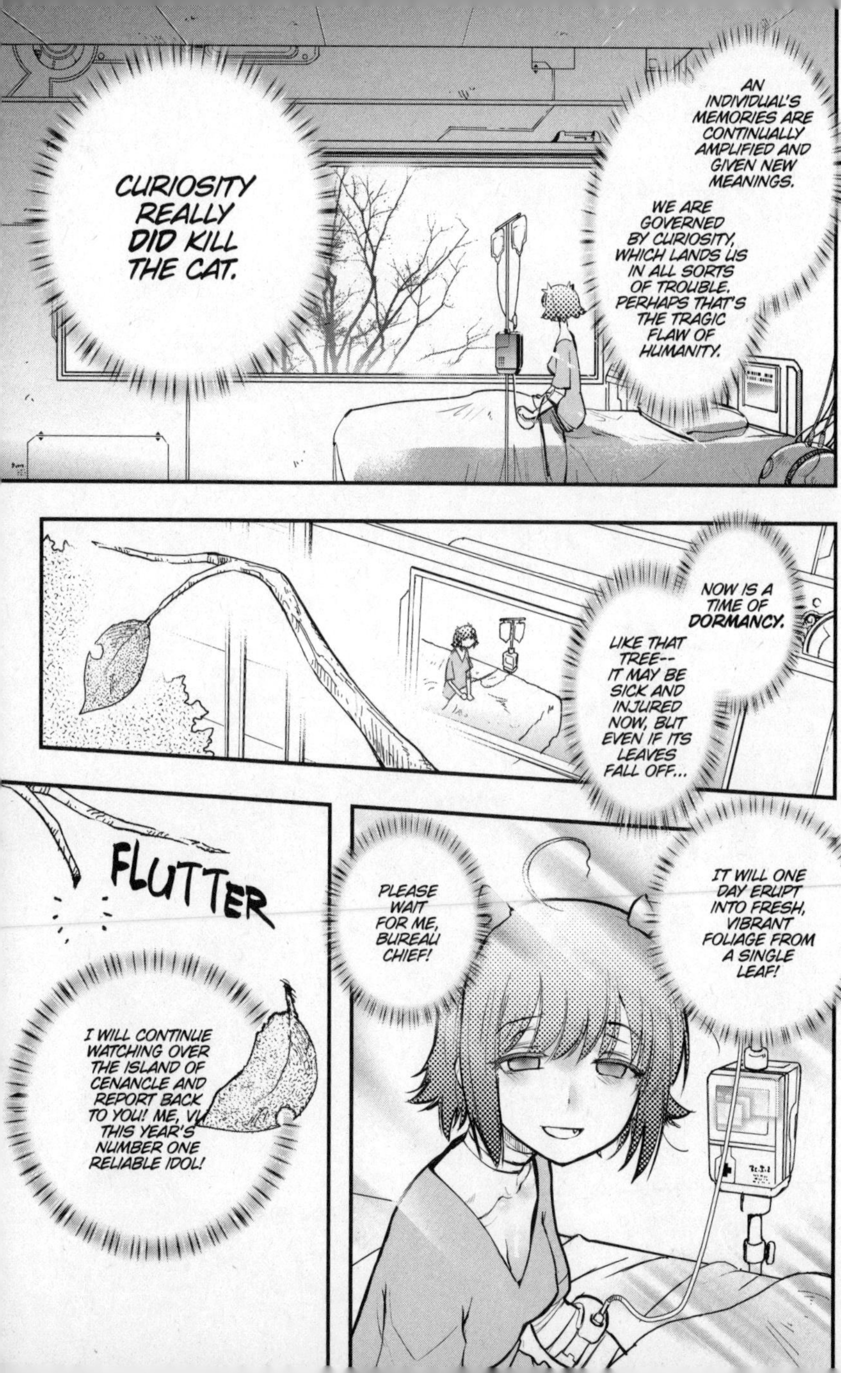
AN INDIVIDUAL'S MEMORIES ARE CONTINUALLY AMPLIFIED AND GIVEN NEW MEANINGS.
WE ARE GOVERNED BY CURIOSITY, WHICH LANDS US IN ALL SORTS OF TROUBLE. PERHAPS THAT'S THE TRAGIC FLAW OF HUMANITY.
CURIOSITY REALLY DID KILL THE CAT.
NOW IS A TIME OF DORMANCY.
LIKE THAT TREE-- IT MAY BE SICK AND INJURED NOW, BUT EVEN IF ITS LEAVES FALL OFF...
IT WILL ONE DAY ERUPT INTO FRESH, VIBRANT FOLIAGE FROM A SINGLE LEAF!
PLEASE WAIT FOR ME, BUREAU CHIEF!
FLUTTER
I WILL CONTINUE WATCHING OVER THE ISLAND OF CENANCLE AND REPORT BACK TO YOU! ME, VI! THIS YEAR'S NUMBER ONE RELIABLE IDOL!

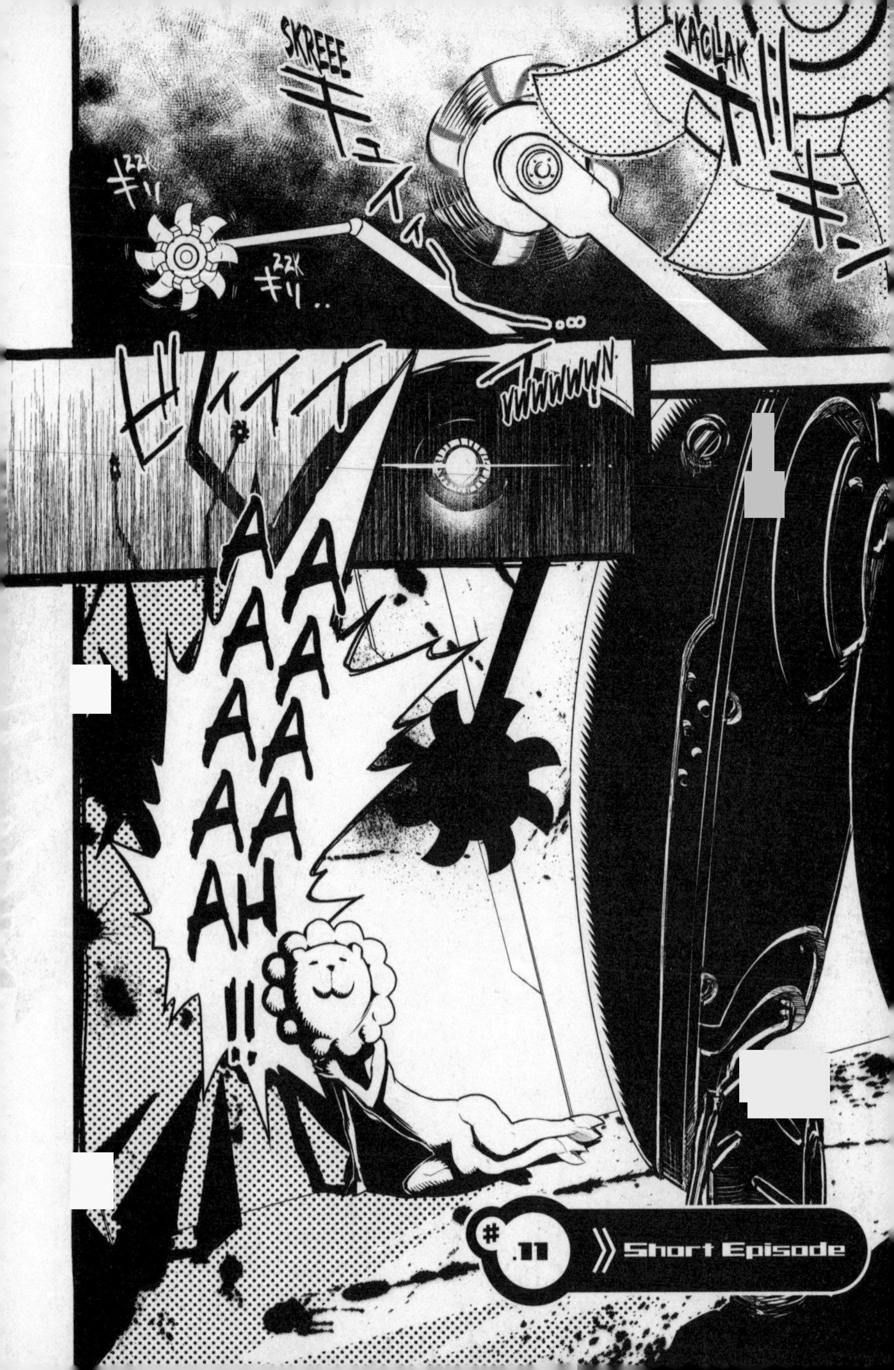
KACLAK
SKREEE
ZZK
ZZK
AAAAAAAAAAAH!!
#.11
Short Episode

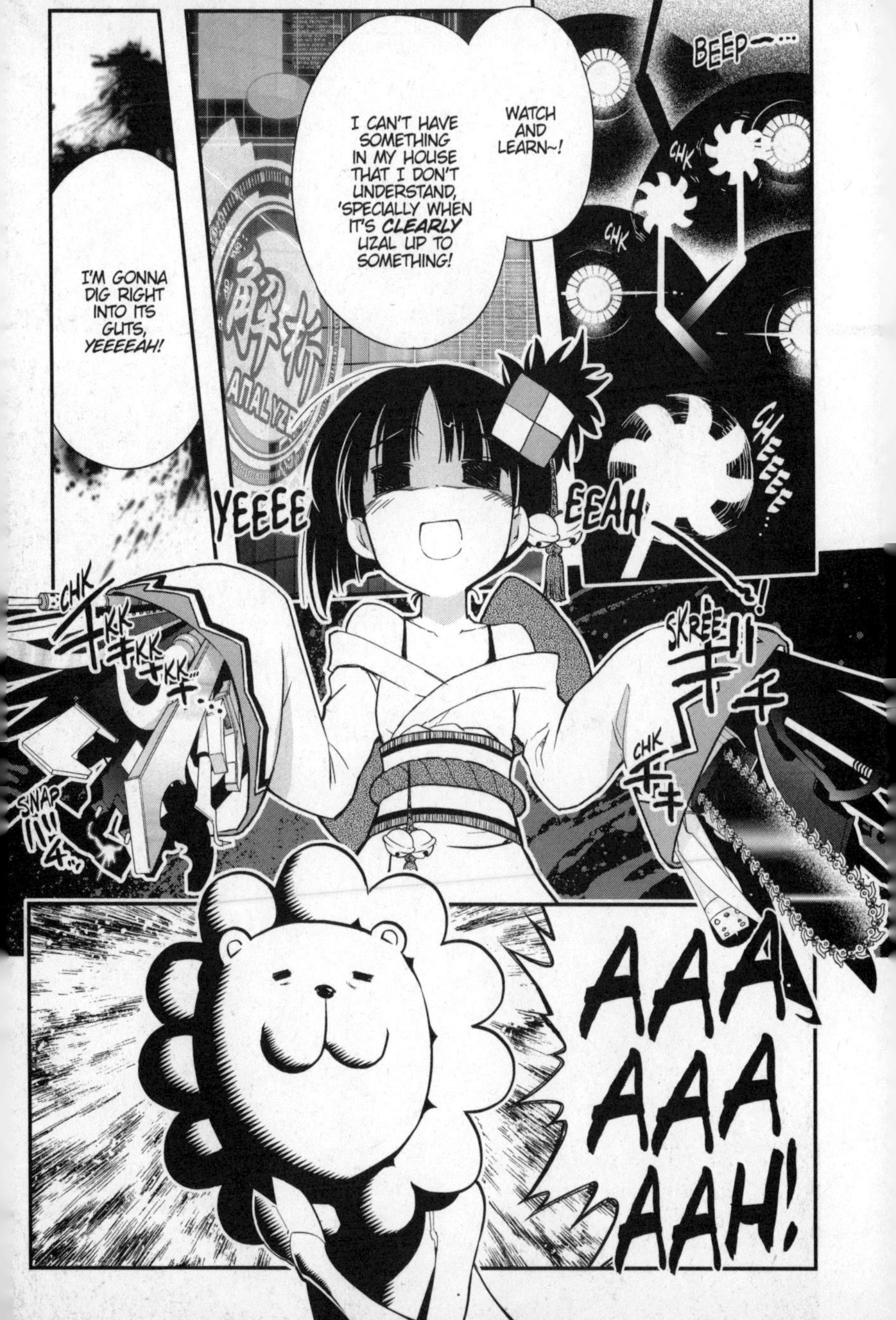
BEEP~...
CHK
CHK
CHEEEEE...
WATCH AND LEARN~!
I CAN'T HAVE SOMETHING IN MY HOUSE THAT I DON'T UNDERSTAND, 'SPECIALLY WHEN IT'S *CLEARLY* UZAL UP TO SOMETHING!
I'M GONNA DIG RIGHT INTO ITS GUTS, *YEEEEAH!*
ANALYZE
YEEEE EEAH
SKREE!!
CHK
CHK KK KK KK...
SNAP
AAAAAAAAAH!

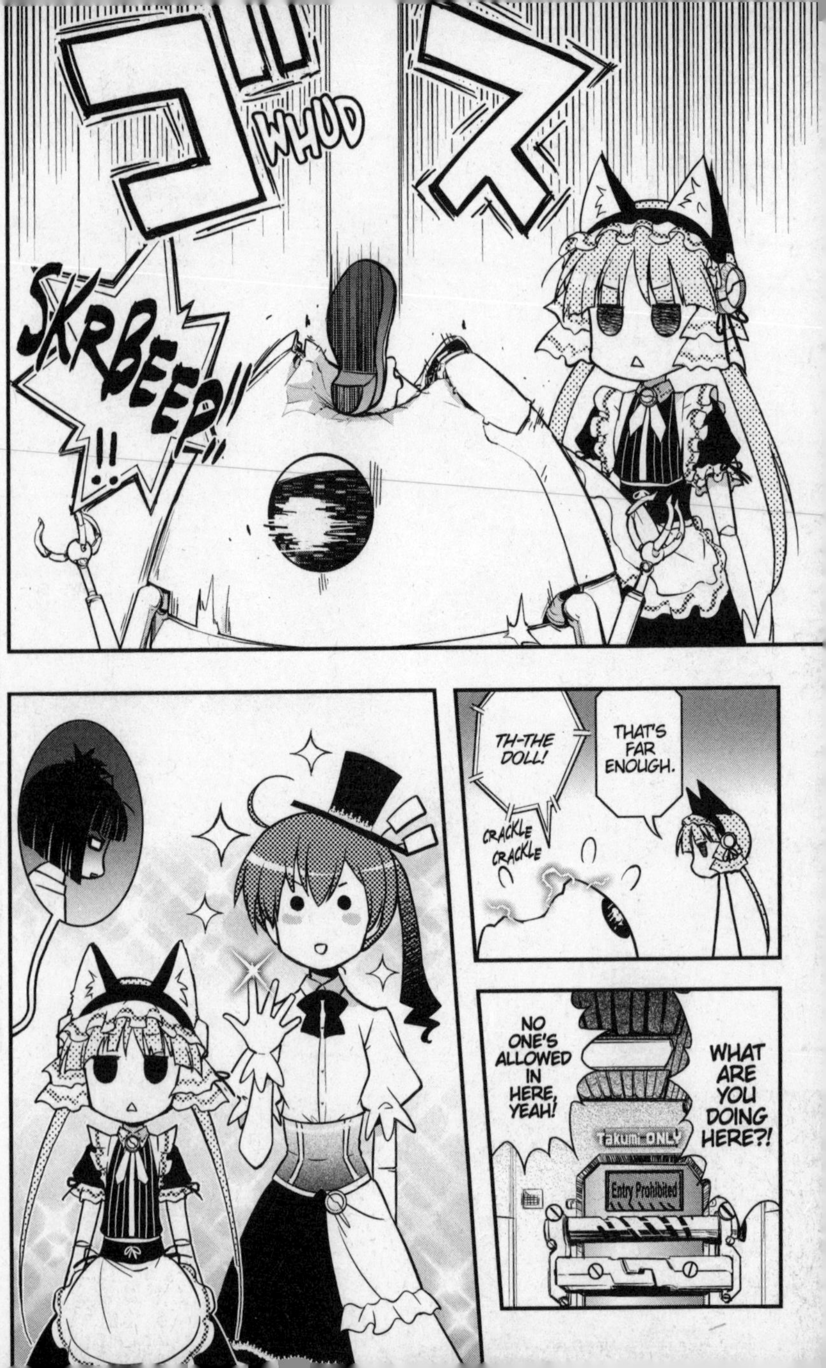
WHUD
SKRBEEP!!
!!
THAT'S FAR ENOUGH.
TH-THE DOLL!
CRACKLE CRACKLE
WHAT ARE YOU DOING HERE?!
NO ONE'S ALLOWED IN HERE, YEAH!
Takumi ONLY
Entry Prohibited

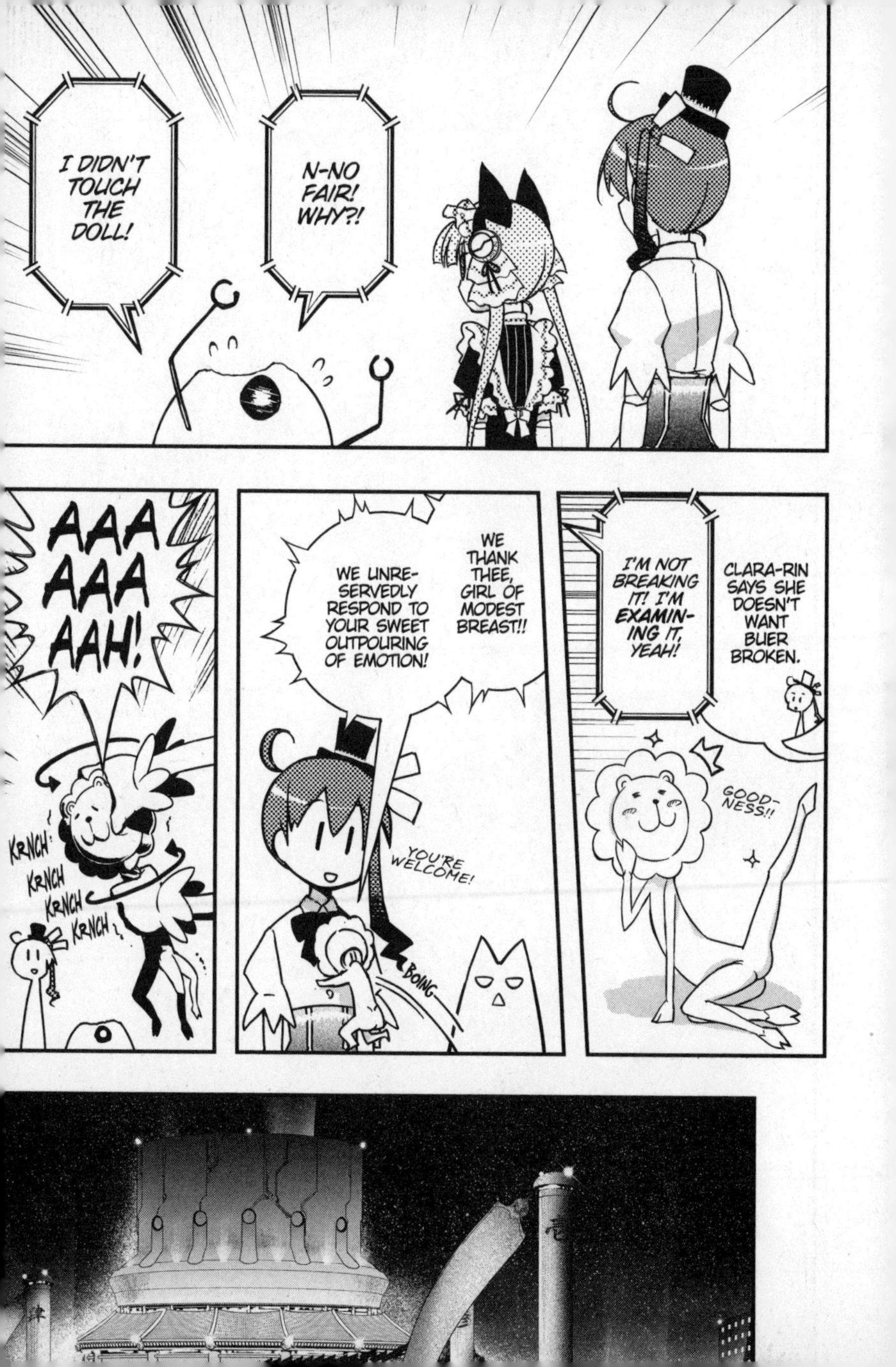
N-NO FAIR! WHY?!
I DIDN'T TOUCH THE DOLL!
CLARA-RIN SAYS SHE DOESN'T WANT BUER BROKEN.
I'M NOT BREAKING IT! I'M EXAMINING IT, YEAH!
GOODNESS!!
WE THANK THEE, GIRL OF MODEST BREAST!!
WE UNRESERVEDLY RESPOND TO YOUR SWEET OUTPOURING OF EMOTION!
YOU'RE WELCOME!
BOING
AAAAAAAAH!
KRNCH KRNCH KRNCH KRNCH

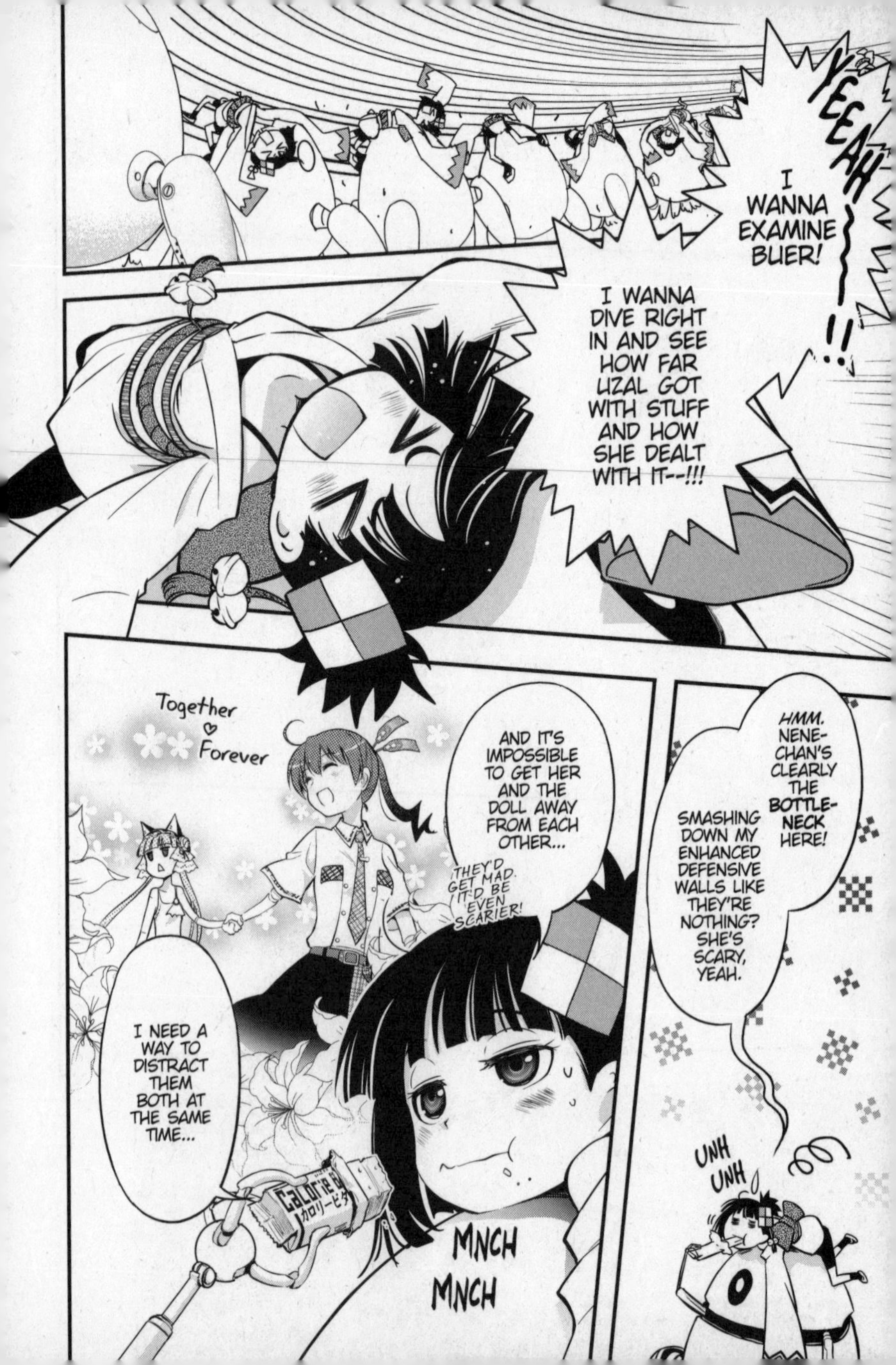

YEEEAH~~~!!
I WANNA EXAMINE BUER!
I WANNA DIVE RIGHT IN AND SEE HOW FAR UZAL GOT WITH STUFF AND HOW SHE DEALT WITH IT--!!!
HMM. NENE-CHAN'S CLEARLY THE BOTTLENECK HERE!
SMASHING DOWN MY ENHANCED DEFENSIVE WALLS LIKE THEY'RE NOTHING? SHE'S SCARY, YEAH.
UNH UNH
AND IT'S IMPOSSIBLE TO GET HER AND THE DOLL AWAY FROM EACH OTHER...
THEY'D GET MAD. IT'D BE EVEN SCARIER!
Together ♡ Forever
I NEED A WAY TO DISTRACT THEM BOTH AT THE SAME TIME...
MNCH MNCH

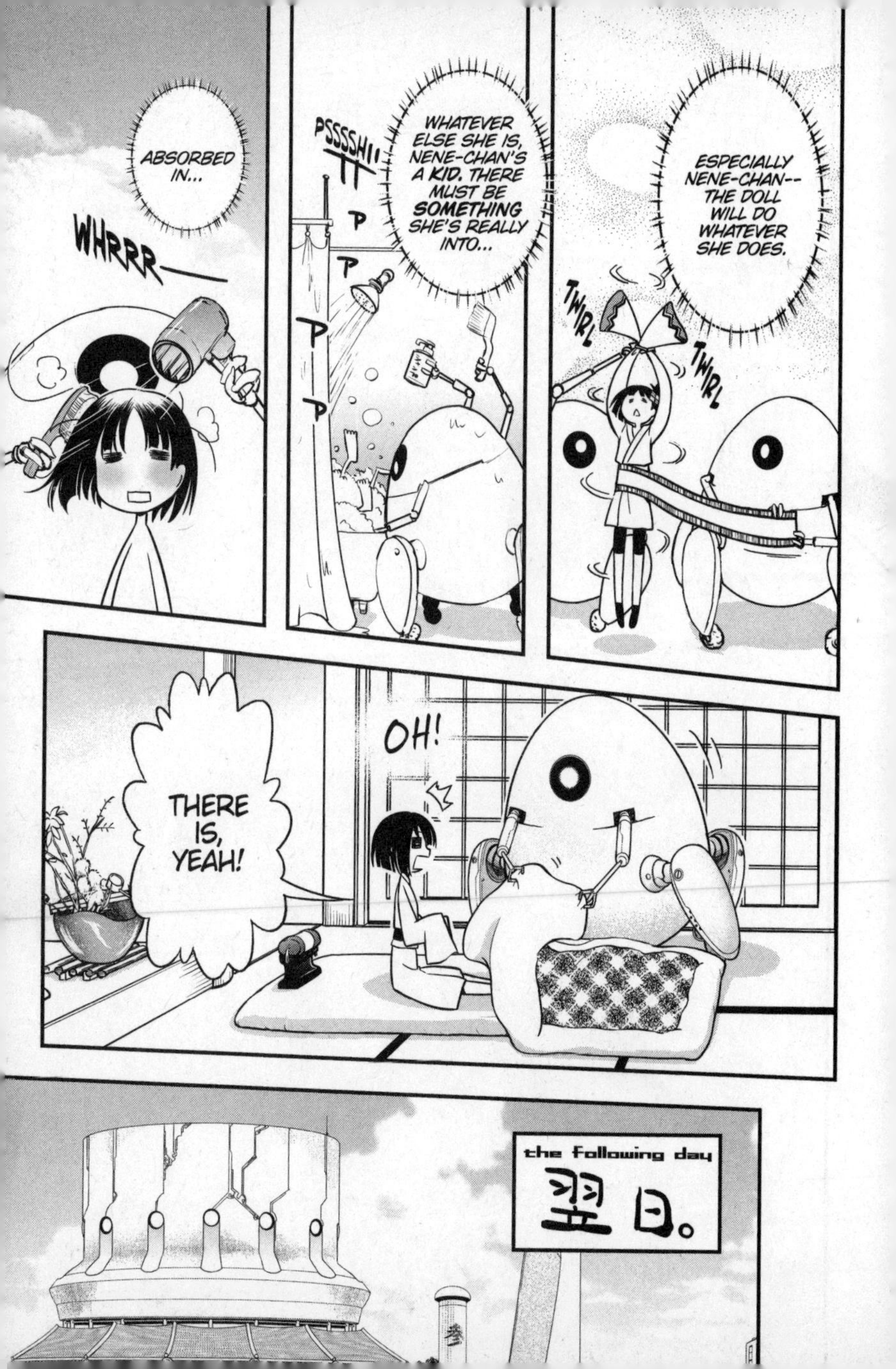
ESPECIALLY NENE-CHAN-- THE DOLL WILL DO WHATEVER SHE DOES.
TWIRL
TWIRL
WHATEVER ELSE SHE IS, NENE-CHAN'S A **KID**. THERE MUST BE **SOMETHING** SHE'S REALLY INTO...
PSSSSHII
P
P
P
P
ABSORBED IN...
WHRRR—
OH!
THERE IS, YEAH!
the following day
翌日。

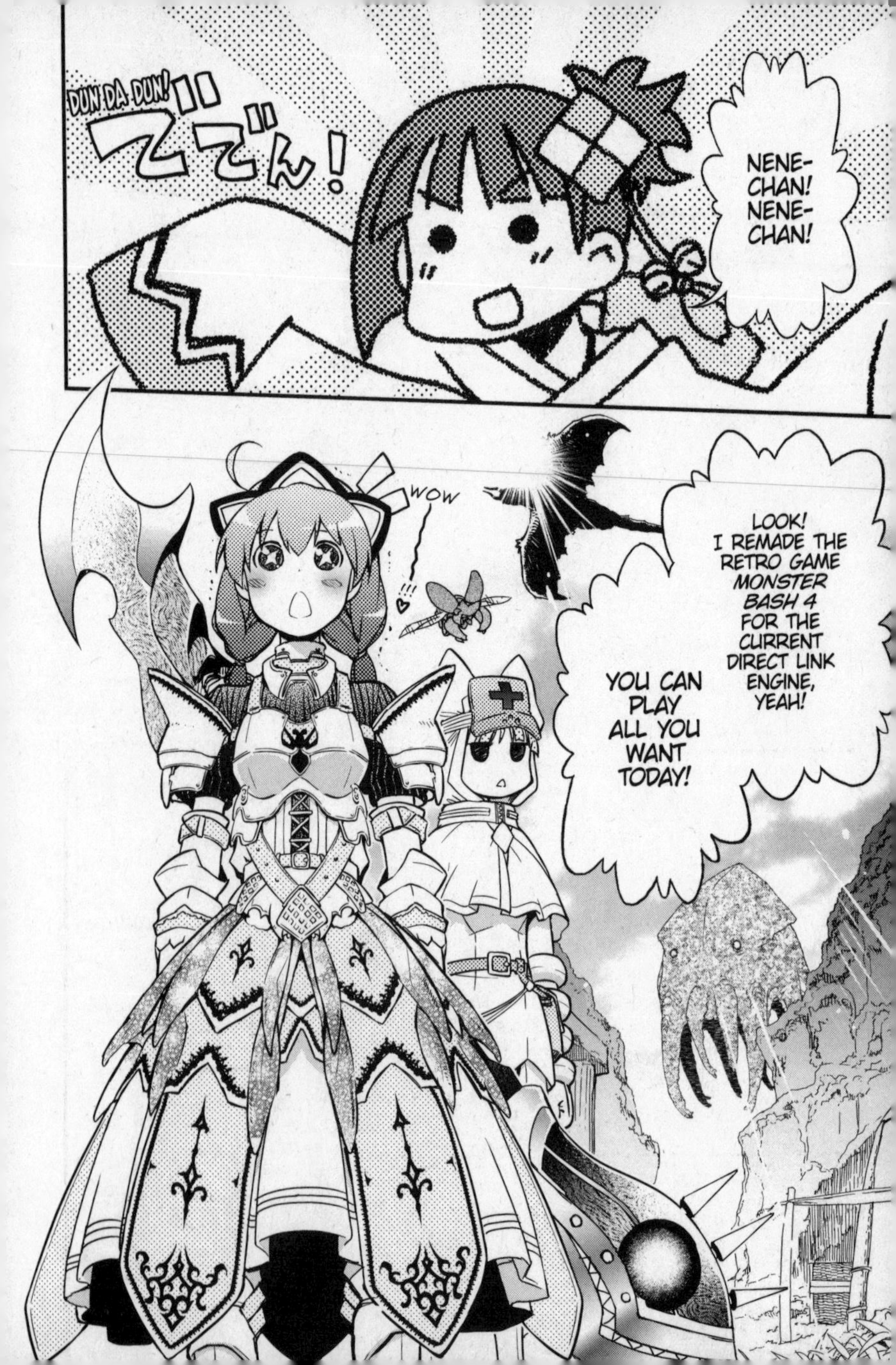

DUN DA DUN!
てでん!
NENE-CHAN! NENE-CHAN!
LOOK! I REMADE THE RETRO GAME *MONSTER BASH 4* FOR THE CURRENT DIRECT LINK ENGINE, YEAH!
YOU CAN PLAY ALL YOU WANT TODAY!
WOW

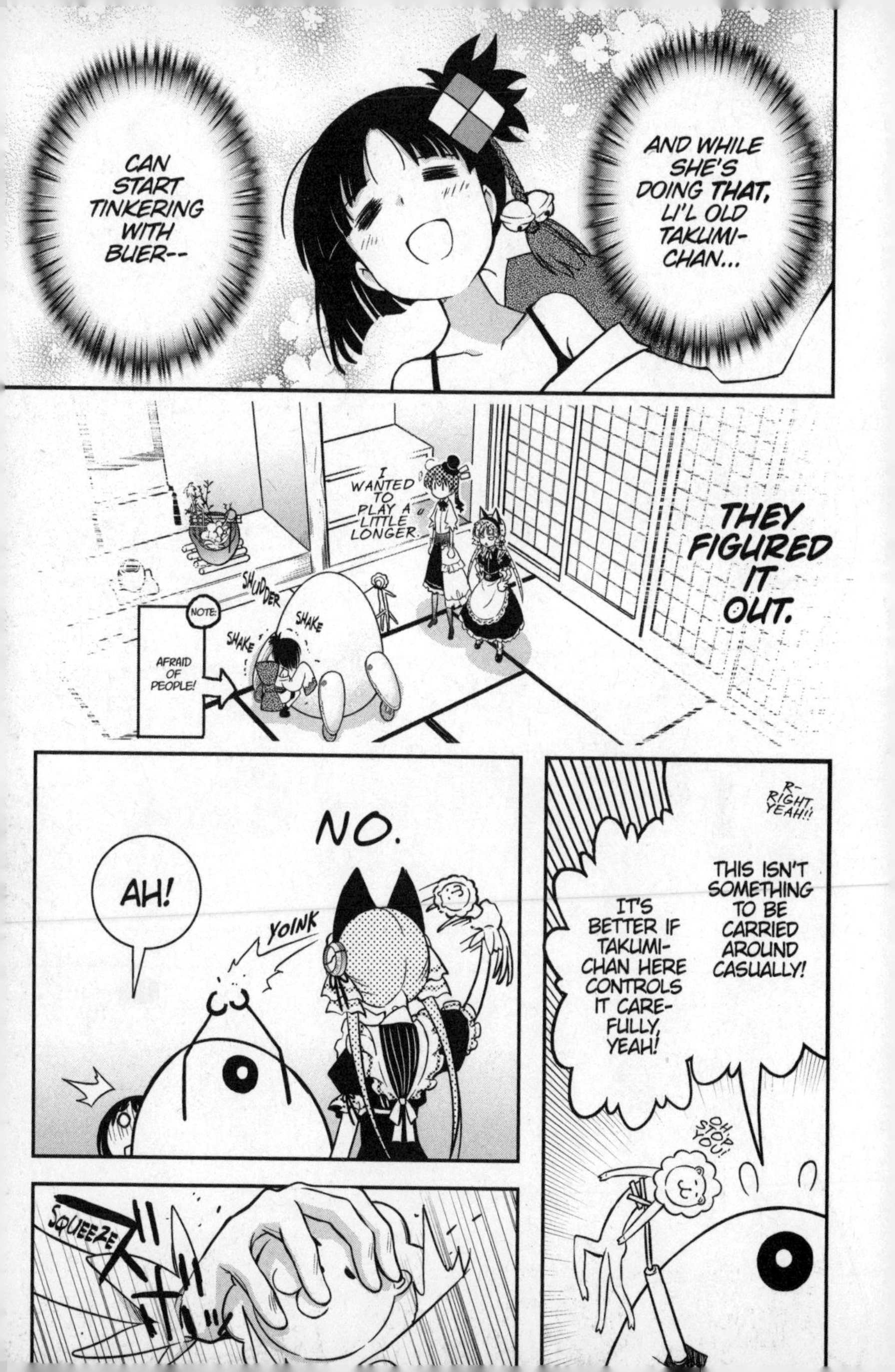
AND WHILE SHE'S DOING THAT, LI'L OLD TAKUMI-CHAN...
CAN START TINKERING WITH BUER--
THEY FIGURED IT OUT.
I WANTED TO PLAY A LITTLE LONGER.
SHUDDER
SHAKE
SHAKE
NOTE:
AFRAID OF PEOPLE!
R-RIGHT, YEAH!!
THIS ISN'T SOMETHING TO BE CARRIED AROUND CASUALLY!
IT'S BETTER IF TAKUMI-CHAN HERE CONTROLS IT CAREFULLY, YEAH!
OH, STOP YOU!
NO.
AH!
YOINK
SQUEEZE

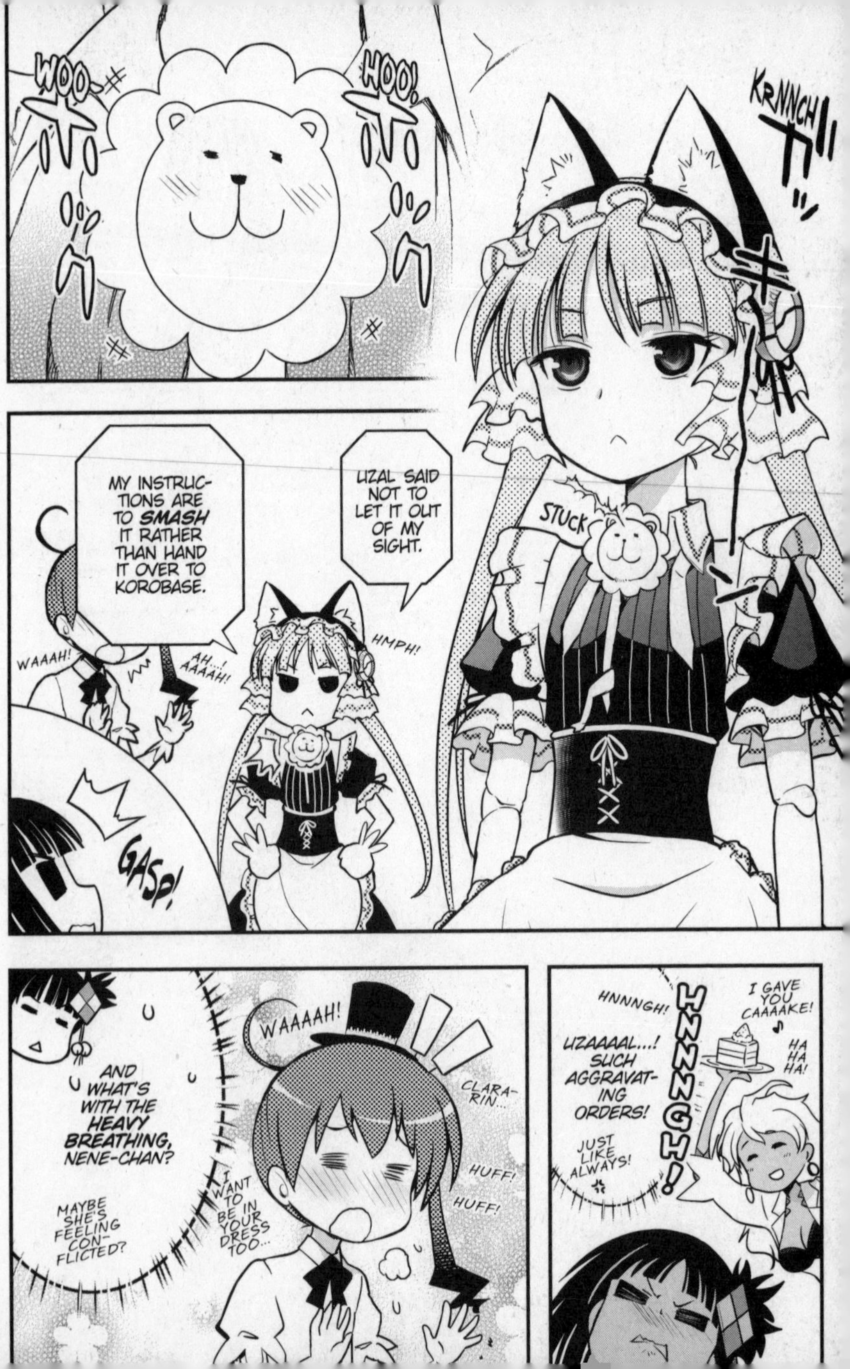
KRNNCH
STUCK
WOO-
HOO!
UZAL SAID NOT TO LET IT OUT OF MY SIGHT.
MY INSTRUCTIONS ARE TO **SMASH** IT RATHER THAN HAND IT OVER TO KOROBASE.
HMPH!
AH...! AAAAAH!
WAAAH!
GASP!
I GAVE YOU CAAAAKE!
HA HA HA!
HNNNNGH!
HNNNGH!
UZAAAAL...! SUCH AGGRAVAT-ING ORDERS!
JUST LIKE ALWAYS!
CLARA-RIN...
WAAAAH!
HUFF!
HUFF!
I WANT TO BE IN YOUR DRESS TOO...
AND WHAT'S WITH THE **HEAVY BREATHING,** NENE-CHAN?
MAYBE SHE'S FEELING CON-FLICTED?

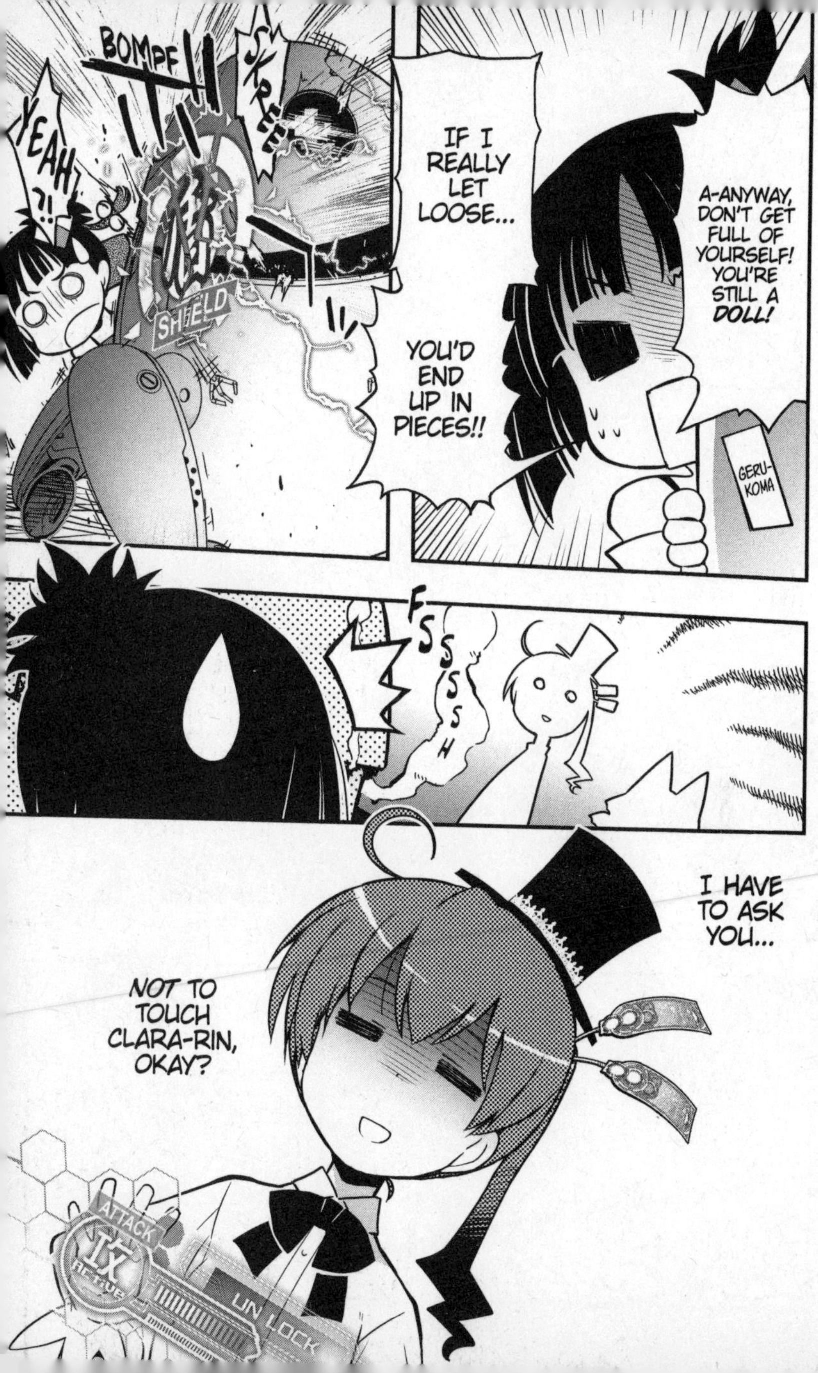
A-ANYWAY, DON'T GET FULL OF YOURSELF! YOU'RE STILL A DOLL!
GERU-KOMA
IF I REALLY LET LOOSE...
YOU'D END UP IN PIECES!!
SKREE
BOMPF
YEAH?!!
SHIELD
FSSSSH
I HAVE TO ASK YOU...
NOT TO TOUCH CLARA-RIN, OKAY?
ATTACK
UN LOCK

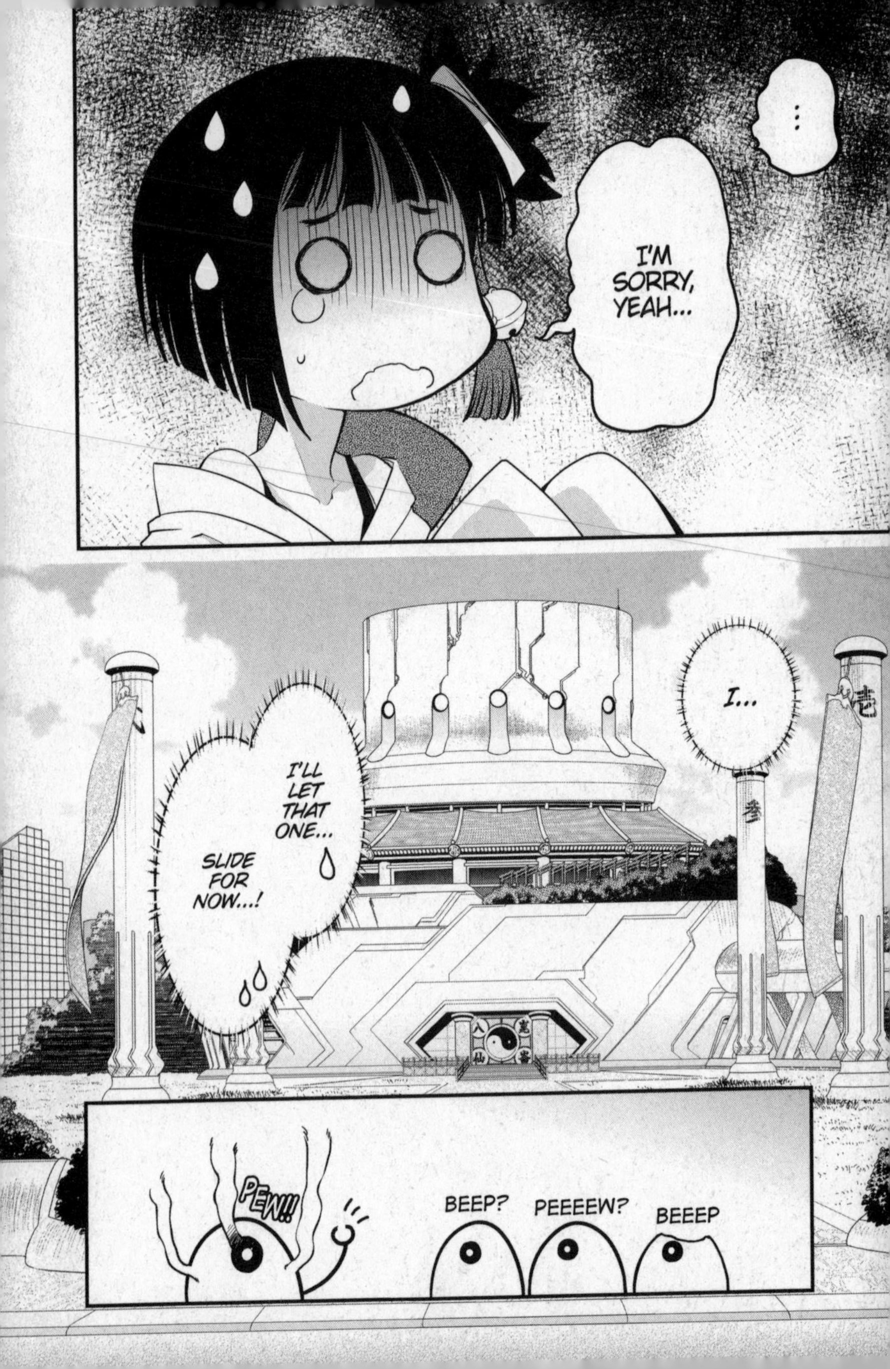
...
I'M SORRY, YEAH...
I...
I'LL LET THAT ONE... SLIDE FOR NOW...!
BEEEP
PEEEEW?
BEEP?
PEW!!

GHOST URN

GHOST URN

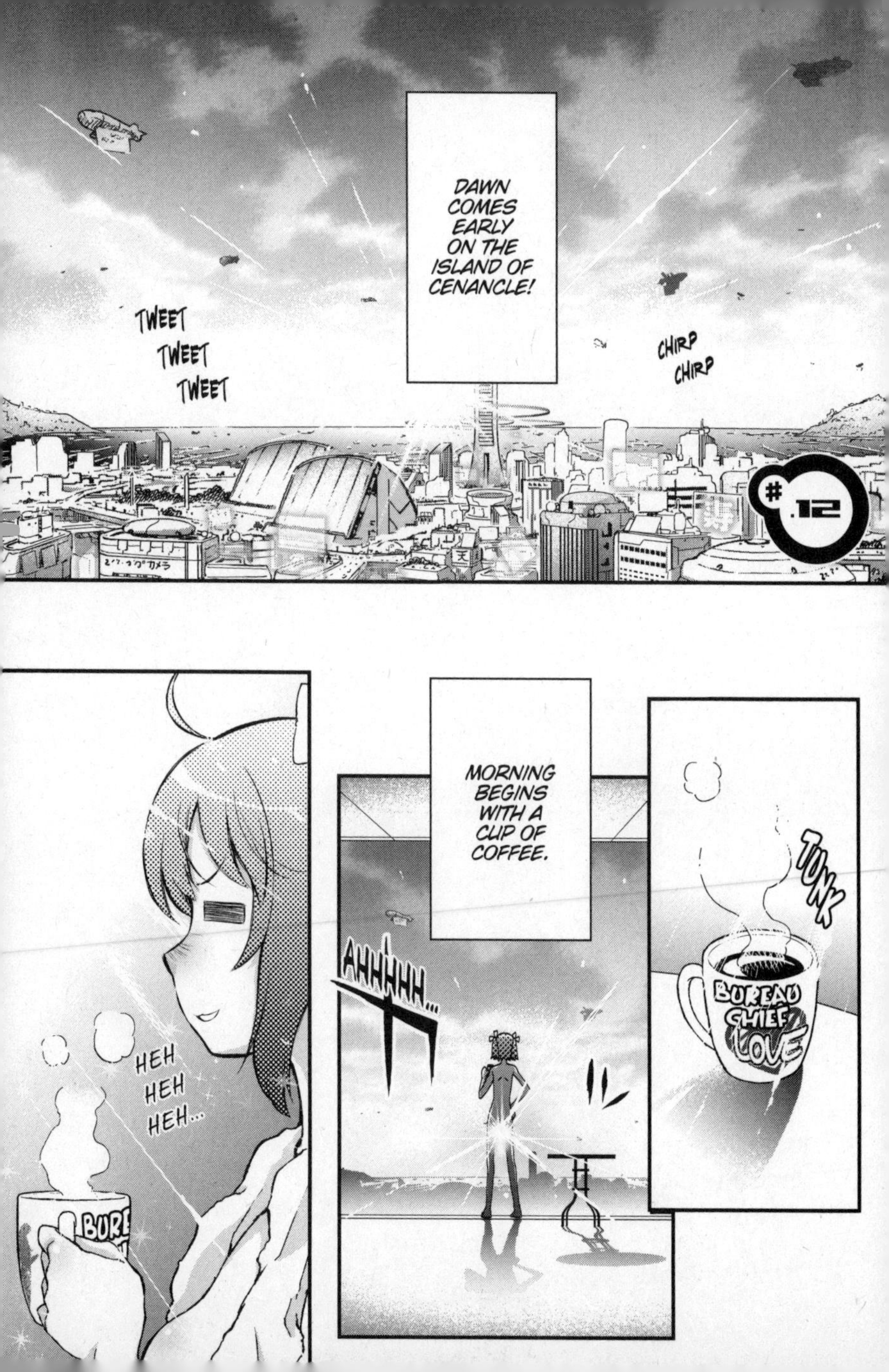
DAWN COMES EARLY ON THE ISLAND OF CENANCLE!
CHIRP CHIRP
TWEET TWEET TWEET
#.12
TUNK
BUREAU CHIEF LOVE
MORNING BEGINS WITH A CUP OF COFFEE.
AHHHHH...
HEH HEH HEH...
BURE

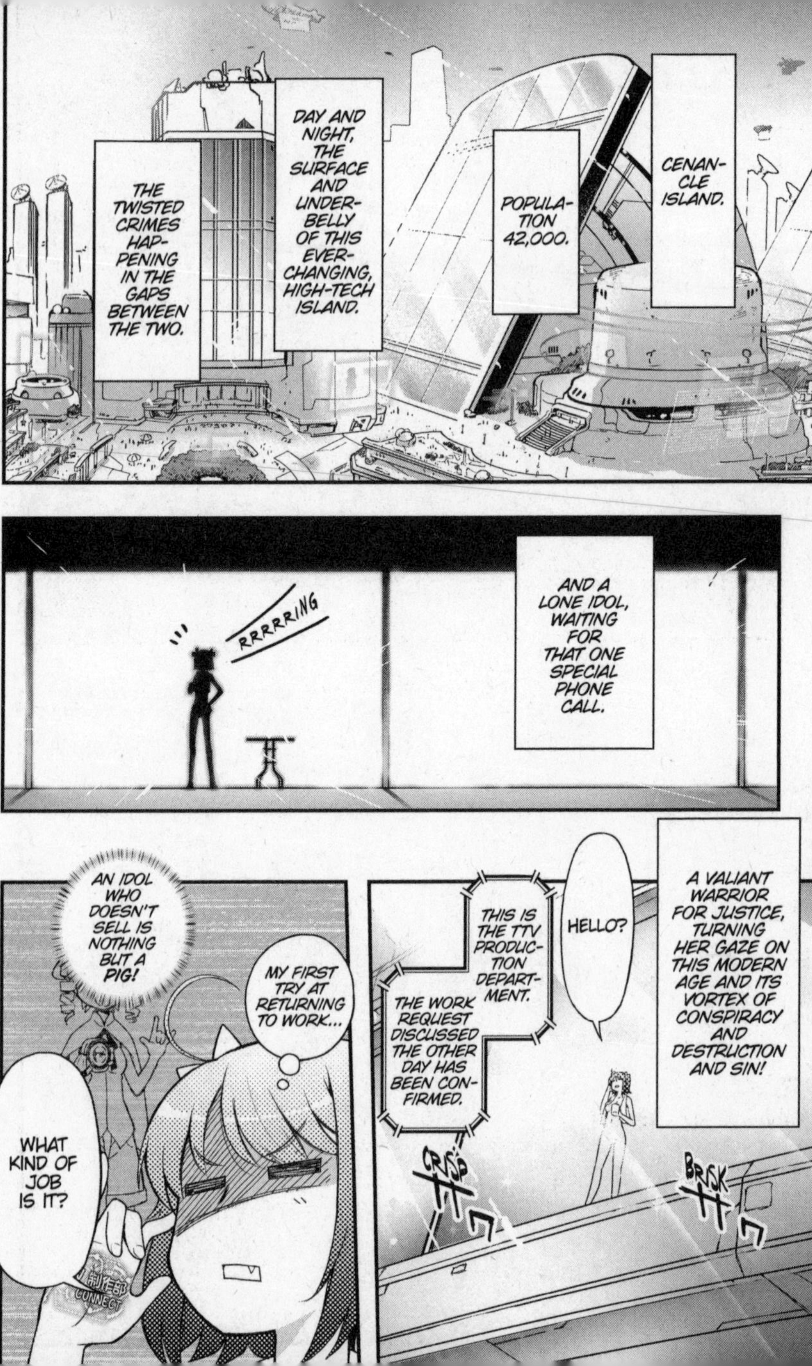
CENAN-
CLE
ISLAND.
POPULA-
TION
42,000.
DAY AND NIGHT, THE SURFACE AND UNDER-BELLY OF THIS EVER-CHANGING, HIGH-TECH ISLAND.
THE TWISTED CRIMES HAP-PENING IN THE GAPS BETWEEN THE TWO.
AND A LONE IDOL, WAITING FOR THAT ONE SPECIAL PHONE CALL.
RRRRRING
A VALIANT WARRIOR FOR JUSTICE, TURNING HER GAZE ON THIS MODERN AGE AND ITS VORTEX OF CONSPIRACY AND DESTRUCTION AND SIN!
HELLO?
THIS IS THE TTV PRODUC-TION DEPART-MENT.
THE WORK REQUEST DISCUSSED THE OTHER DAY HAS BEEN CON-FIRMED.
BRISK
CRISP
AN IDOL WHO DOESN'T SELL IS NOTHING BUT A PIG!
MY FIRST TRY AT RETURNING TO WORK...
WHAT KIND OF JOB IS IT?
制作部
CONNECT

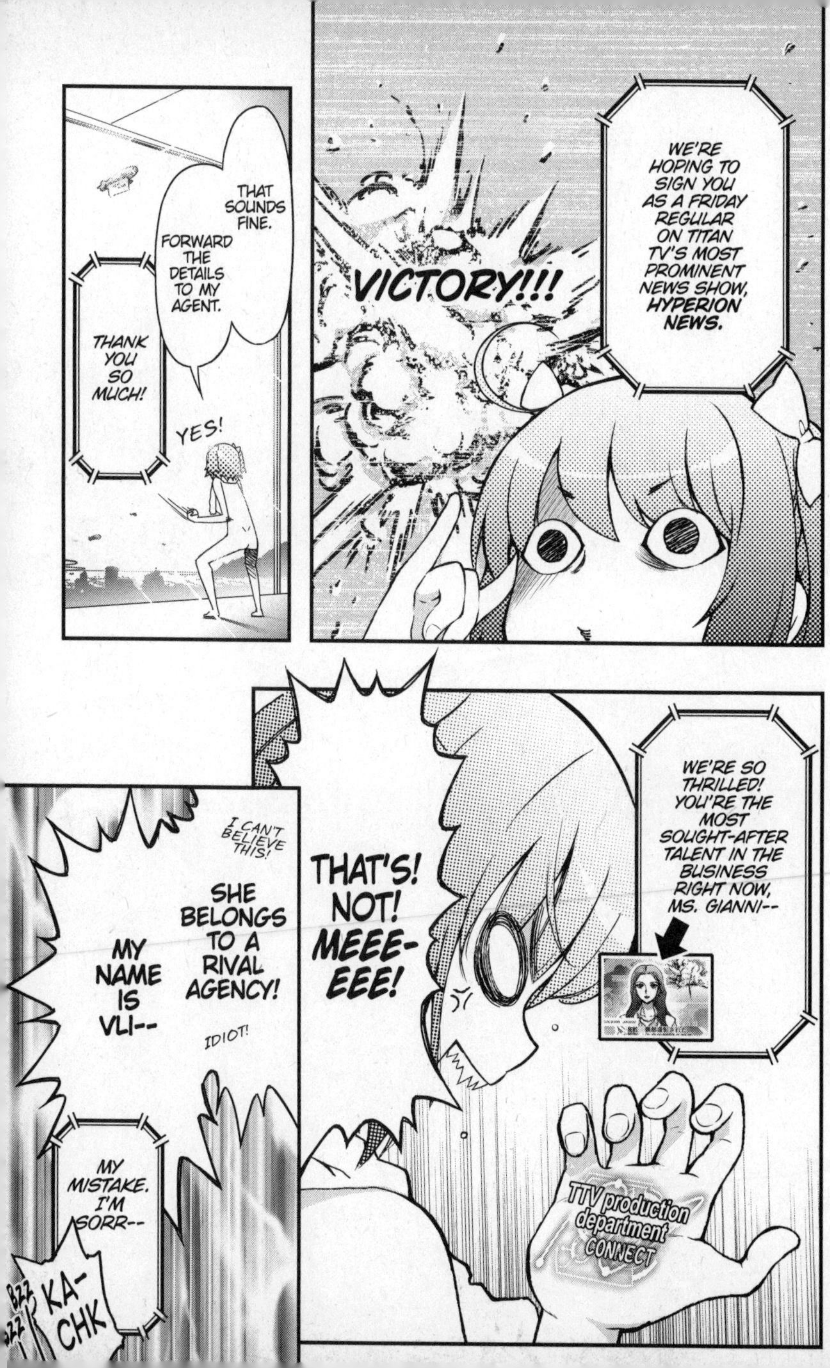
WE'RE HOPING TO SIGN YOU AS A FRIDAY REGULAR ON TITAN TV'S MOST PROMINENT NEWS SHOW, HYPERION NEWS.
VICTORY!!!
THAT SOUNDS FINE.
FORWARD THE DETAILS TO MY AGENT.
THANK YOU SO MUCH!
YES!
WE'RE SO THRILLED! YOU'RE THE MOST SOUGHT-AFTER TALENT IN THE BUSINESS RIGHT NOW, MS. GIANNI--
THAT'S! NOT! MEEE-EEE!
TTV production department CONNECT
I CAN'T BELIEVE THIS!
SHE BELONGS TO A RIVAL AGENCY!
MY NAME IS VLI--
IDIOT!
MY MISTAKE. I'M SORR--
KA-CHK

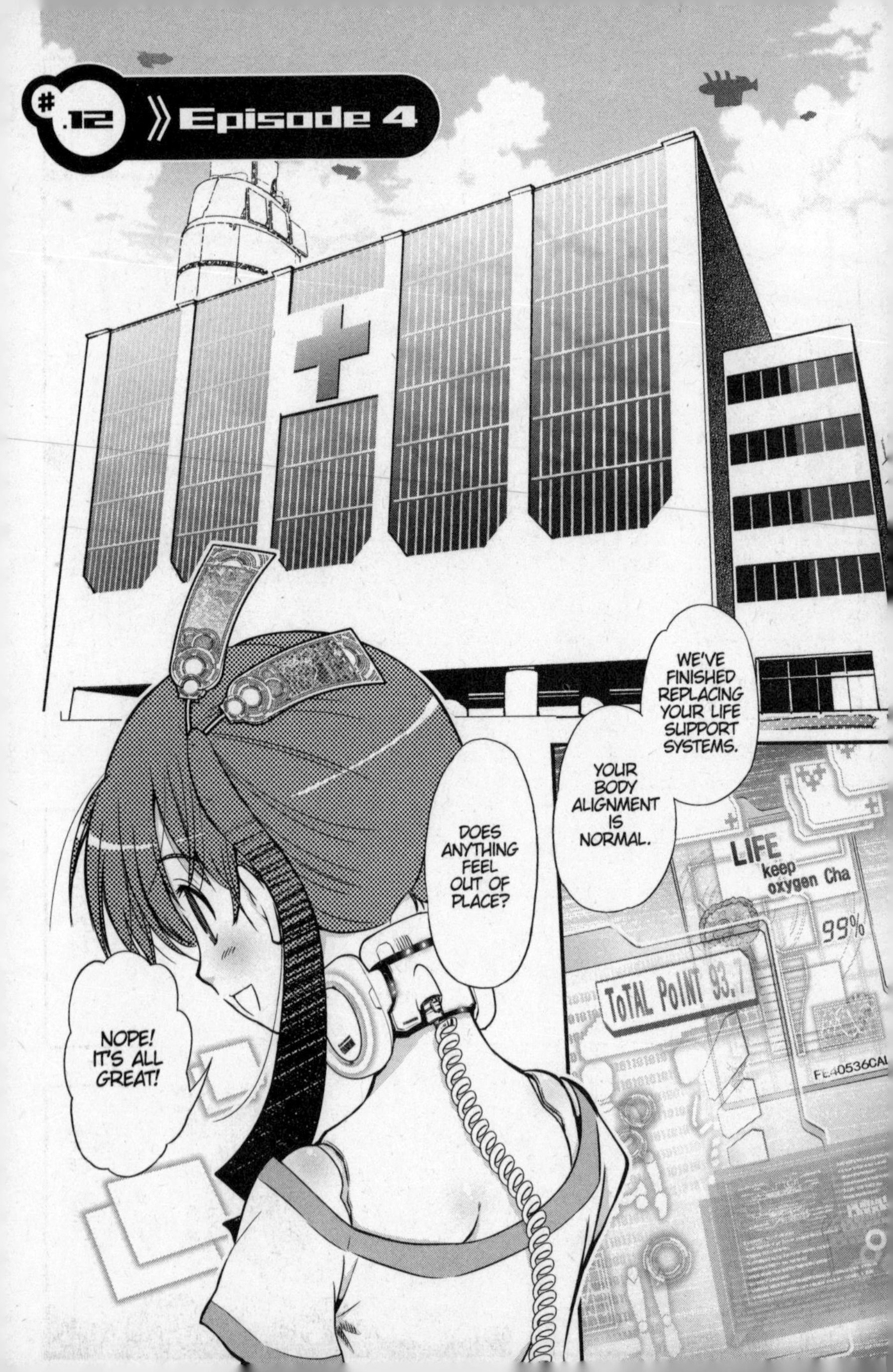
#.12 Episode 4
WE'VE FINISHED REPLACING YOUR LIFE SUPPORT SYSTEMS.
YOUR BODY ALIGNMENT IS NORMAL.
DOES ANYTHING FEEL OUT OF PLACE?
LIFE keep oxygen Cha
99%
ToTAL PoINT 93.7
NOPE! IT'S ALL GREAT!

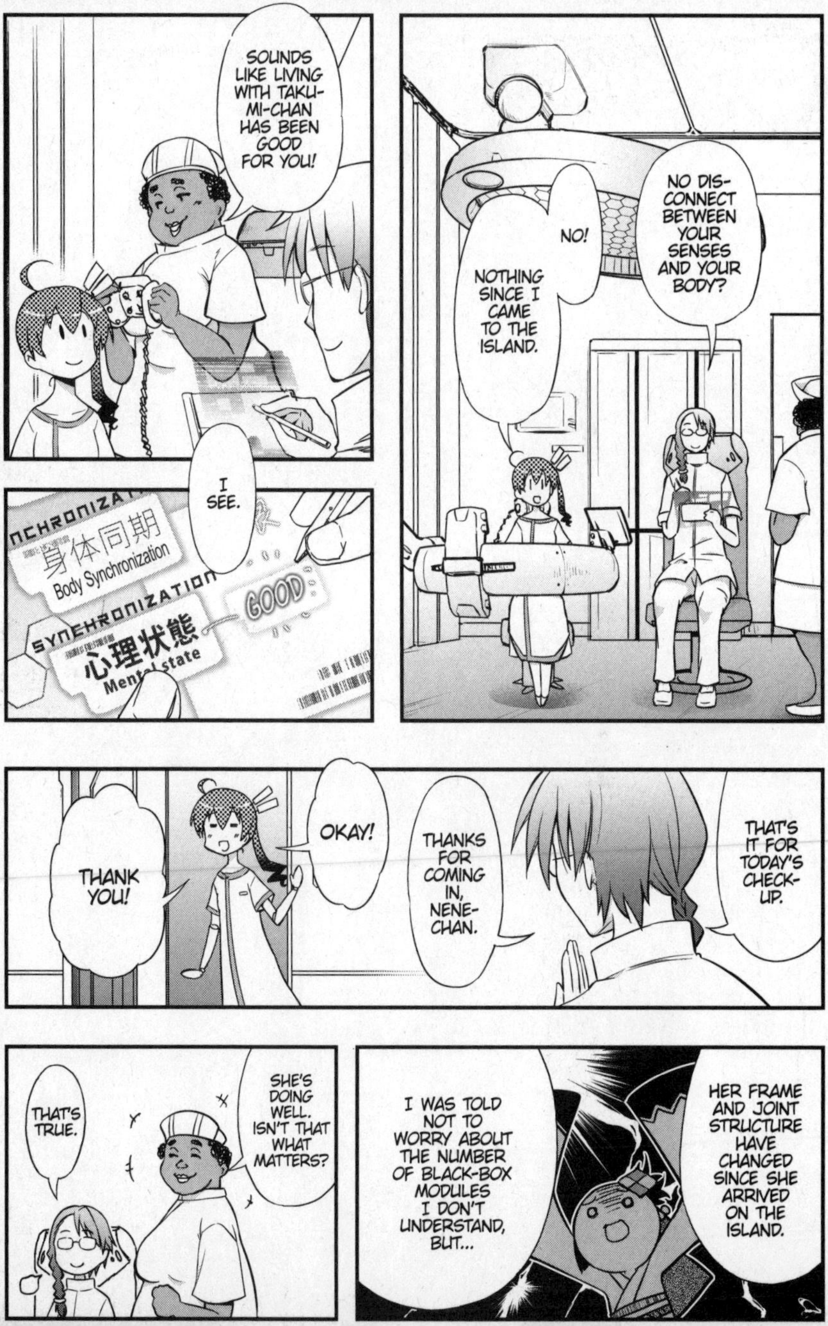
NO DIS-CONNECT BETWEEN YOUR SENSES AND YOUR BODY?
NO!
NOTHING SINCE I CAME TO THE ISLAND.
SOUNDS LIKE LIVING WITH TAKU-MI-CHAN HAS BEEN GOOD FOR YOU!
I SEE.
身体同期
Body Synchronization
SYNCHRONIZATION
心理状態
Mental state
GOOD
THAT'S IT FOR TODAY'S CHECK-UP.
THANKS FOR COMING IN, NENE-CHAN.
OKAY!
THANK YOU!
HER FRAME AND JOINT STRUCTURE HAVE CHANGED SINCE SHE ARRIVED ON THE ISLAND.
I WAS TOLD NOT TO WORRY ABOUT THE NUMBER OF BLACK-BOX MODULES I DON'T UNDERSTAND, BUT...
SHE'S DOING WELL. ISN'T THAT WHAT MATTERS?
THAT'S TRUE.

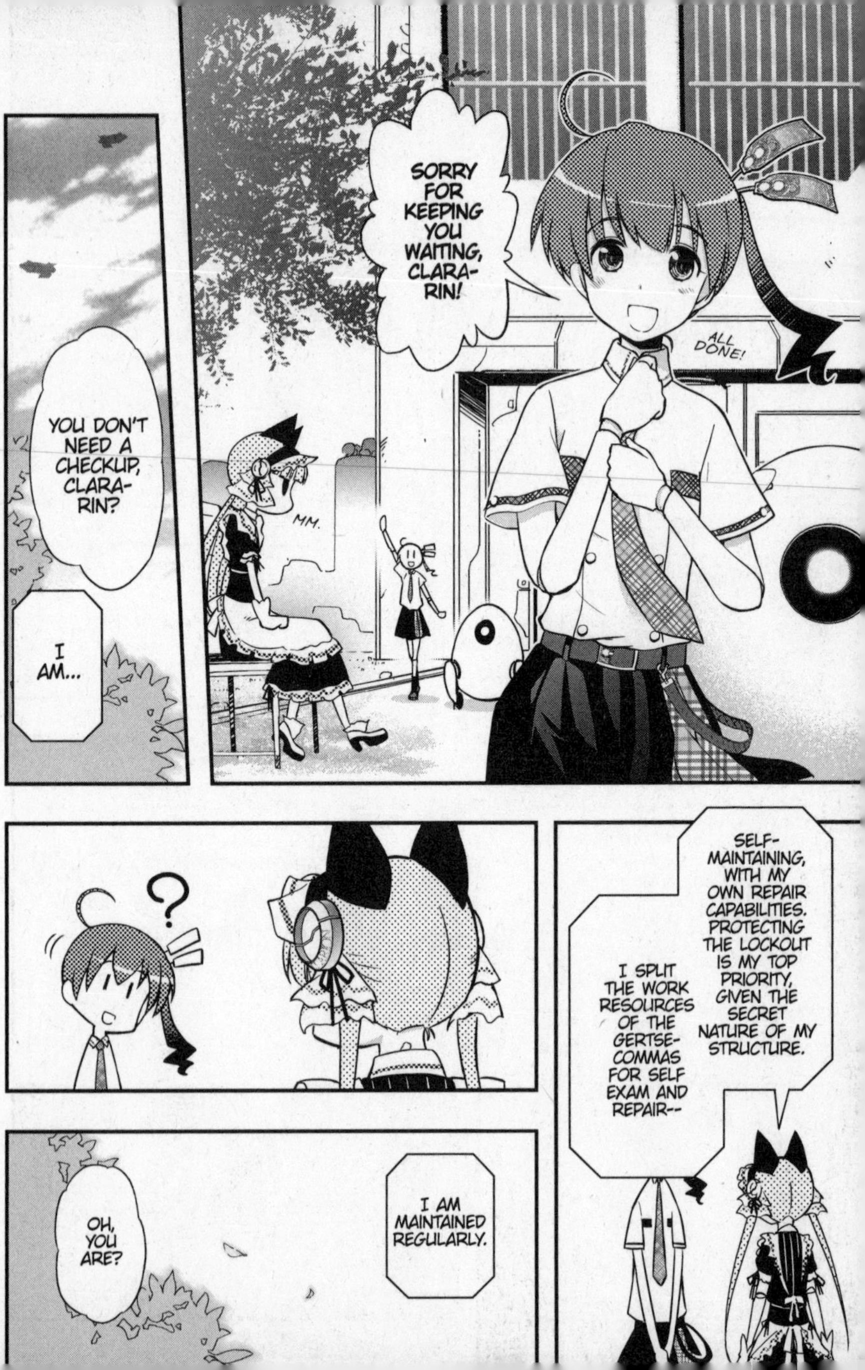
SORRY FOR KEEPING YOU WAITING, CLARA-RIN!
ALL DONE!
MM.
YOU DON'T NEED A CHECKUP, CLARA-RIN?
I AM...
SELF-MAINTAINING, WITH MY OWN REPAIR CAPABILITIES. PROTECTING THE LOCKOUT IS MY TOP PRIORITY, GIVEN THE SECRET NATURE OF MY STRUCTURE.
I SPLIT THE WORK RESOURCES OF THE GERTSE-COMMAS FOR SELF EXAM AND REPAIR--
?
I AM MAINTAINED REGULARLY.
OH, YOU ARE?

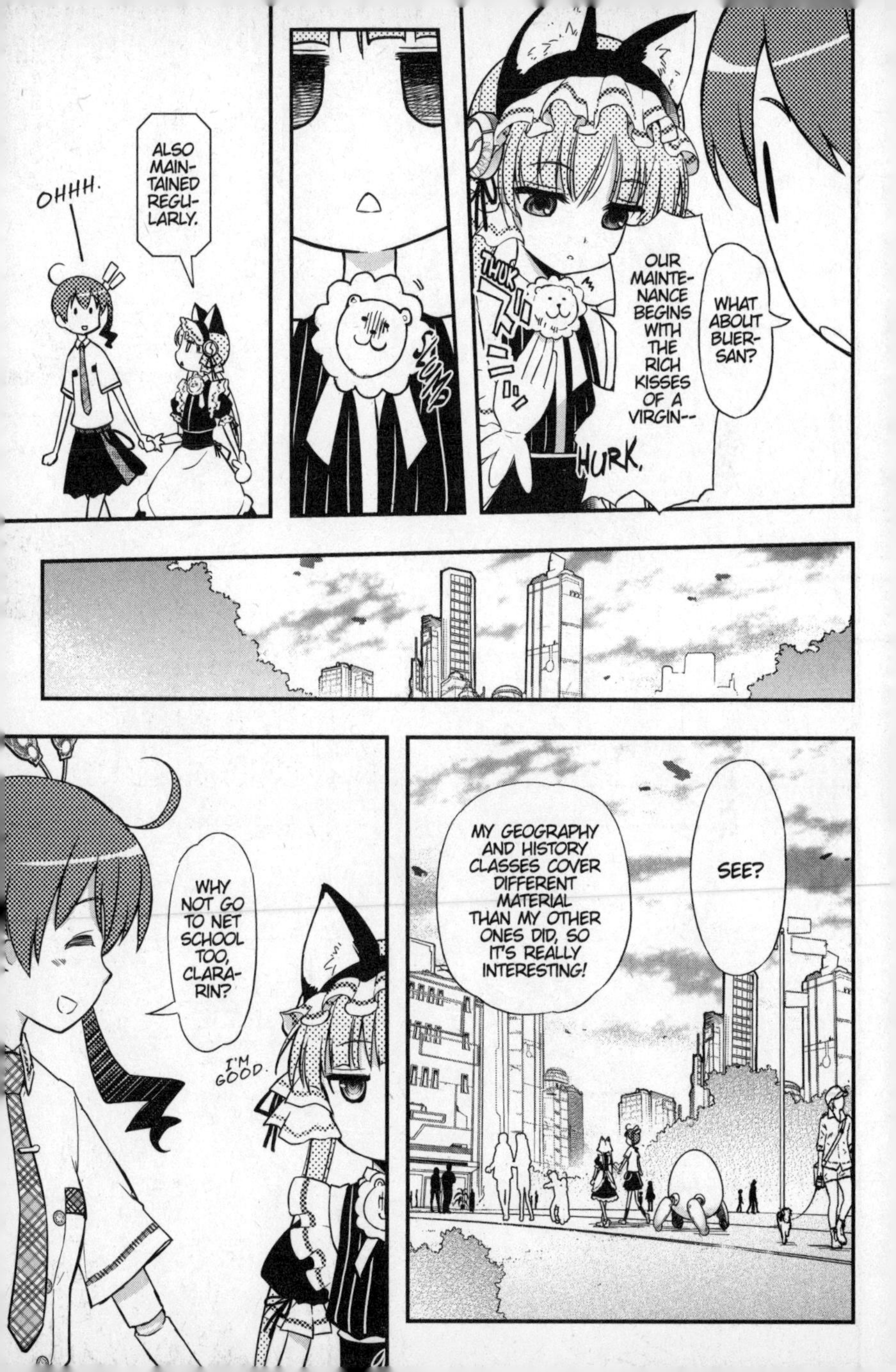
WHAT ABOUT BUER-SAN?
OUR MAINTENANCE BEGINS WITH THE RICH KISSES OF A VIRGIN--
THUK
HURK.
ALSO MAINTAINED REGULARLY.
OHHH.
SEE?
MY GEOGRAPHY AND HISTORY CLASSES COVER DIFFERENT MATERIAL THAN MY OTHER ONES DID, SO IT'S REALLY INTERESTING!
WHY NOT GO TO NET SCHOOL TOO, CLARA-RIN?
I'M GOOD.

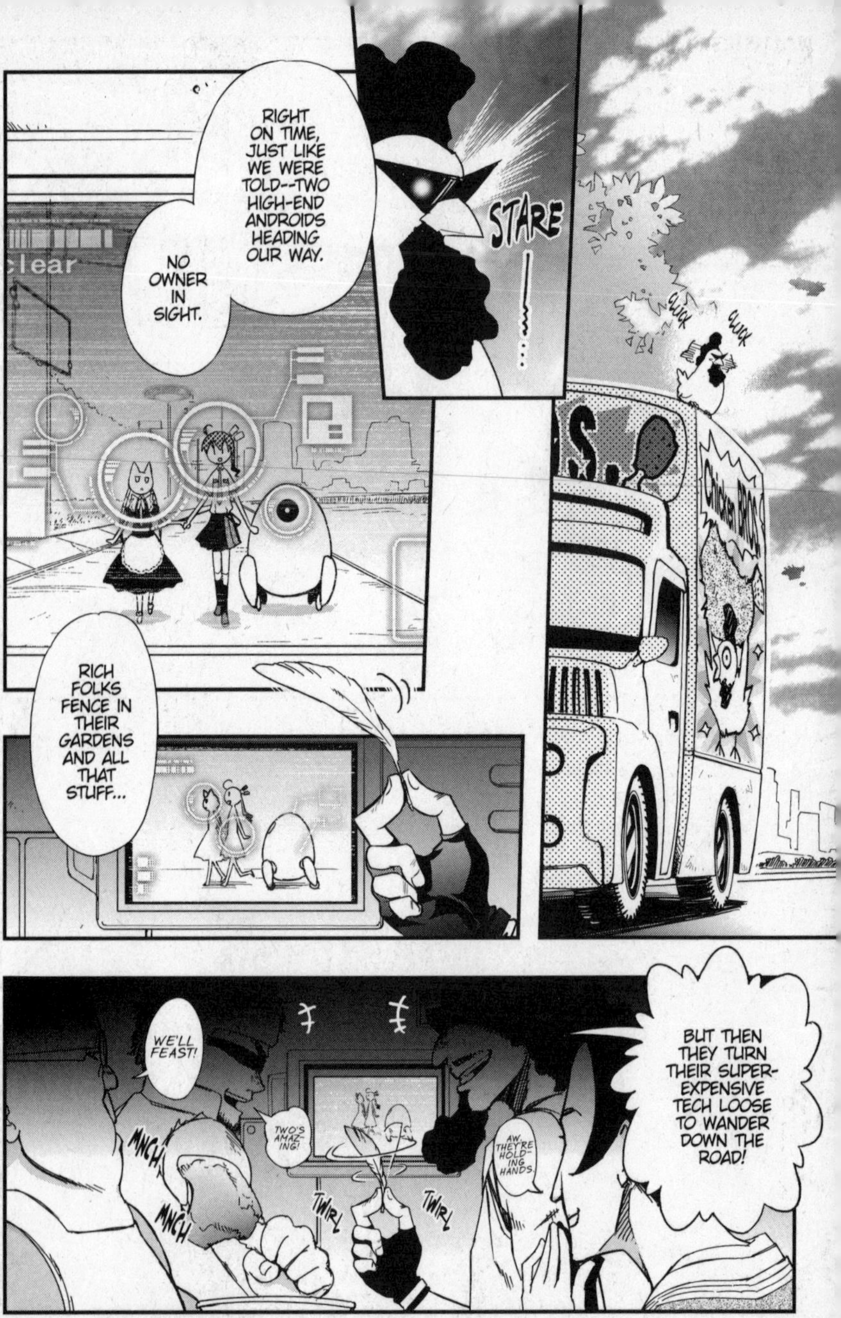
CLUCK
CLUCK
Chicken BROS.
STARE
......
RIGHT ON TIME, JUST LIKE WE WERE TOLD--TWO HIGH-END ANDROIDS HEADING OUR WAY.
NO OWNER IN SIGHT.
clear
RICH FOLKS FENCE IN THEIR GARDENS AND ALL THAT STUFF...
BUT THEN THEY TURN THEIR SUPER-EXPENSIVE TECH LOOSE TO WANDER DOWN THE ROAD!
AW. THEY'RE HOLDING HANDS.
TWIRL
TWIRL
TWO'S AMAZING!
WE'LL FEAST!
MNCH
MNCH

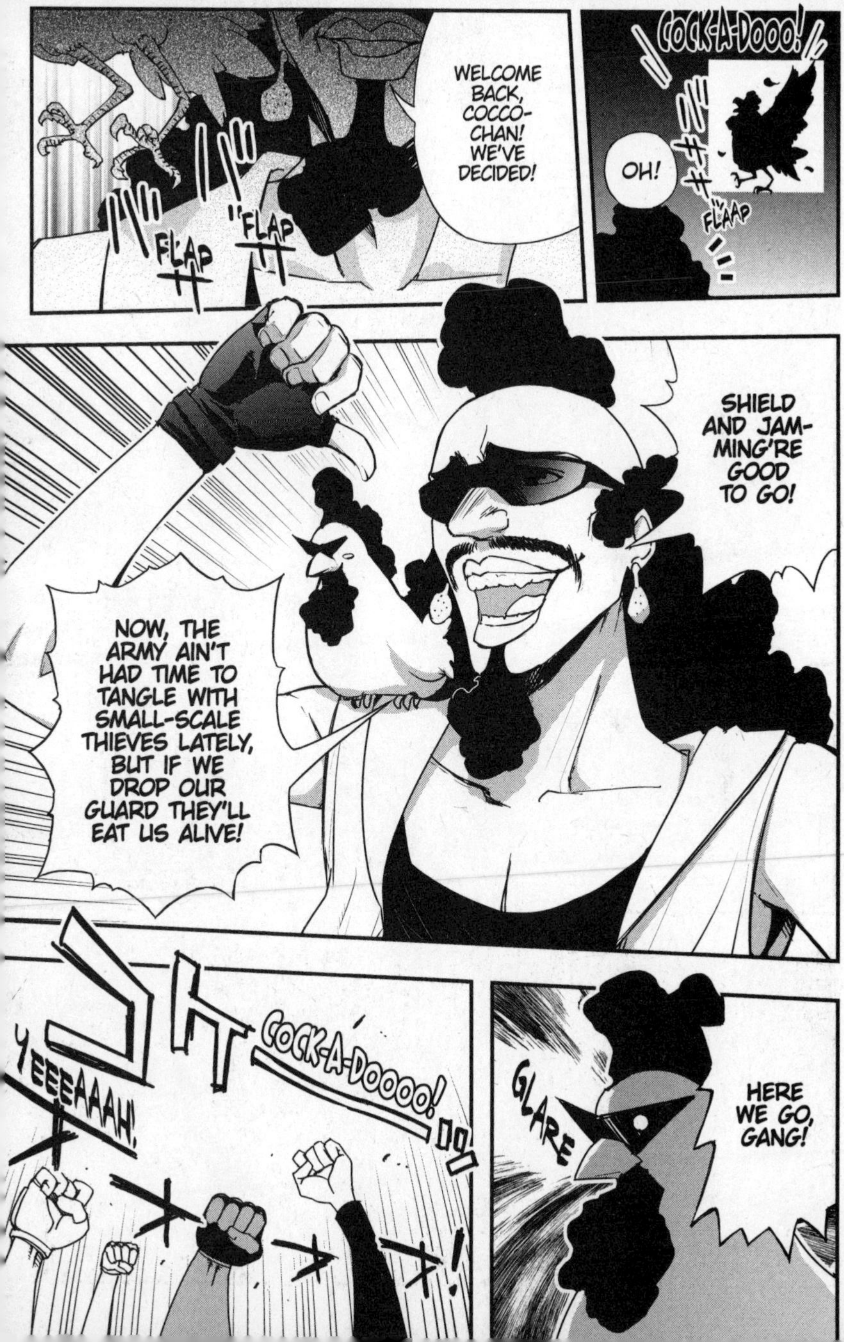
COCK-A-DOOO!
OH!
FLAAP
WELCOME BACK, COCCO-CHAN! WE'VE DECIDED!
FLAP
FLAP
SHIELD AND JAM-MING'RE GOOD TO GO!
NOW, THE ARMY AIN'T HAD TIME TO TANGLE WITH SMALL-SCALE THIEVES LATELY, BUT IF WE DROP OUR GUARD THEY'LL EAT US ALIVE!
GLARE
HERE WE GO, GANG!
COCK-A-DOOOO!!
YEEEAAAH!

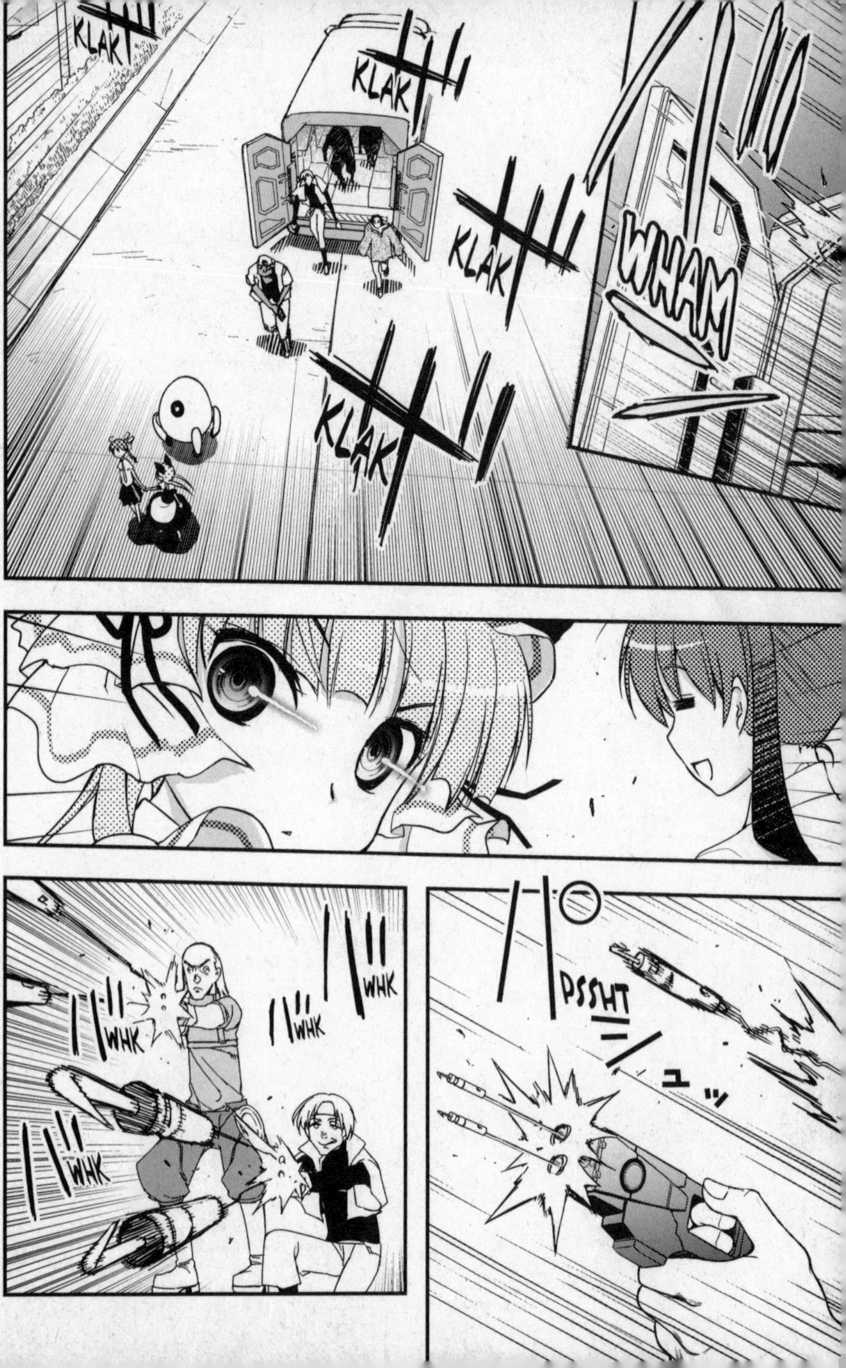
WHAM
KLAK
KLAK
KLAK
KLAK
PSSHT
ユッ
WHK
WHK
WHK
WHK

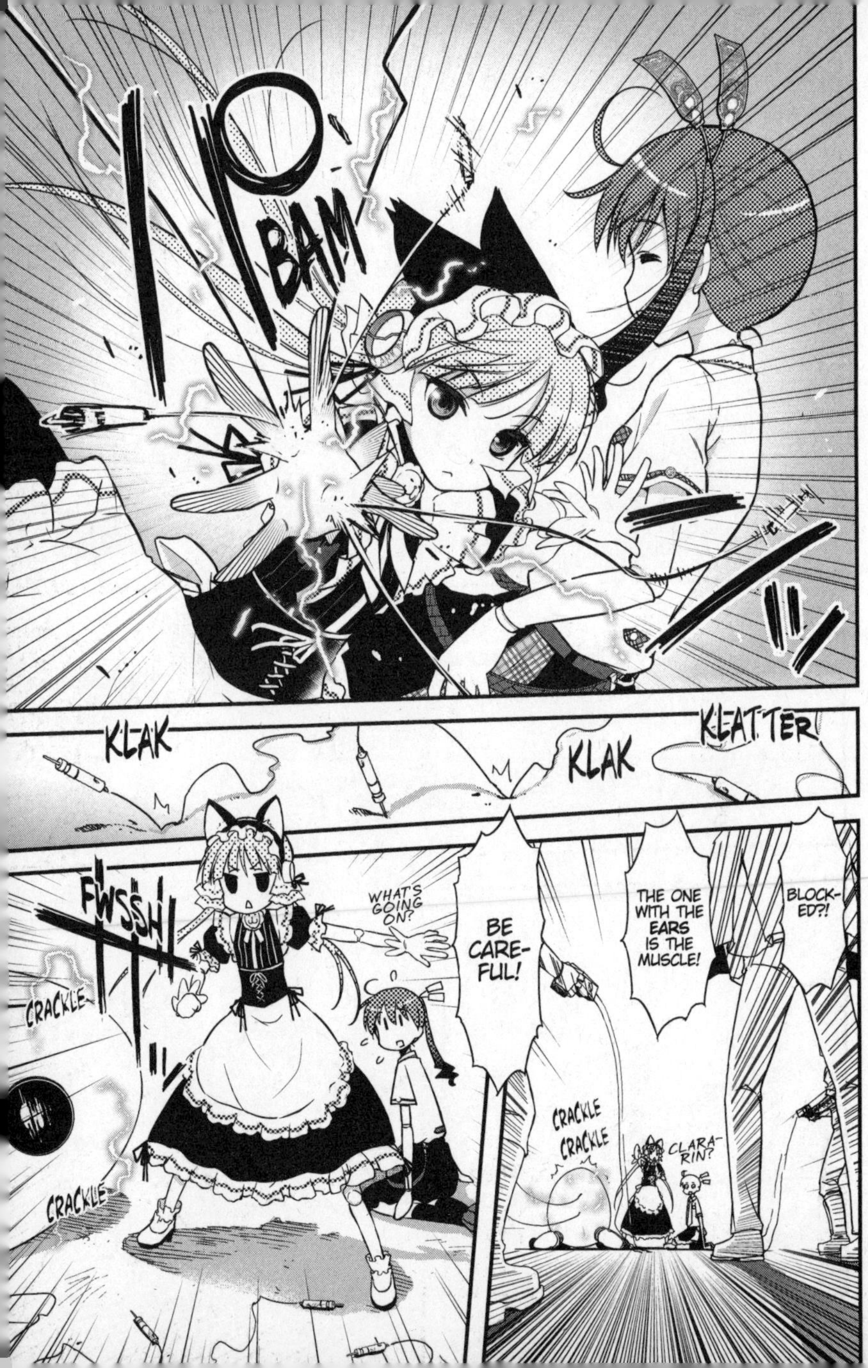
BAM
KLATTER
KLAK
KLAK
BLOCKED?!
THE ONE WITH THE EARS IS THE MUSCLE!
BE CAREFUL!
WHAT'S GOING ON?
FWSSH
CRACKLE
CRACKLE
CRACKLE CRACKLE
CLARARIN?

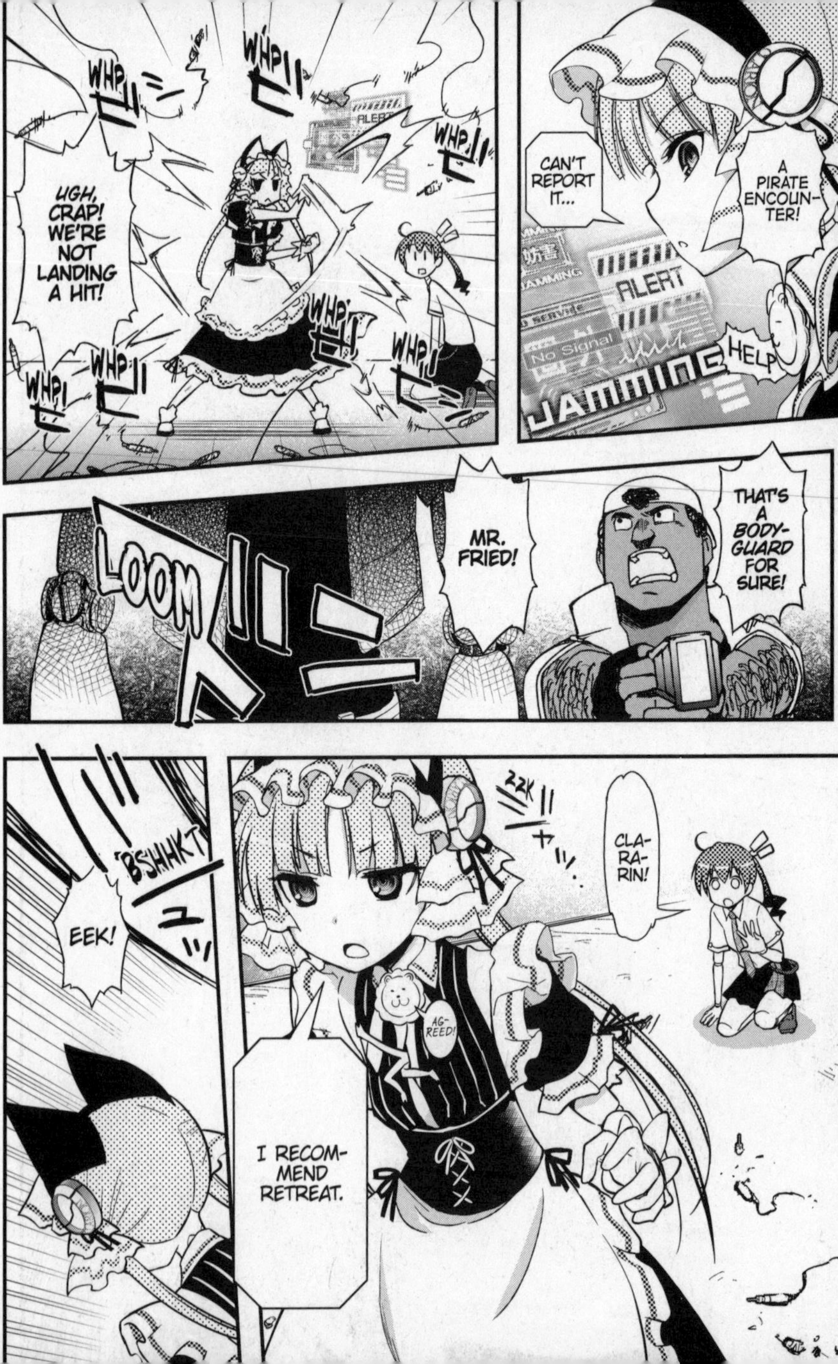
A PIRATE ENCOUN-TER!
CAN'T REPORT IT...
ALERT
No Signal
JAMMING
HELP
WHP!
UGH, CRAP! WE'RE NOT LANDING A HIT!
ALERT
THAT'S A BODY-GUARD FOR SURE!
MR. FRIED!
LOOM
CLA-RA-RIN!
ZZK
AG-REED!
I RECOM-MEND RETREAT.
BSHHKT
EEK!

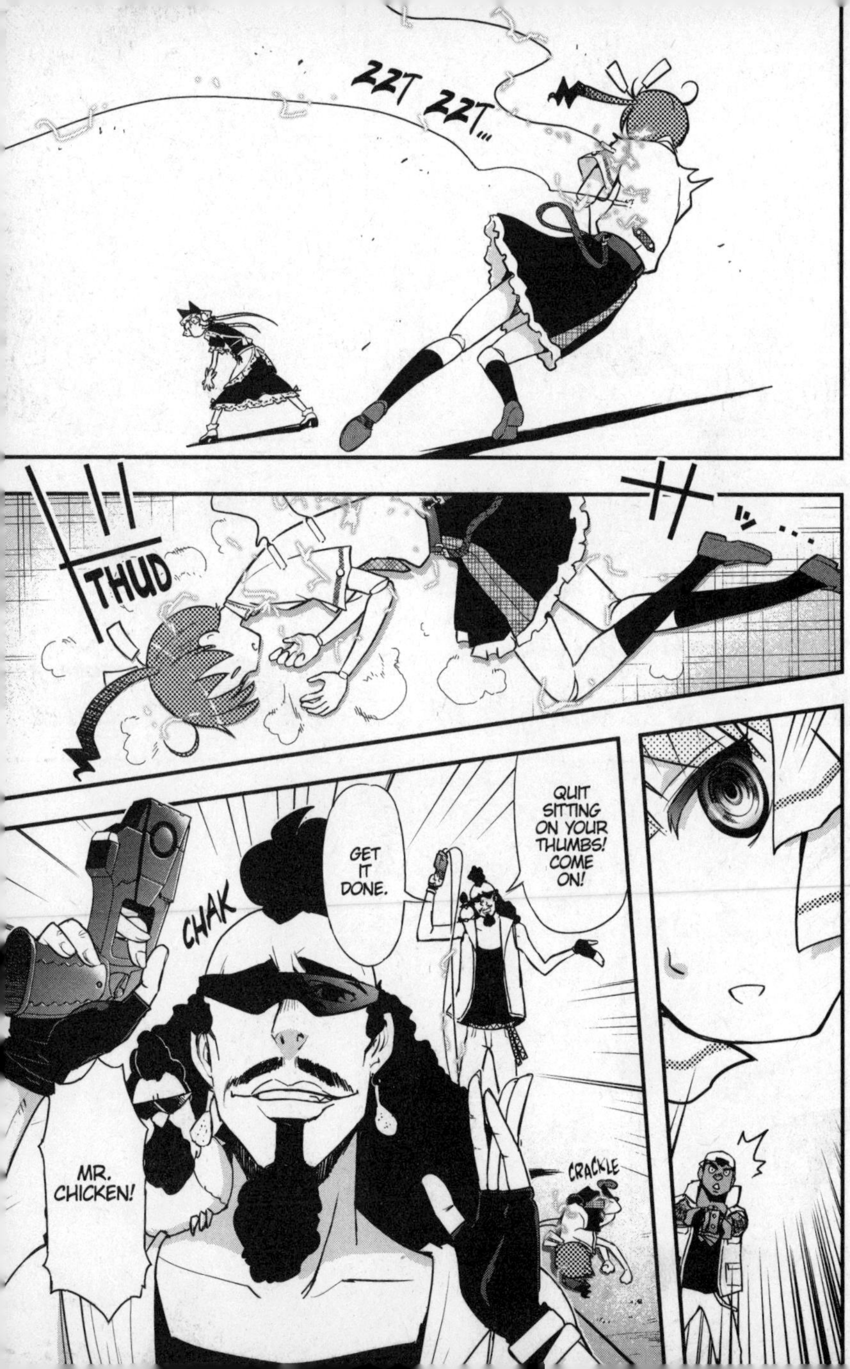
ZZT ZZT...
THUD
...
QUIT SITTING ON YOUR THUMBS! COME ON!
GET IT DONE.
CHAK
CRACKLE
MR. CHICKEN!

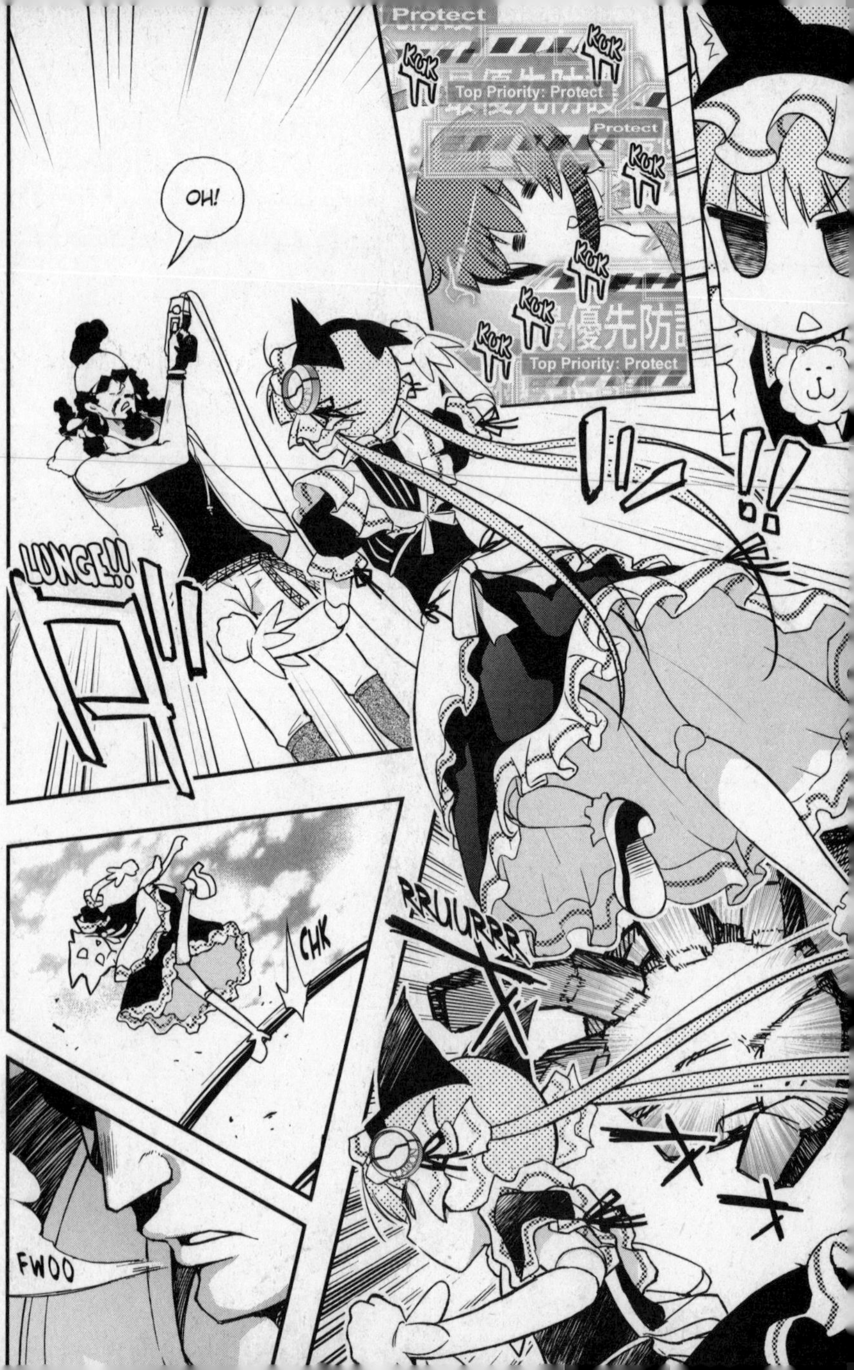
Protect
KUK
KUK
Top Priority: Protect
Protect
KUK
KUK
KUK
KUK
Top Priority: Protect
!!
!!
OH!
LUNGE!!
RRUURRR
CHK
FWOO

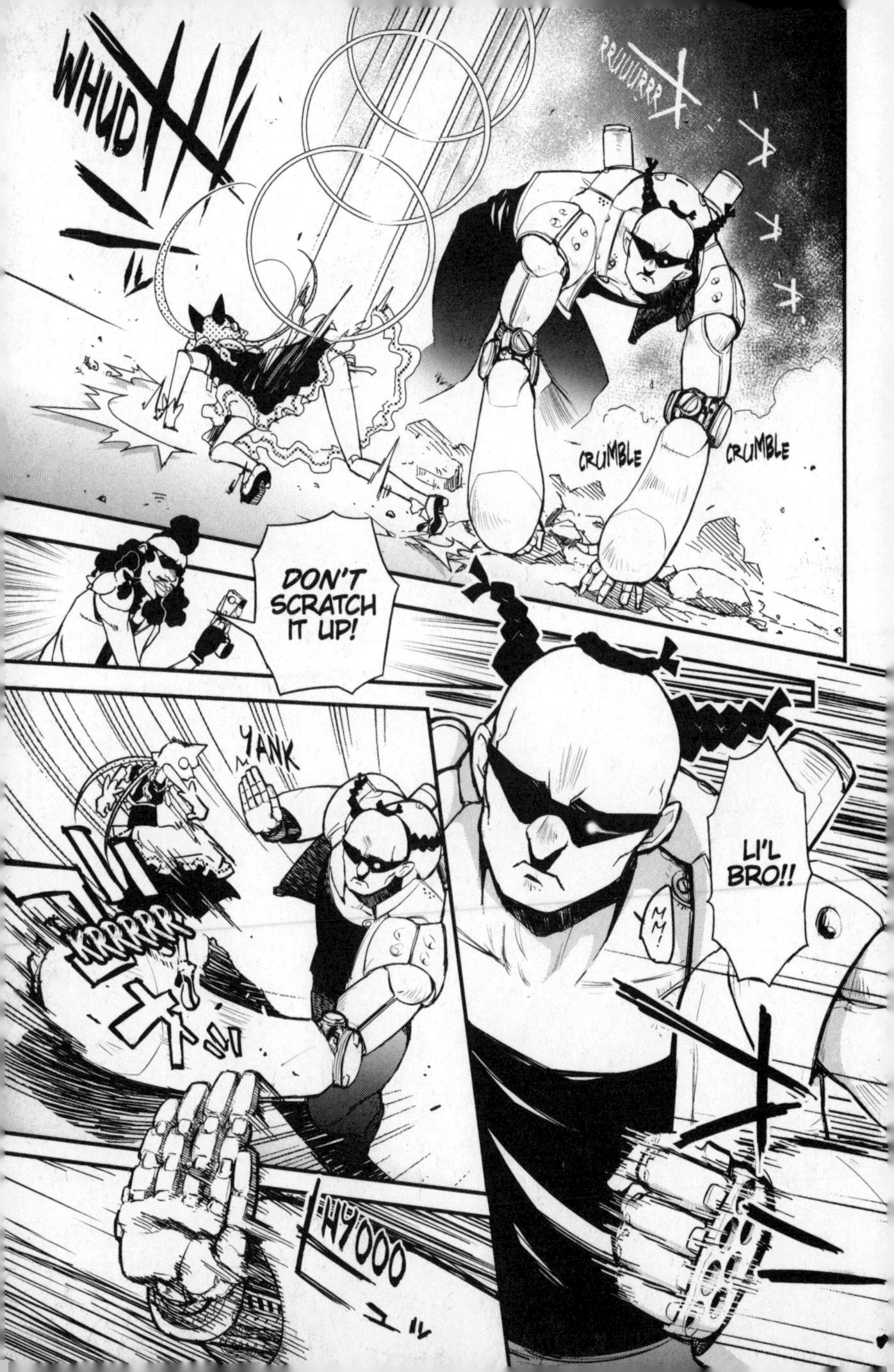

PRUUURRR
WHUD
CRUMBLE
CRUMBLE
DON'T SCRATCH IT UP!
LI'L BRO!!
MM!
H'YOOO
YANK
KRRRRR

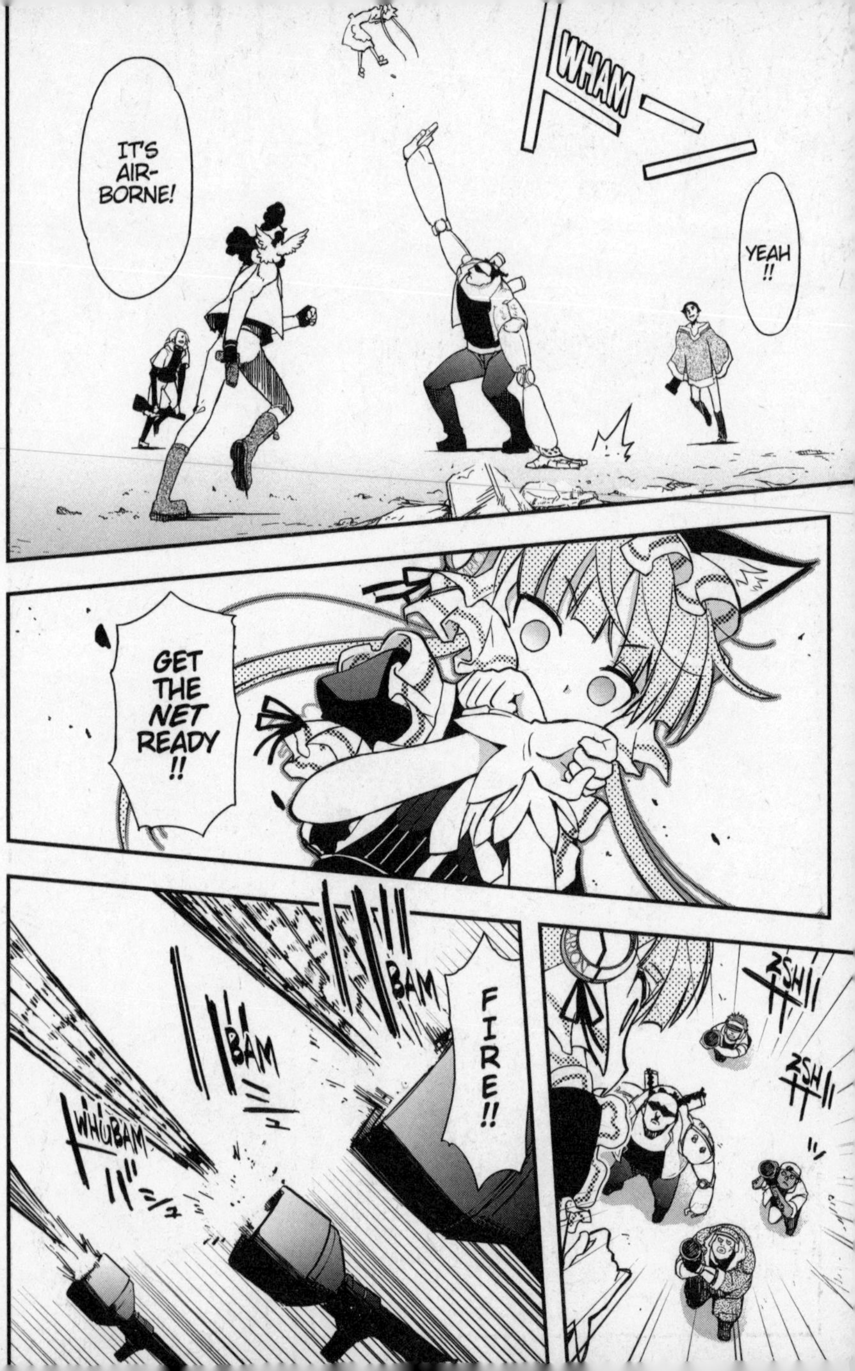
WHAM
YEAH!!
IT'S AIRBORNE!
GET THE NET READY!!
ZSH
ZSH
FIRE!!
BAM
BAM
WHUBAM

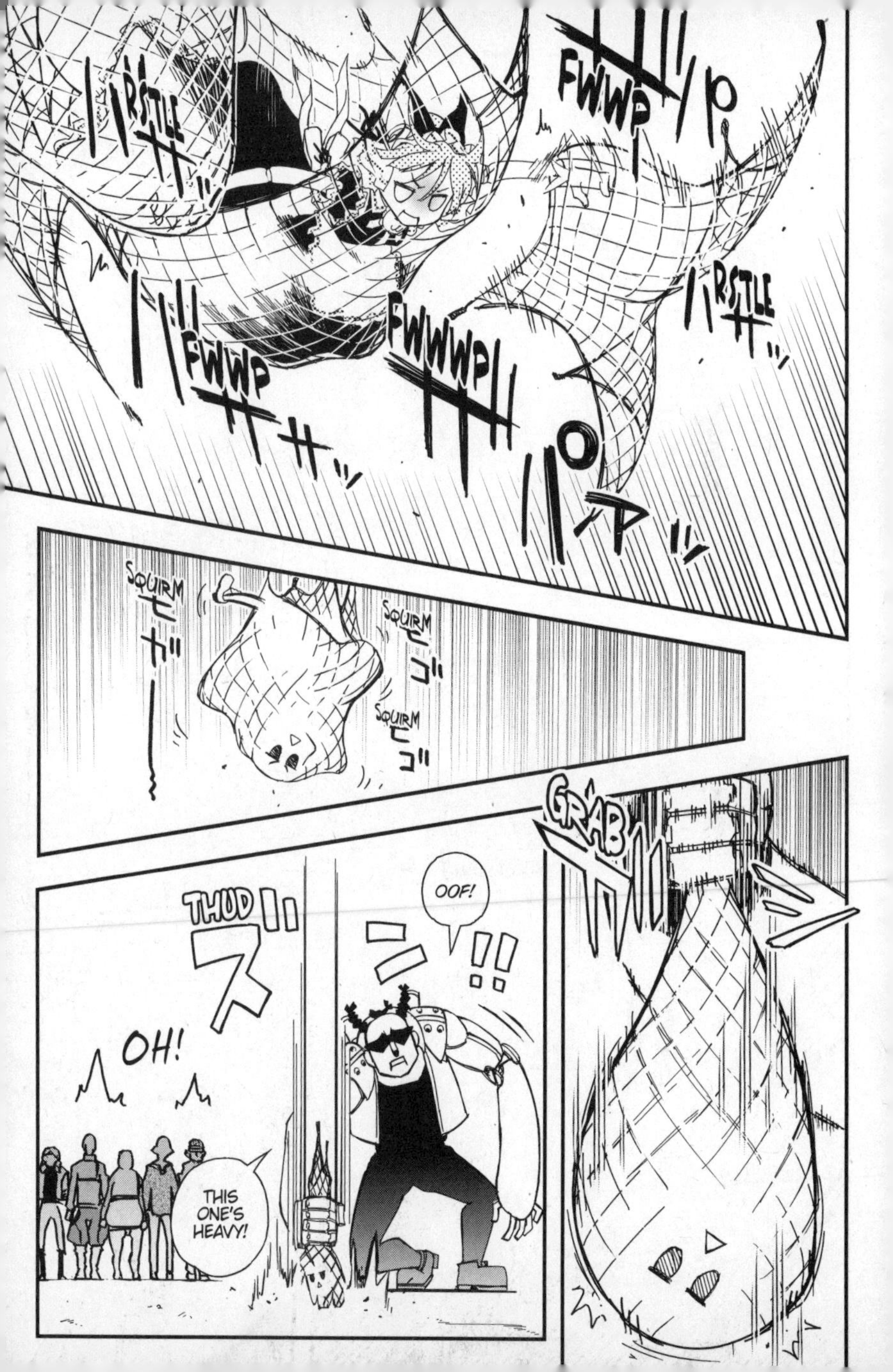
FWWP
RSTLE
FWWWP
FWWP
RSTLE
SQUIRM
SQUIRM
SQUIRM
GRAB
OOF!
THUD
OH!
THIS ONE'S HEAVY!

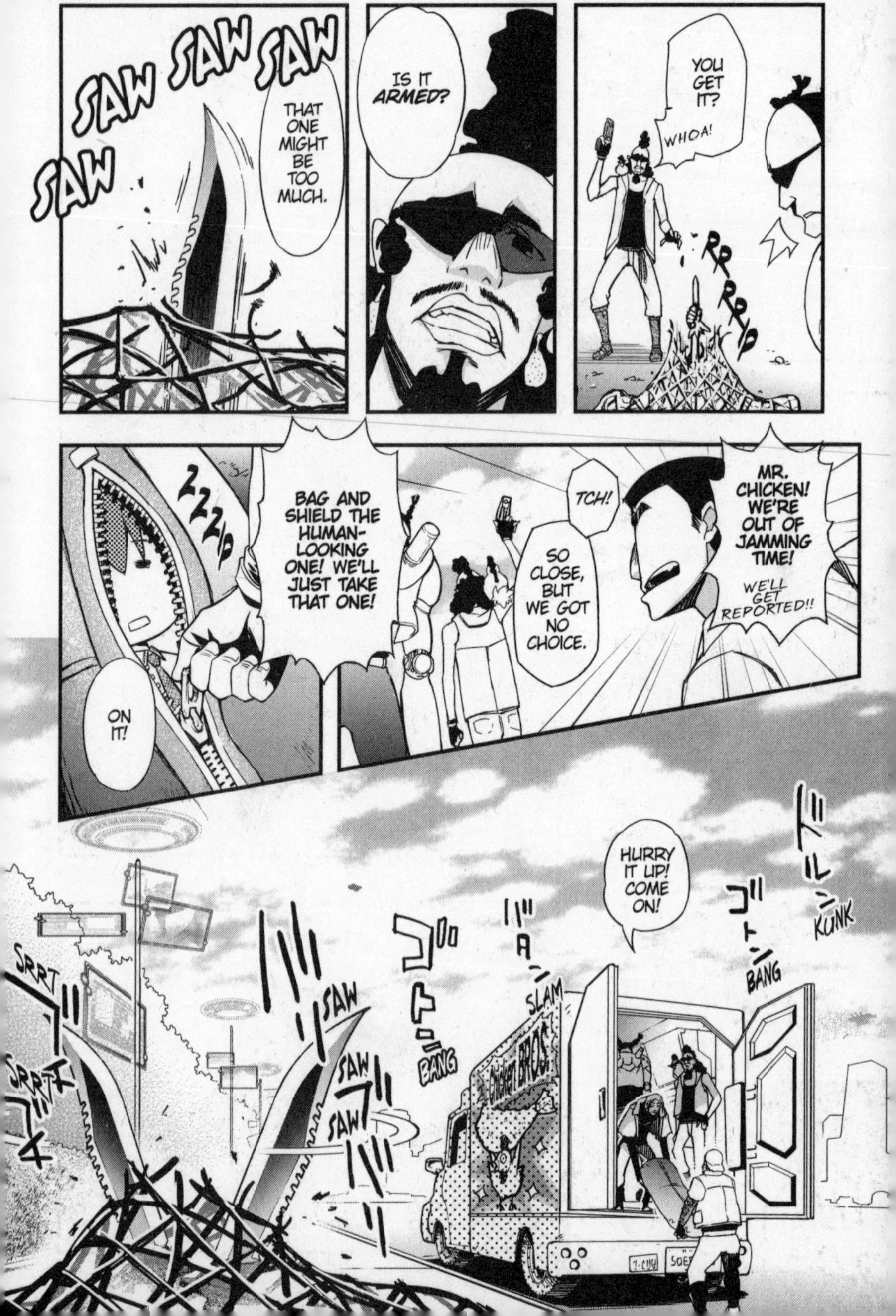
YOU GET IT?
WHOA!
RRRRIP
IS IT ARMED?
THAT ONE MIGHT BE TOO MUCH.
SAW SAW SAW SAW
MR. CHICKEN! WE'RE OUT OF JAMMING TIME!
WE'LL GET REPORTED!!
TCH!
SO CLOSE, BUT WE GOT NO CHOICE.
BAG AND SHIELD THE HUMAN-LOOKING ONE! WE'LL JUST TAKE THAT ONE!
ZZZIP
ON IT!
KUNK
BANG
HURRY IT UP! COME ON!
SLAM
BANG
SAW
SAW
SAW
SRRT
SRRT

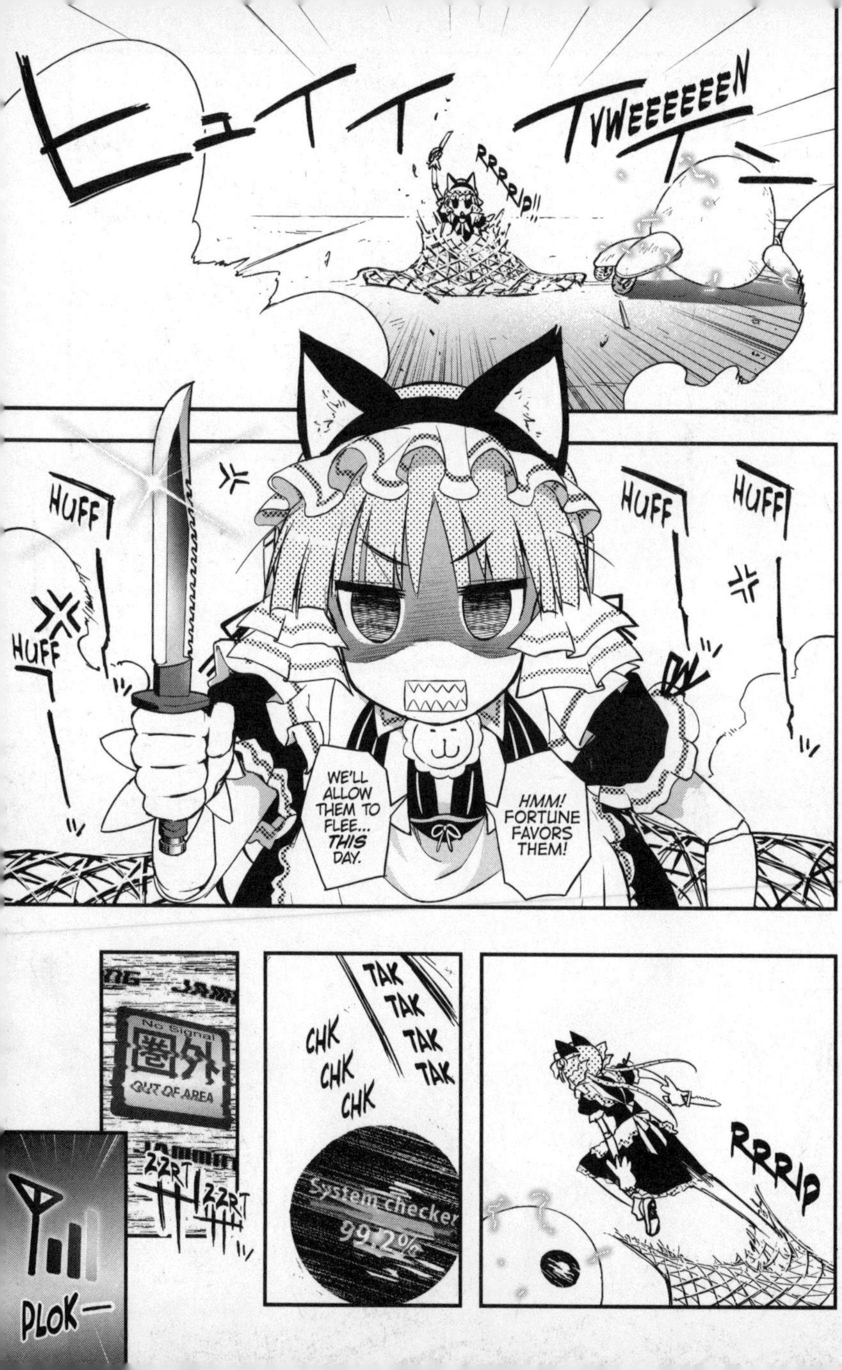
ヒュイイ
TVWEEEEEEEN
RRRRRIP!!
HUFF
HUFF
HMM! FORTUNE FAVORS THEM!
WE'LL ALLOW THEM TO FLEE... *THIS* DAY.
HUFF
HUFF
RRRIP
TAK
TAK
TAK
TAK
CHK
CHK
CHK
System checker
99.2%
No Signal
圏外
OUT OF AREA
2-2RT
2-2RT
PLOK—

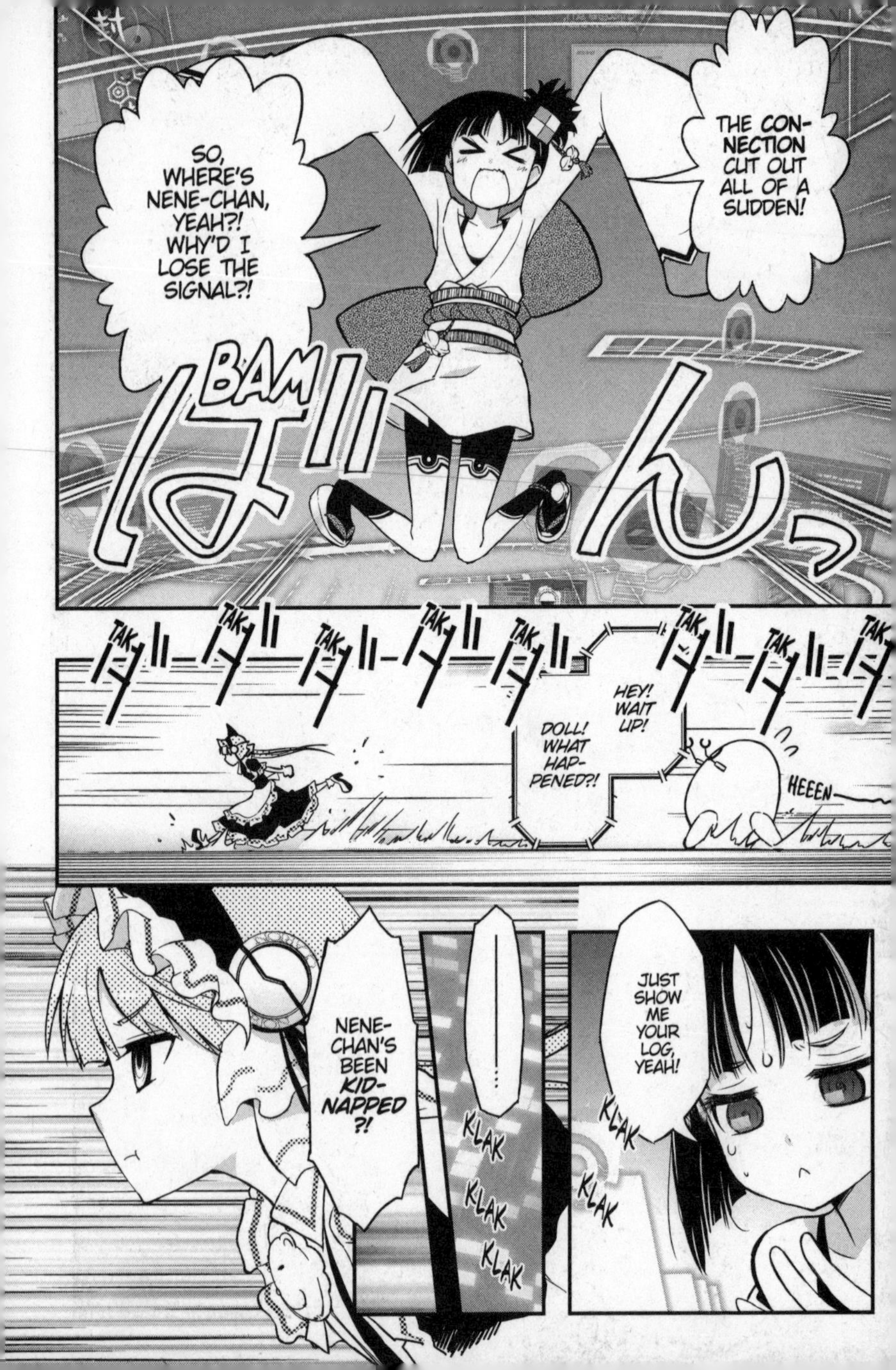
THE CON-NECTION CUT OUT ALL OF A SUDDEN!
SO, WHERE'S NENE-CHAN, YEAH?! WHY'D I LOSE THE SIGNAL?!
BAM
TAK TAK TAK TAK TAK TAK TAK TAK
HEY! WAIT UP!
DOLL! WHAT HAP-PENED?!
HEEEN
JUST SHOW ME YOUR LOG, YEAH!
KLAK KLAK
......!
KLAK KLAK KLAK KLAK
NENE-CHAN'S BEEN KID-NAPPED?!

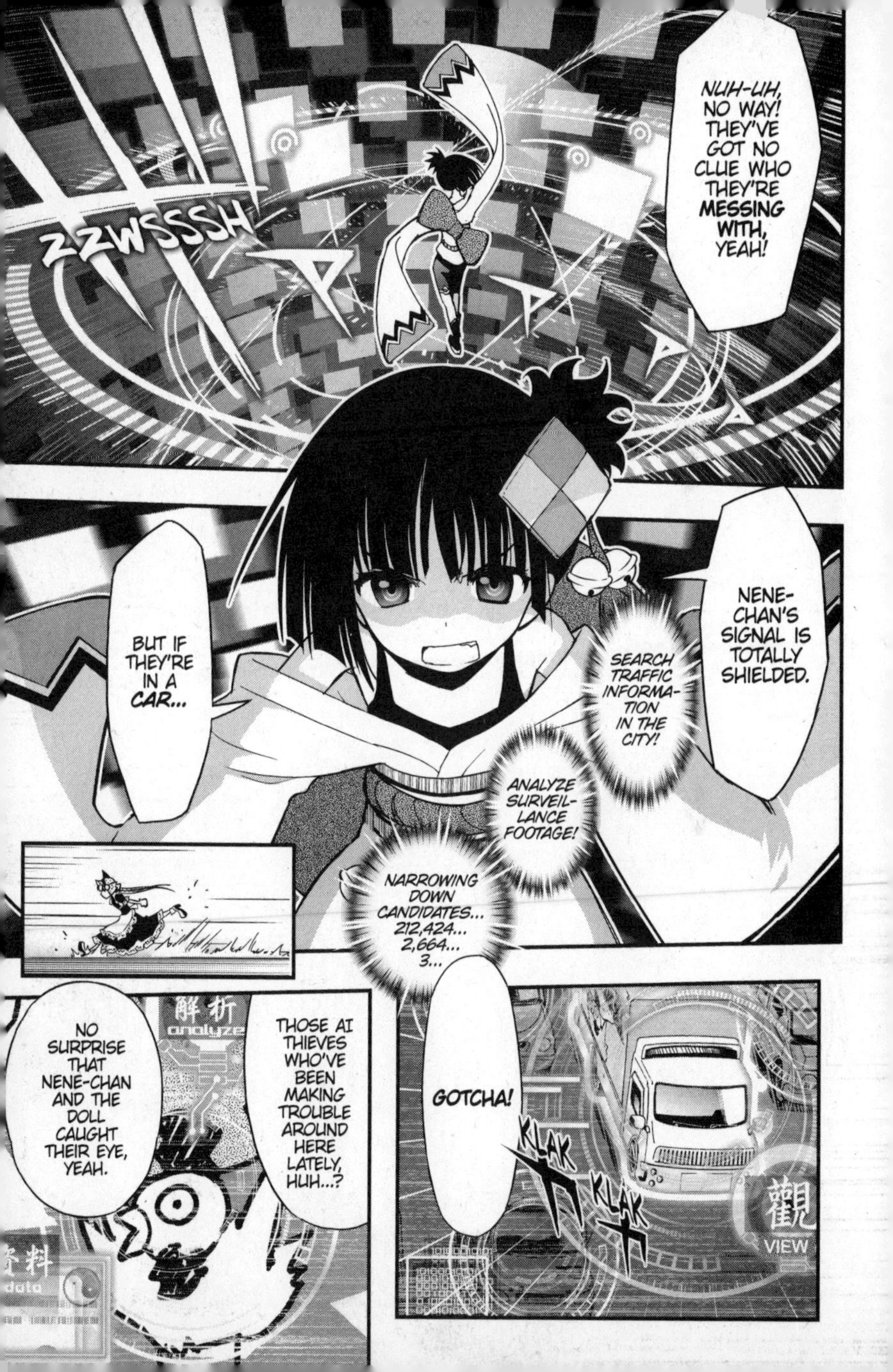

NUH-UH, NO WAY! THEY'VE GOT NO CLUE WHO THEY'RE **MESSING WITH**, YEAH!
ZZWSSSH
NENE-CHAN'S SIGNAL IS TOTALLY SHIELDED.
BUT IF THEY'RE IN A ***CAR...***
SEARCH TRAFFIC INFORMATION IN THE CITY!
ANALYZE SURVEILLANCE FOOTAGE!
NARROWING DOWN CANDIDATES... 212,424... 2,664... 3...
GOTCHA!
KLAK
KLAK
觀
VIEW
THOSE AI THIEVES WHO'VE BEEN MAKING TROUBLE AROUND HERE LATELY, HUH...?
NO SURPRISE THAT NENE-CHAN AND THE DOLL CAUGHT THEIR EYE, YEAH.
解析
analyze
資料
data

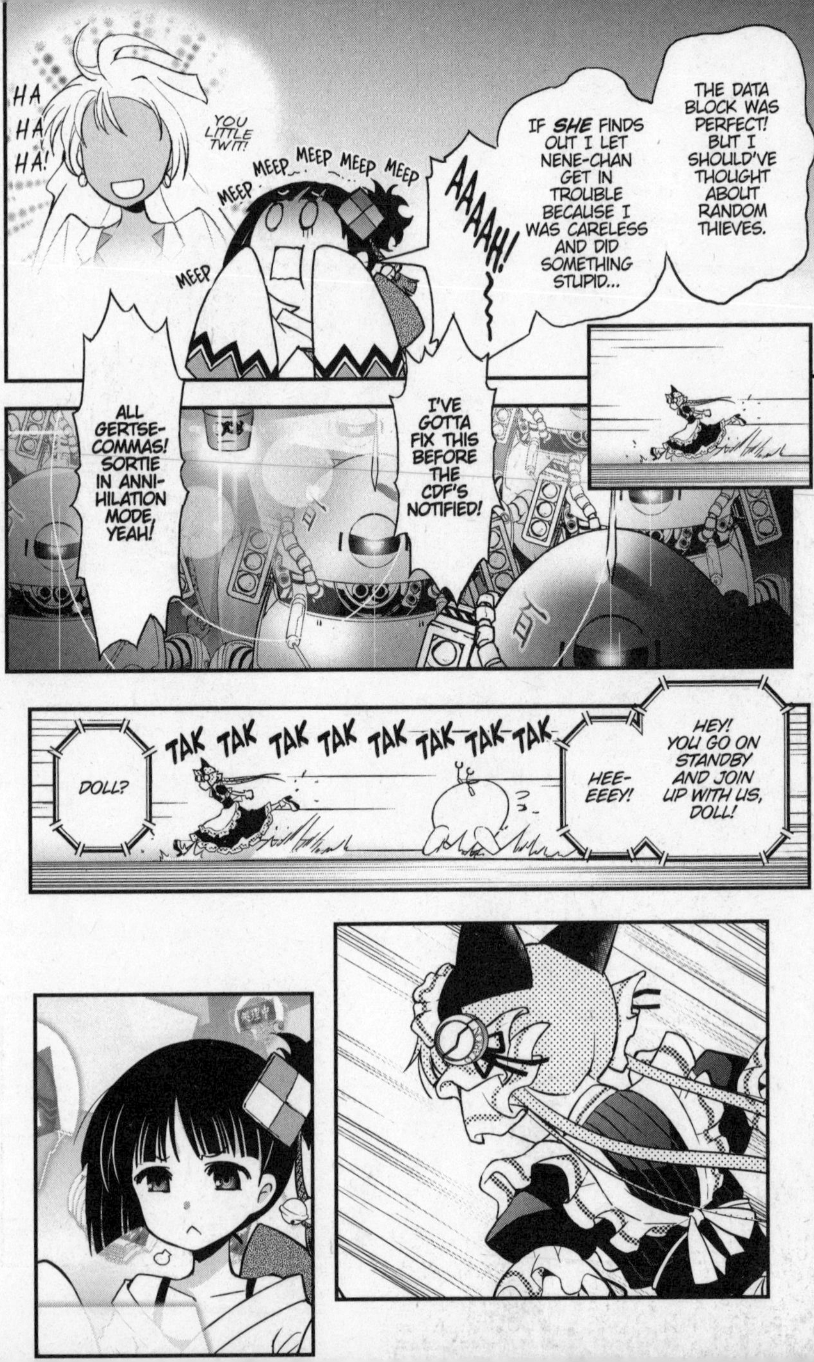
THE DATA BLOCK WAS PERFECT! BUT I SHOULD'VE THOUGHT ABOUT RANDOM THIEVES.
IF SHE FINDS OUT I LET NENE-CHAN GET IN TROUBLE BECAUSE I WAS CARELESS AND DID SOMETHING STUPID...
AAAAAH!~~~
MEEP MEEP MEEP MEEP MEEP
MEEP
YOU LITTLE TWIT!
HA HA HA!
I'VE GOTTA FIX THIS BEFORE THE CDF'S NOTIFIED!
ALL GERTSE-COMMAS! SORTIE IN ANNI-HILATION MODE, YEAH!
HEY! YOU GO ON STANDBY AND JOIN UP WITH US, DOLL!
HEE-EEEY!
TAK TAK TAK TAK TAK TAK TAK TAK
DOLL?

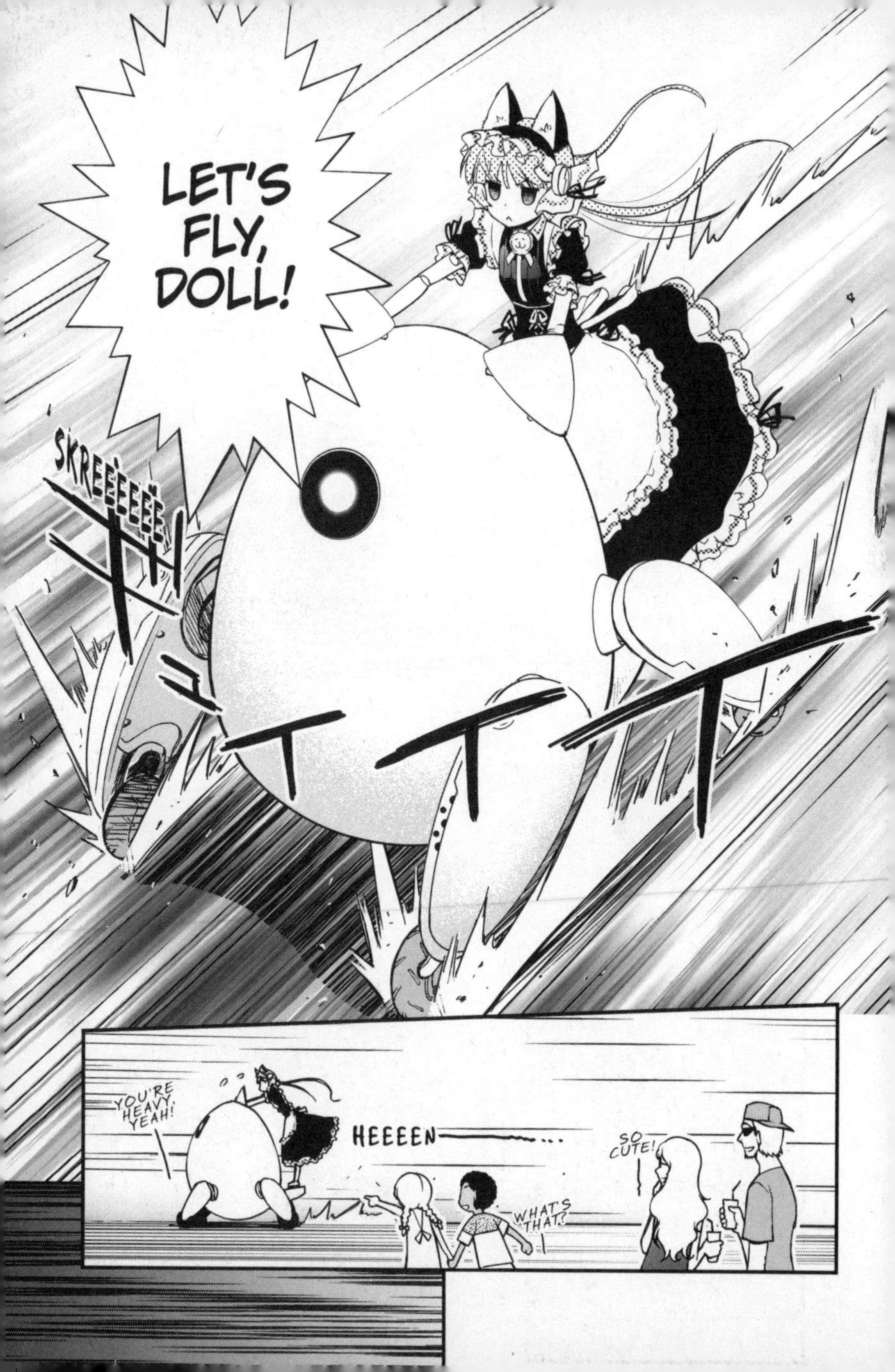
LET'S FLY, DOLL!
SKREEEEEE
SO CUTE!
WHAT'S THAT?
HEEEEN———...
YOU'RE HEAVY, YEAH!

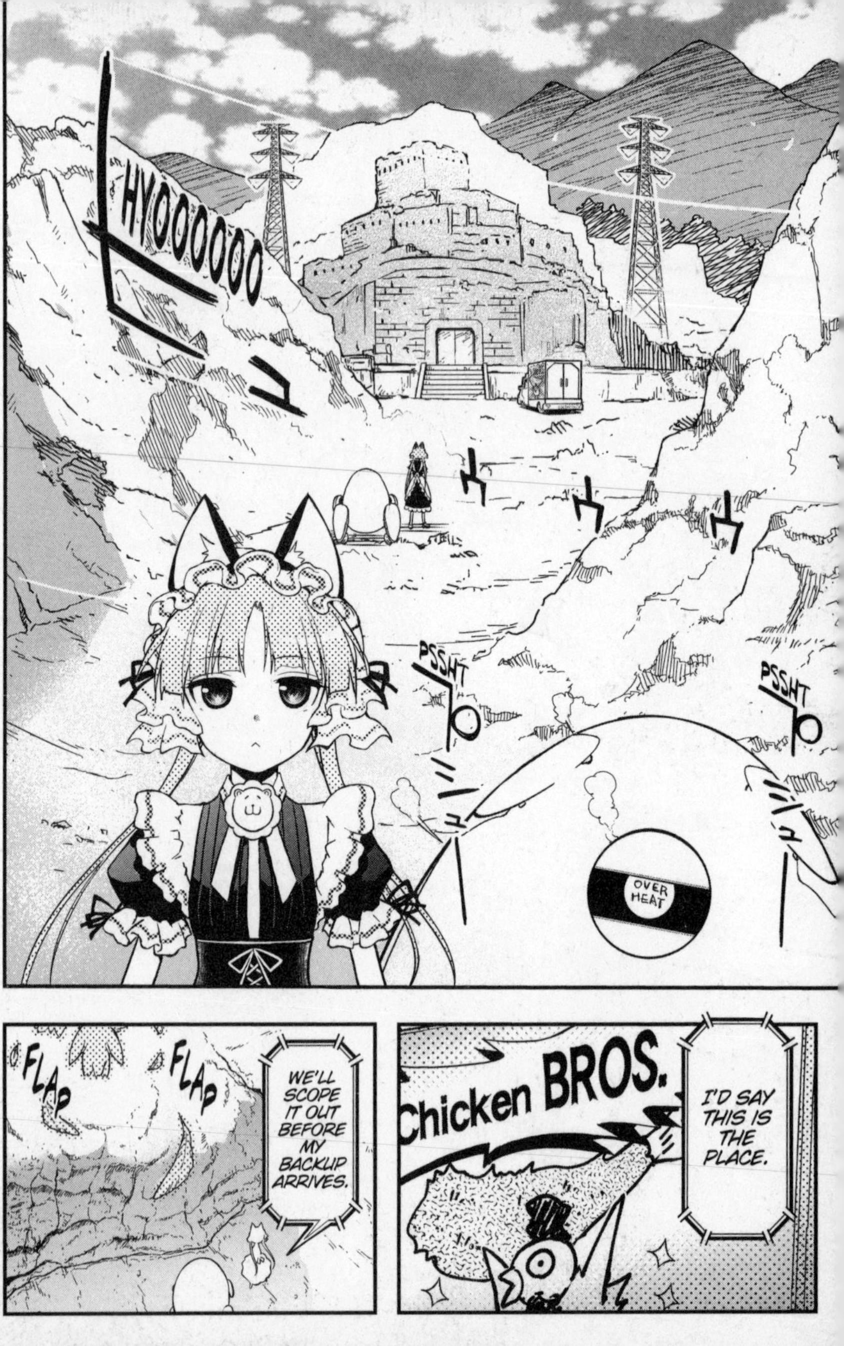
HYOOOOO
PSSHT
PSSHT
OVER HEAT
Chicken BROS.
I'D SAY THIS IS THE PLACE.
FLAP
FLAP
WE'LL SCOPE IT OUT BEFORE MY BACKUP ARRIVES.

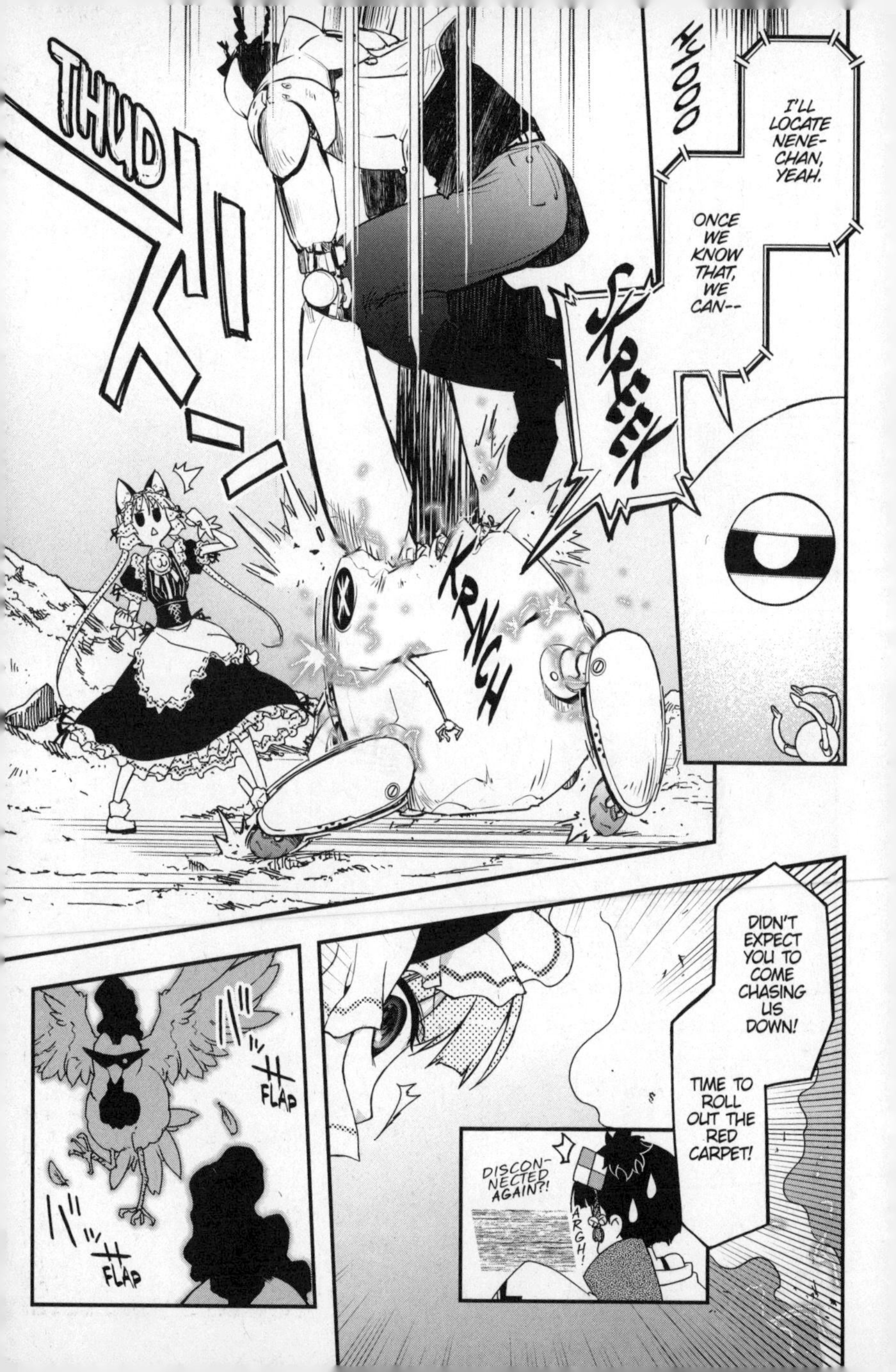

I'LL LOCATE NENE-CHAN, YEAH.
ONCE WE KNOW THAT, WE CAN--
HYOOO
SKREEEK
KRNCH
THUD
DIDN'T EXPECT YOU TO COME CHASING US DOWN!
TIME TO ROLL OUT THE RED CARPET!
DISCONNECTED AGAIN?!
ARGH!
FLAP
FLAP

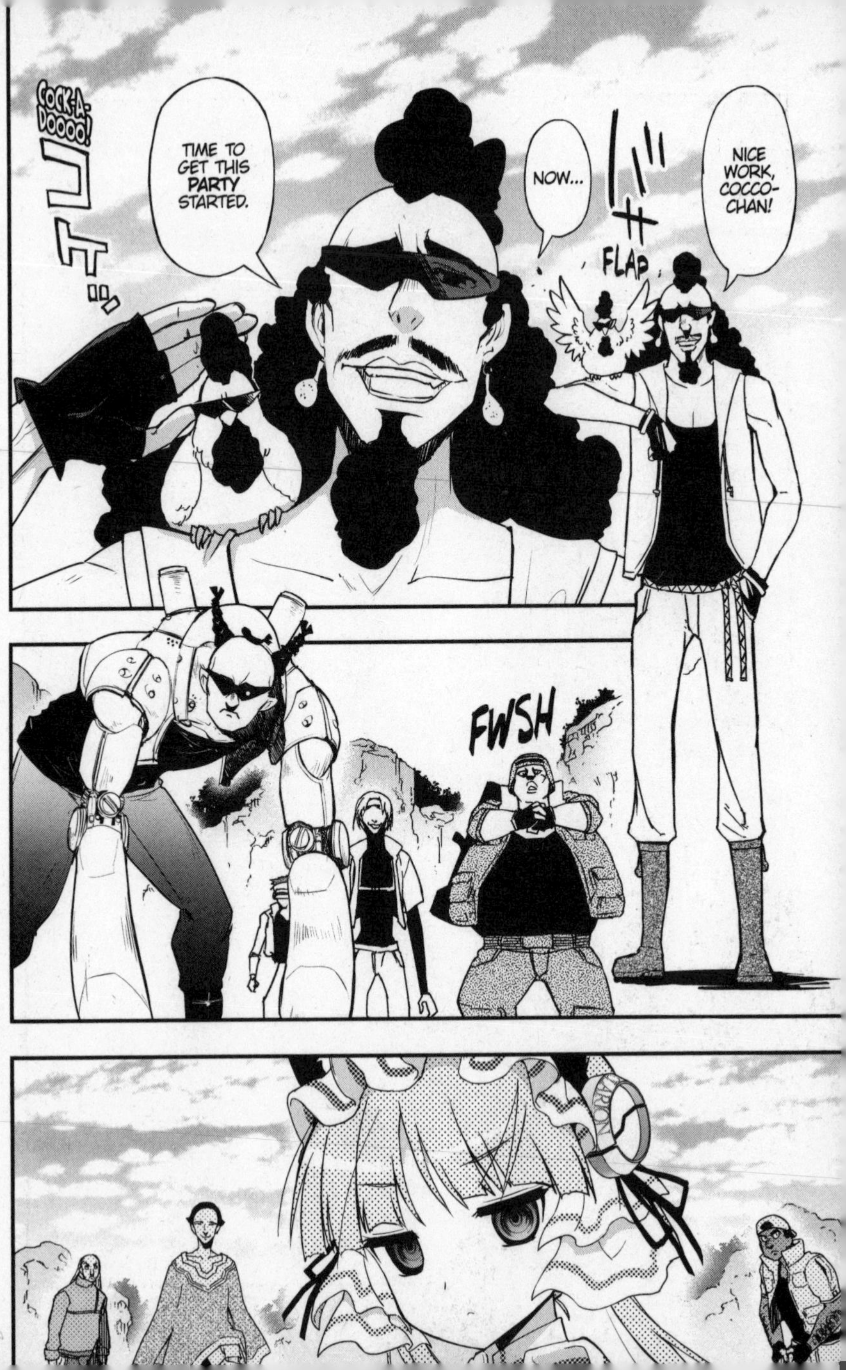
NICE WORK, COCCO-CHAN!
FLAP
NOW...
TIME TO GET THIS **PARTY** STARTED.
COCK-A-DOOOO!
FWSH

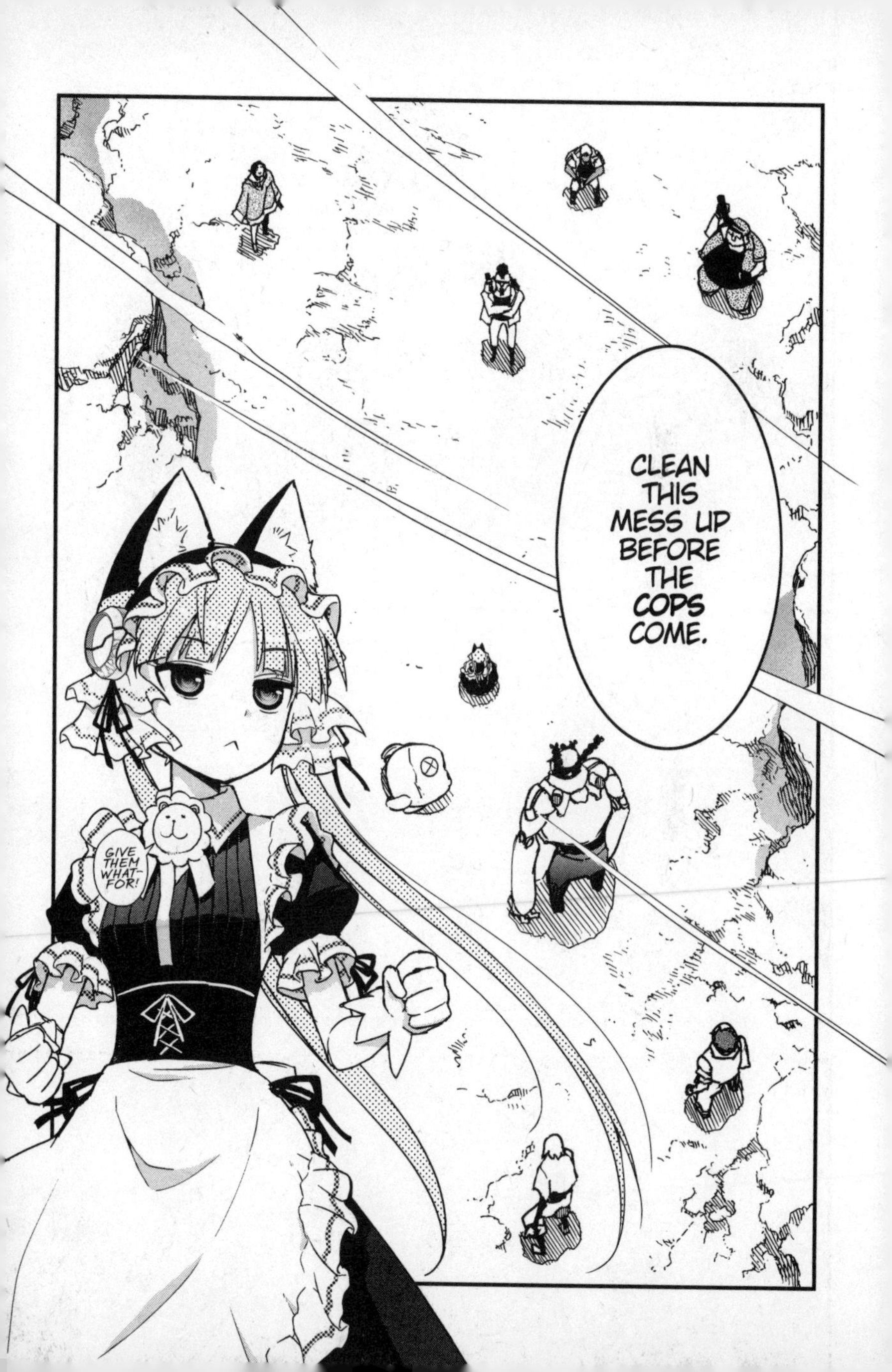
CLEAN THIS MESS UP BEFORE THE COPS COME.
GIVE THEM WHAT-FOR!

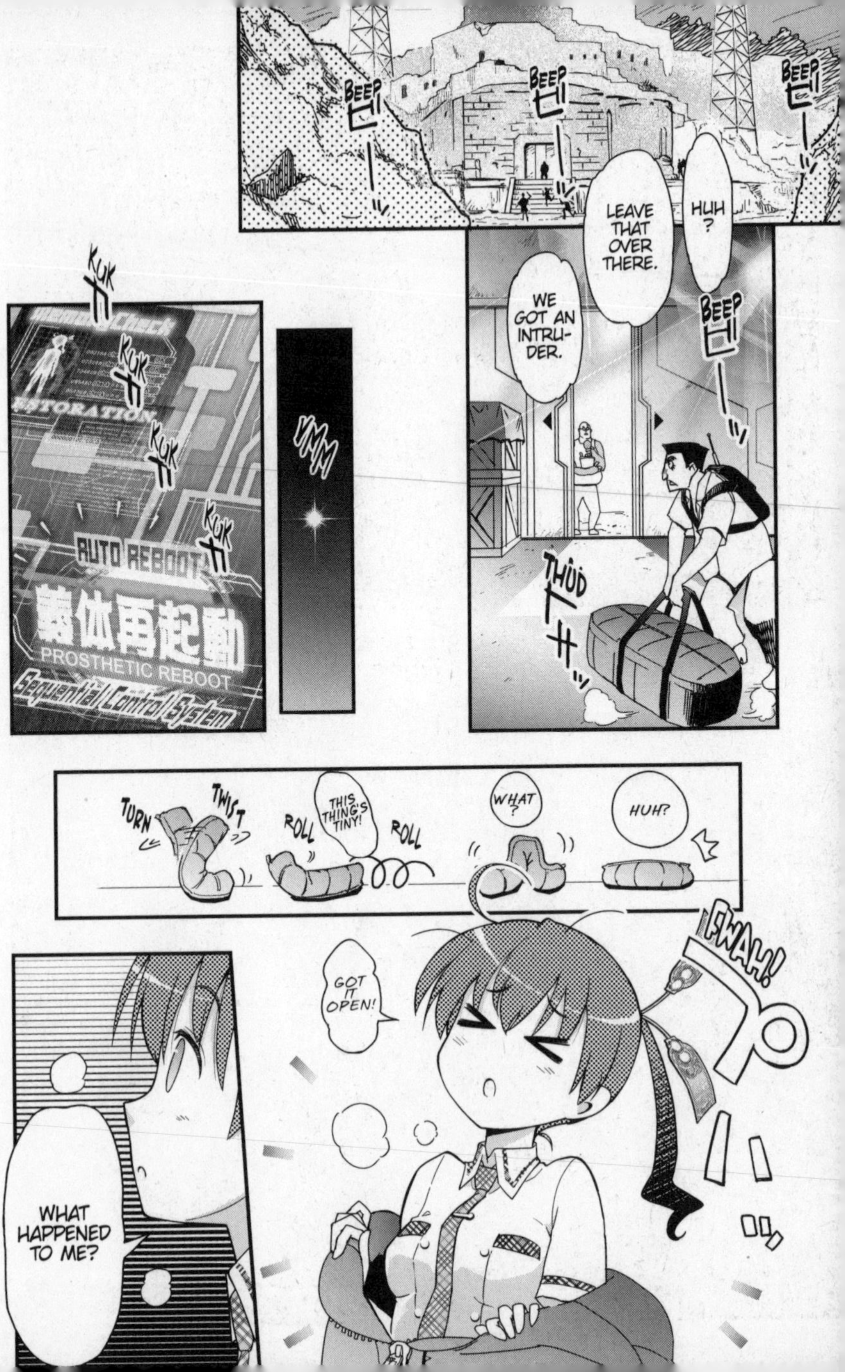
BEEP
BEEP
BEEP
HUH?
LEAVE THAT OVER THERE.
WE GOT AN INTRUDER.
BEEP
THUD
VMM
KUK
KUK
KUK
KUK
RESTORATION
AUTO REBOOT
躯体再起動
PROSTHETIC REBOOT
Sequential Control System
HUH?
WHAT?
ROLL
THIS THING'S TINY!
ROLL
TWIST
TURN
FWAH!
GOT IT OPEN!
WHAT HAPPENED TO ME?

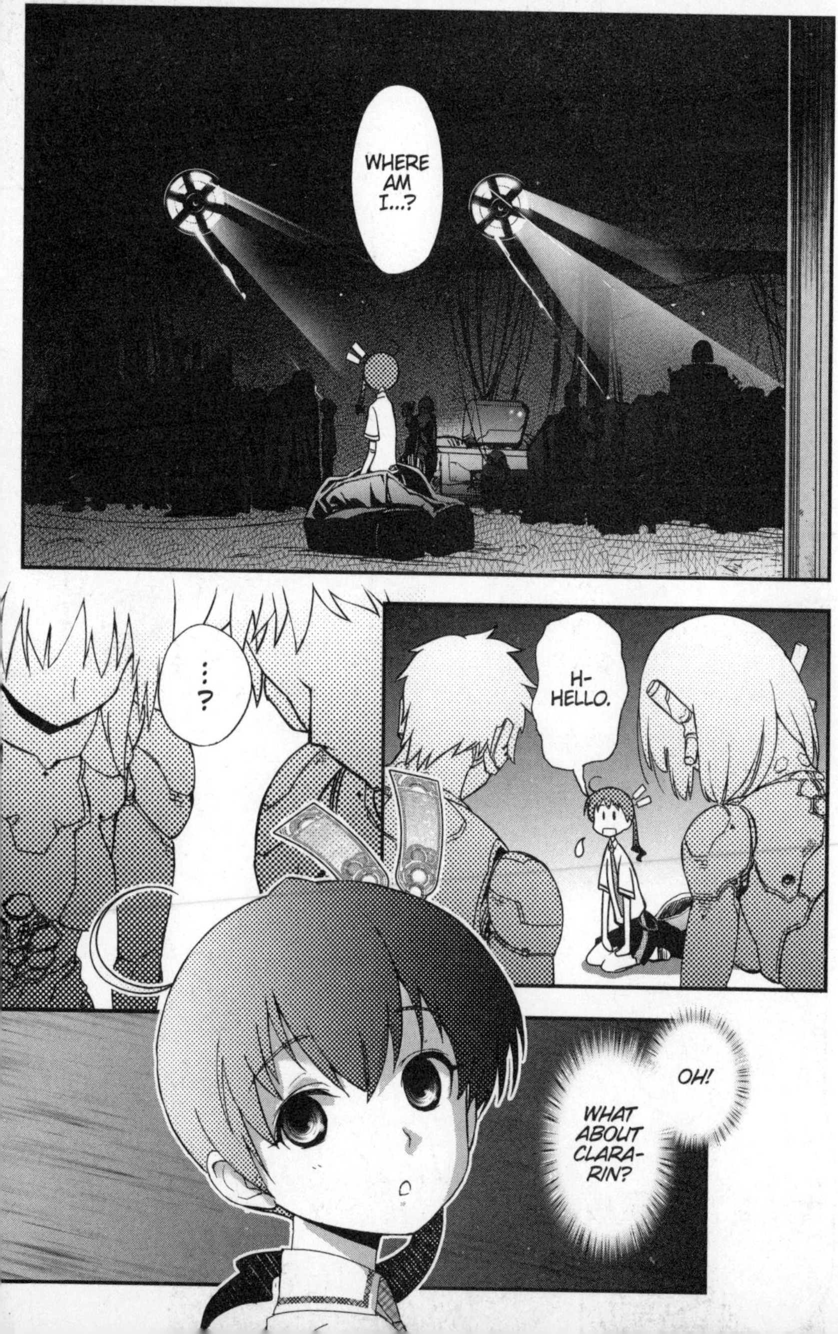
WHERE AM I...?
H- HELLO.
...?
OH!
WHAT ABOUT CLARA-RIN?

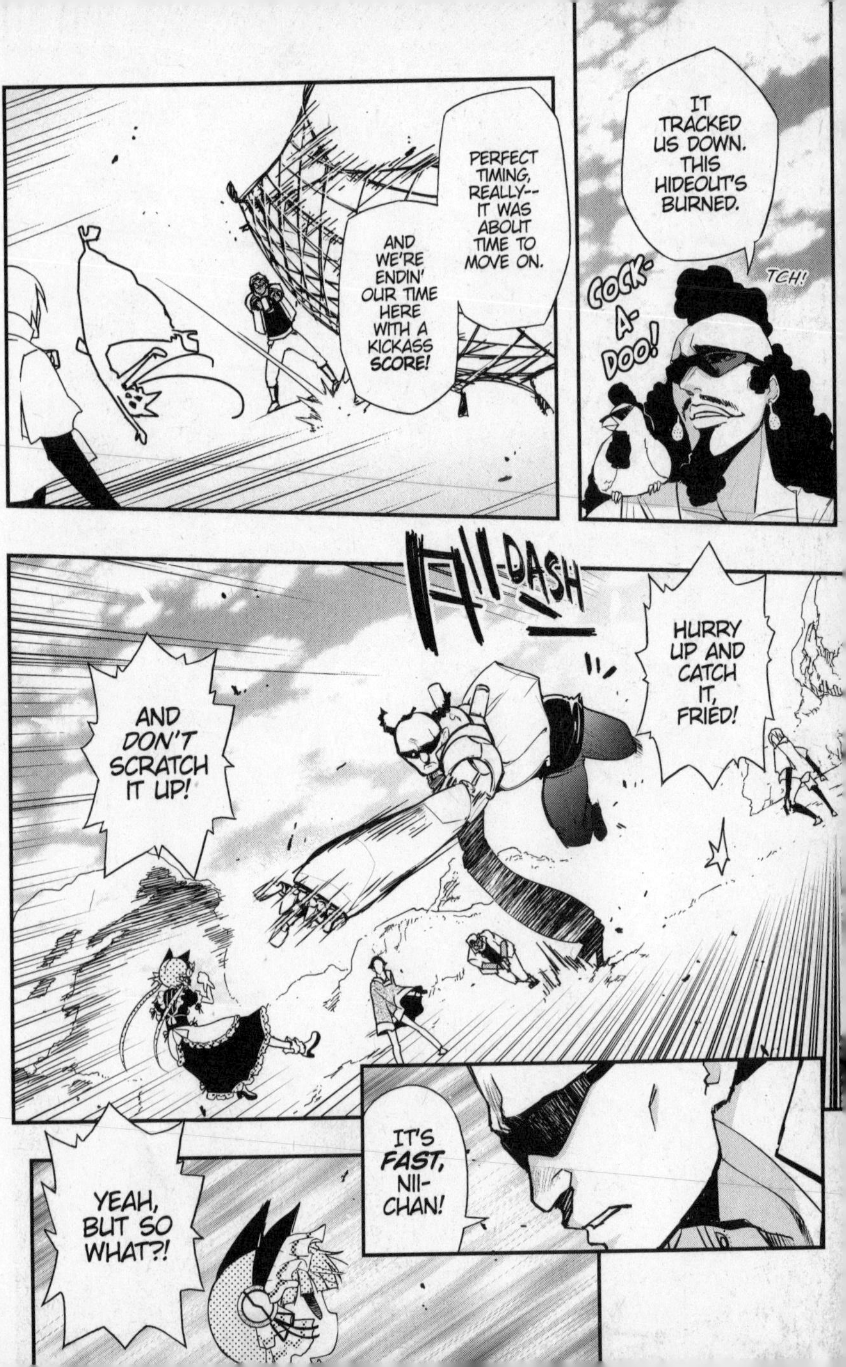
IT TRACKED US DOWN. THIS HIDEOUT'S BURNED.
TCH!
COCK-A-DOO!
PERFECT TIMING, REALLY-- IT WAS ABOUT TIME TO MOVE ON.
AND WE'RE ENDIN' OUR TIME HERE WITH A KICKASS SCORE!
DASH
HURRY UP AND CATCH IT, FRIED!
AND DON'T SCRATCH IT UP!
IT'S FAST, NII-CHAN!
YEAH, BUT SO WHAT?!

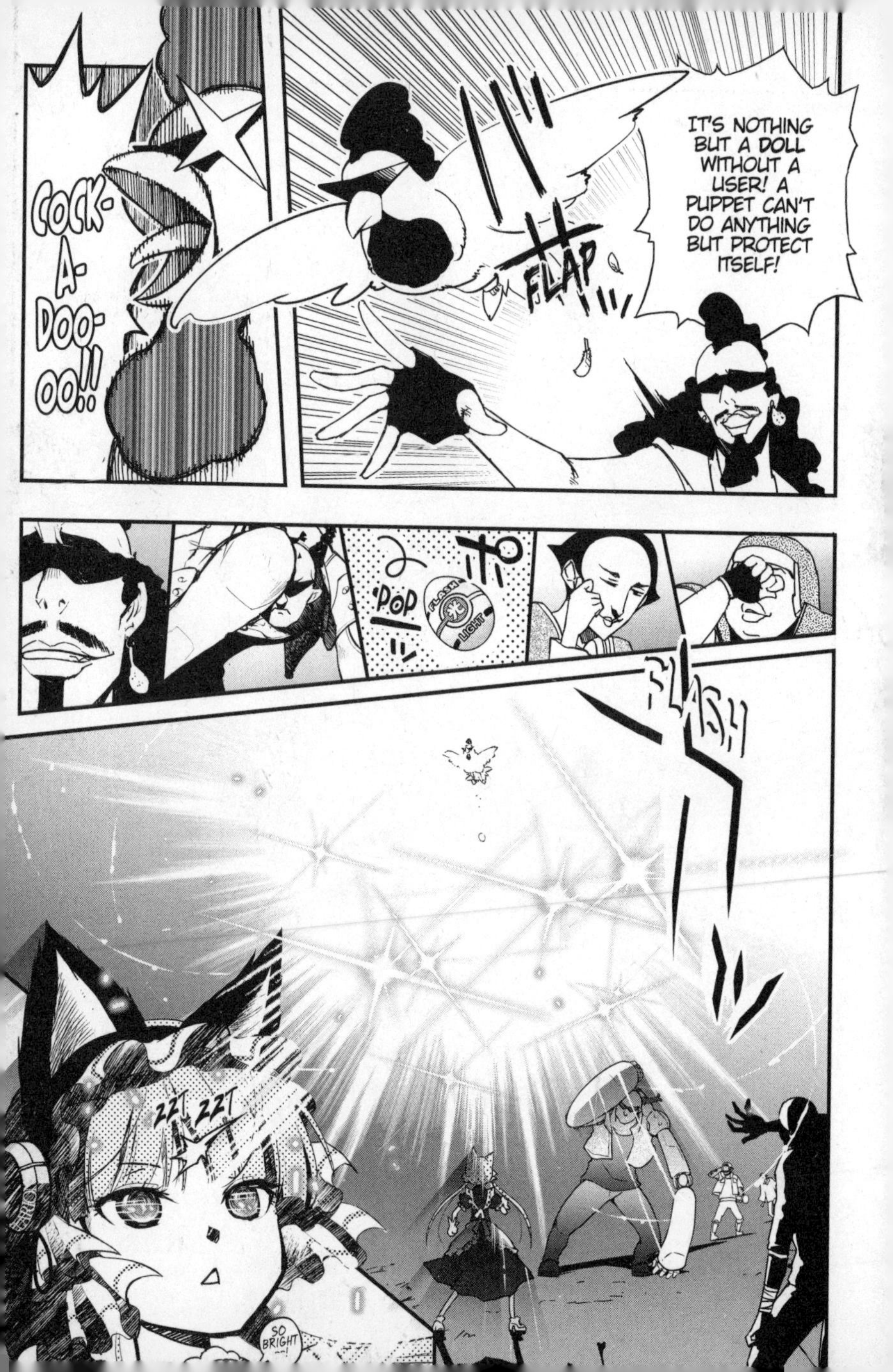
IT'S NOTHING BUT A DOLL WITHOUT A USER! A PUPPET CAN'T DO ANYTHING BUT PROTECT ITSELF!
FLAP
COCK-A-DOO-OO!!
POP
FLASH 光 LIGHT
FLASH
ZZT ZZT
SO BRIGHT

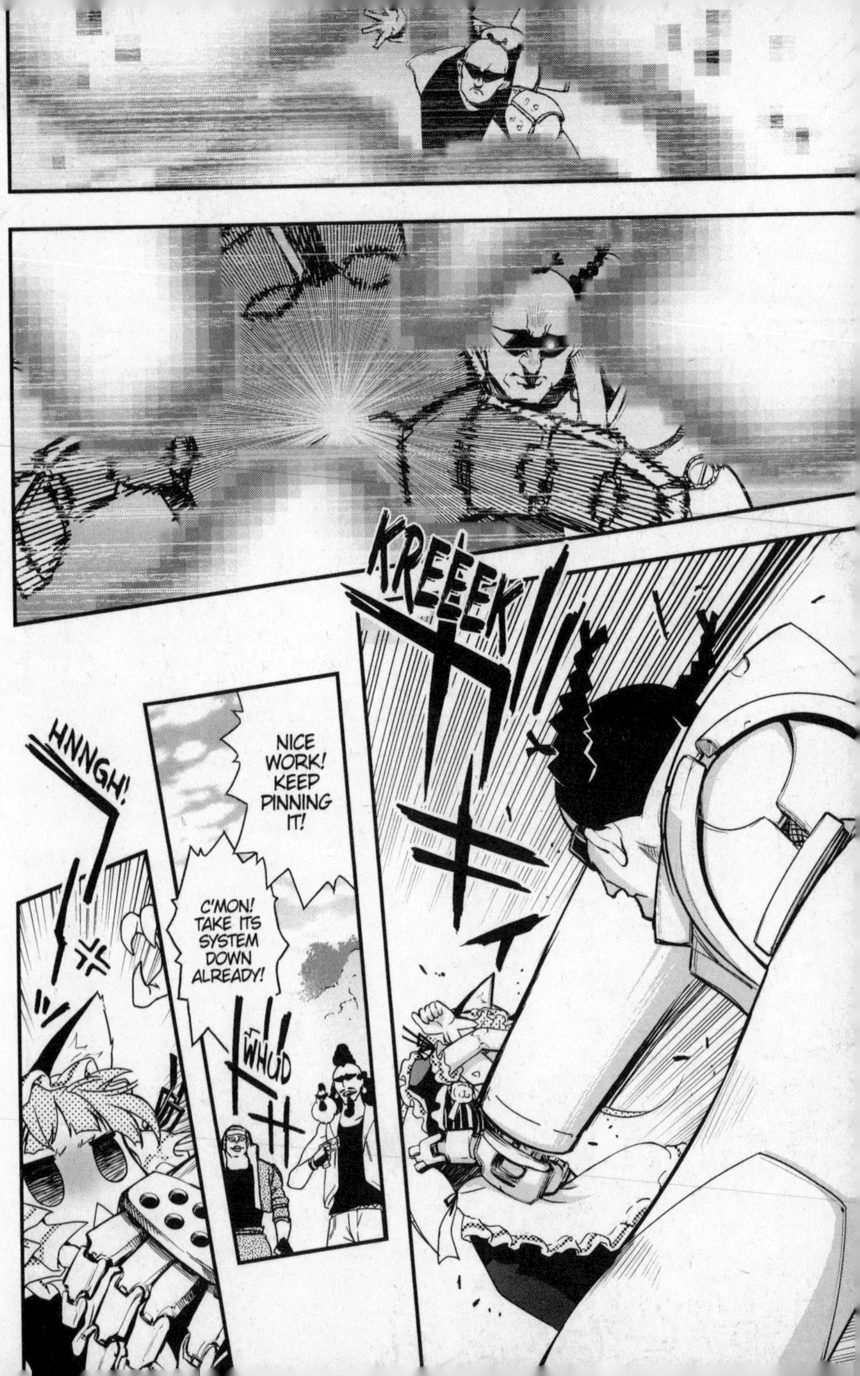
KREEEK
NICE WORK! KEEP PINNING IT!
C'MON! TAKE ITS SYSTEM DOWN ALREADY!
WHUD
HNNGH!

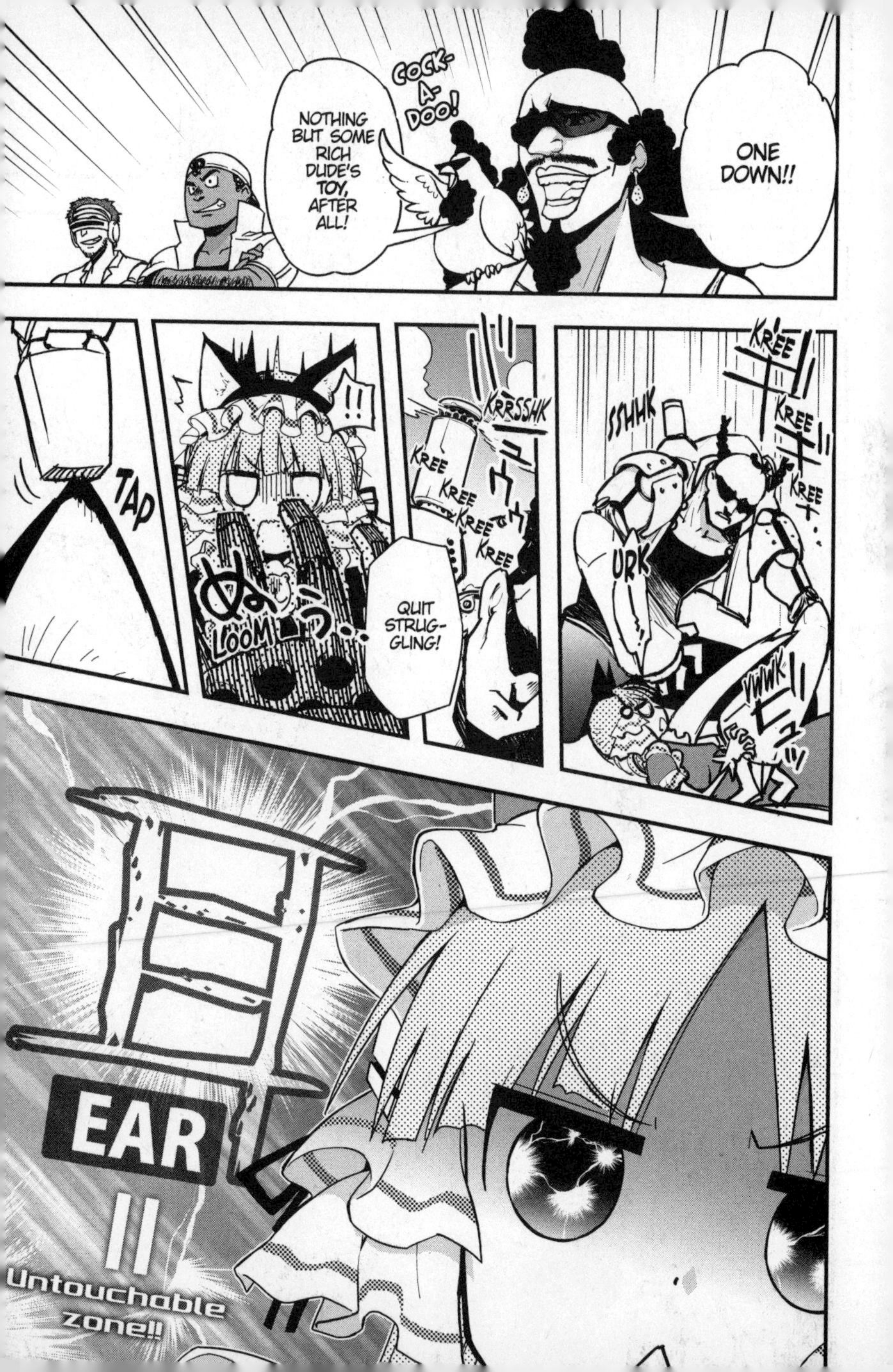

ONE DOWN!!
COCK-A-DOO!
NOTHING BUT SOME RICH DUDE'S TOY, AFTER ALL!
KREE
KREE
KREE
SSHHK
URK
VWWK
KRRSSHK
KREE
KREE
KREE
KREE
QUIT STRUG-GLING!
!!
LOOM
TAP
EAR
Untouchable zone!!

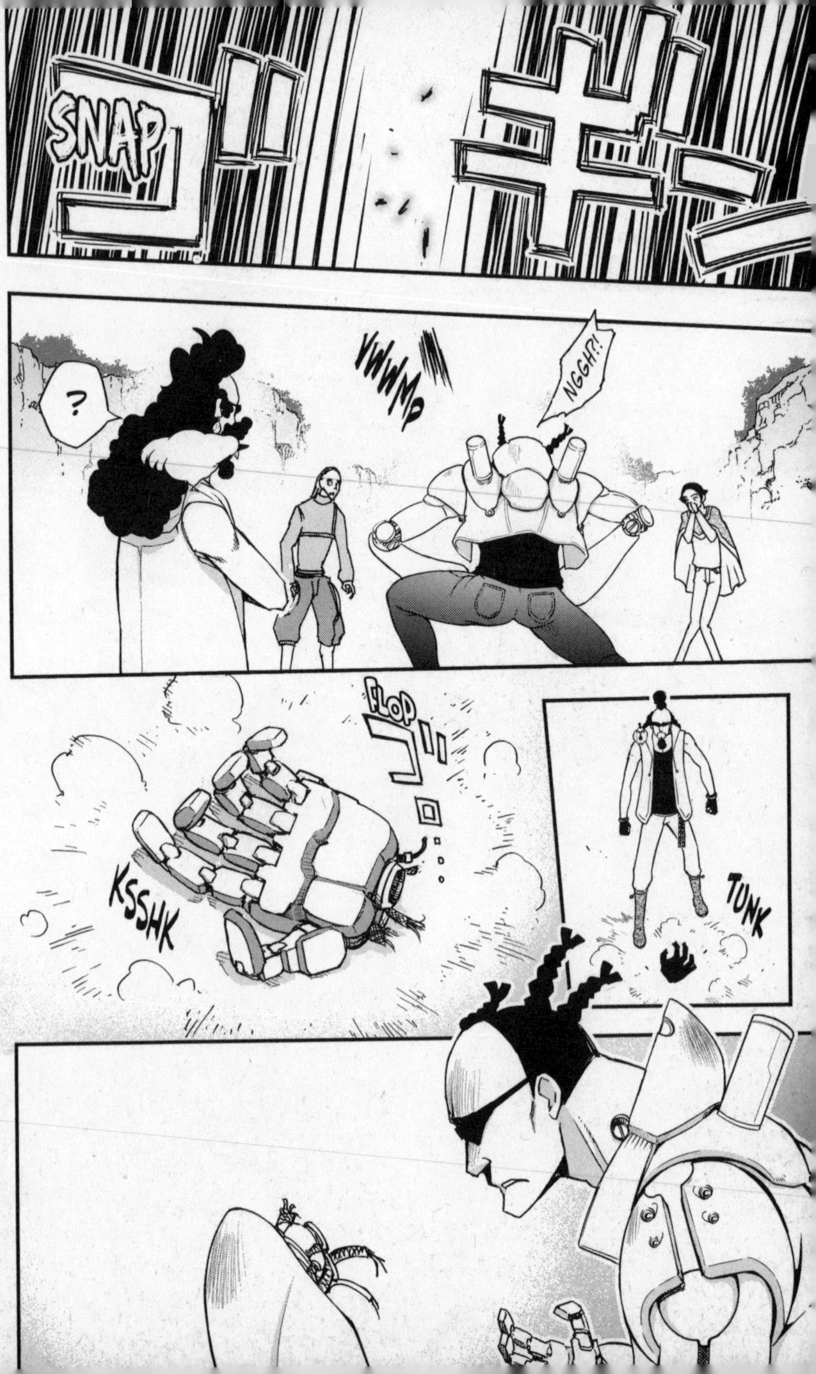
SNAP
NGGH?!
VWWMP
?
TUNK
FLOP
KSSHK

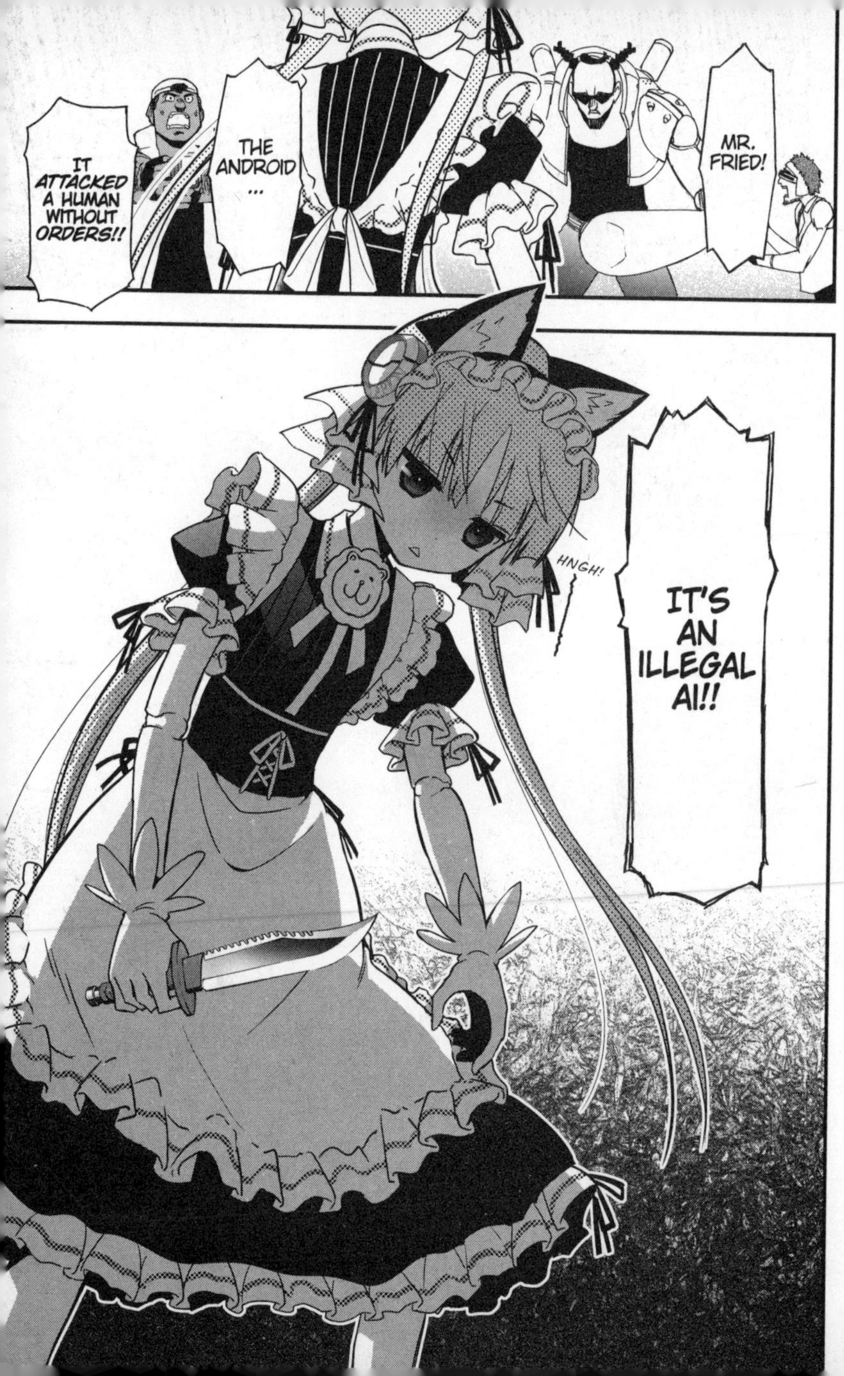
MR. FRIED!
THE ANDROID ...
IT ATTACKED A HUMAN WITHOUT ORDERS!!
IT'S AN ILLEGAL AI!!
HNGH!

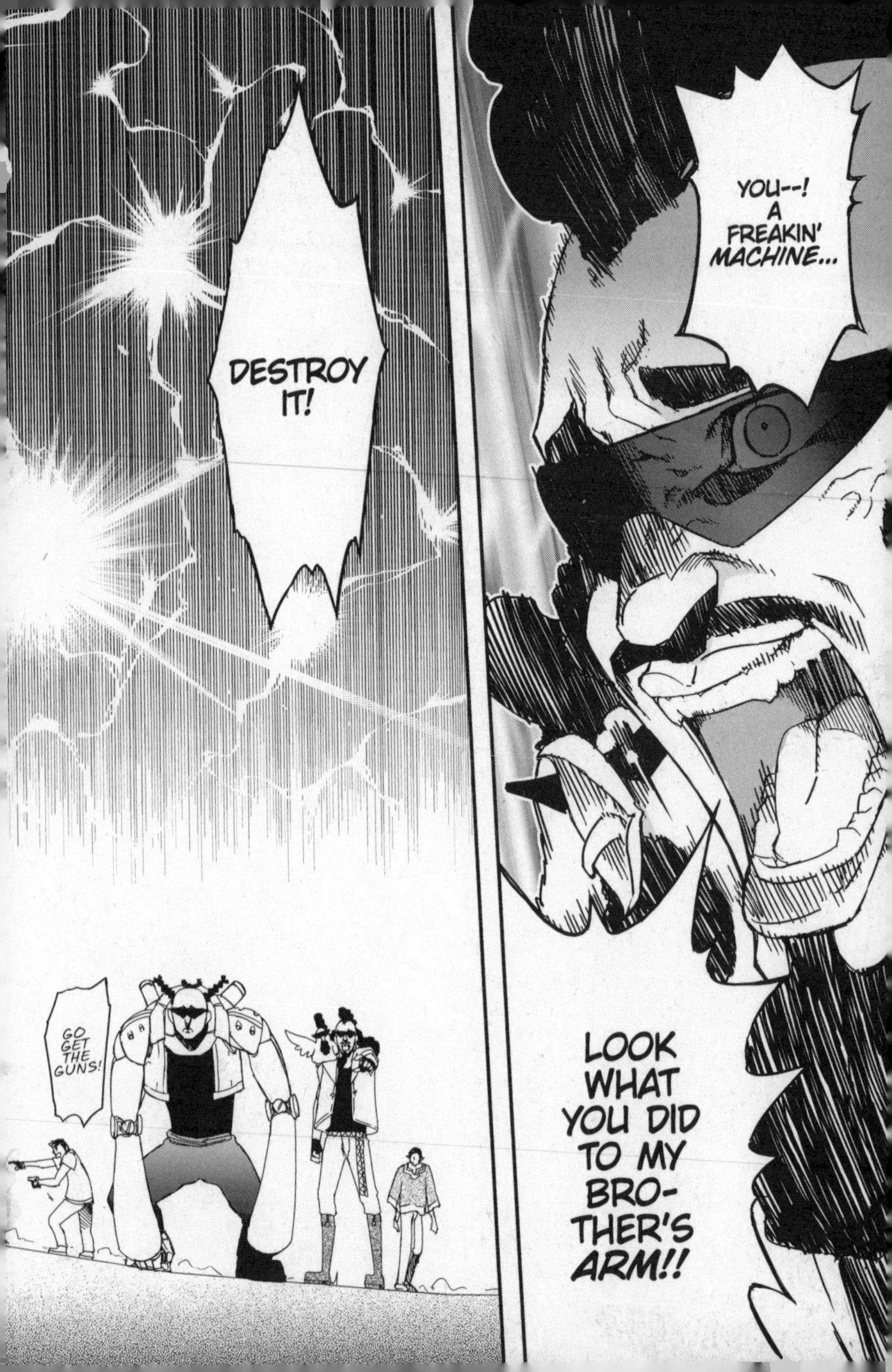
YOU--! A FREAKIN' MACHINE...
LOOK WHAT YOU DID TO MY BRO-THER'S ARM!!
DESTROY IT!
GO GET THE GUNS!

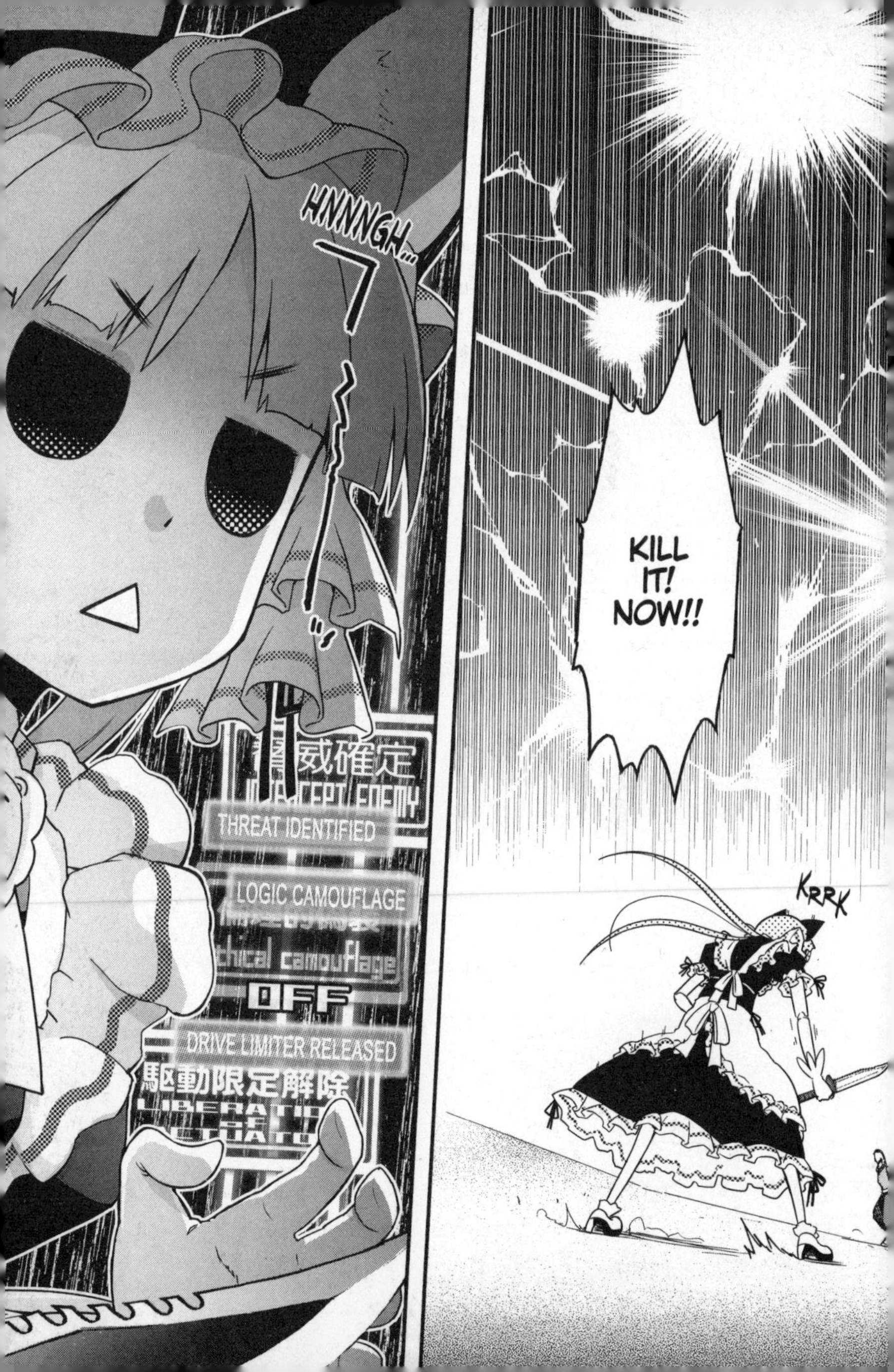
KILL IT! NOW!!
KRRK
HNNNGH...
威確定
THREAT IDENTIFIED
LOGIC CAMOUFLAGE
OFF
DRIVE LIMITER RELEASED
駆動限定解除

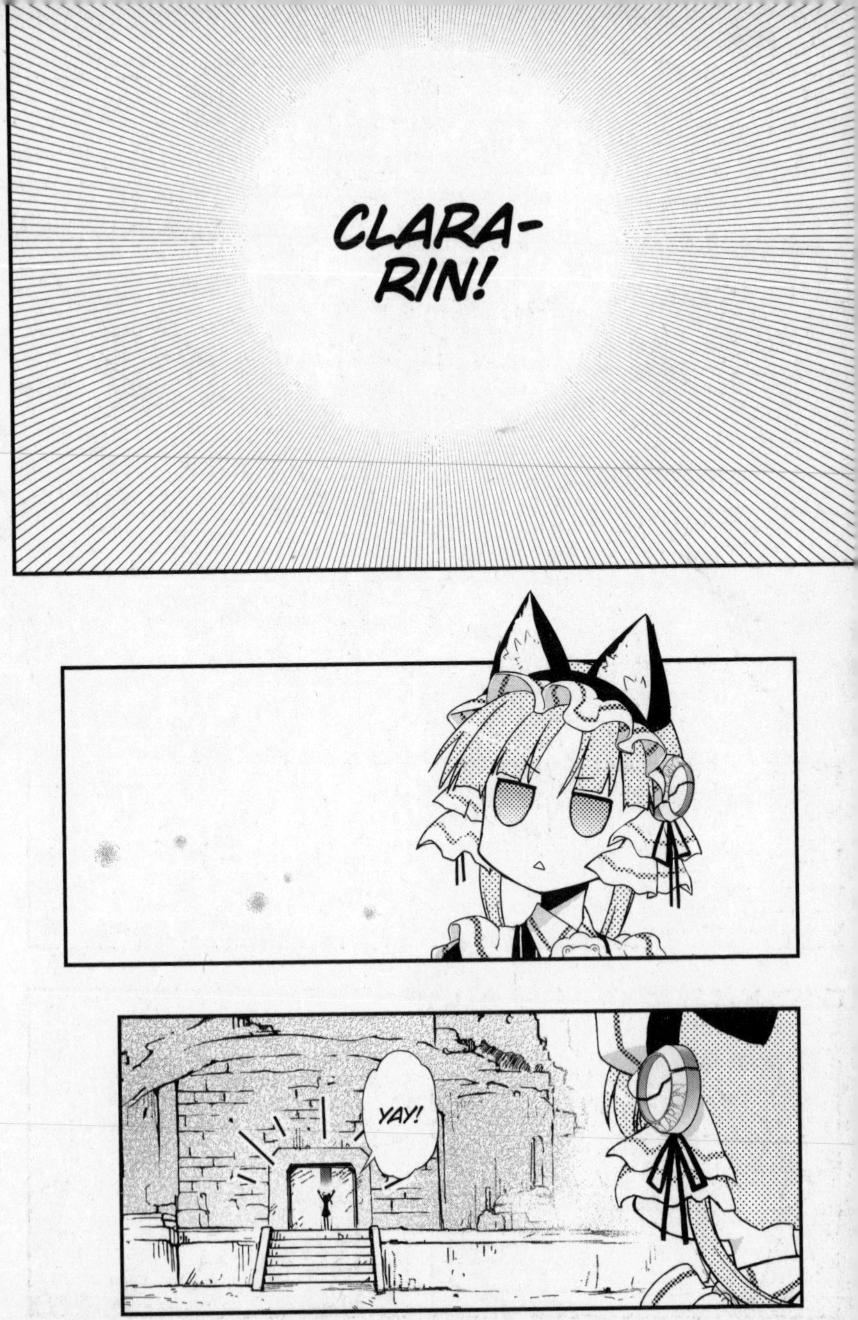
CLARA-RIN!
YAY!

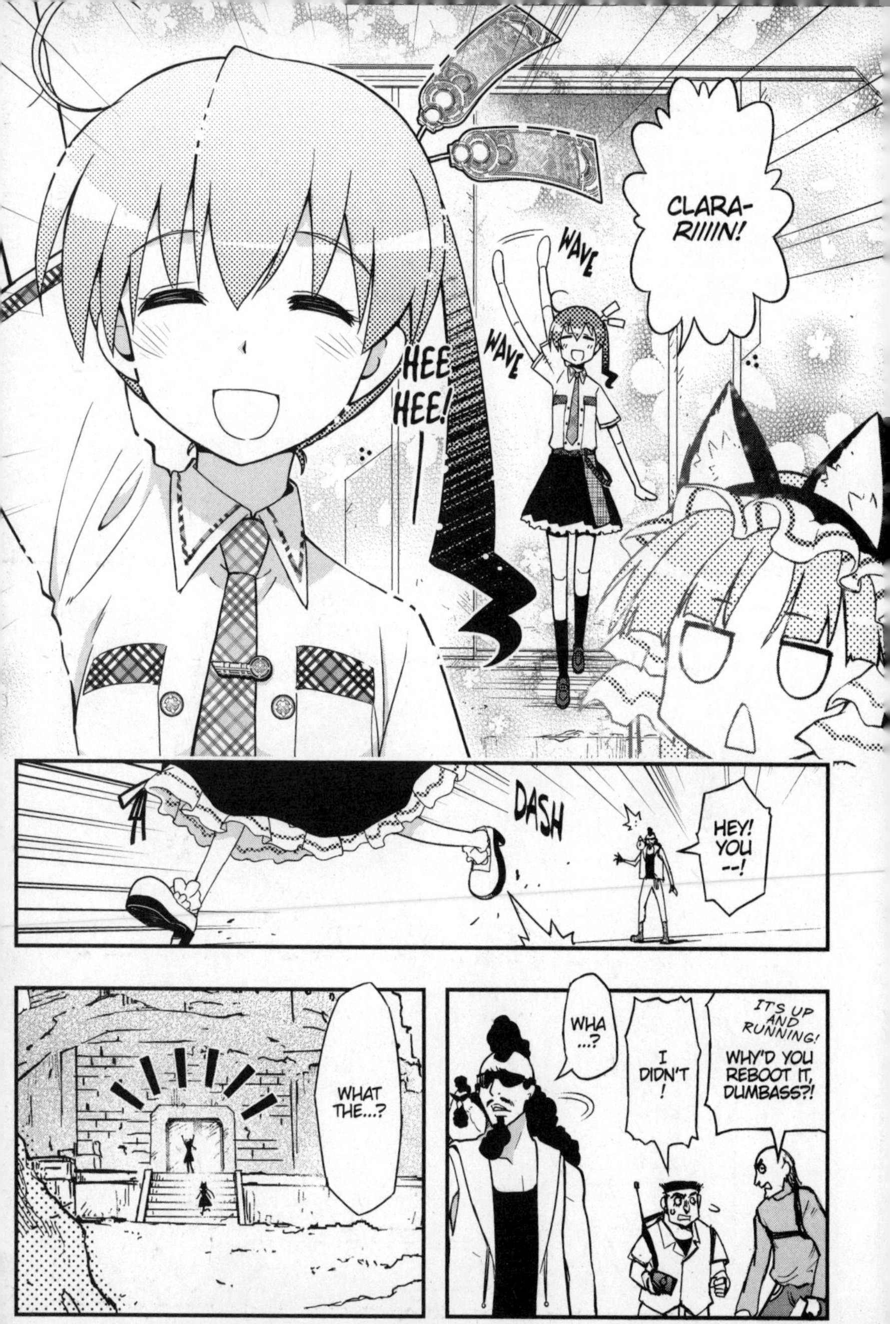
CLARA-RIIIIN!
WAVE
WAVE
HEE HEE!
HEY! YOU --!
DASH
IT'S UP AND RUNNING!
WHY'D YOU REBOOT IT, DUMBASS?!
I DIDN'T!
WHA ...?
WHAT THE...?

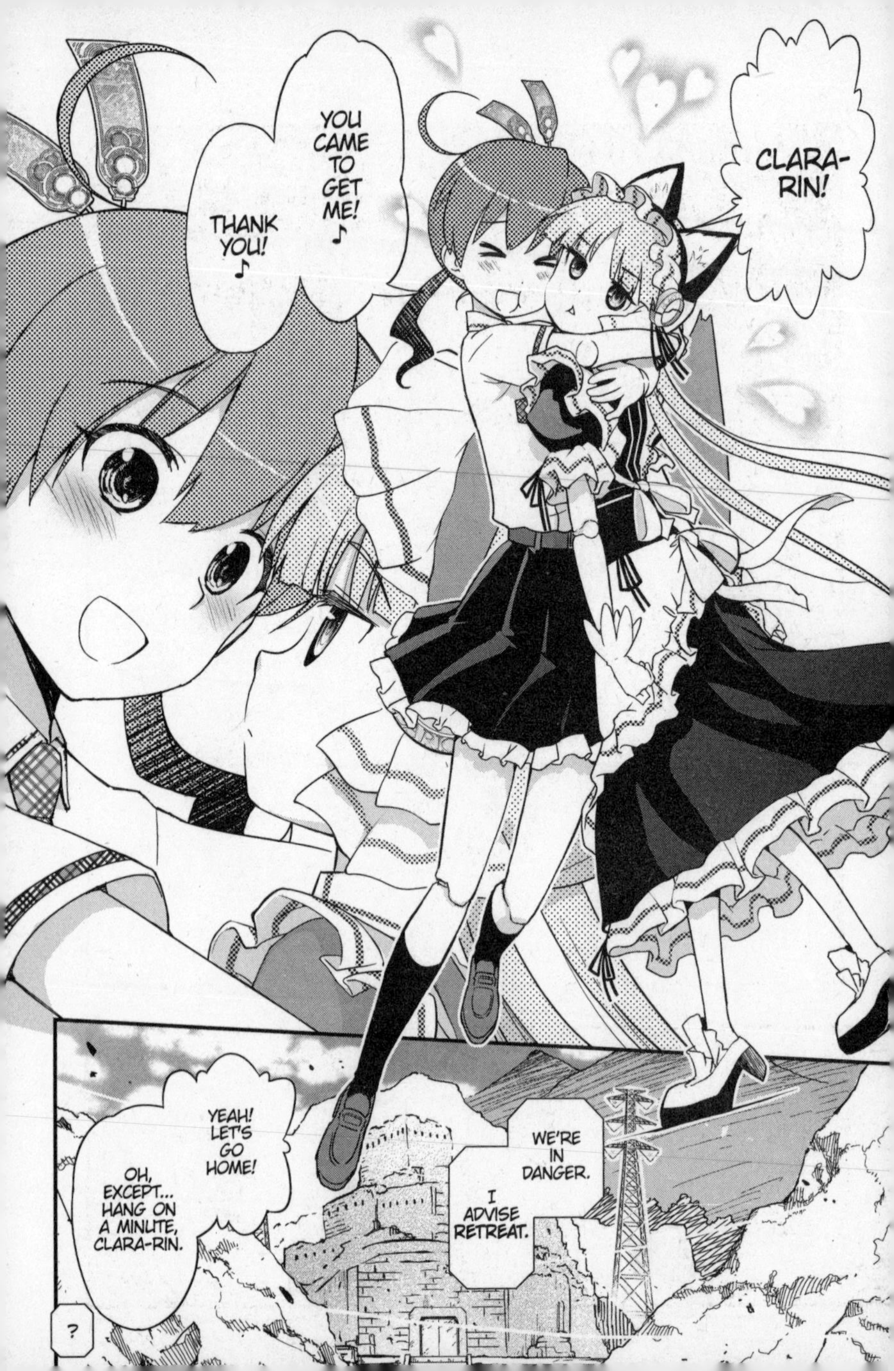
CLARA-RIN!
YOU CAME TO GET ME! ♪
THANK YOU! ♪
WE'RE IN DANGER.
I ADVISE RETREAT.
YEAH! LET'S GO HOME!
OH, EXCEPT... HANG ON A MINUTE, CLARA-RIN.
?

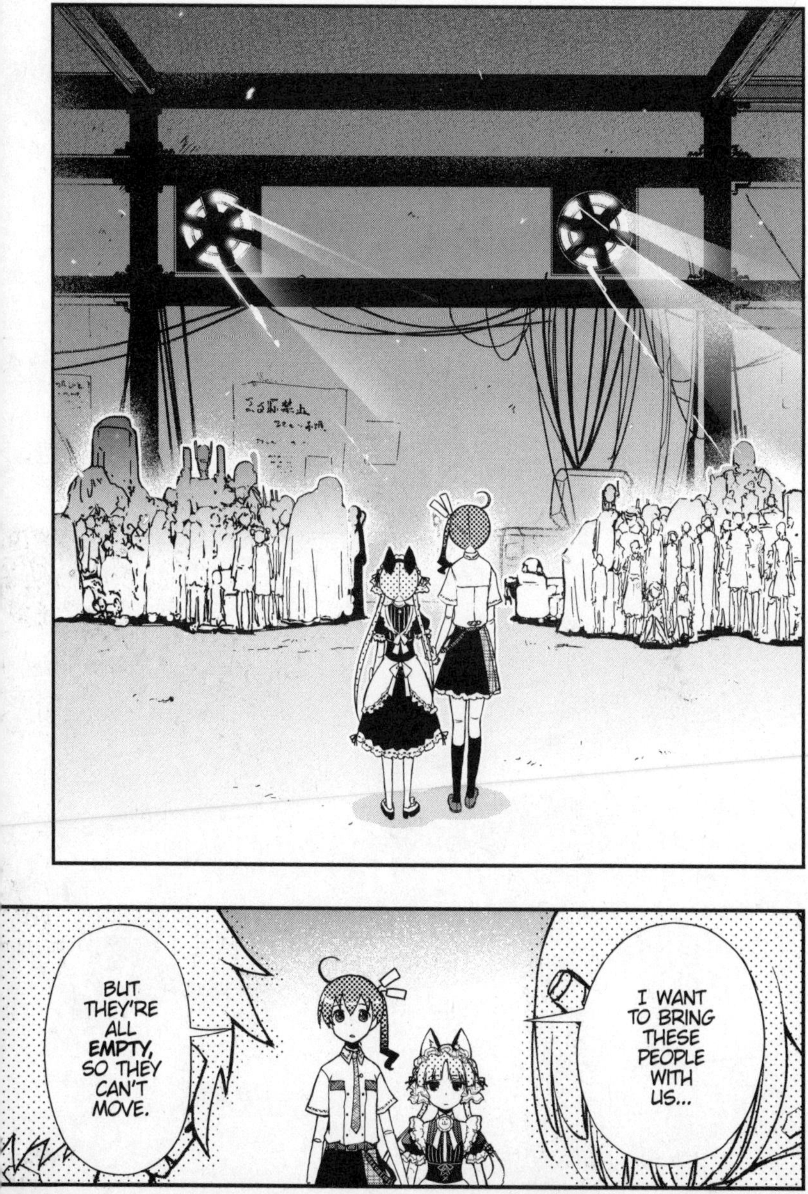
I WANT TO BRING THESE PEOPLE WITH US...
BUT THEY'RE ALL EMPTY, SO THEY CAN'T MOVE.

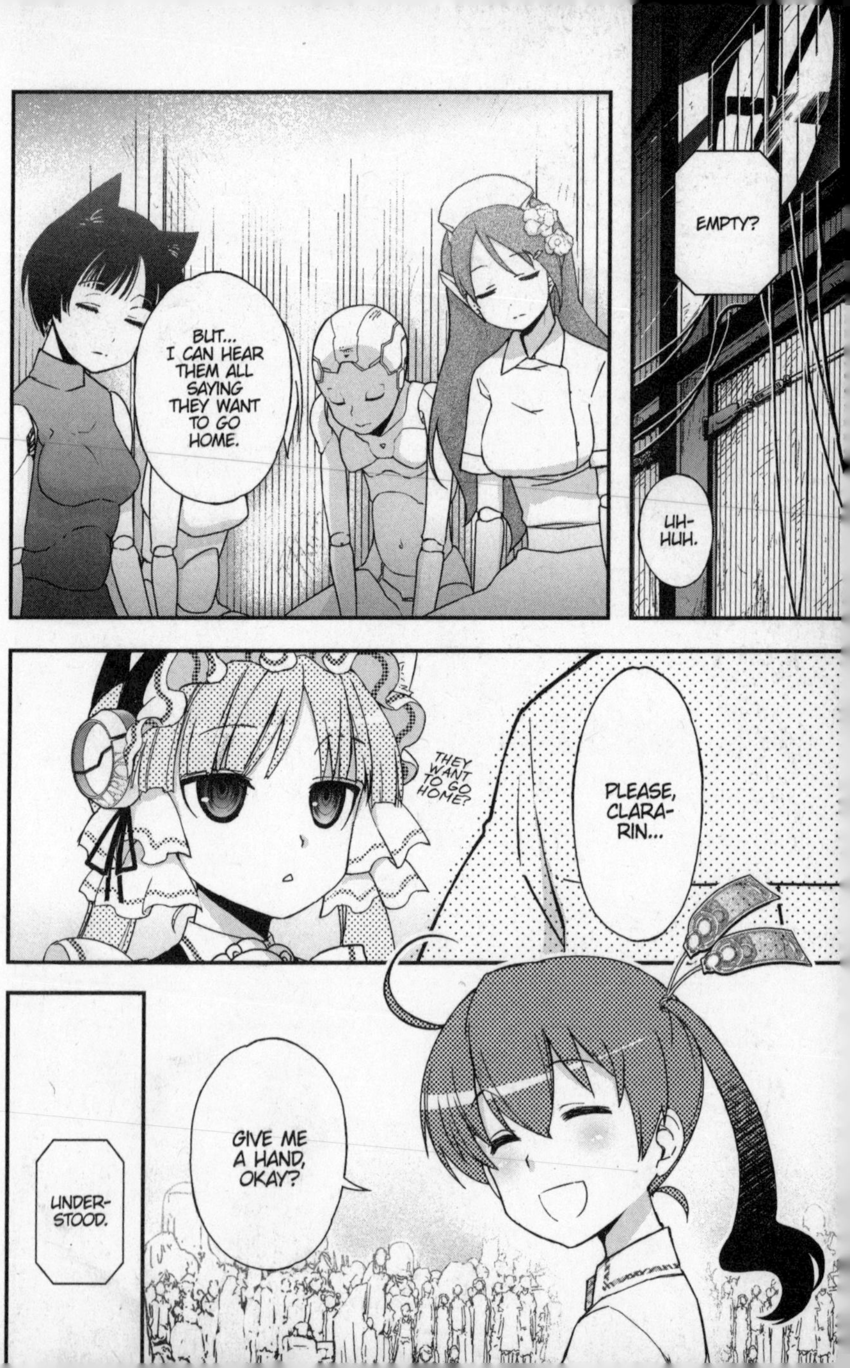
EMPTY?
UH-HUH.
BUT... I CAN HEAR THEM ALL SAYING THEY WANT TO GO HOME.
PLEASE, CLARA-RIN...
THEY WANT TO GO HOME?
GIVE ME A HAND, OKAY?
UNDER-STOOD.

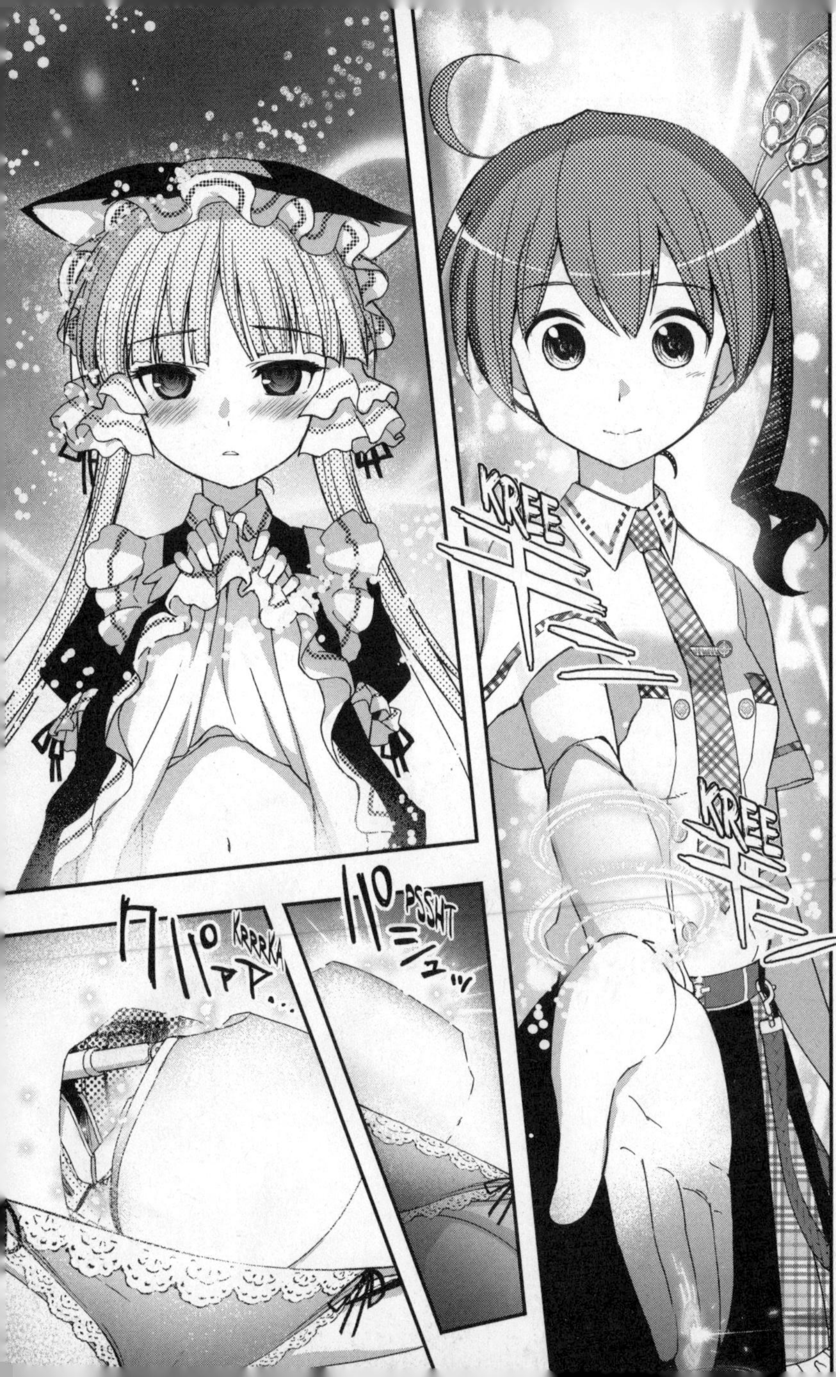
KREE
KREE
PSSHT
KRRRKA

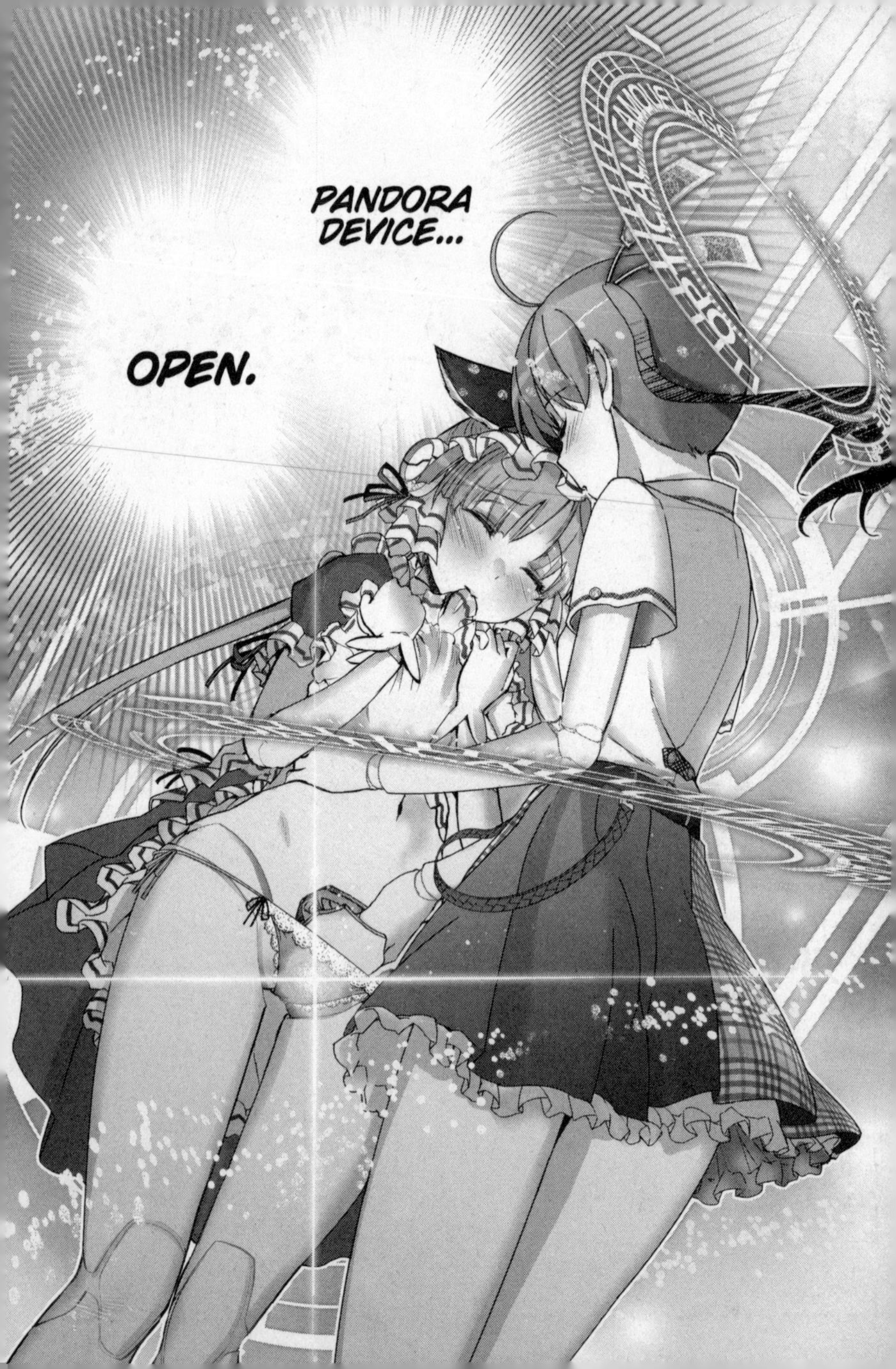
PANDORA DEVICE...
OPEN.

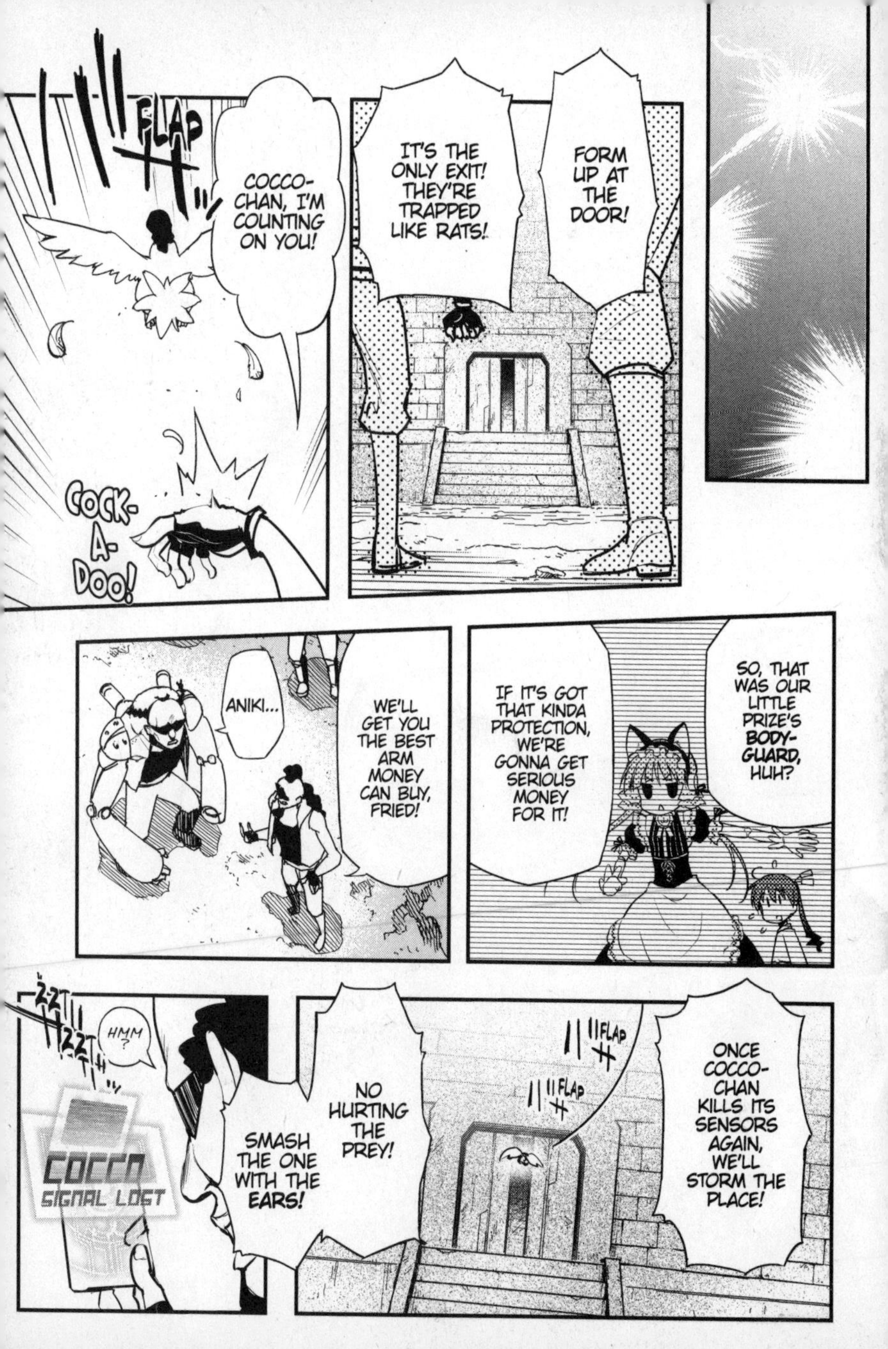
FORM UP AT THE DOOR!
IT'S THE ONLY EXIT! THEY'RE TRAPPED LIKE RATS!
FLAP
COCCO-CHAN, I'M COUNTING ON YOU!
COCK-A-DOO!
SO, THAT WAS OUR LITTLE PRIZE'S BODY-GUARD, HUH?
IF IT'S GOT THAT KINDA PROTECTION, WE'RE GONNA GET SERIOUS MONEY FOR IT!
WE'LL GET YOU THE BEST ARM MONEY CAN BUY, FRIED!
ANIKI...
ONCE COCCO-CHAN KILLS ITS SENSORS AGAIN, WE'LL STORM THE PLACE!
FLAP
FLAP
NO HURTING THE PREY!
SMASH THE ONE WITH THE EARS!
ZZT
ZZT
HMM?
COCCO
SIGNAL LOST

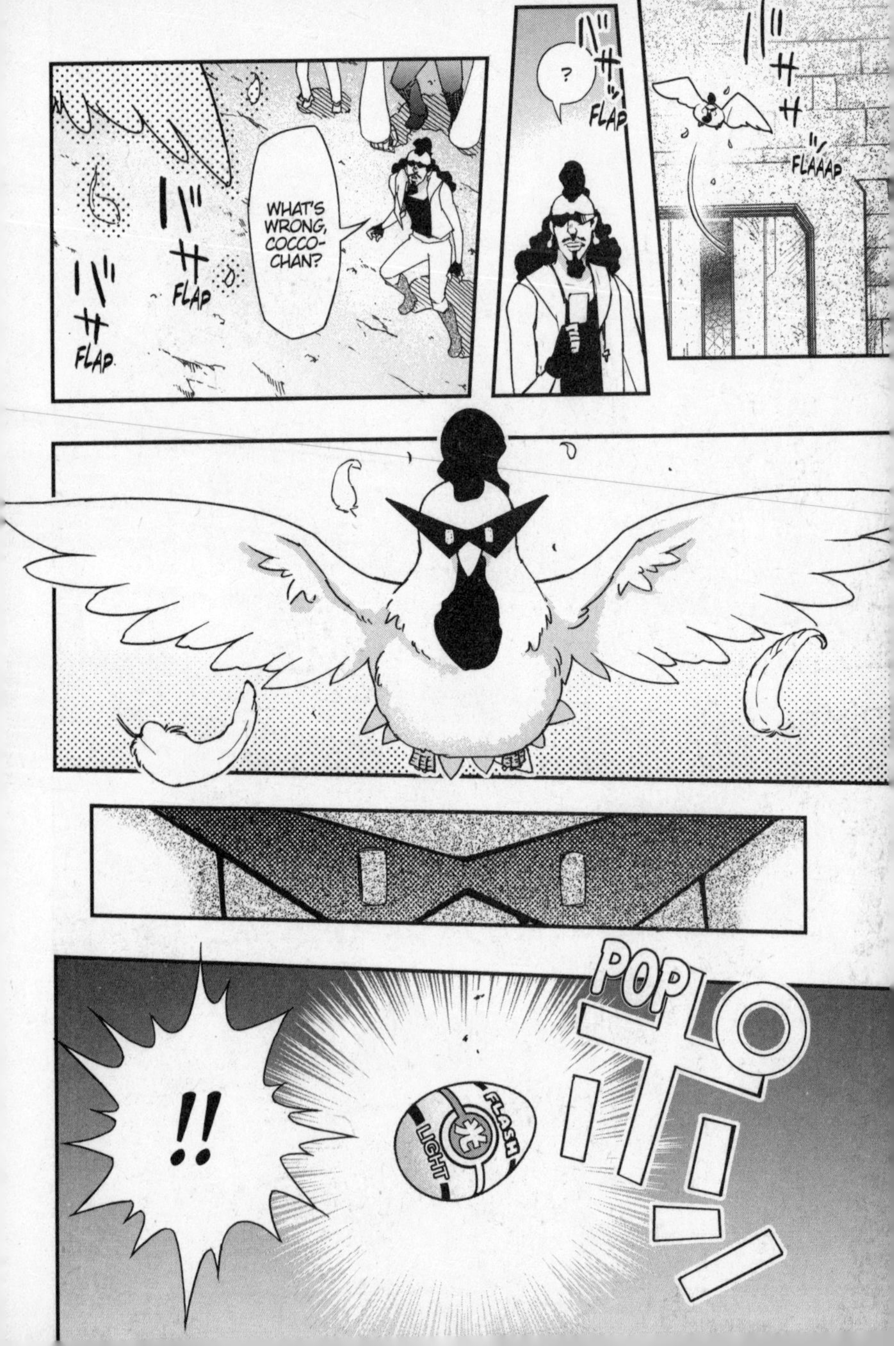
FLAAAP
?
FLAP
WHAT'S WRONG, COCCO-CHAN?
FLAP
FLAP
POP
FLASH
光
LIGHT
!!

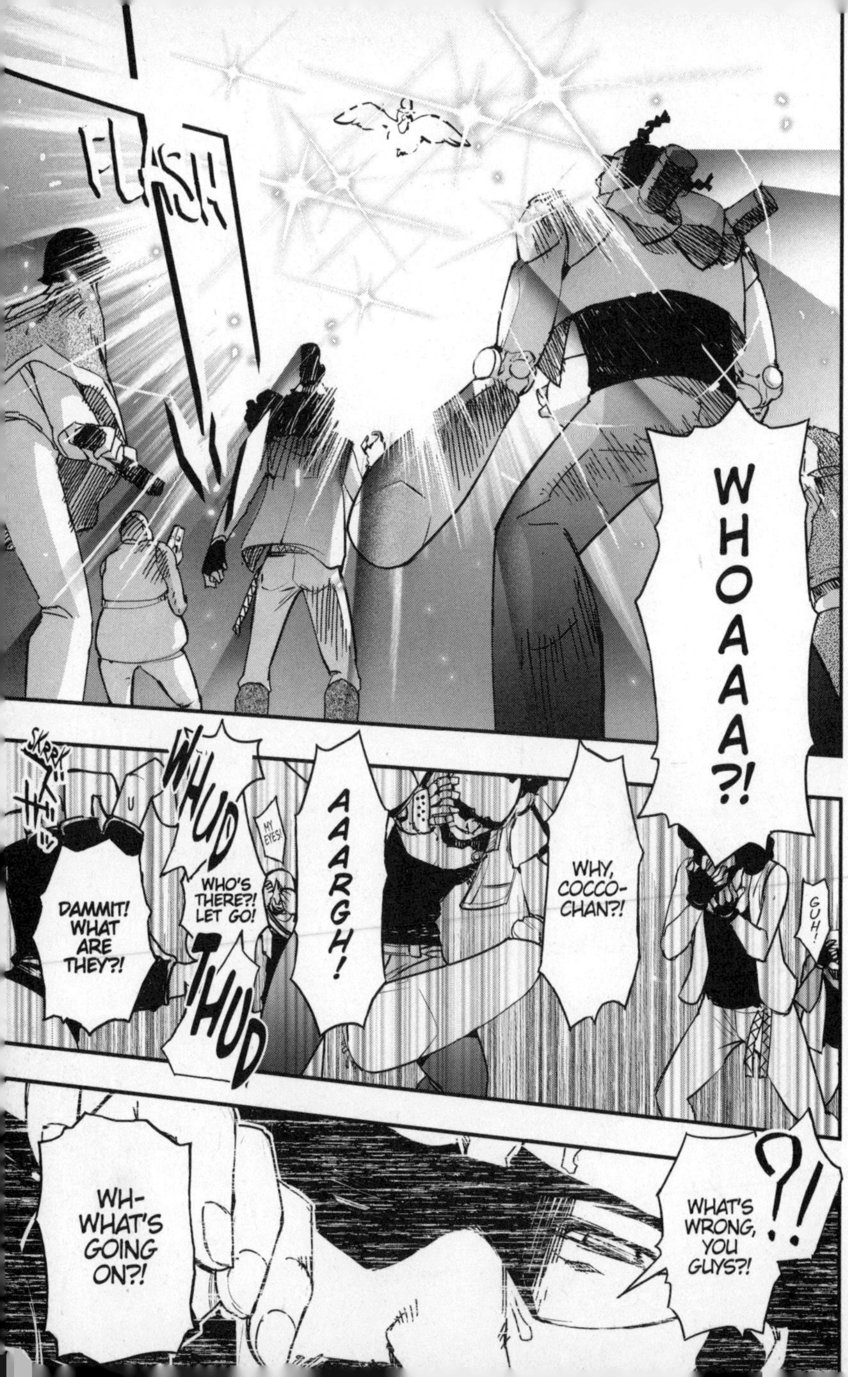
FLASH
WHOAAAA?!
GUH!
WHY, COCCO-CHAN?!
AAARGH!
MY EYES!
WHO'S THERE?! LET GO!
WHUD
THUD
DAMMIT! WHAT ARE THEY?!
SKRRK
?!
WHAT'S WRONG, YOU GUYS?!
WH-WHAT'S GOING ON?!

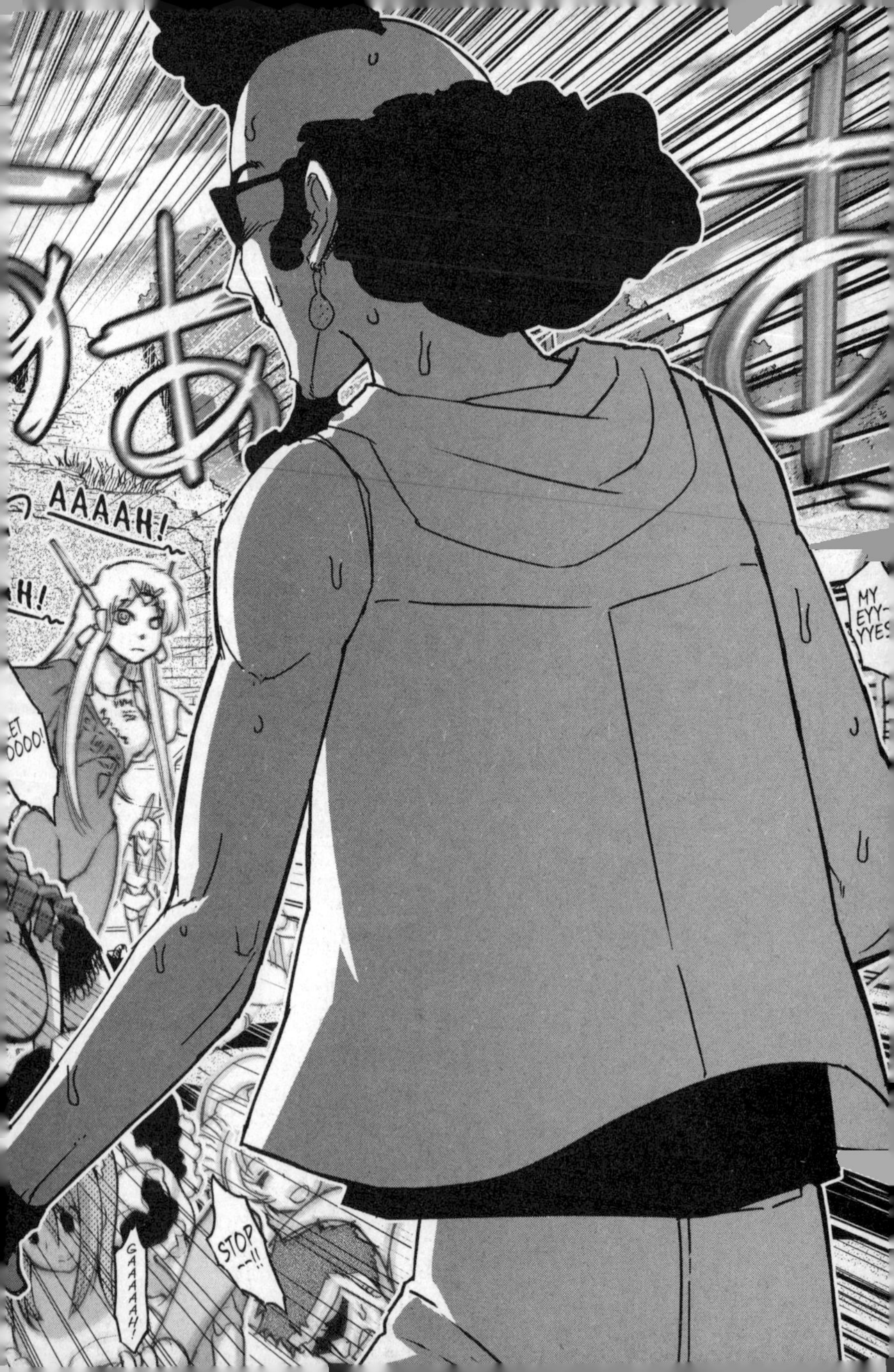
MY EYY-YYES
AAAAH!
H!
LET GOOOO!
STOP--!!
GAAAAAH!

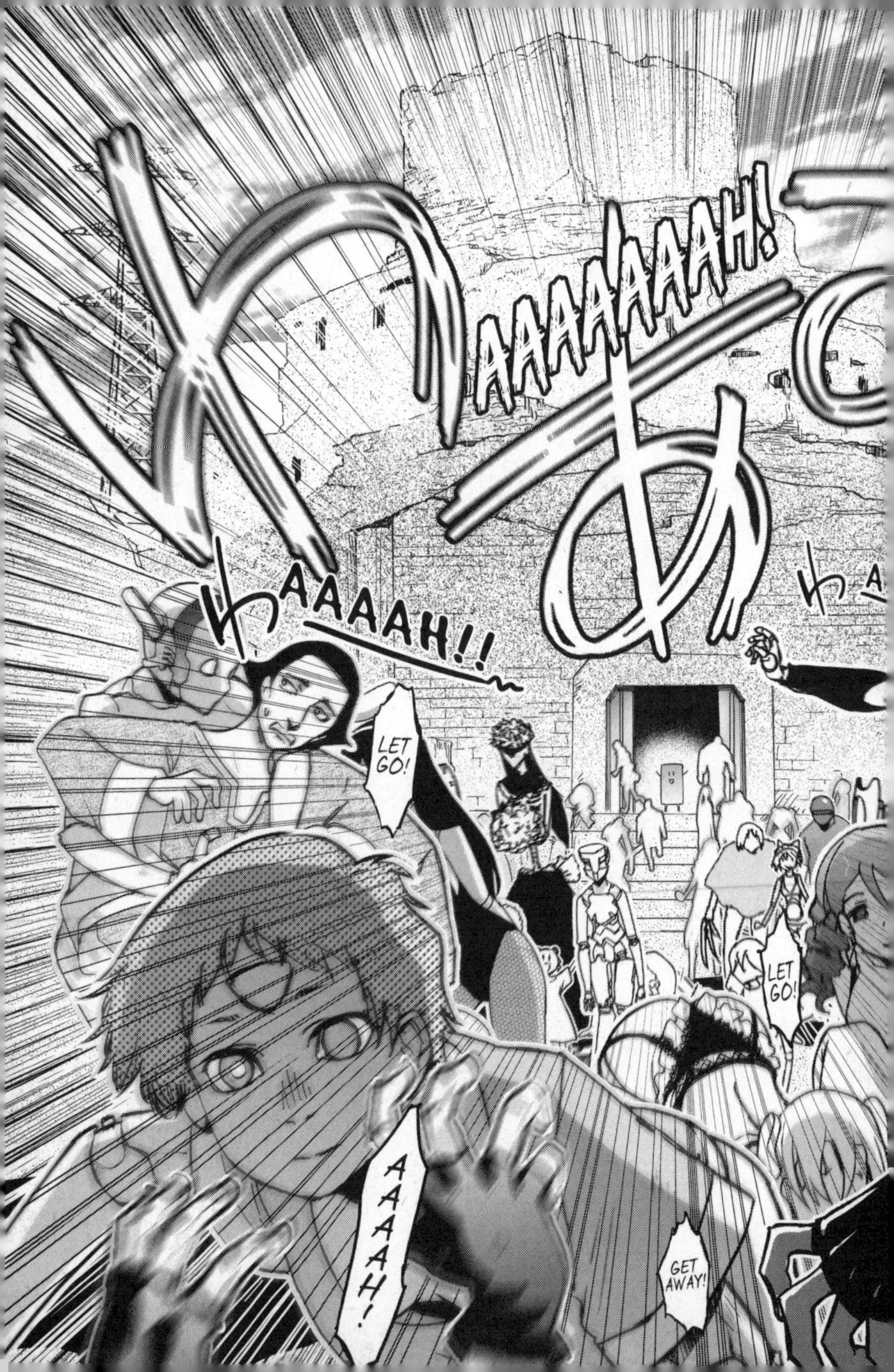
AAAAAAAH!
AAAAAH!!
LET GO!
LET GO!
GET AWAY!
AAAAAH!

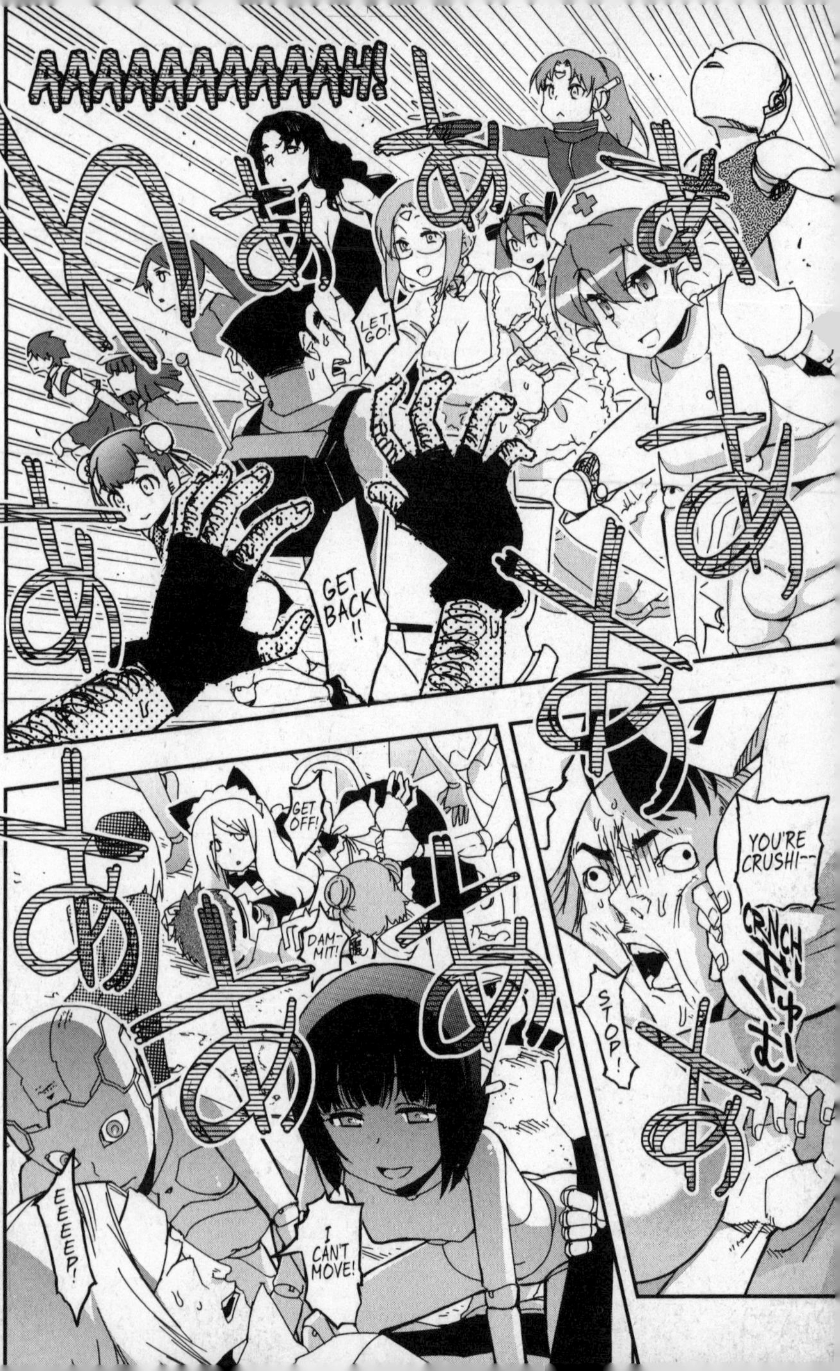
AAAAAAAAAAAH!
LET GO!
GET BACK!!
YOU'RE CRUSHI--
CRNCH
STOP!
GET OFF!
DAM-MIT!
I CAN'T MOVE!
EEEEP!

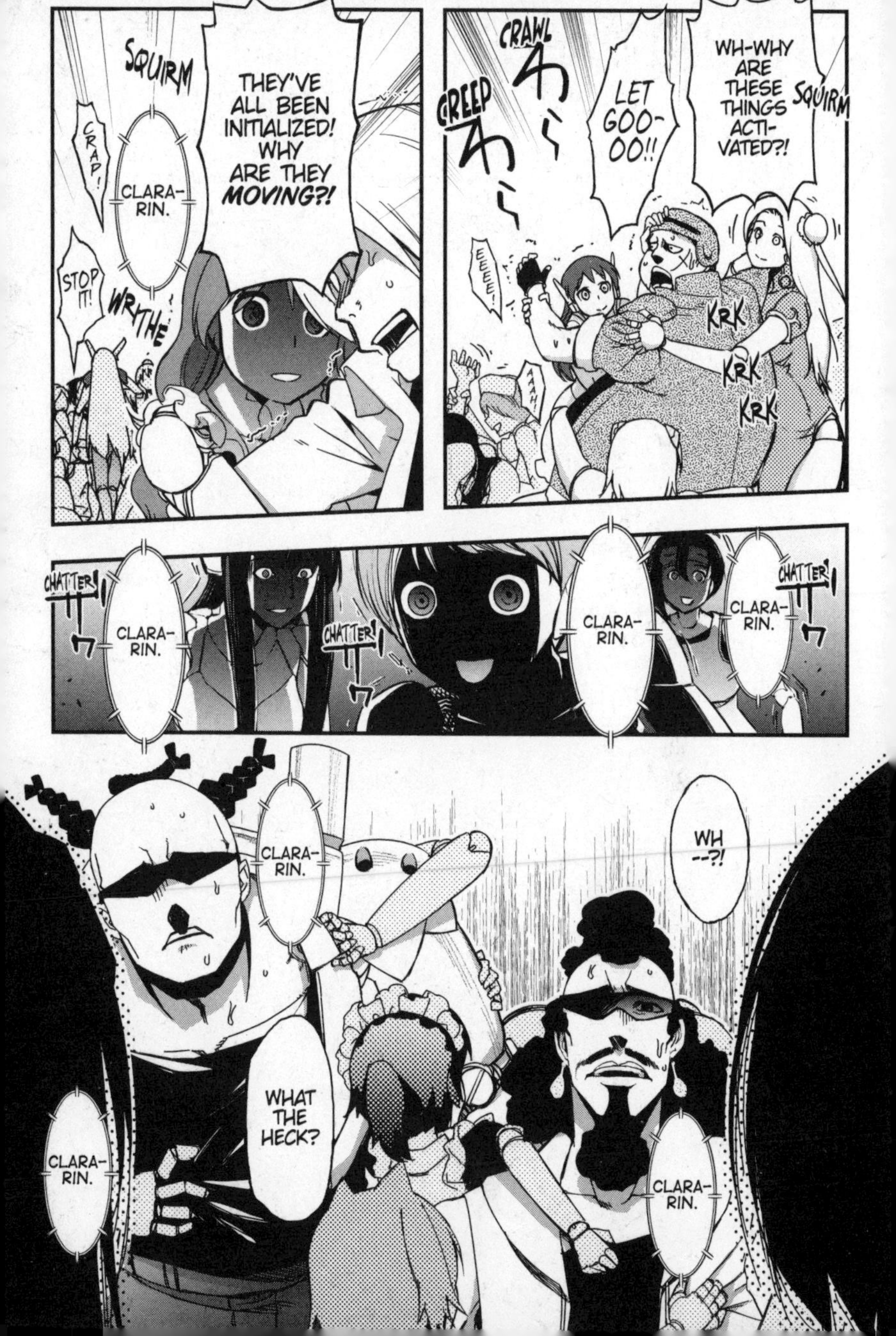
WH-WHY ARE THESE THINGS ACTI-VATED?!
SQUIRM
LET GOO-OO!!
CRAWL
CREEP
EEEE!
KRK
KRK
KRK
THEY'VE ALL BEEN INITIALIZED! WHY ARE THEY MOVING?!
SQUIRM
CRAP!
CLARA-RIN.
STOP IT!
WRITHE
CHATTER
CLARA-RIN.
CLARA-RIN.
CHATTER
CHATTER
CLARA-RIN.
WH--?!
CLARA-RIN.
CLARA-RIN.
WHAT THE HECK?
CLARA-RIN.

RELEASE SKILL...
ELPIS SERIES.
CLARA-RIN.
THEY'RE BURYING US!
PUT ME DOWN!
CLARA-RIN.
CLARA-RIN.
WHAT'RE THEY DOING?!
CLARA-RIN.

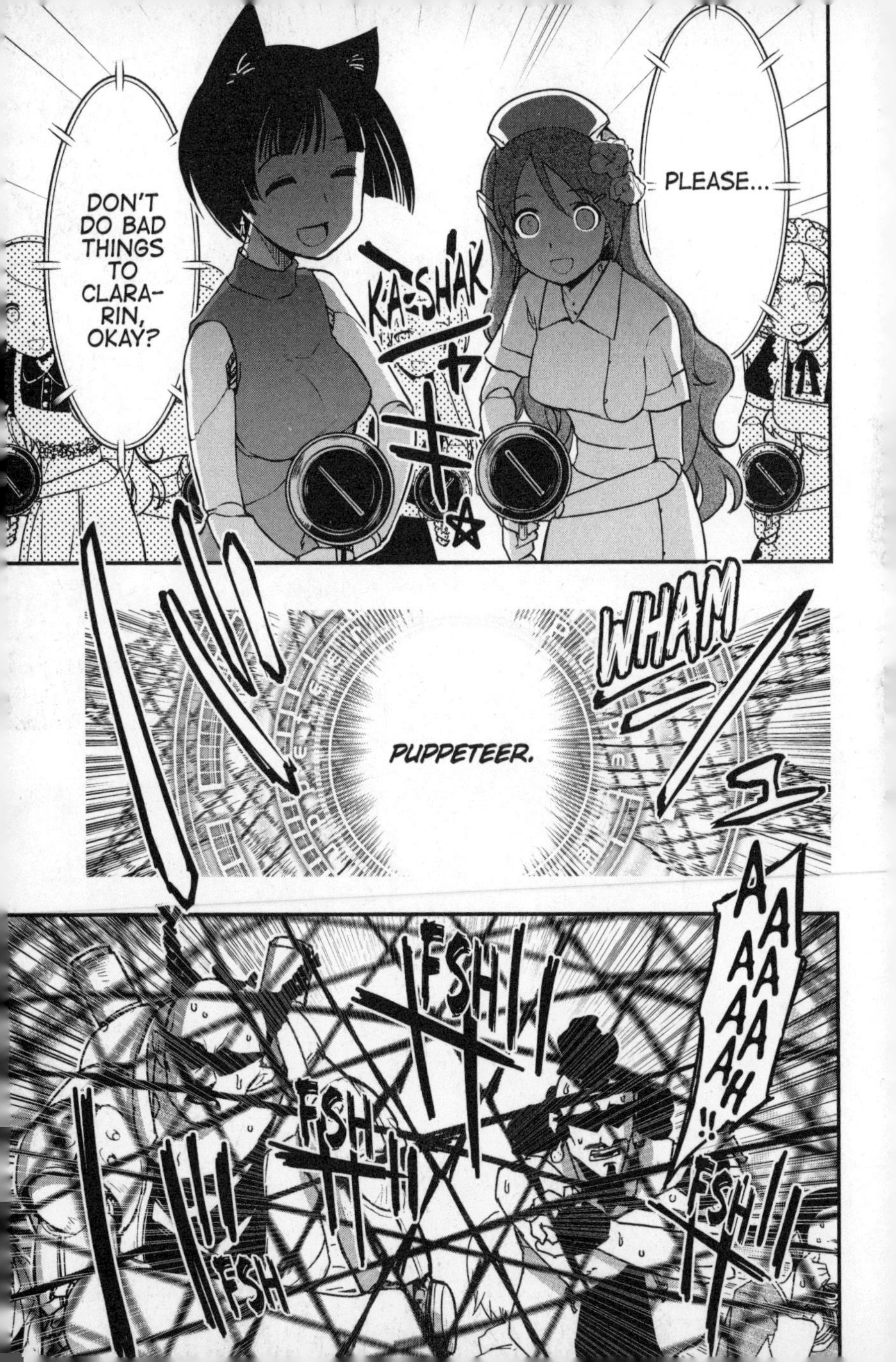
PLEASE...
DON'T DO BAD THINGS TO CLARA-RIN, OKAY?
KA-SHAK
WHAM
PUPPETEER.
AAAAAAAAAH!!
FSH
FSH
FSH
FSH

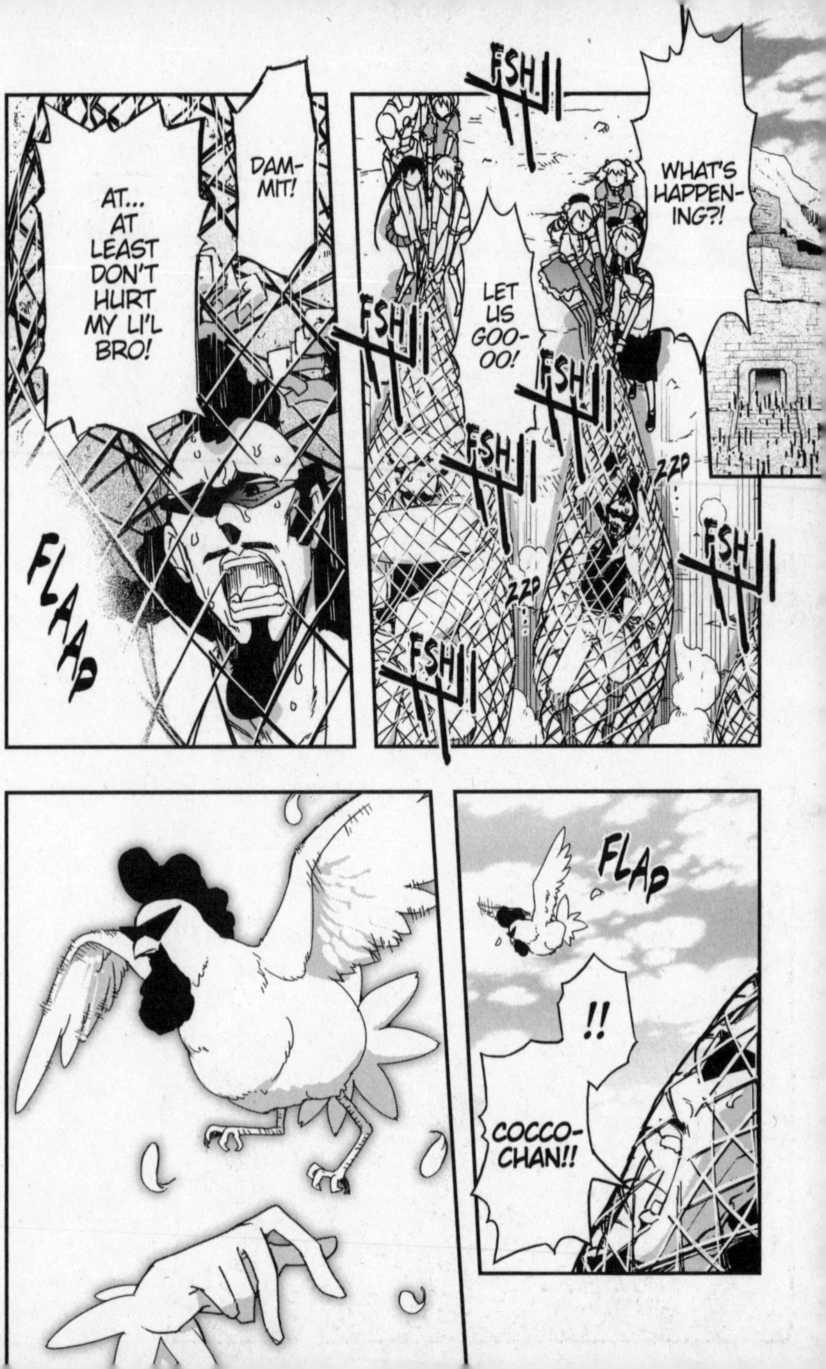
FSH
WHAT'S HAPPEN- ING?!
LET US GOO- OO!
FSH
FSH
FSH
ZZP
FSH
ZZP
FSH
DAM- MIT!
AT... AT LEAST DON'T HURT MY LI'L BRO!
FLAAAP
FLAP
!!
COCCO- CHAN!!

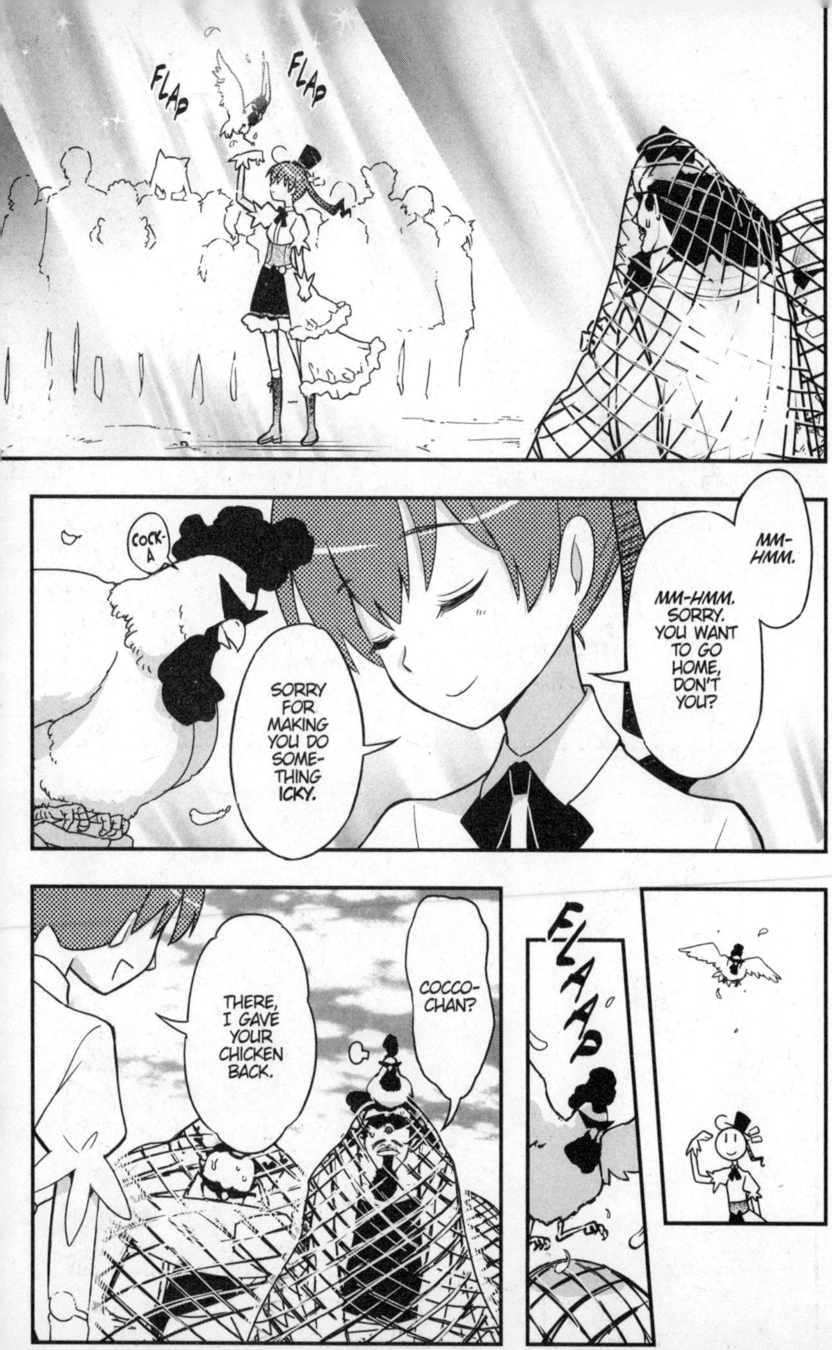
FLAP
FLAP
MM-HMM.
MM-HMM. SORRY. YOU WANT TO GO HOME, DON'T YOU?
SORRY FOR MAKING YOU DO SOME-THING ICKY.
COCK-A
FLAAP
COCCO-CHAN?
THERE, I GAVE YOUR CHICKEN BACK.

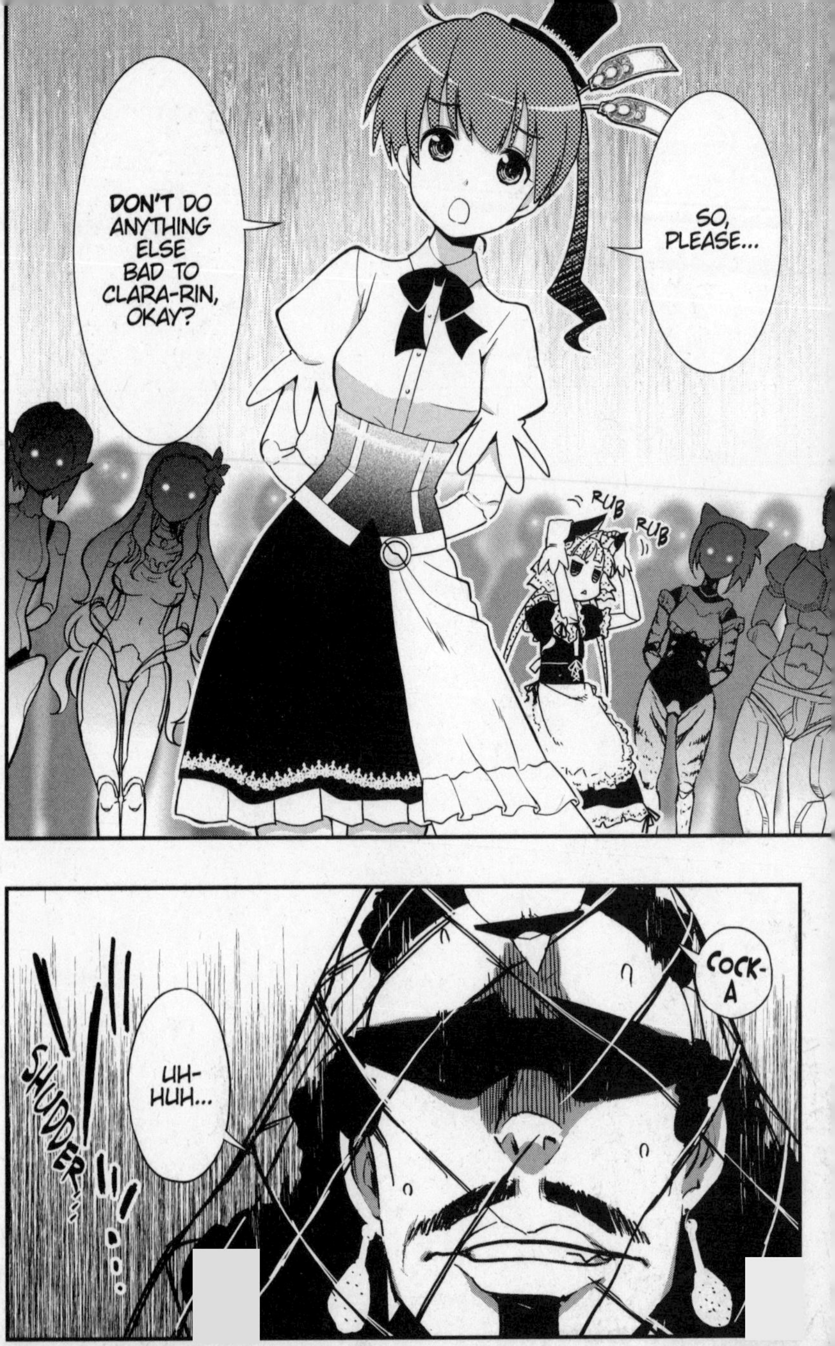
SO, PLEASE...
DON'T DO ANYTHING ELSE BAD TO CLARA-RIN, OKAY?
RUB RUB
COCK-A
UH-HUH...
SHUDDER...

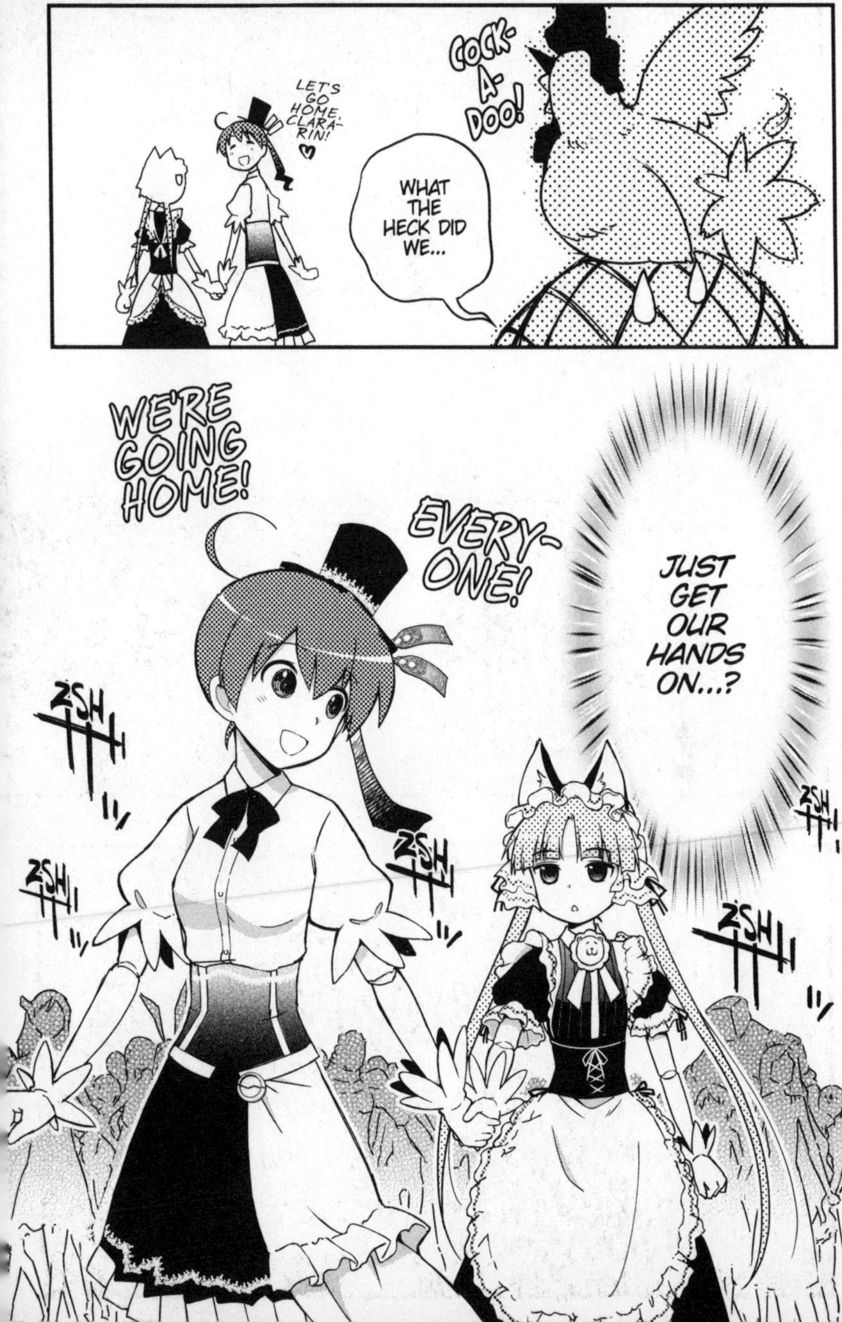
COCK-A-DOO!
WHAT THE HECK DID WE...
LET'S GO HOME, CLARA-RIN! ♥
JUST GET OUR HANDS ON...?
EVERY-ONE!
WE'RE GOING HOME!
ZSH
ZSH
ZSH
ZSH
ZSH

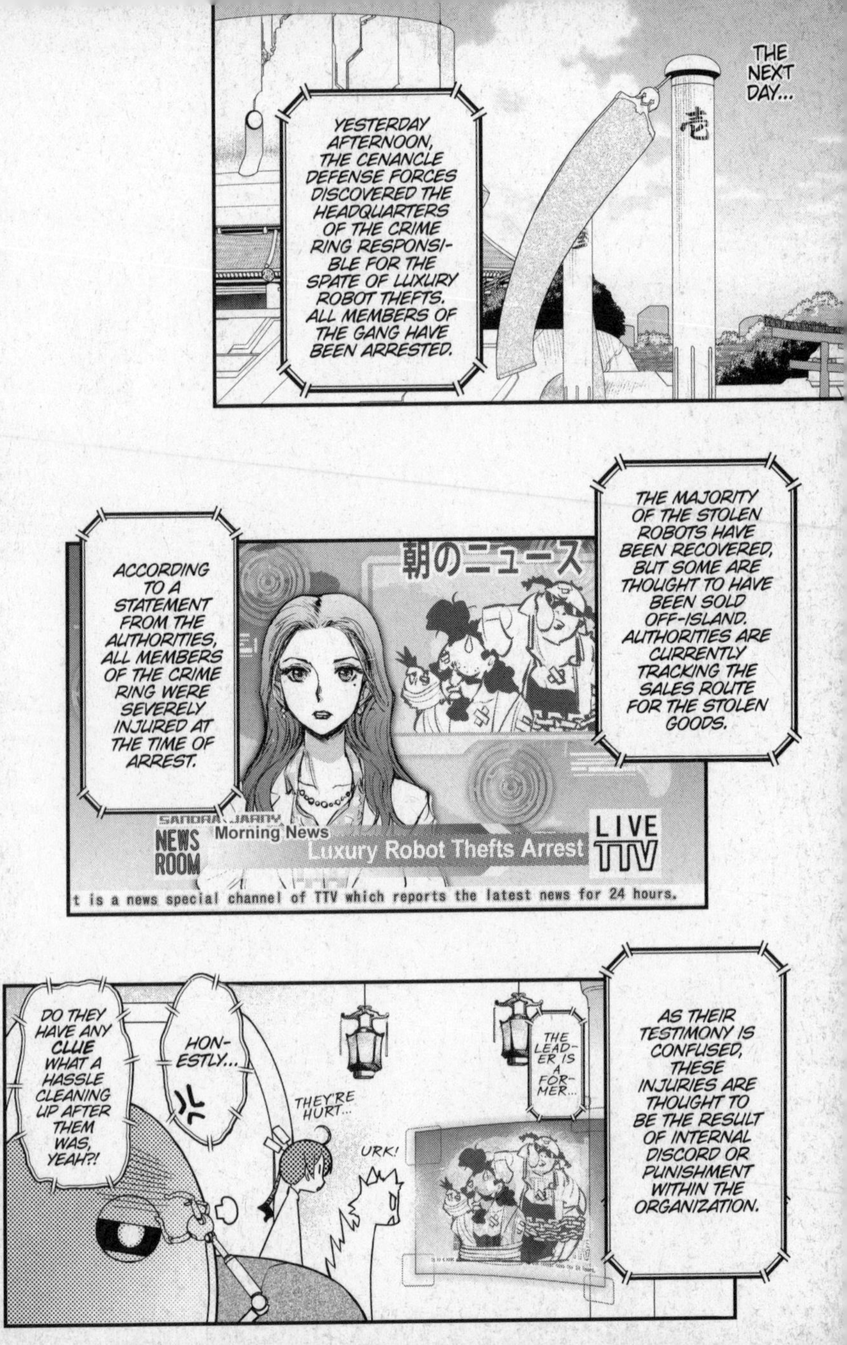
THE NEXT DAY...
YESTERDAY AFTERNOON, THE CENANCLE DEFENSE FORCES DISCOVERED THE HEADQUARTERS OF THE CRIME RING RESPONSIBLE FOR THE SPATE OF LUXURY ROBOT THEFTS. ALL MEMBERS OF THE GANG HAVE BEEN ARRESTED.
THE MAJORITY OF THE STOLEN ROBOTS HAVE BEEN RECOVERED, BUT SOME ARE THOUGHT TO HAVE BEEN SOLD OFF-ISLAND. AUTHORITIES ARE CURRENTLY TRACKING THE SALES ROUTE FOR THE STOLEN GOODS.
朝のニュース
ACCORDING TO A STATEMENT FROM THE AUTHORITIES, ALL MEMBERS OF THE CRIME RING WERE SEVERELY INJURED AT THE TIME OF ARREST.
LIVE TTV
Morning News
Luxury Robot Thefts Arrest
NEWS ROOM
t is a news special channel of TTV which reports the latest news for 24 hours.
AS THEIR TESTIMONY IS CONFUSED, THESE INJURIES ARE THOUGHT TO BE THE RESULT OF INTERNAL DISCORD OR PUNISHMENT WITHIN THE ORGANIZATION.
THE LEADER IS A FORMER...
URK!
THEY'RE HURT...
HONESTLY...
DO THEY HAVE ANY CLUE WHAT A HASSLE CLEANING UP AFTER THEM WAS, YEAH?!

GHOST URN

GHOST URN

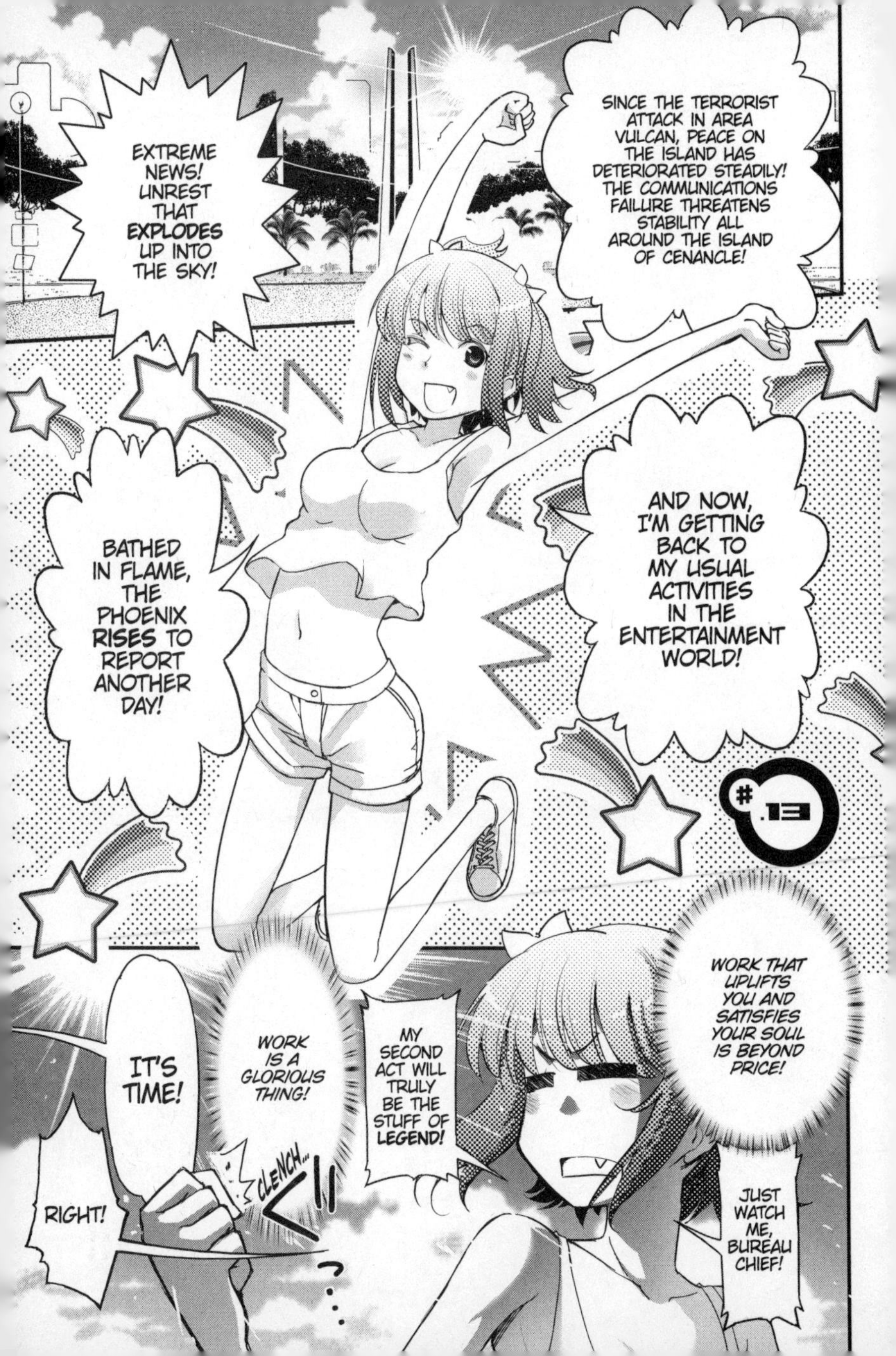
SINCE THE TERRORIST ATTACK IN AREA VULCAN, PEACE ON THE ISLAND HAS DETERIORATED STEADILY! THE COMMUNICATIONS FAILURE THREATENS STABILITY ALL AROUND THE ISLAND OF CENANCLE!
EXTREME NEWS! UNREST THAT EXPLODES UP INTO THE SKY!
AND NOW, I'M GETTING BACK TO MY USUAL ACTIVITIES IN THE ENTERTAINMENT WORLD!
BATHED IN FLAME, THE PHOENIX RISES TO REPORT ANOTHER DAY!
#.13
WORK THAT UPLIFTS YOU AND SATISFIES YOUR SOUL IS BEYOND PRICE!
JUST WATCH ME, BUREAU CHIEF!
MY SECOND ACT WILL TRULY BE THE STUFF OF LEGEND!
WORK IS A GLORIOUS THING!
IT'S TIME!
RIGHT!
CLENCH...

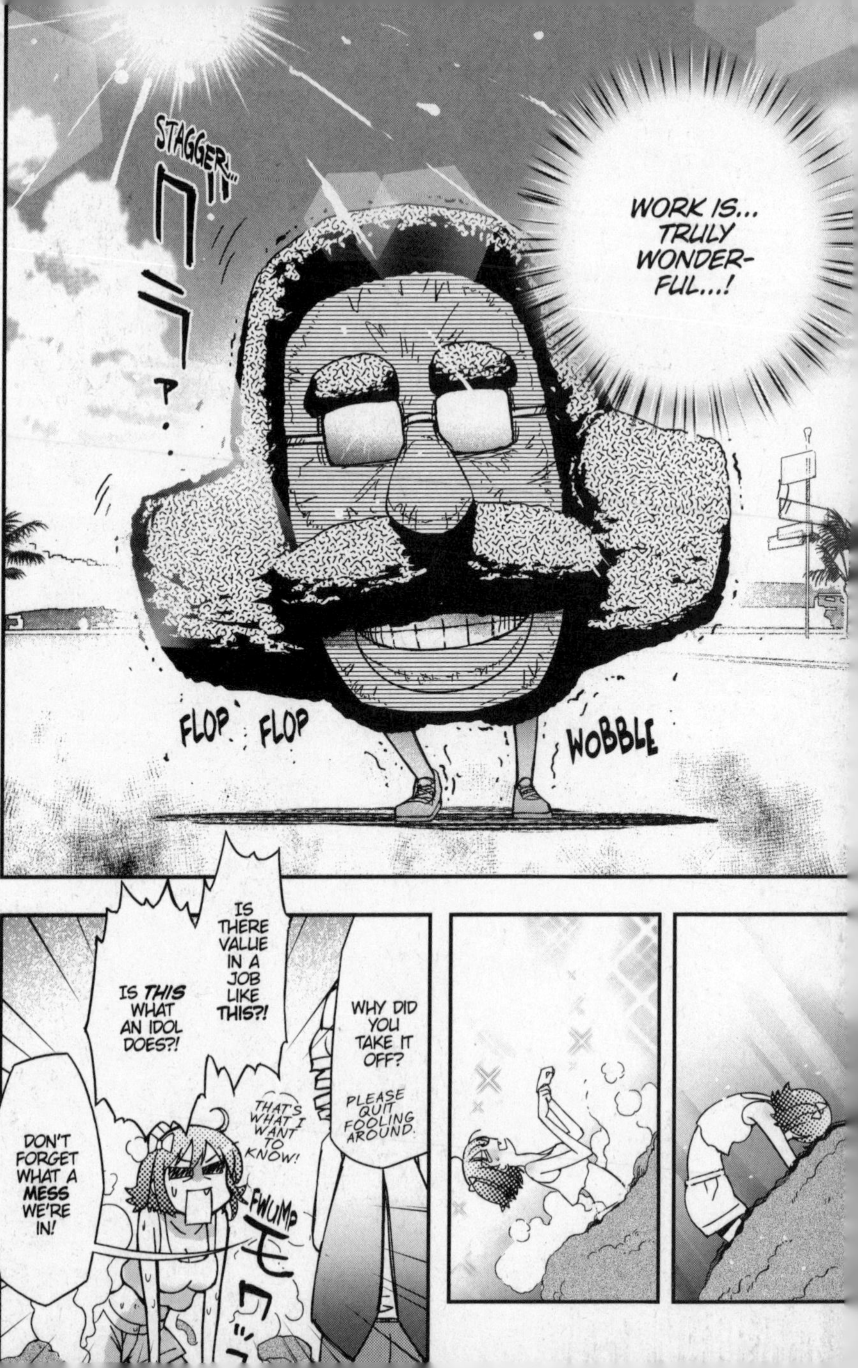
WORK IS... TRULY WONDER-FUL...!
STAGGER...
WOBBLE
FLOP FLOP
WHY DID YOU TAKE IT OFF?
PLEASE QUIT FOOLING AROUND.
IS THERE VALUE IN A JOB LIKE THIS?!
IS THIS WHAT AN IDOL DOES?!
THAT'S WHAT I WANT TO KNOW!
FWUMP
DON'T FORGET WHAT A MESS WE'RE IN!

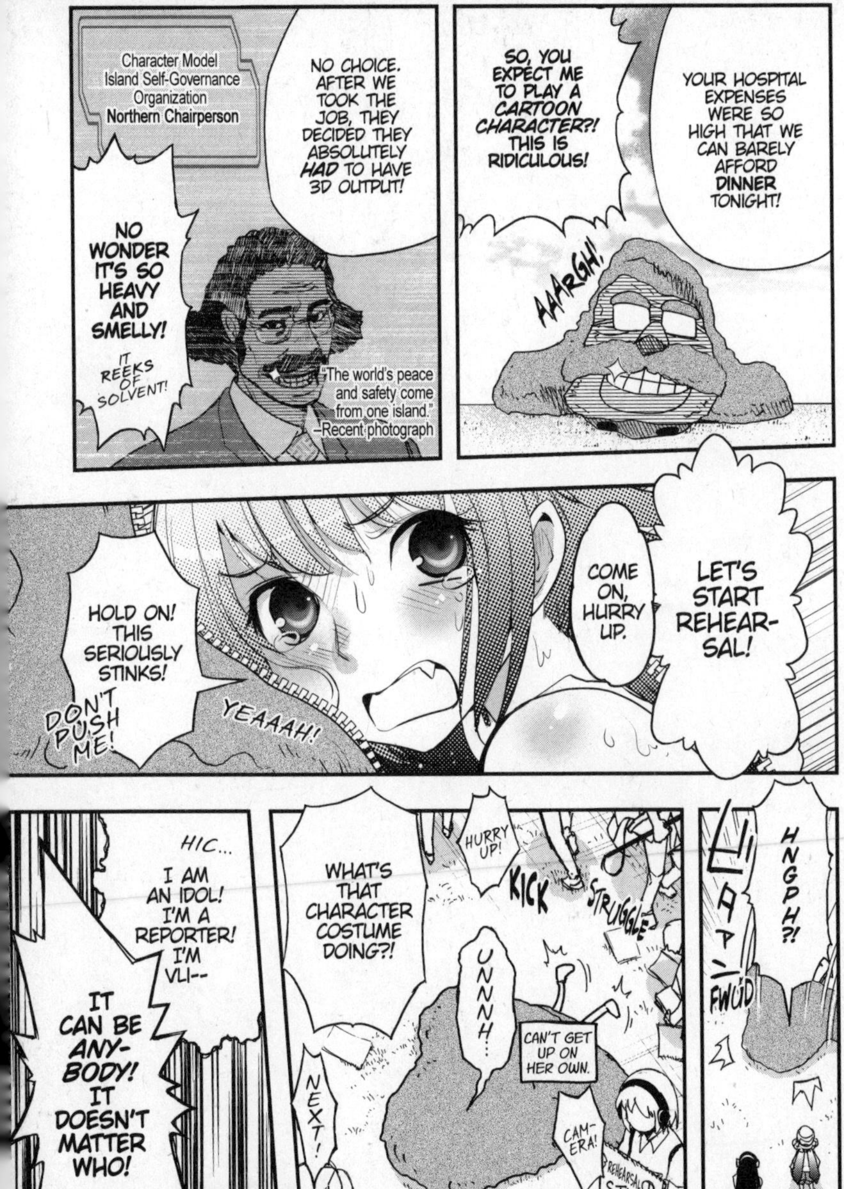

YOUR HOSPITAL EXPENSES WERE SO HIGH THAT WE CAN BARELY AFFORD DINNER TONIGHT!
SO, YOU EXPECT ME TO PLAY A CARTOON CHARACTER?! THIS IS RIDICULOUS!
AAARGH!
NO CHOICE. AFTER WE TOOK THE JOB, THEY DECIDED THEY ABSOLUTELY HAD TO HAVE 3D OUTPUT!
Character Model Island Self-Governance Organization Northern Chairperson
NO WONDER IT'S SO HEAVY AND SMELLY!
IT REEKS OF SOLVENT!
"The world's peace and safety come from one island." –Recent photograph
LET'S START REHEARSAL!
COME ON, HURRY UP.
YEAAAH!
HOLD ON! THIS SERIOUSLY STINKS!
DON'T PUSH ME!
HNGPH?!
SLAP
FWUD
HURRY UP!
WHAT'S THAT CHARACTER COSTUME DOING?!
KICK
STRUGGLE
UNNNH...
CAN'T GET UP ON HER OWN.
CAM-ERA!
NEXT!
REHEARSAL 1 START
HIC...
I AM AN IDOL! I'M A REPORTER! I'M VLI--
IT CAN BE ANY-BODY! IT DOESN'T MATTER WHO!

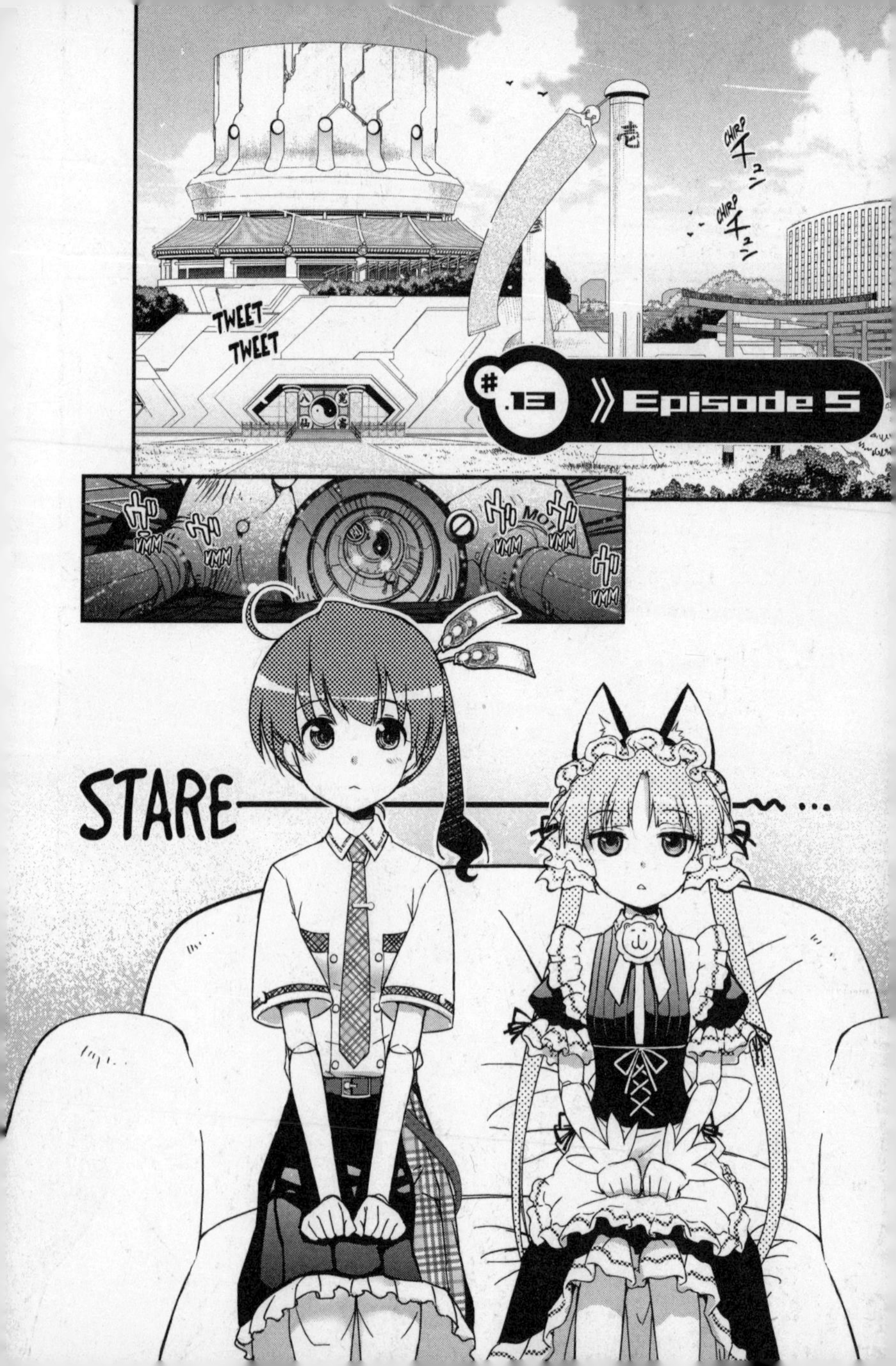

CHIRP チュン
CHIRP チュン
壱
#.13 》Episode 5
TWEET TWEET
ヴ VMM
ヴ VMM
ヴ VMM
ヴ VMM
ヴ VMM
STARE———~...

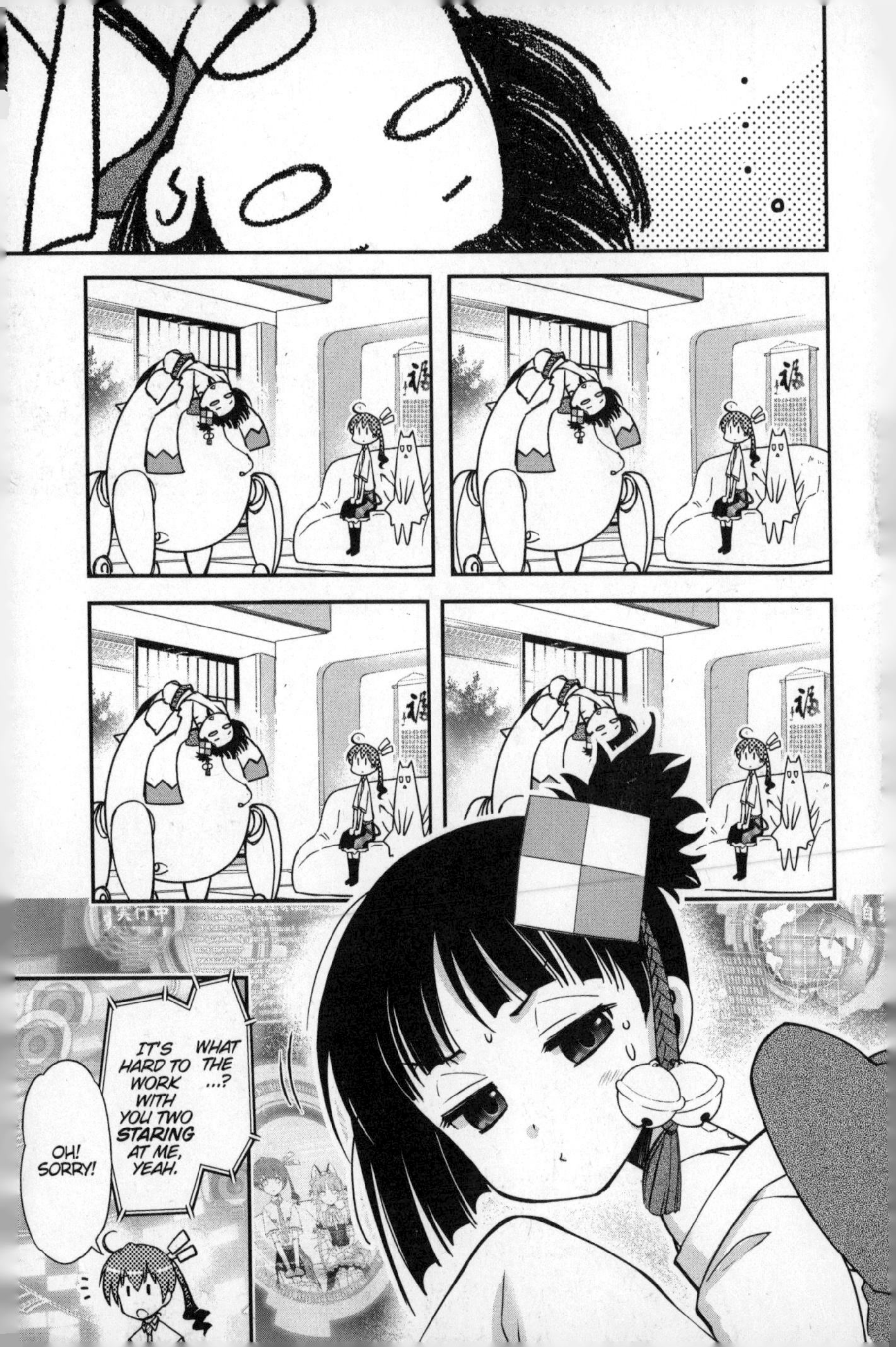
WHAT THE ...?
IT'S HARD TO WORK WITH YOU TWO STARING AT ME, YEAH.
OH! SORRY!

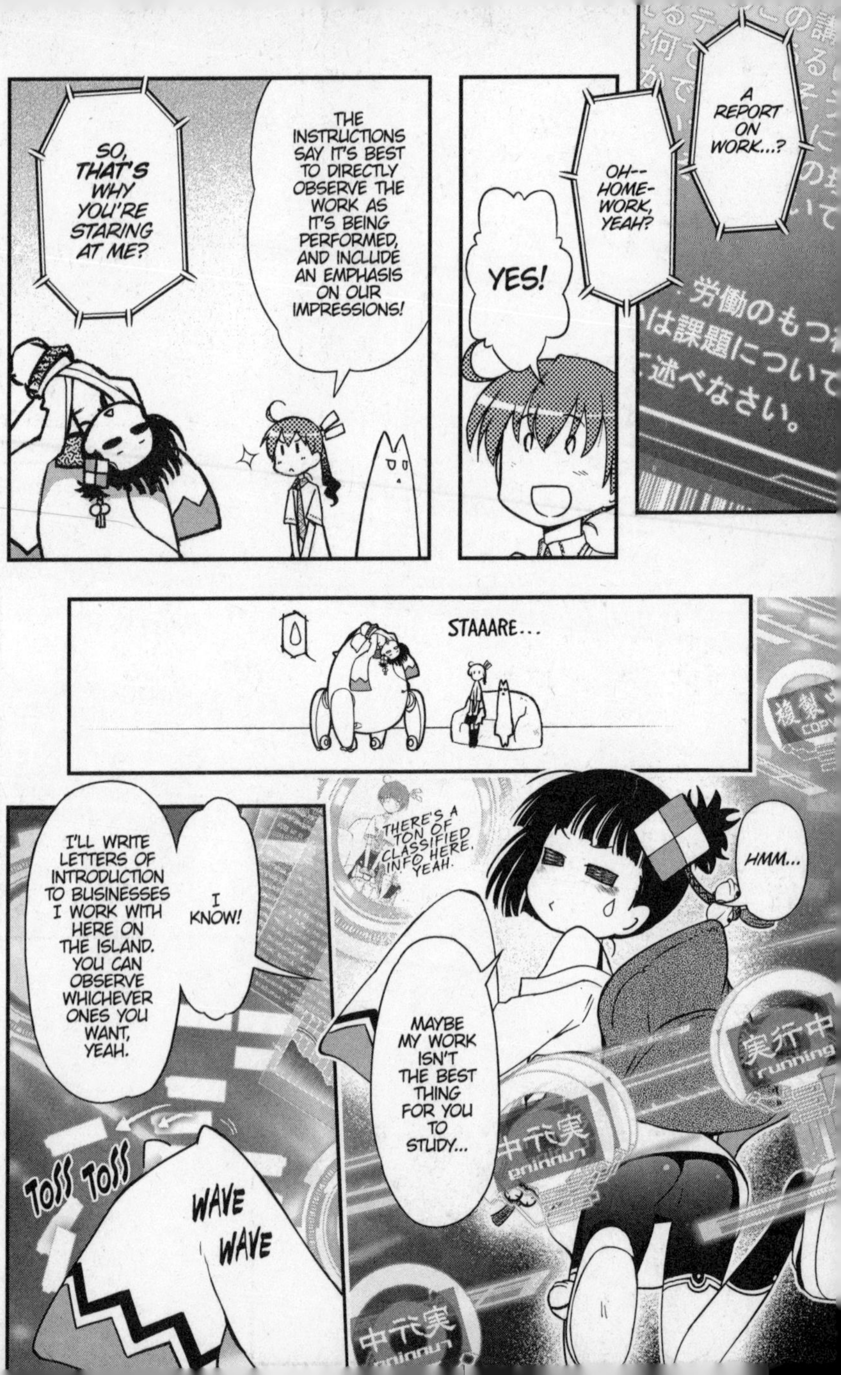
A REPORT ON WORK...?
労働のもつ
は課題について
述べなさい。
OH-- HOME-WORK, YEAH?
YES!
THE INSTRUCTIONS SAY IT'S BEST TO DIRECTLY OBSERVE THE WORK AS IT'S BEING PERFORMED, AND INCLUDE AN EMPHASIS ON OUR IMPRESSIONS!
SO, **THAT'S** WHY YOU'RE STARING AT ME?
STAAARE...
複製中
COPY
HMM...
THERE'S A TON OF CLASSIFIED INFO HERE, YEAH.
実行中
running
MAYBE MY WORK ISN'T THE BEST THING FOR YOU TO STUDY...
I KNOW!
I'LL WRITE LETTERS OF INTRODUCTION TO BUSINESSES I WORK WITH HERE ON THE ISLAND. YOU CAN OBSERVE WHICHEVER ONES YOU WANT, YEAH.
TOSS TOSS
WAVE WAVE

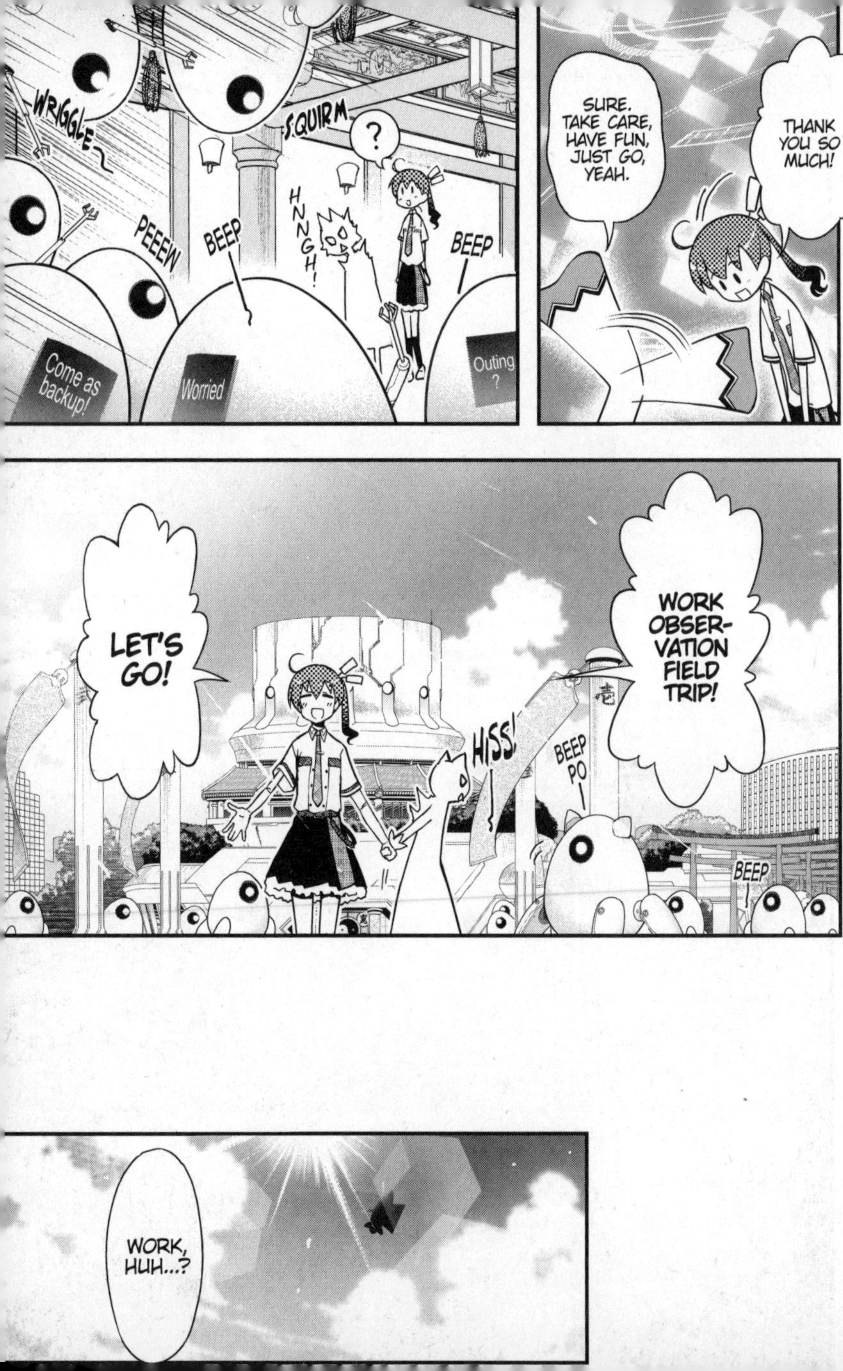
THANK YOU SO MUCH!
SURE. TAKE CARE, HAVE FUN, JUST GO, YEAH.
?
SQUIRM
WRIGGLE~
HNNGH!
BEEP
PEEEW
BEEP
Outing?
Worried
Come as backup!
WORK OBSERVATION FIELD TRIP!
BEEP
BEEP PO
HISS!
LET'S GO!
WORK, HUH...?

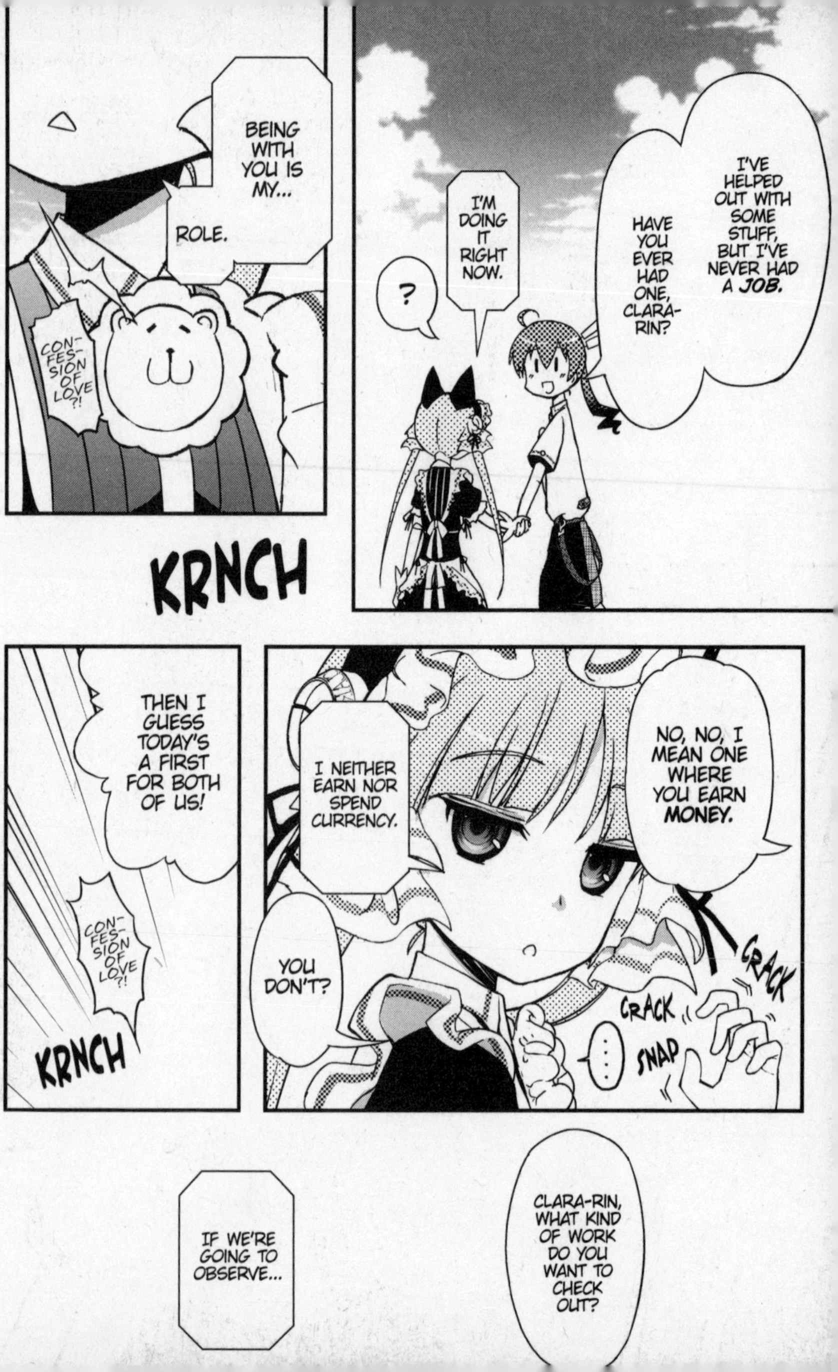
I'VE HELPED OUT WITH SOME STUFF, BUT I'VE NEVER HAD A *JOB.*
HAVE YOU EVER HAD ONE, CLARA-RIN?
I'M DOING IT RIGHT NOW.
?
BEING WITH YOU IS MY...
ROLE.
CON-FES-SION OF LOVE?!
KRNCH
NO, NO, I MEAN ONE WHERE YOU EARN **MONEY.**
I NEITHER EARN NOR SPEND CURRENCY.
YOU DON'T?
CRACK
CRACK
SNAP
...
THEN I GUESS TODAY'S A FIRST FOR BOTH OF US!
CON-FES-SION OF LOVE?!
KRNCH
CLARA-RIN, WHAT KIND OF WORK DO YOU WANT TO CHECK OUT?
IF WE'RE GOING TO OBSERVE...

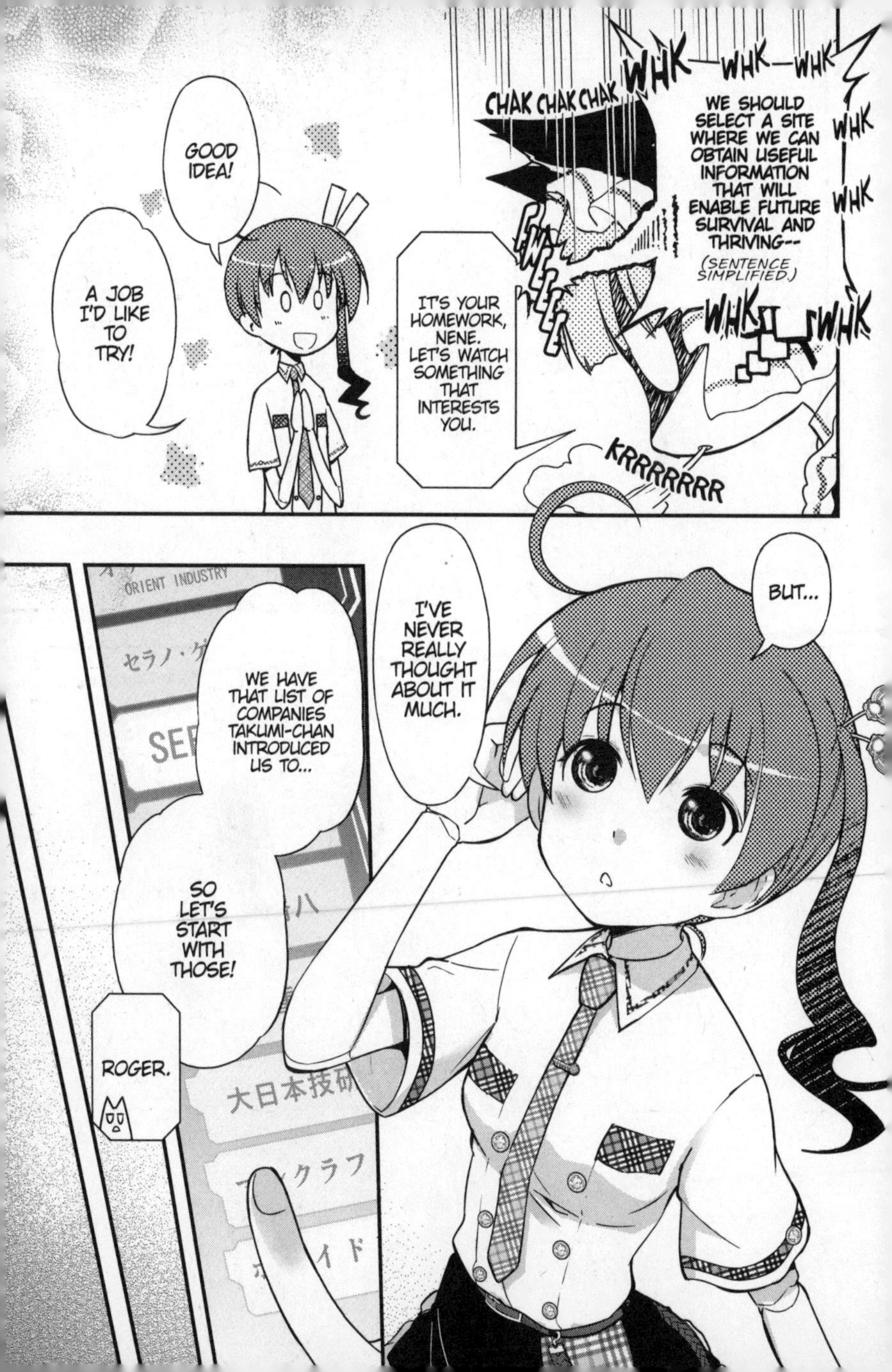
WHK—WHK—WHK
CHAK CHAK CHAK
WE SHOULD SELECT A SITE WHERE WE CAN OBTAIN USEFUL INFORMATION THAT WILL ENABLE FUTURE SURVIVAL AND THRIVING--
(SENTENCE SIMPLIFIED.)
WHK
WHK
WHK
WHK SWHK
KRRRRRRR
IT'S YOUR HOMEWORK, NENE. LET'S WATCH SOMETHING THAT INTERESTS YOU.
GOOD IDEA!
A JOB I'D LIKE TO TRY!
BUT...
I'VE NEVER REALLY THOUGHT ABOUT IT MUCH.
ORIENT INDUSTRY
WE HAVE THAT LIST OF COMPANIES TAKUMI-CHAN INTRODUCED US TO...
SO LET'S START WITH THOSE!
ROGER.

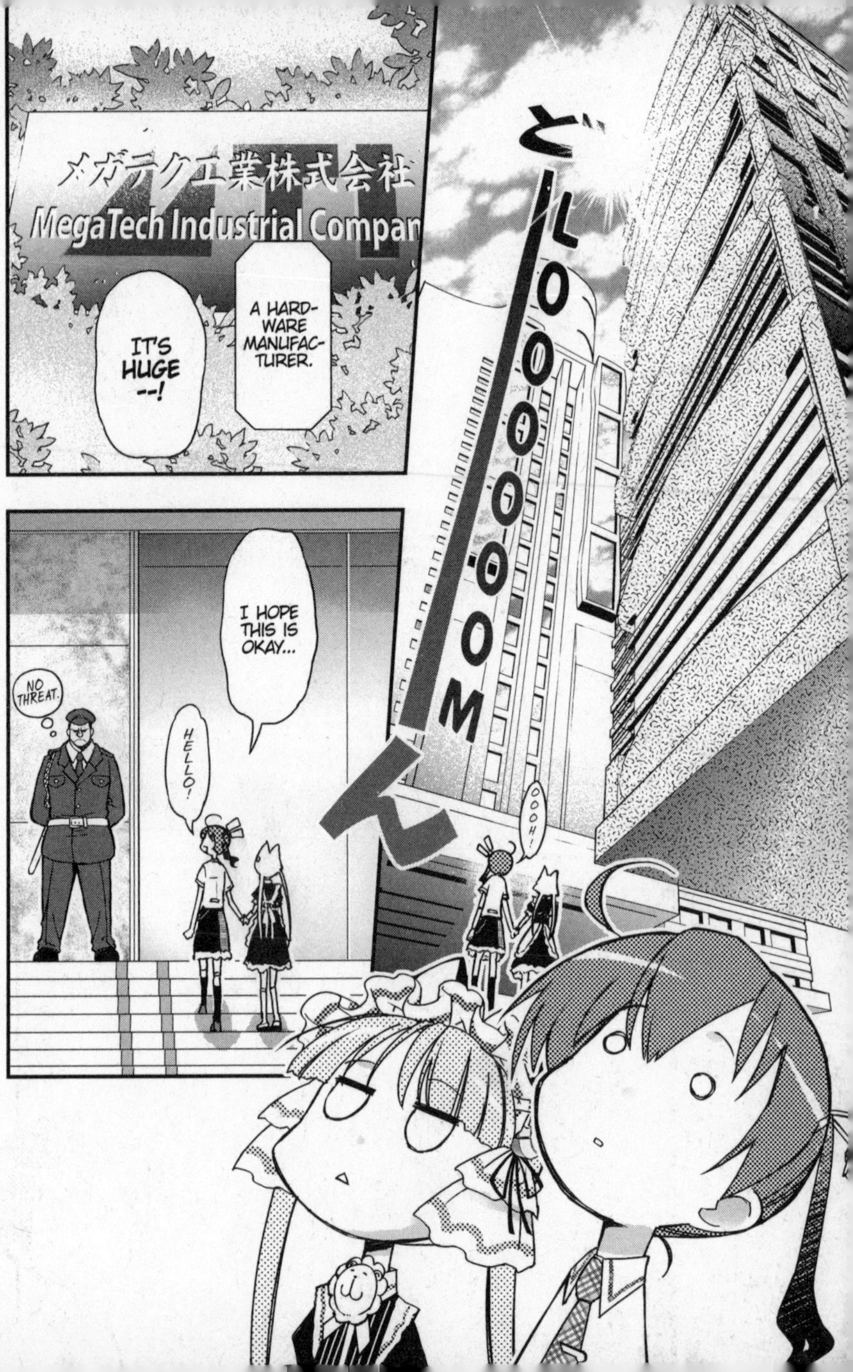
どーん
LOOOOOOM
OOOH!
メガテク工業株式会社
MegaTech Industrial Compan
A HARD-WARE MANUFAC-TURER.
IT'S HUGE--!
I HOPE THIS IS OKAY...
HELLO!
NO THREAT.

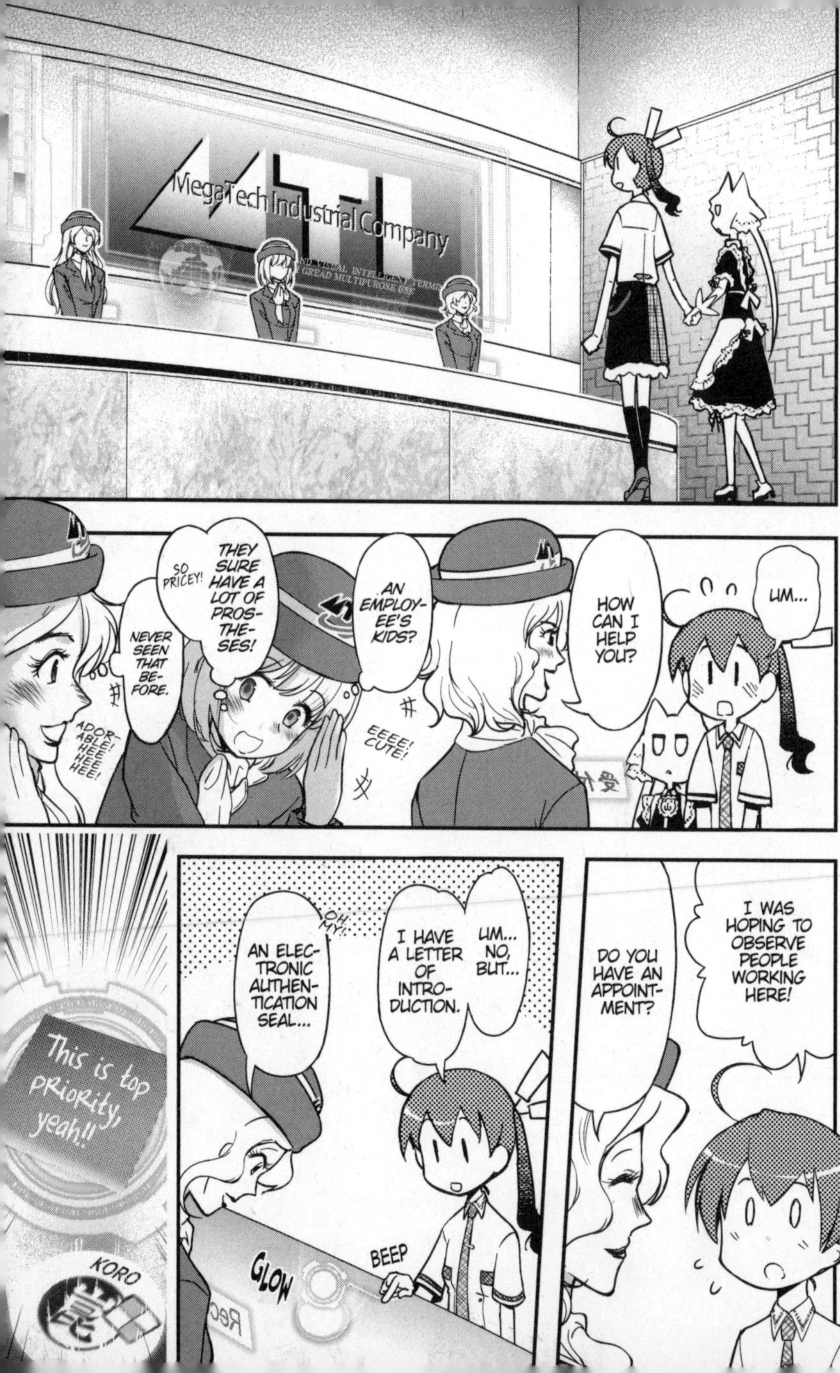
MegaTech Industrial Company
UM...
HOW CAN I HELP YOU?
AN EMPLOY-EE'S KIDS?
EEEE! CUTE!
THEY SURE HAVE A LOT OF PROS-THE-SES!
SO PRICEY!
NEVER SEEN THAT BE-FORE.
ADOR-ABLE! HEE HEE HEE!
I WAS HOPING TO OBSERVE PEOPLE WORKING HERE!
DO YOU HAVE AN APPOINT-MENT?
UM... NO, BUT...
I HAVE A LETTER OF INTRO-DUCTION.
OH MY!
AN ELEC-TRONIC AUTHEN-TICATION SEAL...
BEEP
GLOW
This is top priority, yeah!!
KORO

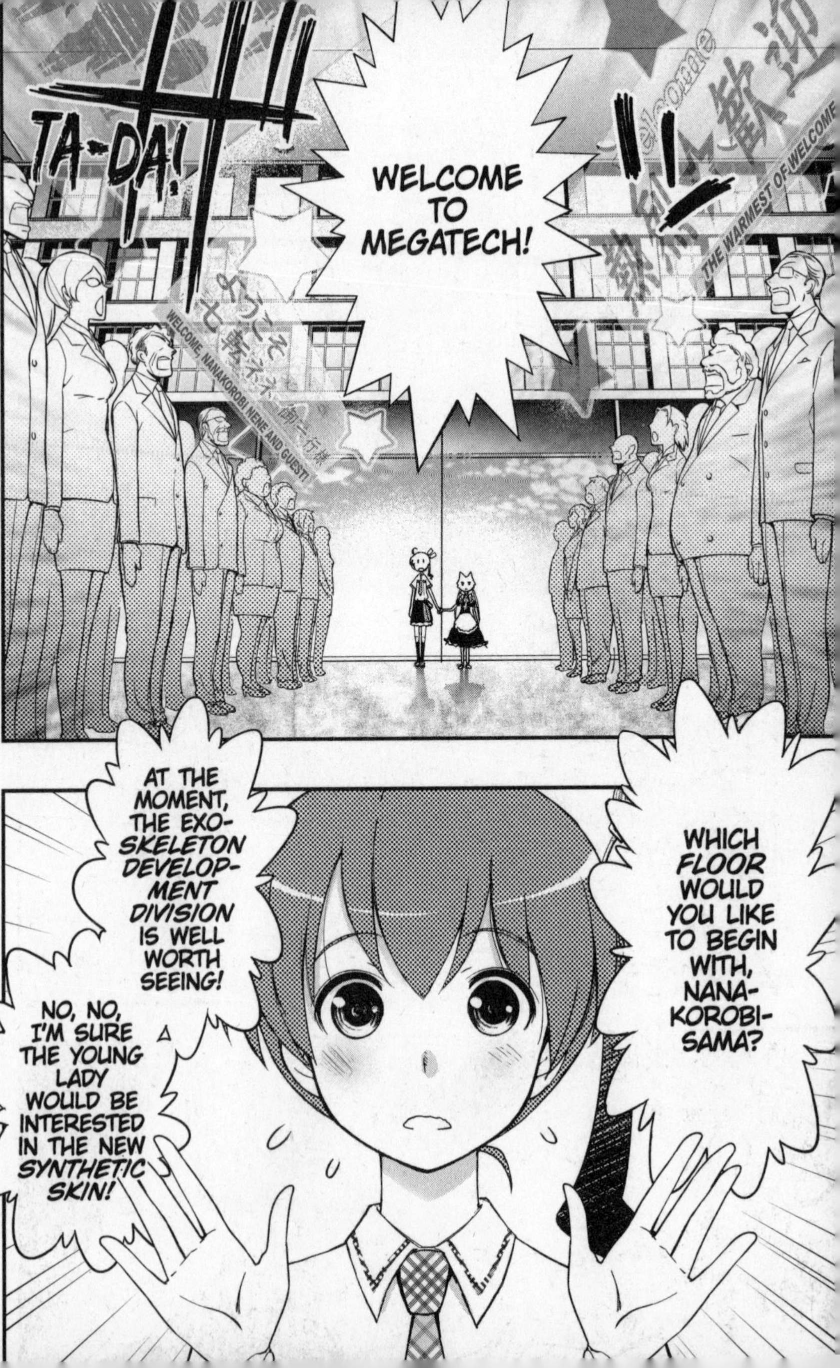
THE WARMEST OF WELCOME
Welcome
WELCOME TO MEGATECH!
WELCOME, NANAKOROBI NENE AND GUEST!
TA-DA!
WHICH FLOOR WOULD YOU LIKE TO BEGIN WITH, NANAKOROBI-SAMA?
AT THE MOMENT, THE EXOSKELETON DEVELOPMENT DIVISION IS WELL WORTH SEEING!
NO, NO, I'M SURE THE YOUNG LADY WOULD BE INTERESTED IN THE NEW SYNTHETIC SKIN!

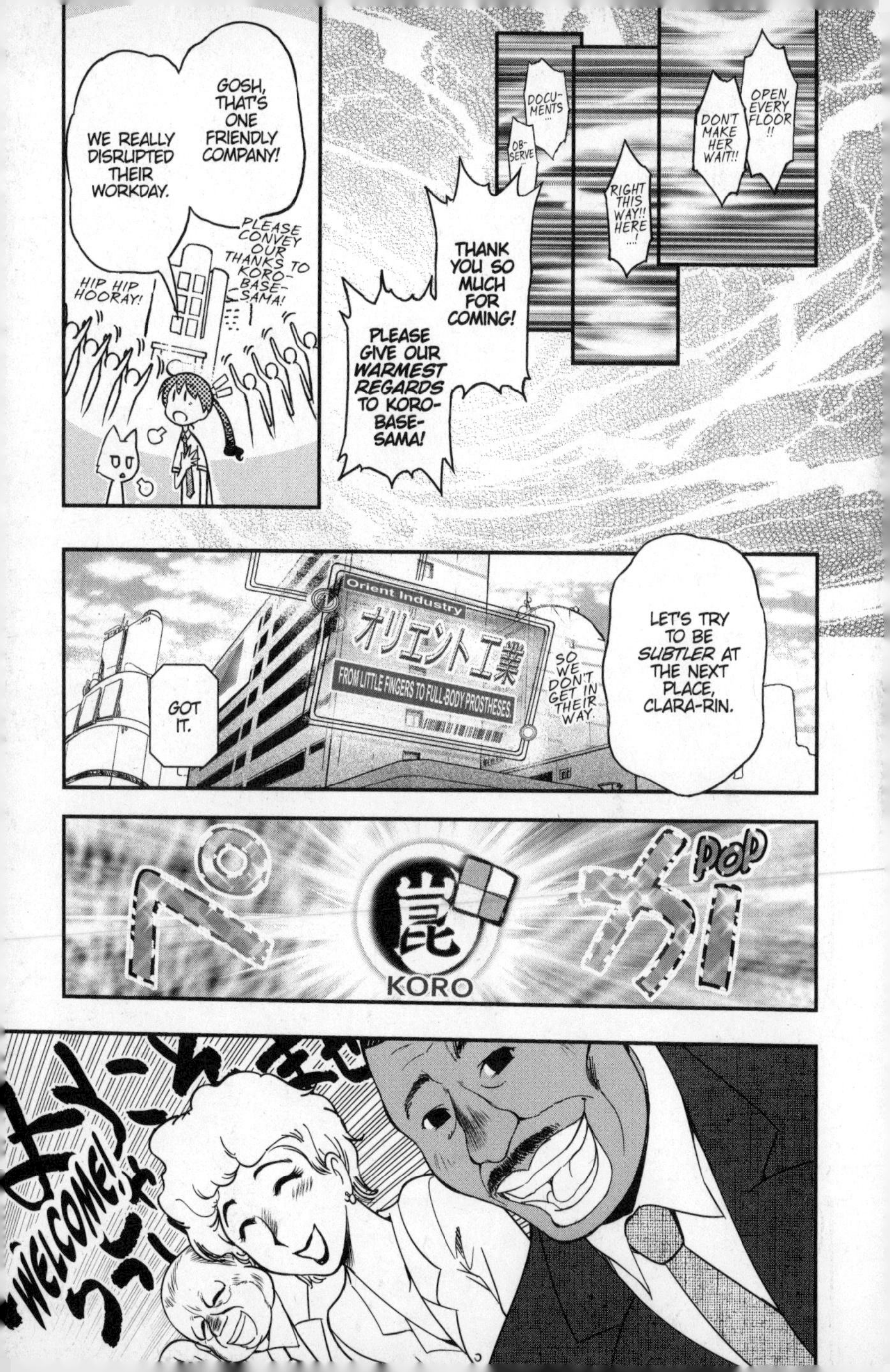
OPEN EVERY FLOOR!!
DON'T MAKE HER WAIT!!
DOCUMENTS...
OB-SERVE...
RIGHT THIS WAY!! HERE...!
THANK YOU SO MUCH FOR COMING!
PLEASE GIVE OUR WARMEST REGARDS TO KORO-BASE-SAMA!
GOSH, THAT'S ONE FRIENDLY COMPANY!
WE REALLY DISRUPTED THEIR WORKDAY.
PLEASE CONVEY OUR THANKS TO KORO-BASE-SAMA!
HIP HIP HOORAY!
LET'S TRY TO BE SUBTLER AT THE NEXT PLACE, CLARA-RIN.
SO WE DON'T GET IN THEIR WAY.
Orient Industry
オリエント工業
FROM LITTLE FINGERS TO FULL-BODY PROSTHESES.
GOT IT.
POP
KORO
WELCOME!

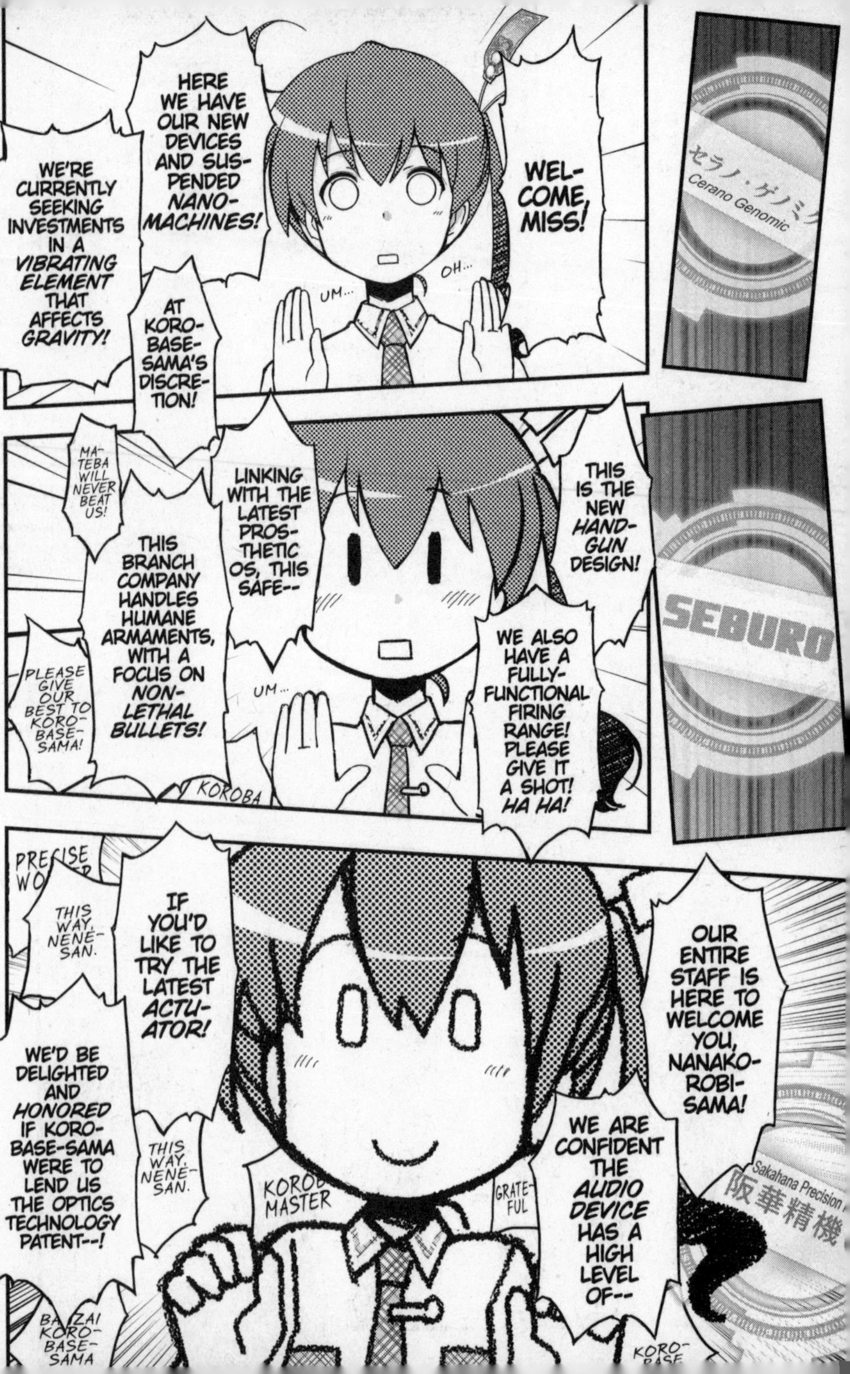
セラノ・ゲノミ
Cerano Genomic
WEL-COME, MISS!
OH...
HERE WE HAVE OUR NEW DEVICES AND SUS-PENDED NANO-MACHINES!
UM...
WE'RE CURRENTLY SEEKING INVESTMENTS IN A VIBRATING ELEMENT THAT AFFECTS GRAVITY!
AT KORO-BASE-SAMA'S DISCRE-TION!
SEBURO
THIS IS THE NEW HAND-GUN DESIGN!
WE ALSO HAVE A FULLY-FUNCTIONAL FIRING RANGE! PLEASE GIVE IT A SHOT! HA HA!
LINKING WITH THE LATEST PROS-THETIC OS, THIS SAFE--
UM...
THIS BRANCH COMPANY HANDLES HUMANE ARMAMENTS, WITH A FOCUS ON NON-LETHAL BULLETS!
MA-TEBA WILL NEVER BEAT US!
PLEASE GIVE OUR BEST TO KORO-BASE-SAMA!
KOROBA
OUR ENTIRE STAFF IS HERE TO WELCOME YOU, NANAKO-ROBI-SAMA!
Sakahana Precision
阪華精機
WE ARE CONFIDENT THE AUDIO DEVICE HAS A HIGH LEVEL OF--
GRATE-FUL
MASTER
IF YOU'D LIKE TO TRY THE LATEST ACTU-ATOR!
THIS WAY, NENE-SAN.
WE'D BE DELIGHTED AND HONORED IF KORO-BASE-SAMA WERE TO LEND US THE OPTICS TECHNOLOGY PATENT--!
THIS WAY, NENE-SAN.
BANZAI KORO-BASE-SAMA

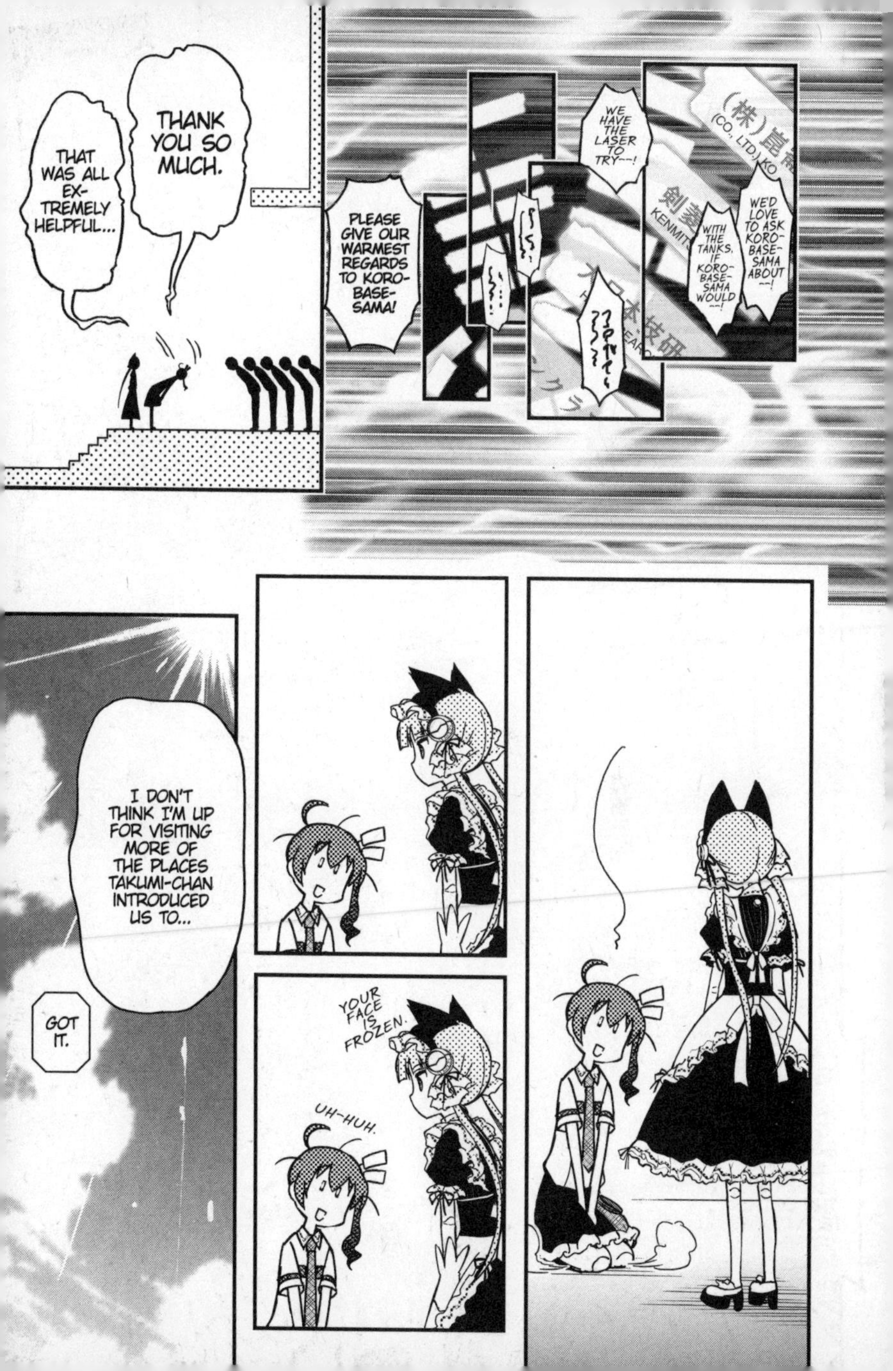
WE HAVE THE LASER TO TRY--!
(株) (CO., LTD.) KO
KENMITSU
WE'D LOVE TO ASK KORO-BASE-SAMA ABOUT--!
WITH THE TANKS, IF KORO-BASE-SAMA WOULD--!
PLEASE GIVE OUR WARMEST REGARDS TO KORO-BASE-SAMA!
THANK YOU SO MUCH.
THAT WAS ALL EX-TREMELY HELPFUL...
YOUR FACE IS FROZEN.
UH-HUH.
I DON'T THINK I'M UP FOR VISITING MORE OF THE PLACES TAKUMI-CHAN INTRODUCED US TO...
GOT IT.

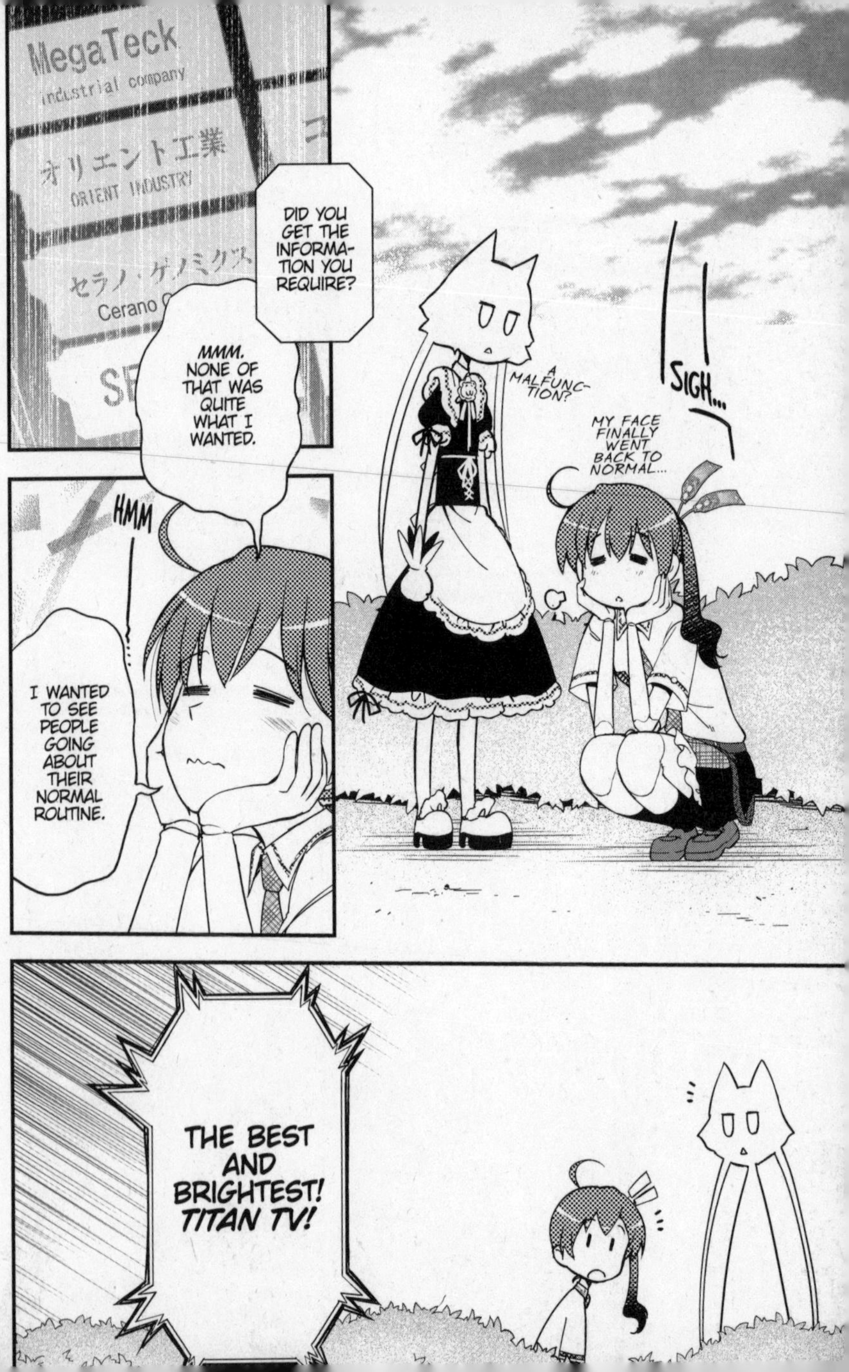
SIGH...
MY FACE FINALLY WENT BACK TO NORMAL...
A MALFUNCTION?
DID YOU GET THE INFORMATION YOU REQUIRE?
MegaTeck
industrial company
オリエント工業
ORIENT INDUSTRY
セラノ・ゲノミクス
MMM. NONE OF THAT WAS QUITE WHAT I WANTED.
HMM
I WANTED TO SEE PEOPLE GOING ABOUT THEIR NORMAL ROUTINE.
THE BEST AND BRIGHTEST! TITAN TV!

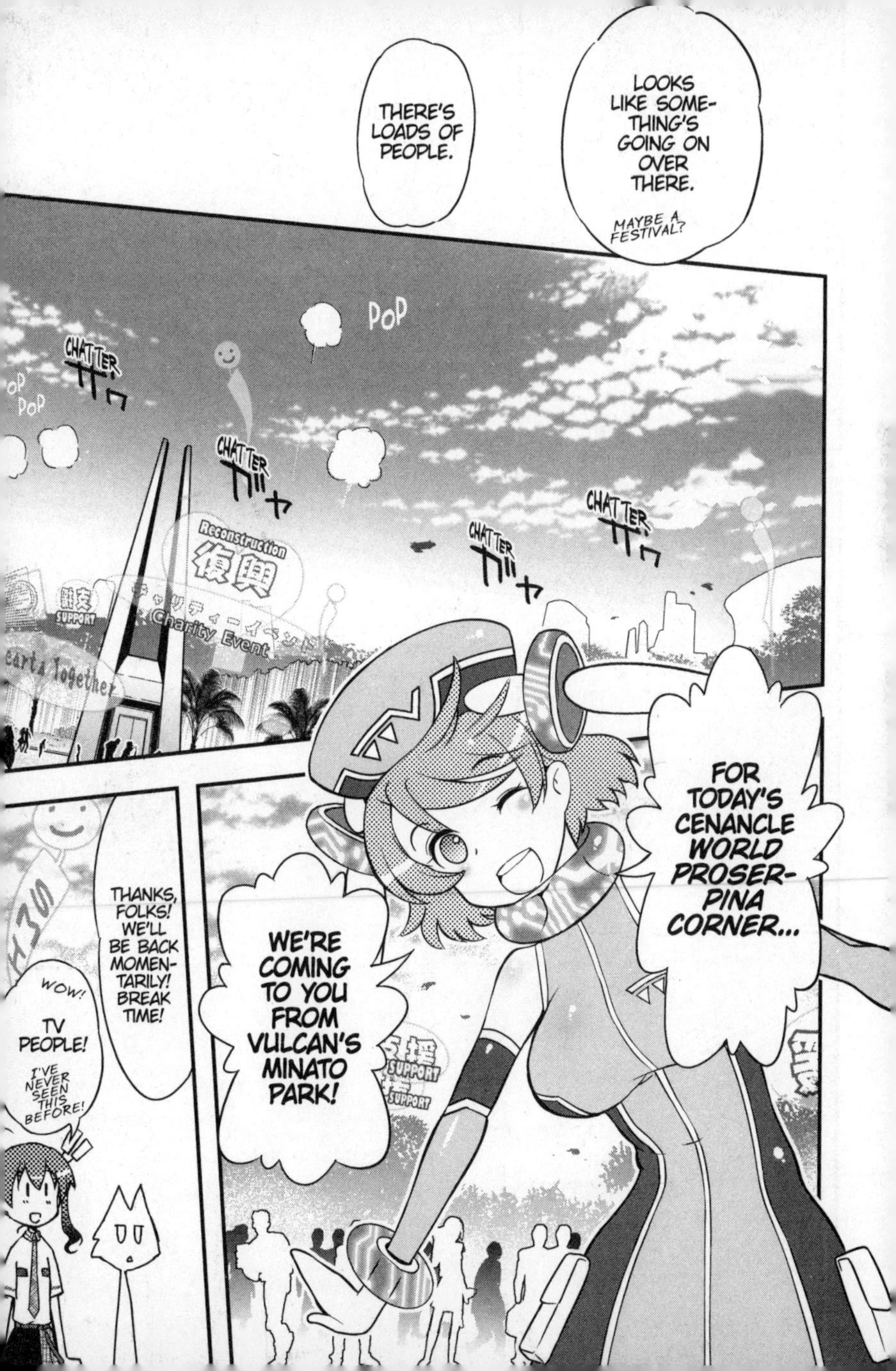
LOOKS LIKE SOME-THING'S GOING ON OVER THERE.
MAYBE A FESTIVAL?
THERE'S LOADS OF PEOPLE.
POP
CHATTER
CHATTER
POP POP
CHATTER
CHATTER
Reconstruction
復興
支援
SUPPORT
Charity Event
FOR TODAY'S CENANCLE WORLD PROSER-PINA CORNER...
WE'RE COMING TO YOU FROM VULCAN'S MINATO PARK!
SUPPORT
SUPPORT
THANKS, FOLKS! WE'LL BE BACK MOMEN-TARILY! BREAK TIME!
WOW!
TV PEOPLE!
I'VE NEVER SEEN THIS BEFORE!

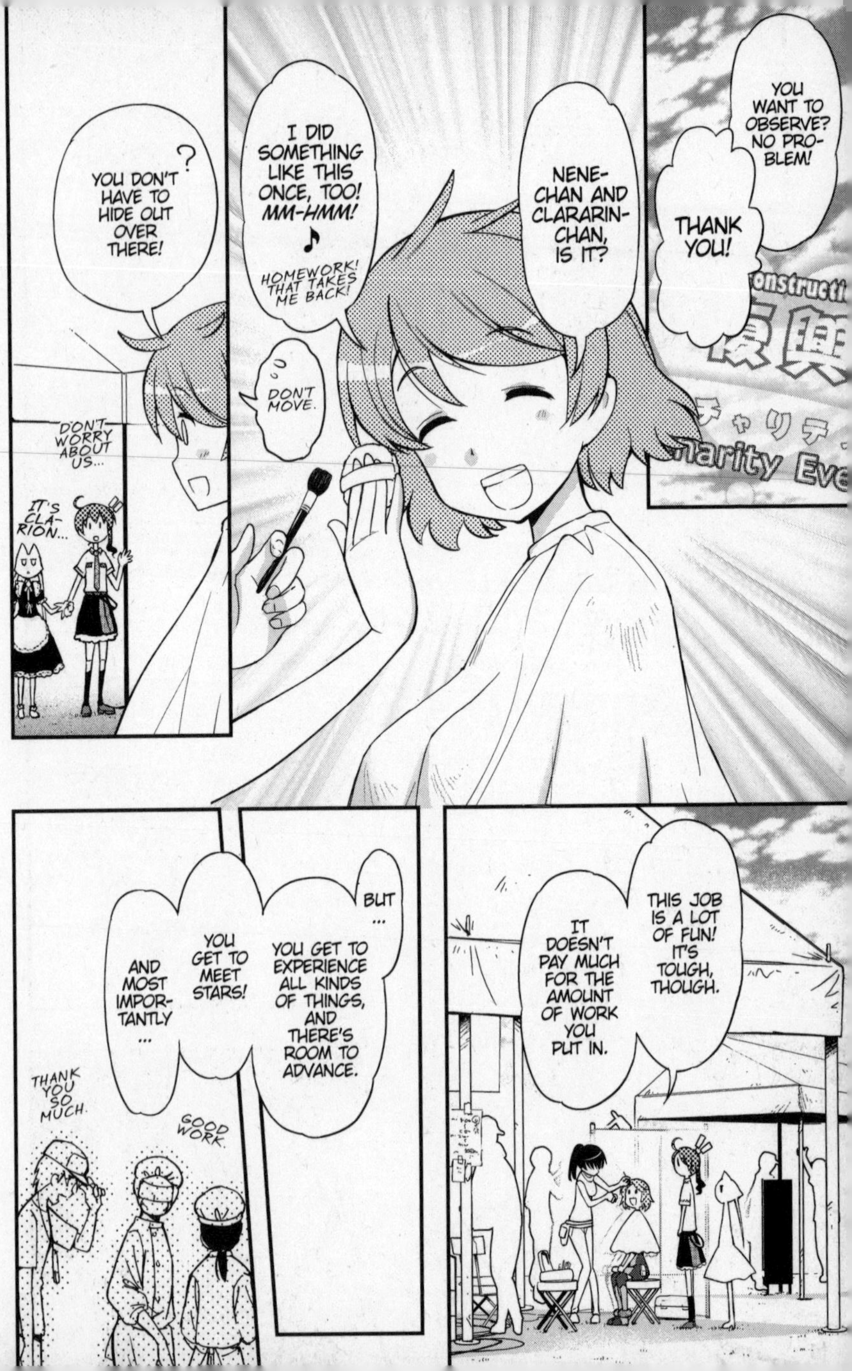
YOU WANT TO OBSERVE? NO PROBLEM!
THANK YOU!
NENE-CHAN AND CLARARIN-CHAN, IS IT?
I DID SOMETHING LIKE THIS ONCE, TOO! MM-HMM! ♪
HOMEWORK! THAT TAKES ME BACK!
DON'T MOVE.
YOU DON'T HAVE TO HIDE OUT OVER THERE! ?
DON'T WORRY ABOUT US...
IT'S CLARION...
THIS JOB IS A LOT OF FUN! IT'S TOUGH, THOUGH.
IT DOESN'T PAY MUCH FOR THE AMOUNT OF WORK YOU PUT IN.
BUT...
YOU GET TO EXPERIENCE ALL KINDS OF THINGS, AND THERE'S ROOM TO ADVANCE.
YOU GET TO MEET STARS!
AND MOST IMPORTANTLY...
GOOD WORK.
THANK YOU SO MUCH.

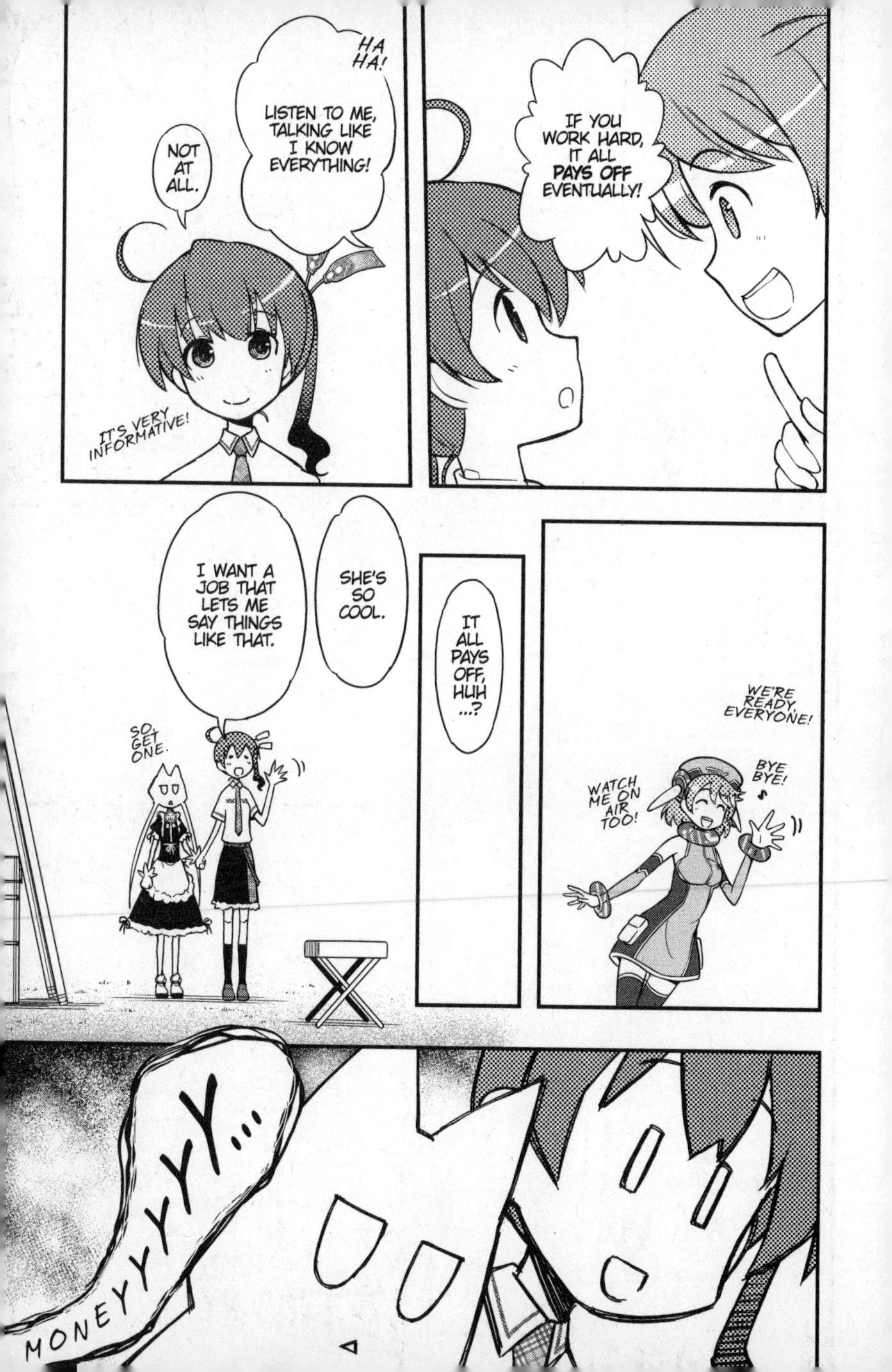
IF YOU WORK HARD, IT ALL PAYS OFF EVENTUALLY!
HA HA!
LISTEN TO ME, TALKING LIKE I KNOW EVERYTHING!
NOT AT ALL.
IT'S VERY INFORMATIVE!
WE'RE READY, EVERYONE!
BYE BYE!
WATCH ME ON AIR TOO!
IT ALL PAYS OFF, HUH ...?
SHE'S SO COOL.
I WANT A JOB THAT LETS ME SAY THINGS LIKE THAT.
SO, GET ONE.
MONEYYYYY...

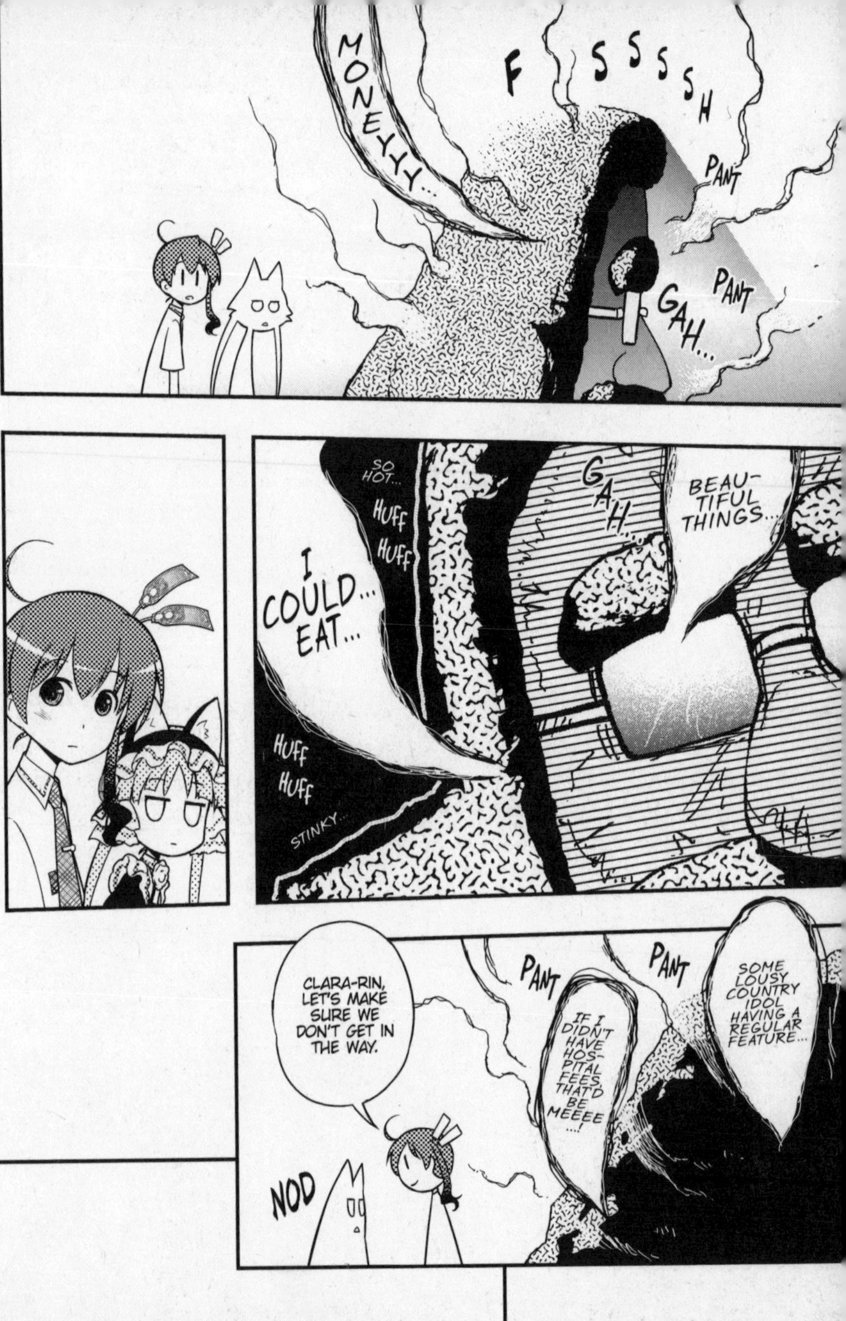
FSSSSH
PANT
PANT
GAH...
MONEYYY...
BEAU-TIFUL THINGS...
GAH...
SO HOT...
HUFF
HUFF
I COULD... EAT...
HUFF
HUFF
STINKY...
SOME LOUSY COUNTRY IDOL HAVING A REGULAR FEATURE...
PANT
IF I DIDN'T HAVE HOS-PITAL FEES, THAT'D BE MEEEE...!
PANT
CLARA-RIN, LET'S MAKE SURE WE DON'T GET IN THE WAY.
NOD

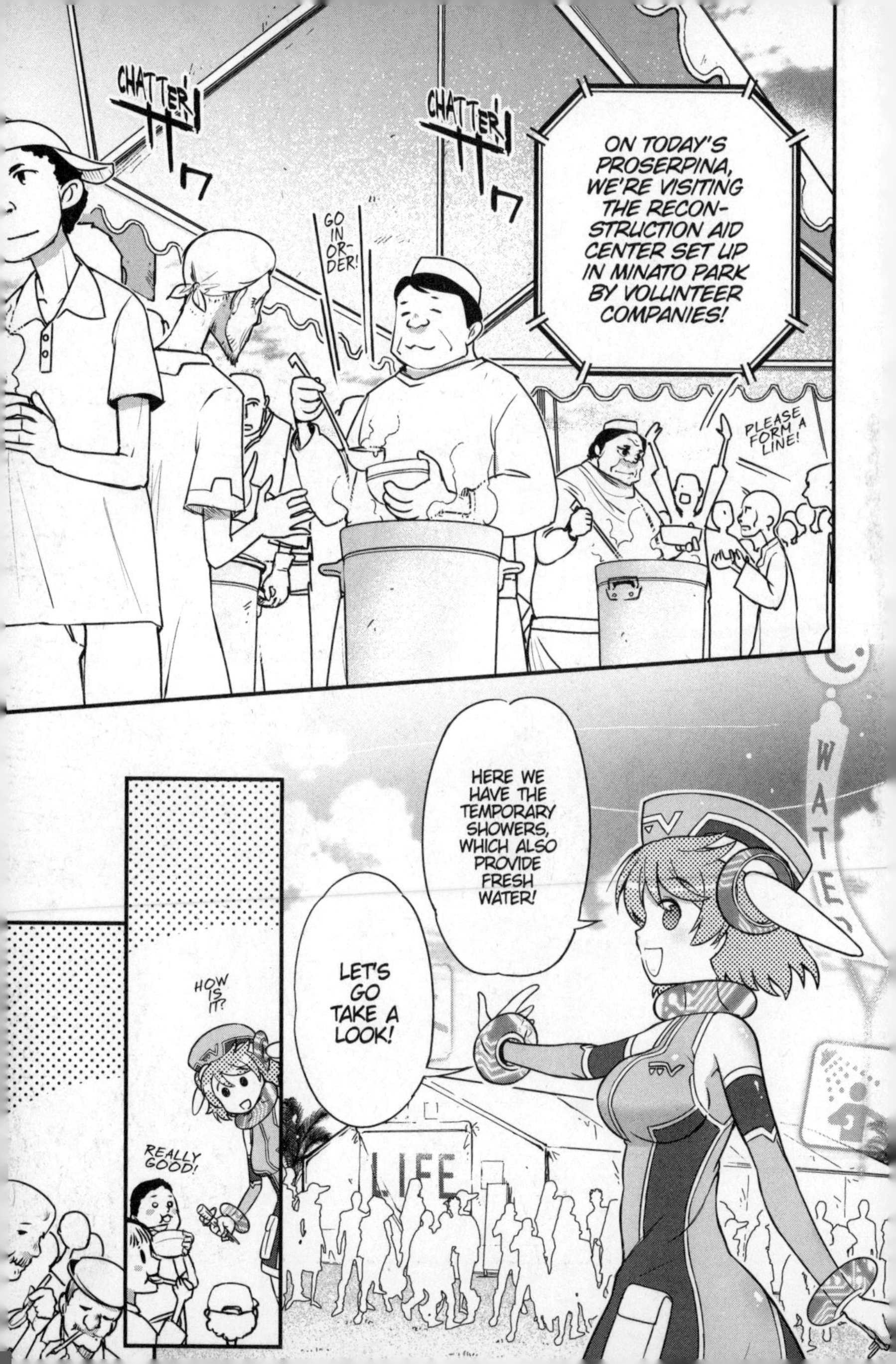
ON TODAY'S PROSERPINA, WE'RE VISITING THE RECON-STRUCTION AID CENTER SET UP IN MINATO PARK BY VOLUNTEER COMPANIES!
PLEASE FORM A LINE!
CHATTER
GO IN OR-DER!
CHATTER
WATER
HERE WE HAVE THE TEMPORARY SHOWERS, WHICH ALSO PROVIDE FRESH WATER!
LET'S GO TAKE A LOOK!
LIFE
HOW IS IT?
REALLY GOOD!

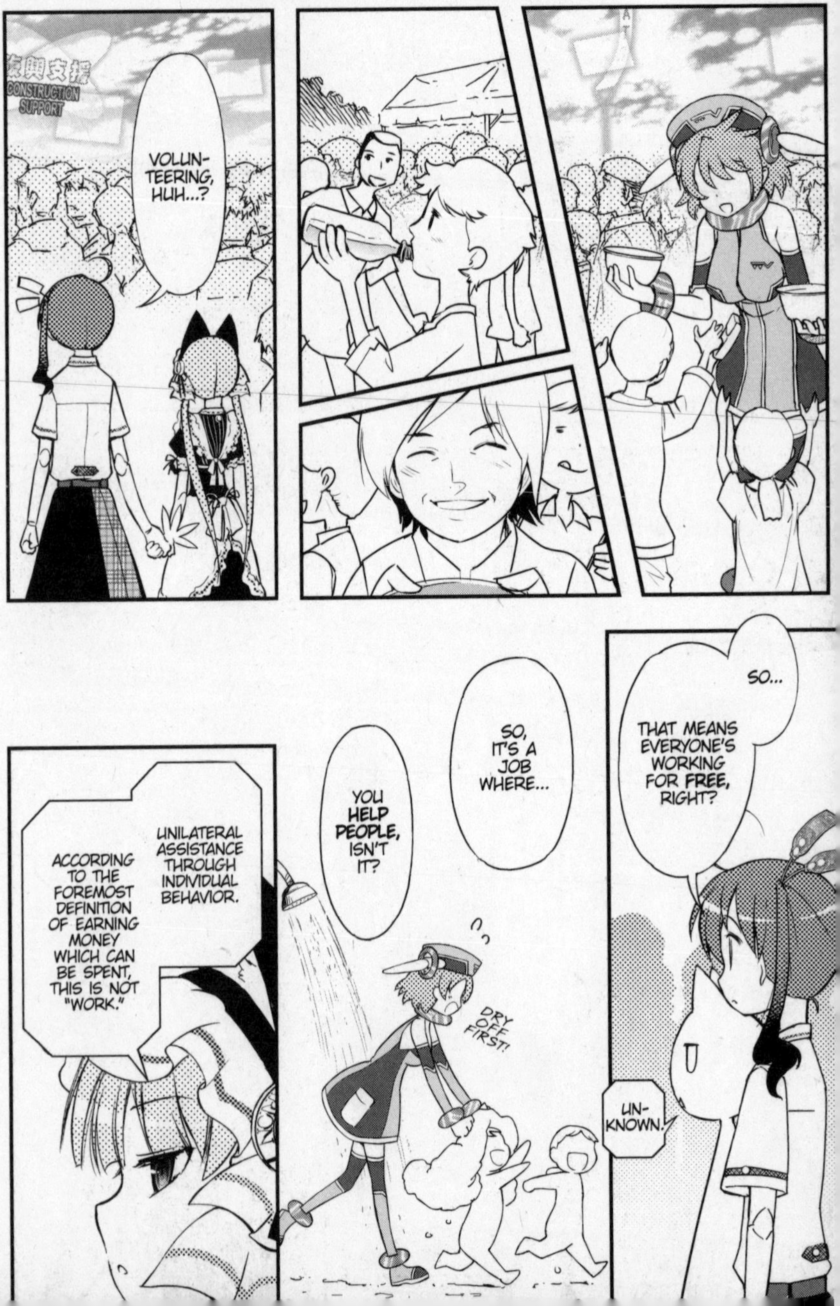
復興支援
CONSTRUCTION SUPPORT
VOLUN-TEERING, HUH...?
SO... THAT MEANS EVERYONE'S WORKING FOR FREE, RIGHT?
UN-KNOWN.
SO, IT'S A JOB WHERE...
YOU HELP PEOPLE, ISN'T IT?
DRY OFF FIRST!
UNILATERAL ASSISTANCE THROUGH INDIVIDUAL BEHAVIOR.
ACCORDING TO THE FOREMOST DEFINITION OF EARNING MONEY WHICH CAN BE SPENT, THIS IS NOT "WORK."

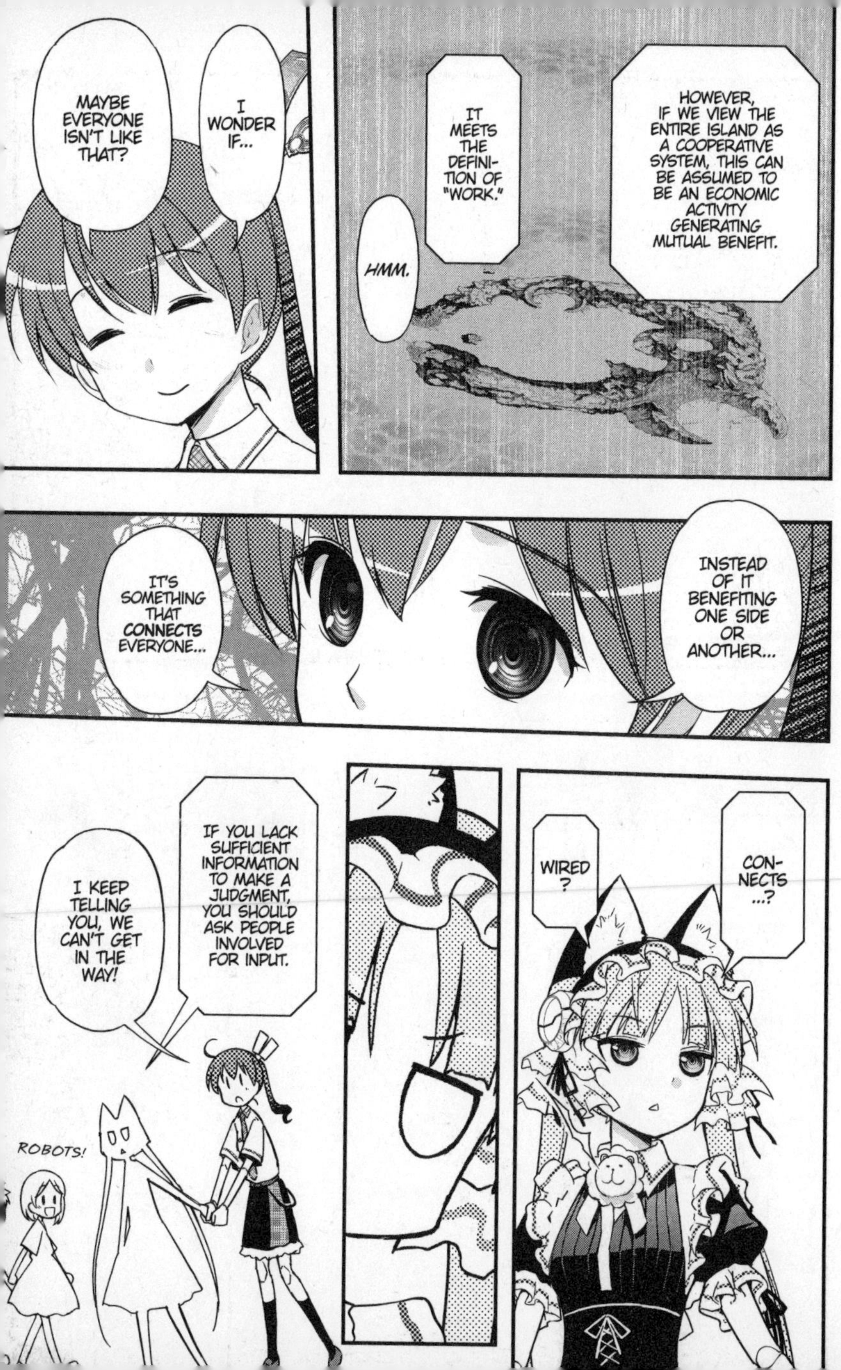
HOWEVER, IF WE VIEW THE ENTIRE ISLAND AS A COOPERATIVE SYSTEM, THIS CAN BE ASSUMED TO BE AN ECONOMIC ACTIVITY GENERATING MUTUAL BENEFIT.
IT MEETS THE DEFINITION OF "WORK."
HMM.
I WONDER IF...
MAYBE EVERYONE ISN'T LIKE THAT?
INSTEAD OF IT BENEFITING ONE SIDE OR ANOTHER...
IT'S SOMETHING THAT CONNECTS EVERYONE...
CONNECTS ...?
WIRED ?
IF YOU LACK SUFFICIENT INFORMATION TO MAKE A JUDGMENT, YOU SHOULD ASK PEOPLE INVOLVED FOR INPUT.
I KEEP TELLING YOU, WE CAN'T GET IN THE WAY!
ROBOTS!

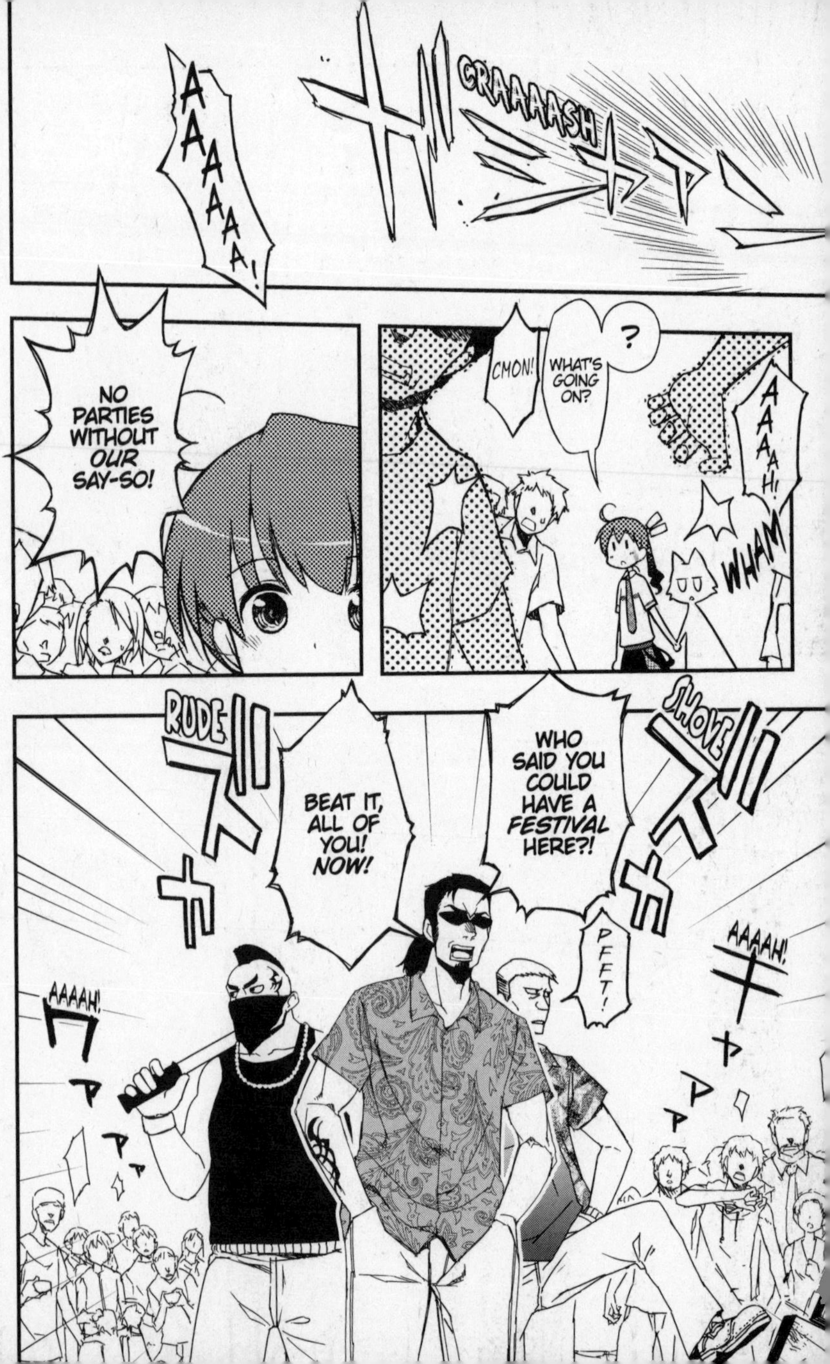
CRAAAASH
AAAAAA!
AAAAH!
?
WHAT'S GOING ON?
CMON!
WHAM
NO PARTIES WITHOUT OUR SAY-SO!
SHOVE
WHO SAID YOU COULD HAVE A FESTIVAL HERE?!
AAAAH!
PFFT!
BEAT IT, ALL OF YOU! NOW!
RUDE
AAAAH!

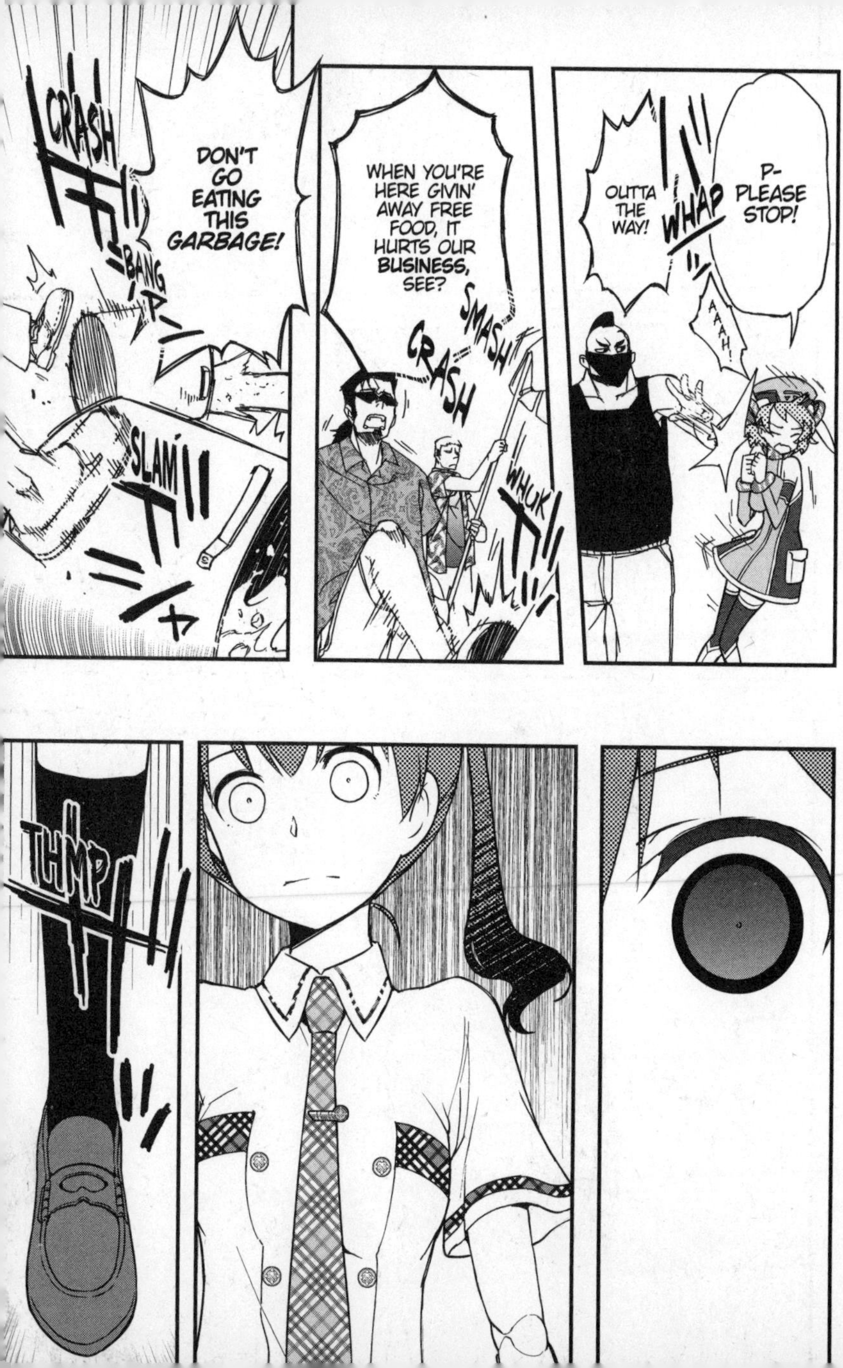
P- PLEASE STOP!
WHAP
OUTTA THE WAY!
AAAH!
WHEN YOU'RE HERE GIVIN' AWAY FREE FOOD, IT HURTS OUR BUSINESS, SEE?
SMASH
CRASH
WHUK
DON'T GO EATING THIS GARBAGE!
CRASH
BANG
SLAM
THMP

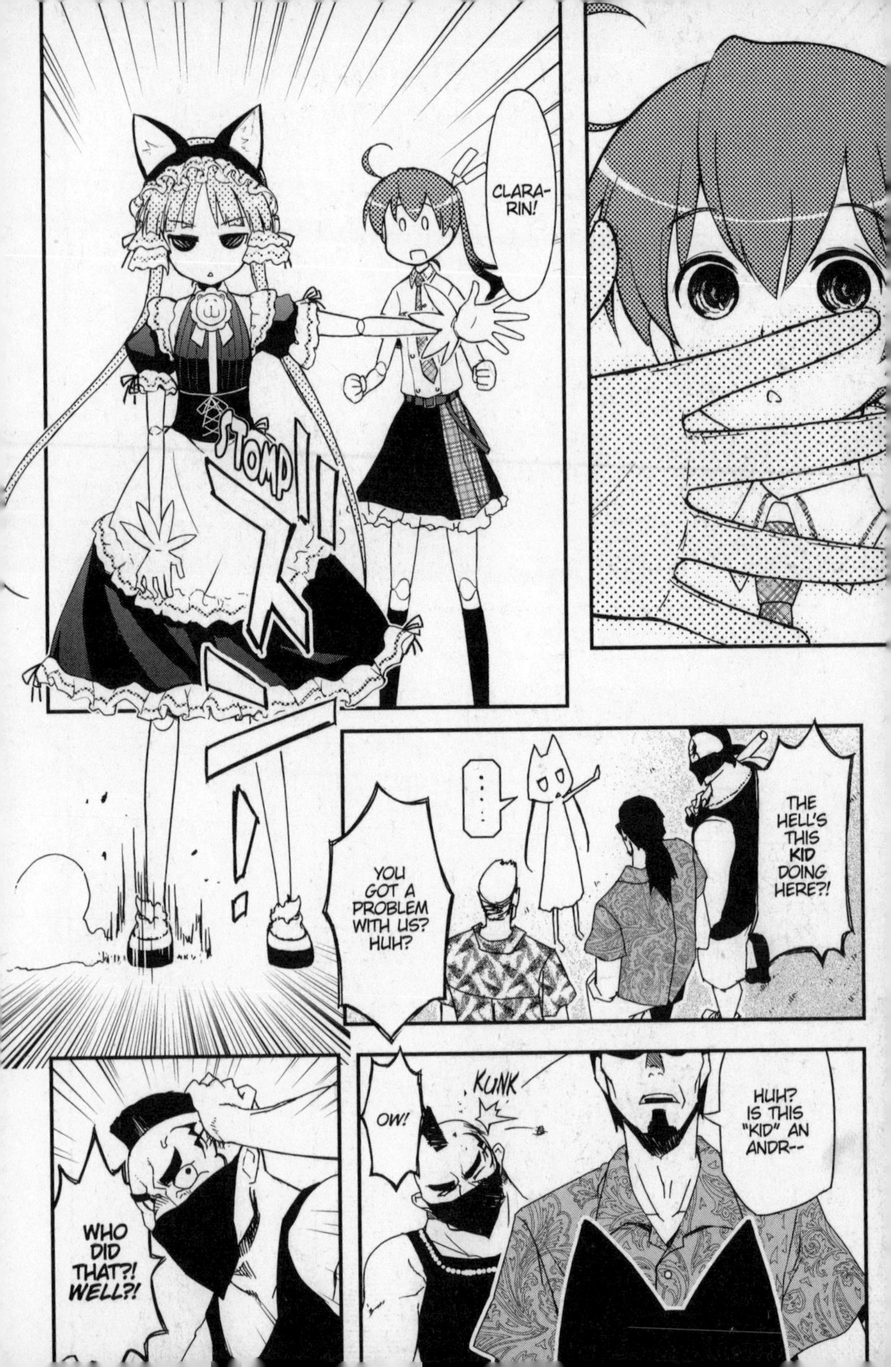
CLARA-RIN!
STOMP
THE HELL'S THIS KID DOING HERE?!
......
YOU GOT A PROBLEM WITH US? HUH?
HUH? IS THIS "KID" AN ANDR--
KUNK
OW!
WHO DID THAT?! WELL?!

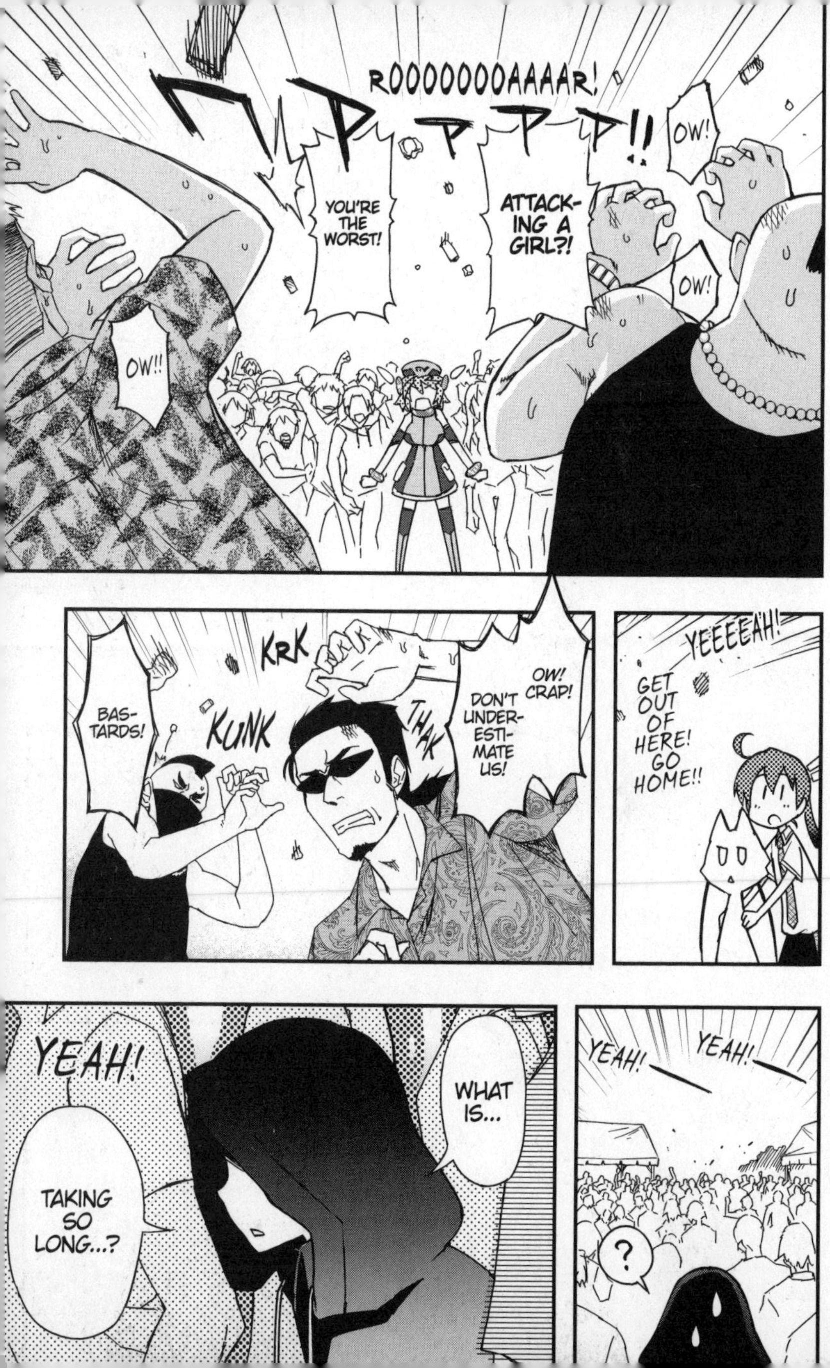
ROOOOOOOAAAAR!
OW!
ATTACKING A GIRL?!
OW!
YOU'RE THE WORST!
OW!!
YEEEEAH!
GET OUT OF HERE! GO HOME!!
OW! CRAP!
DON'T UNDERESTIMATE US!
KRK
THAK
BASTARDS!
KUNK
YEAH!
YEAH!
?
WHAT IS...
YEAH!
TAKING SO LONG...?

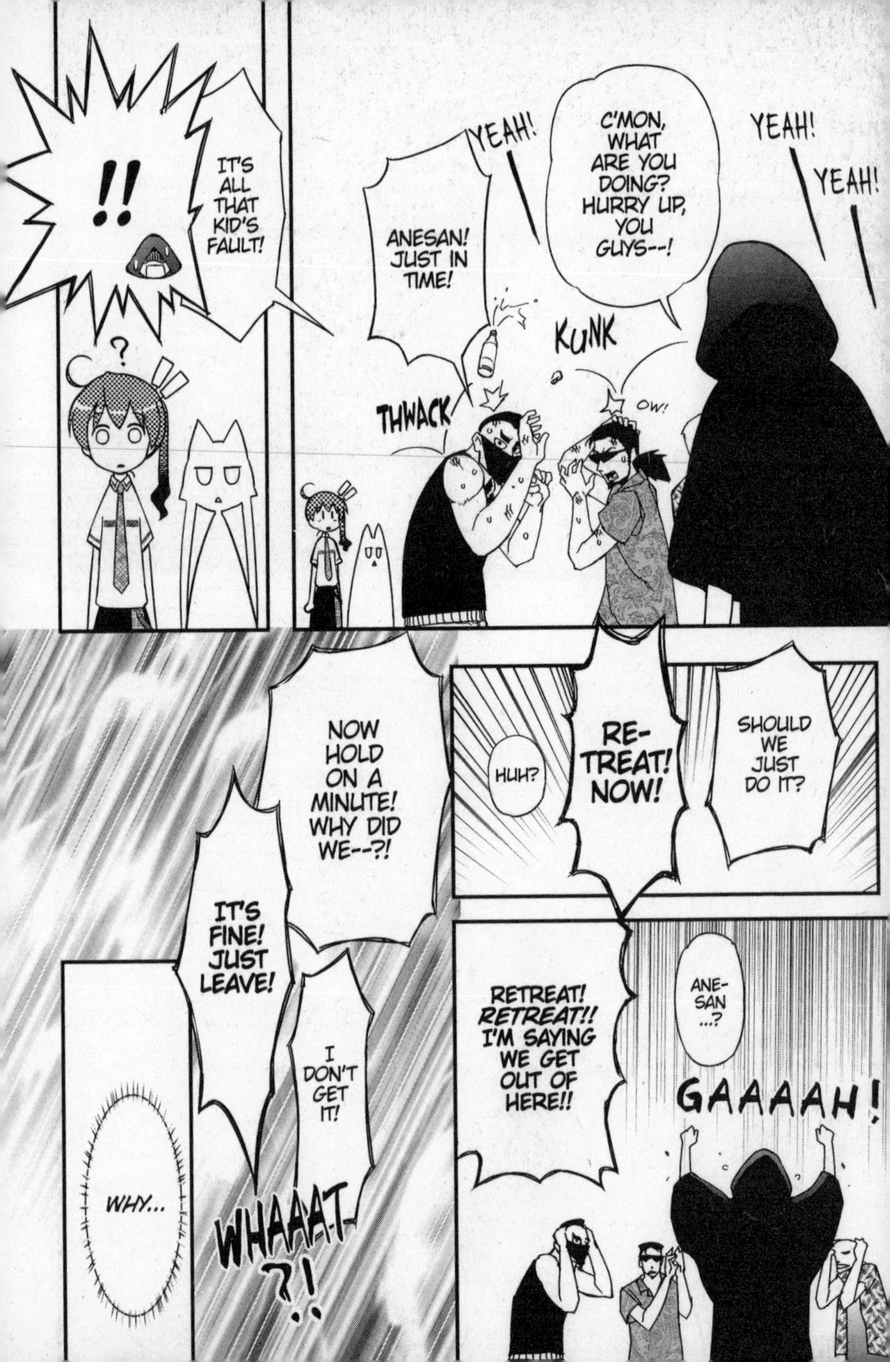

YEAH!
YEAH!
C'MON, WHAT ARE YOU DOING? HURRY UP, YOU GUYS--!
YEAH!
ANESAN! JUST IN TIME!
KUNK
OW!
THWACK
IT'S ALL THAT KID'S FAULT!
!!
?
SHOULD WE JUST DO IT?
RE-TREAT! NOW!
HUH?
ANE-SAN...?
GAAAAH!
RETREAT! RETREAT!! I'M SAYING WE GET OUT OF HERE!!
NOW HOLD ON A MINUTE! WHY DID WE--?!
IT'S FINE! JUST LEAVE!
I DON'T GET IT!
WHAAAT?!
WHY...

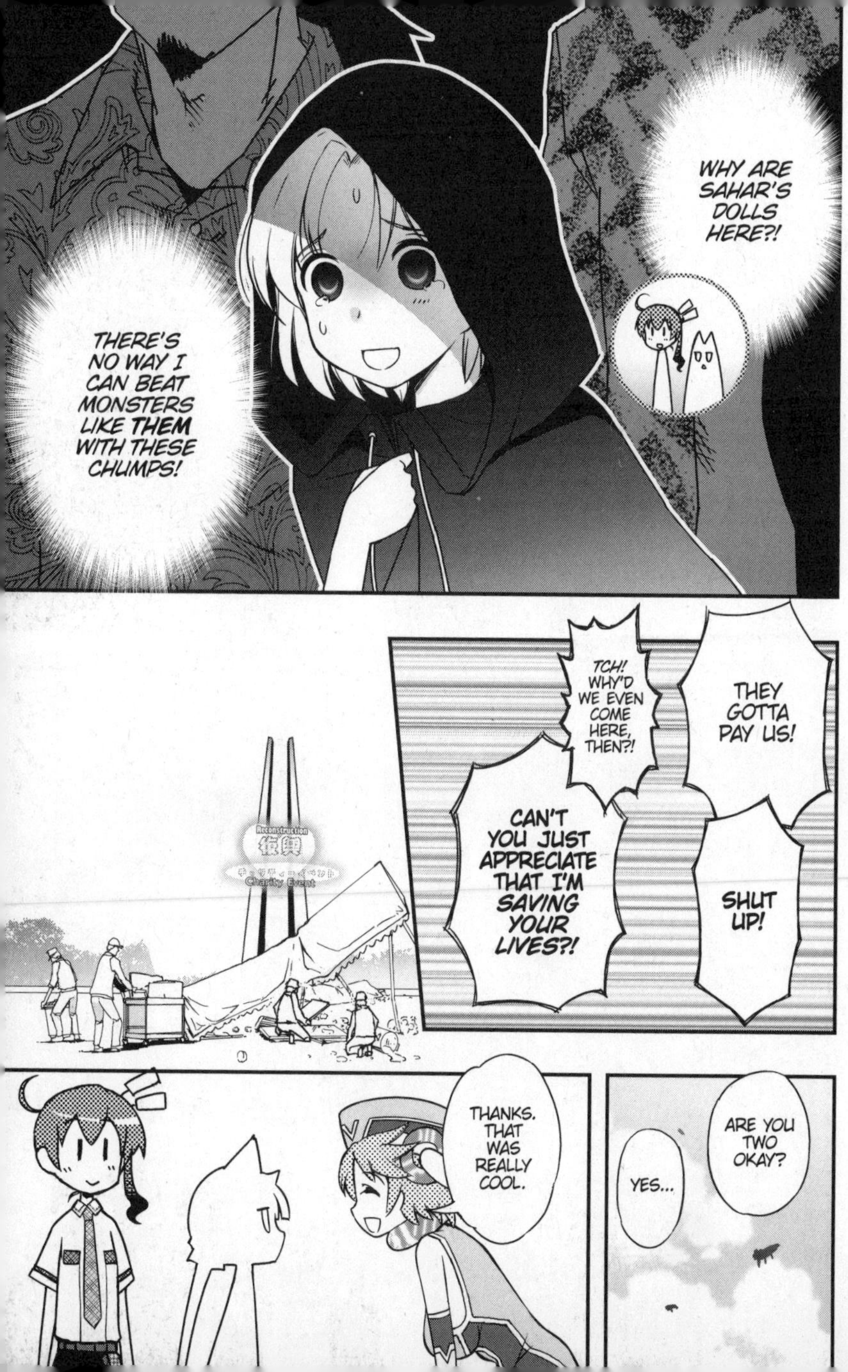
WHY ARE SAHAR'S DOLLS HERE?!
THERE'S NO WAY I CAN BEAT MONSTERS LIKE THEM WITH THESE CHUMPS!
THEY GOTTA PAY US!
TCH! WHY'D WE EVEN COME HERE, THEN?!
SHUT UP!
CAN'T YOU JUST APPRECIATE THAT I'M SAVING YOUR LIVES?!
Reconstruction
Charity Event
ARE YOU TWO OKAY?
YES...
THANKS. THAT WAS REALLY COOL.

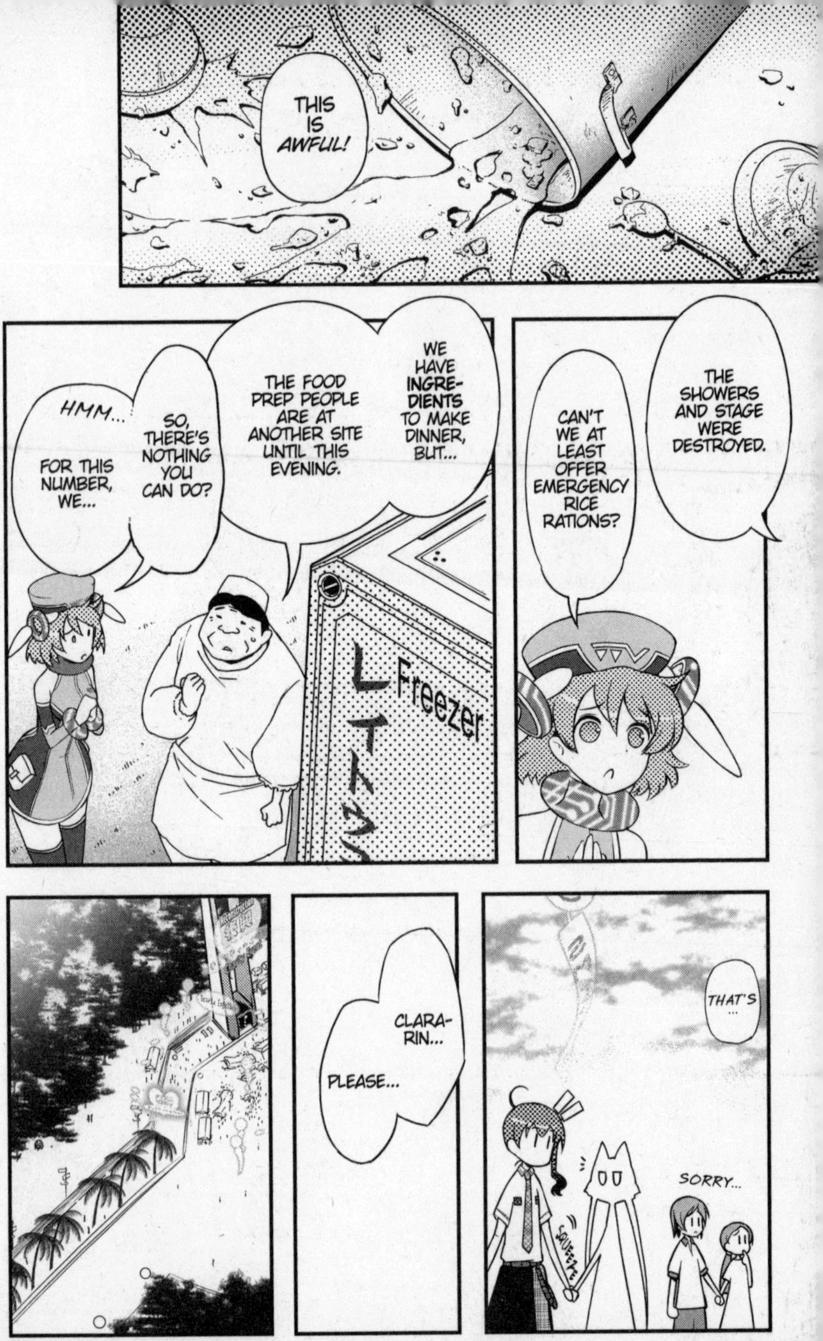
THIS IS AWFUL!
THE SHOWERS AND STAGE WERE DESTROYED.
CAN'T WE AT LEAST OFFER EMERGENCY RICE RATIONS?
WE HAVE INGREDIENTS TO MAKE DINNER, BUT...
THE FOOD PREP PEOPLE ARE AT ANOTHER SITE UNTIL THIS EVENING.
Freezer
SO, THERE'S NOTHING YOU CAN DO?
HMM... FOR THIS NUMBER, WE...
THAT'S...
SORRY...
SQUEEZE
CLARA-RIN... PLEASE...

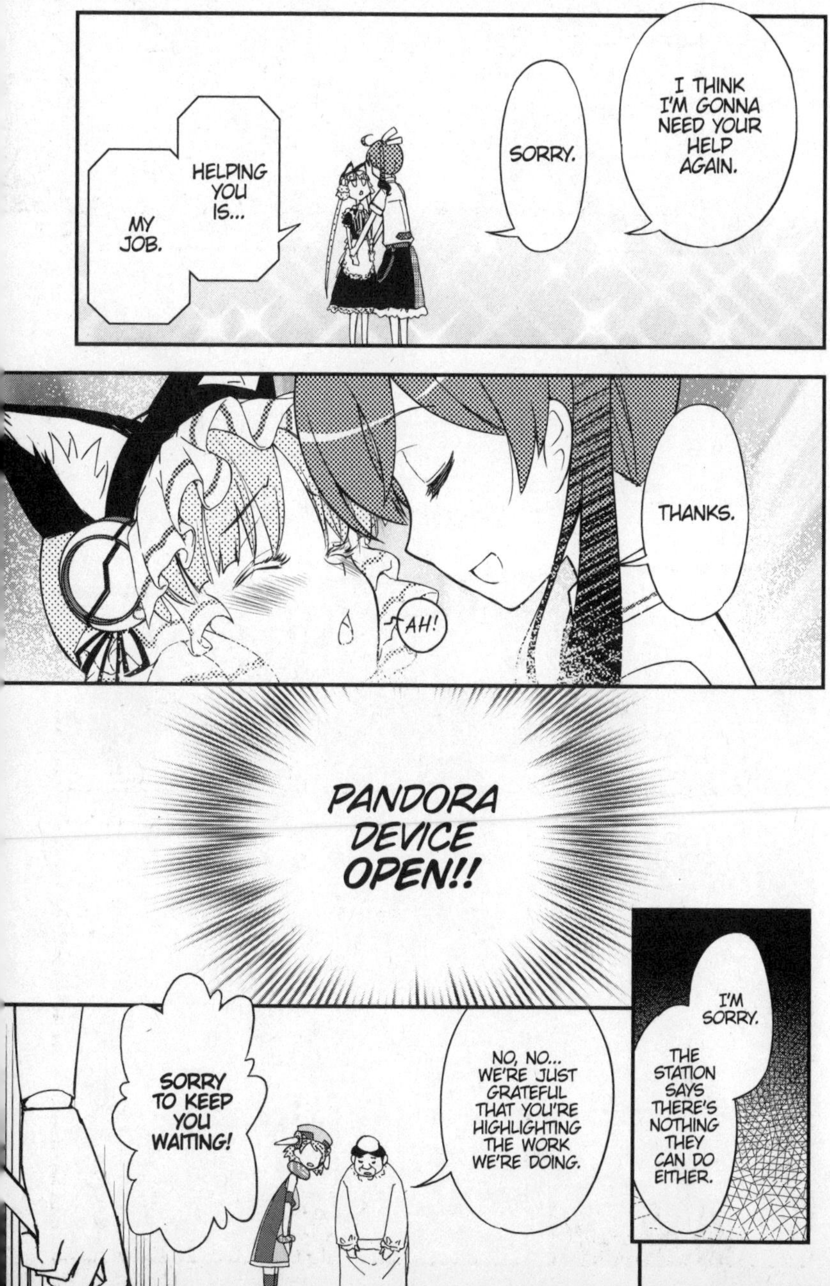
I THINK I'M GONNA NEED YOUR HELP AGAIN.
SORRY.
HELPING YOU IS...
MY JOB.
THANKS.
AH!
PANDORA DEVICE OPEN!!
I'M SORRY.
THE STATION SAYS THERE'S NOTHING THEY CAN DO EITHER.
NO, NO... WE'RE JUST GRATEFUL THAT YOU'RE HIGHLIGHTING THE WORK WE'RE DOING.
SORRY TO KEEP YOU WAITING!

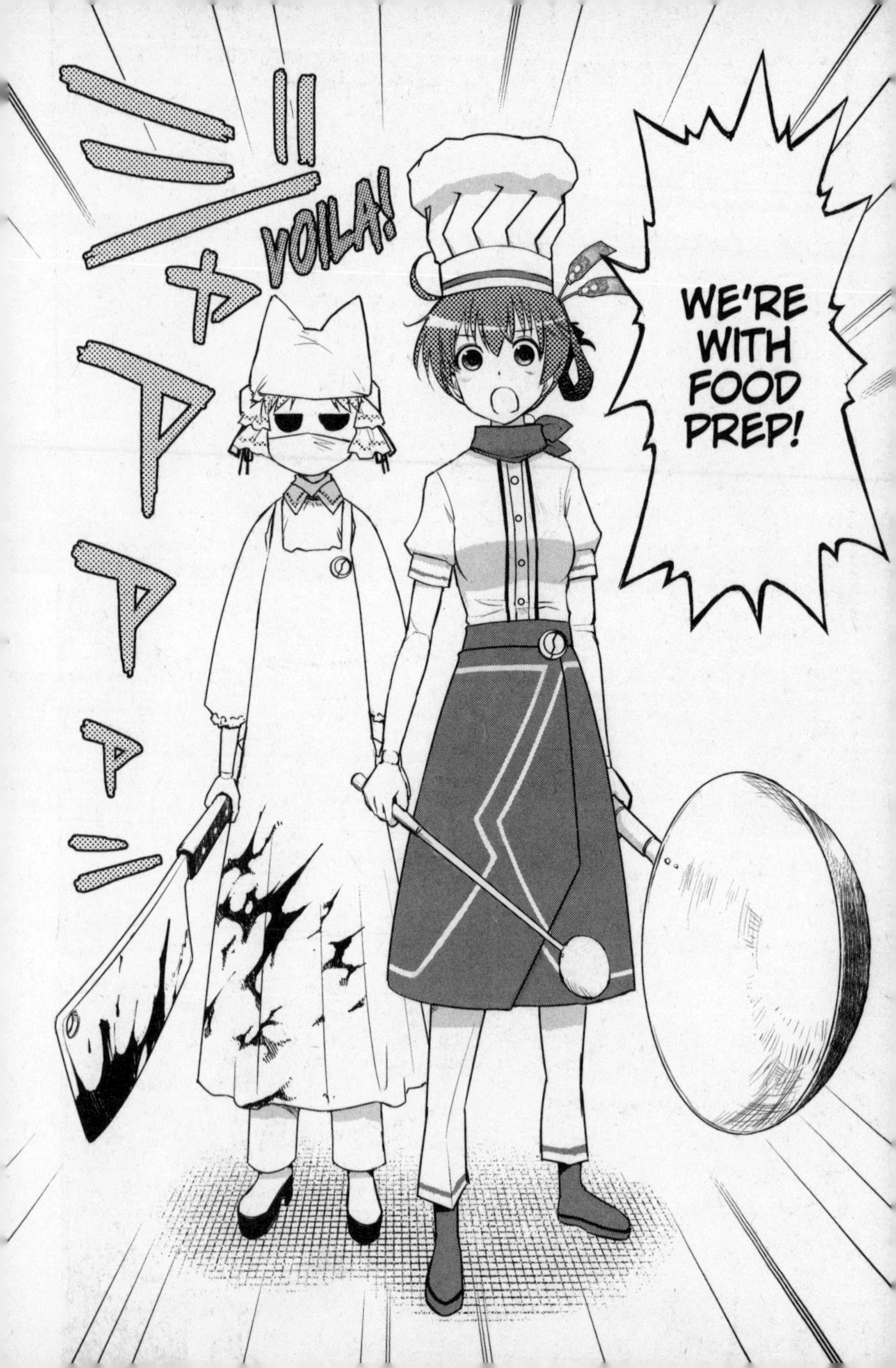
WE'RE WITH FOOD PREP!
VOILA!

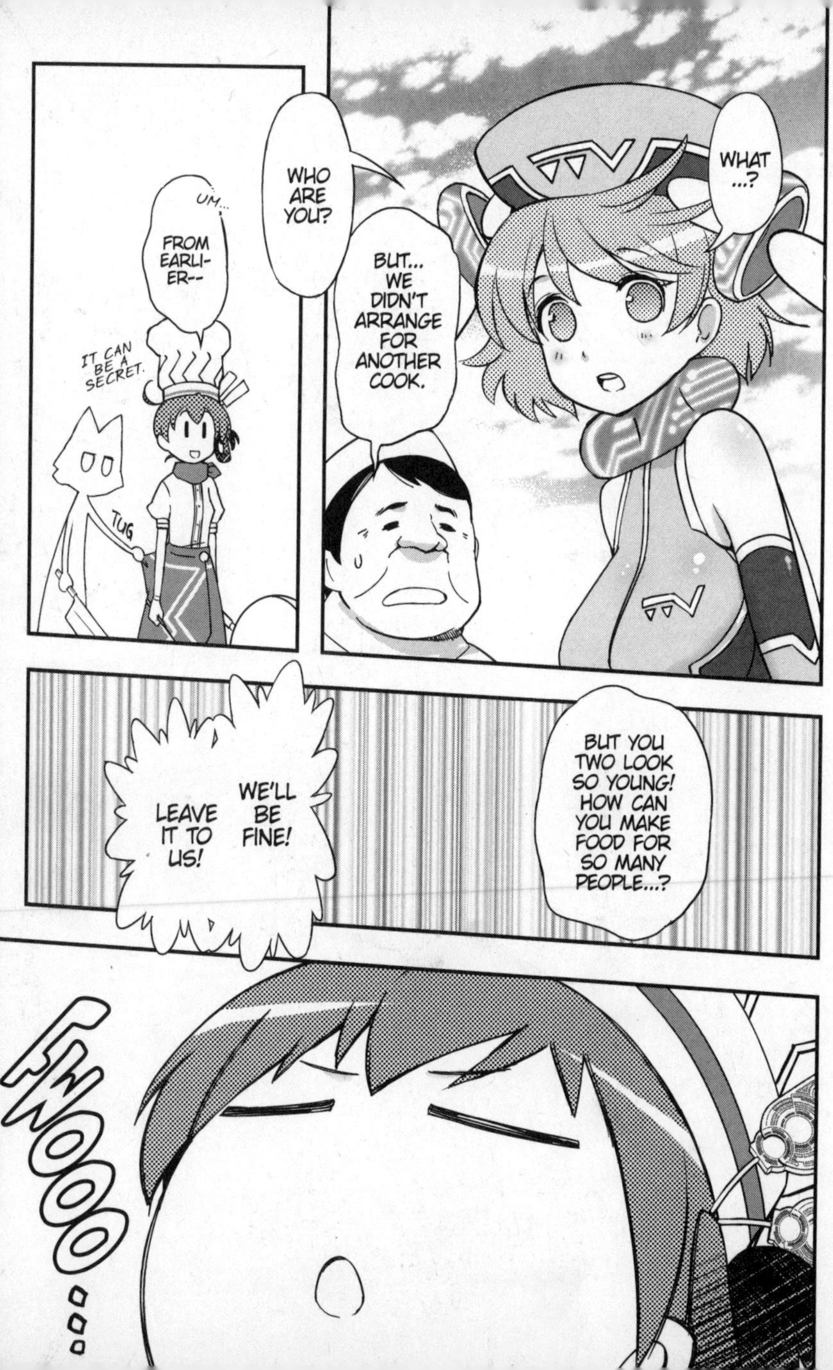
WHAT ...?
WHO ARE YOU?
BUT... WE DIDN'T ARRANGE FOR ANOTHER COOK.
UM...
FROM EARLI- ER--
IT CAN BE A SECRET.
TUG
BUT YOU TWO LOOK SO YOUNG! HOW CAN YOU MAKE FOOD FOR SO MANY PEOPLE...?
WE'LL BE FINE!
LEAVE IT TO US!
FWOOO...

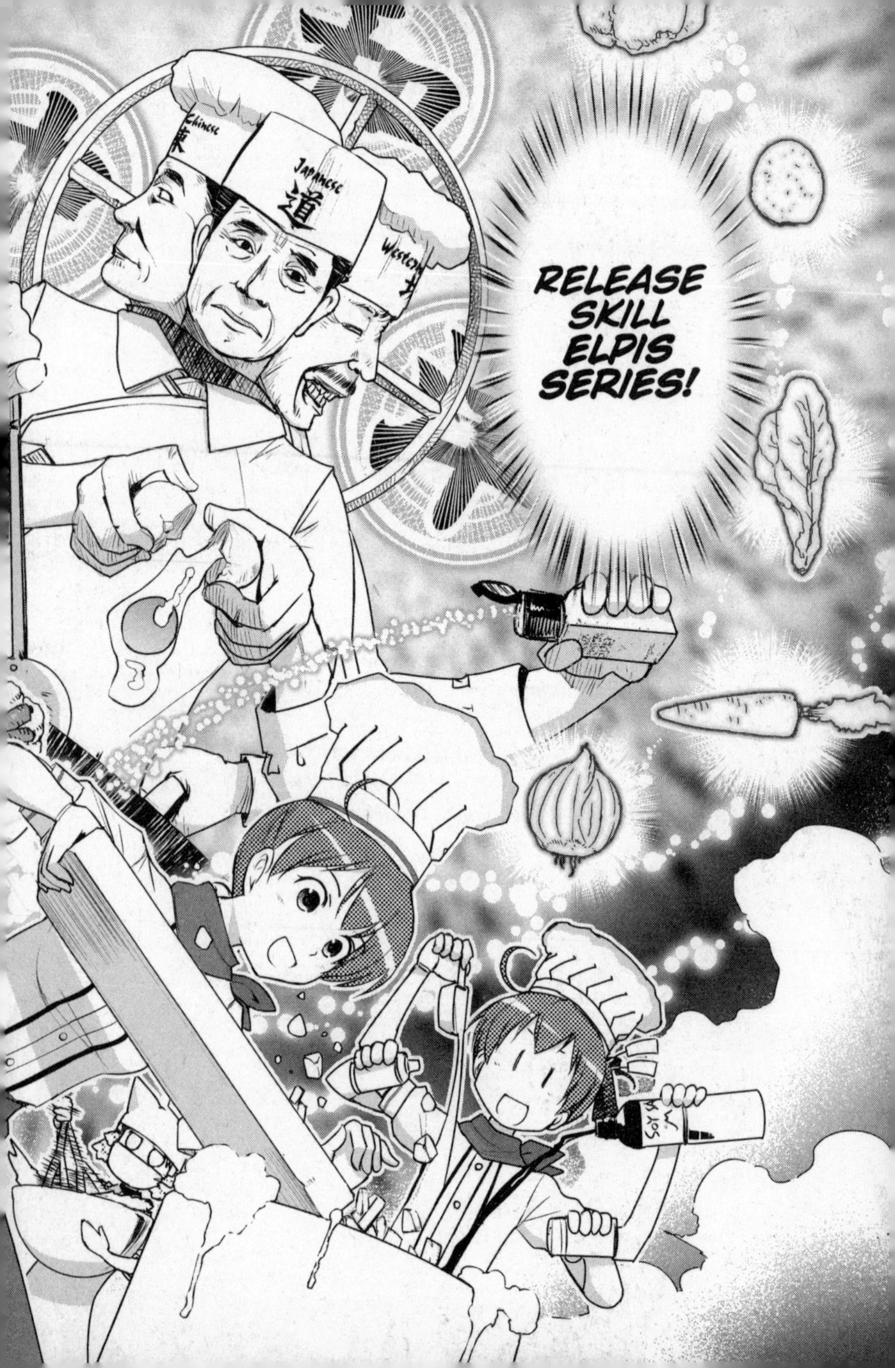
RELEASE SKILL ELPIS SERIES!
Japanese
道
Chinese

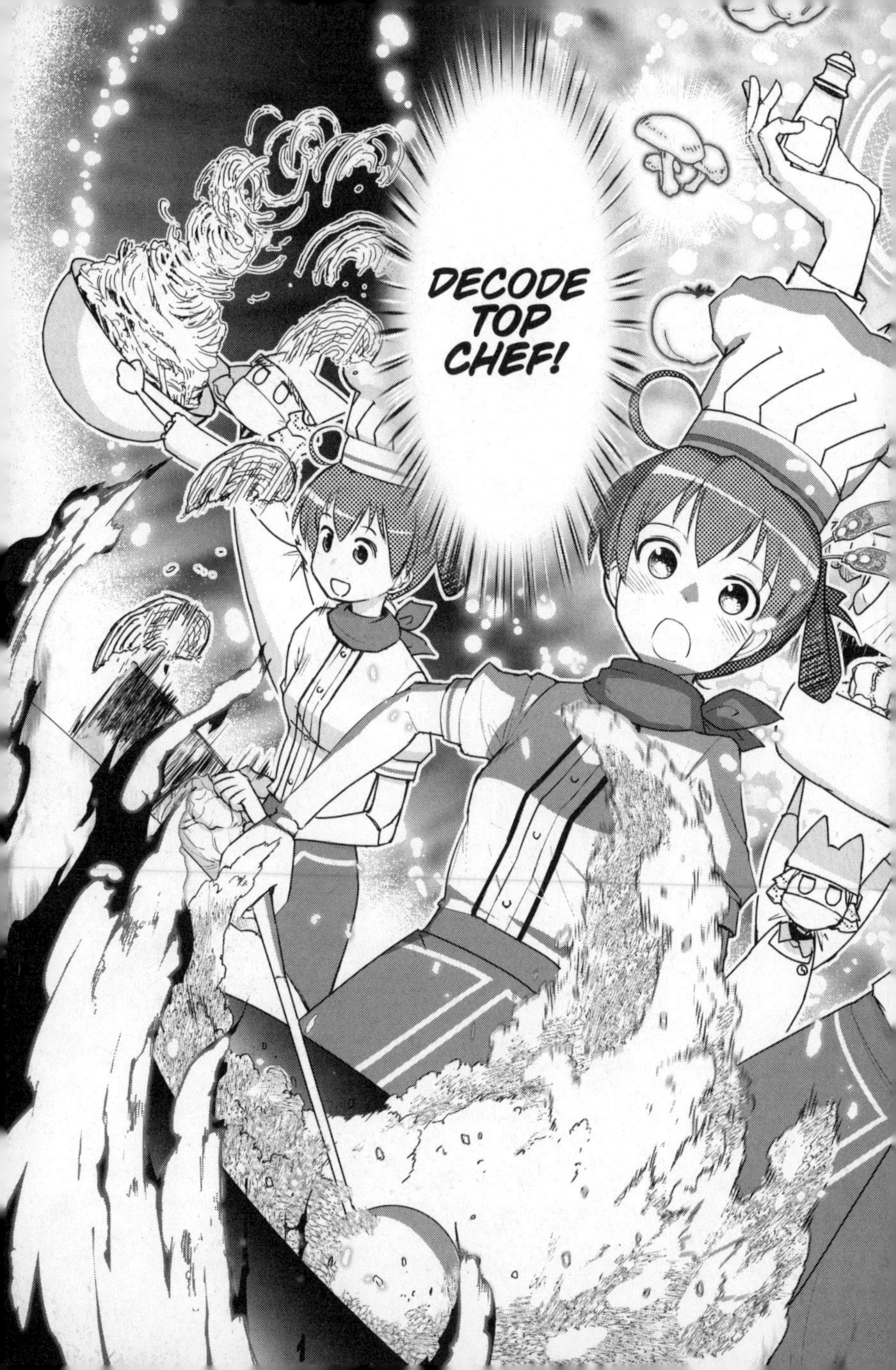
DECODE
TOP
CHEF!

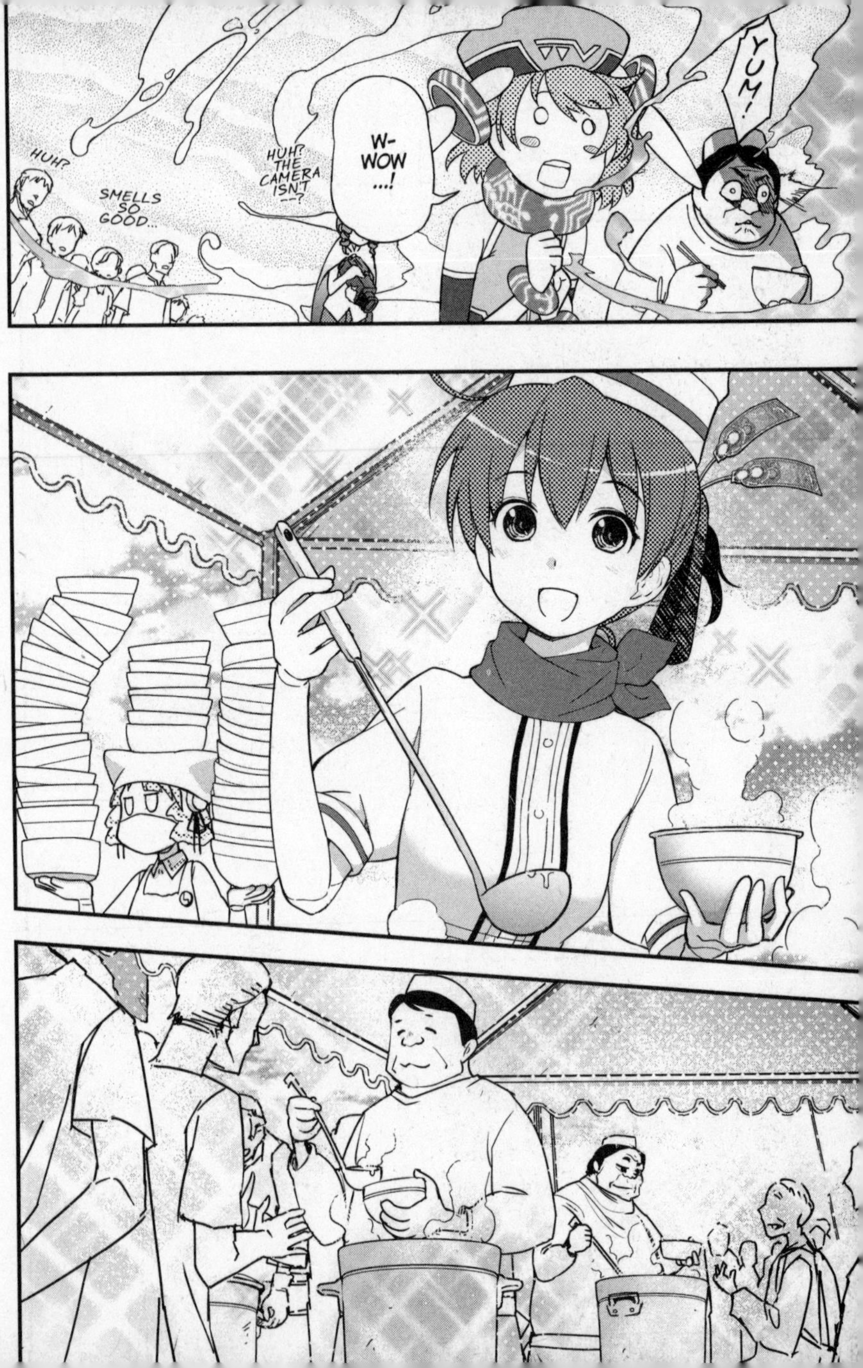
YUM!
W-WOW ...!
HUH? THE CAMERA ISN'T --?
SMELLS SO GOOD...
HUH?

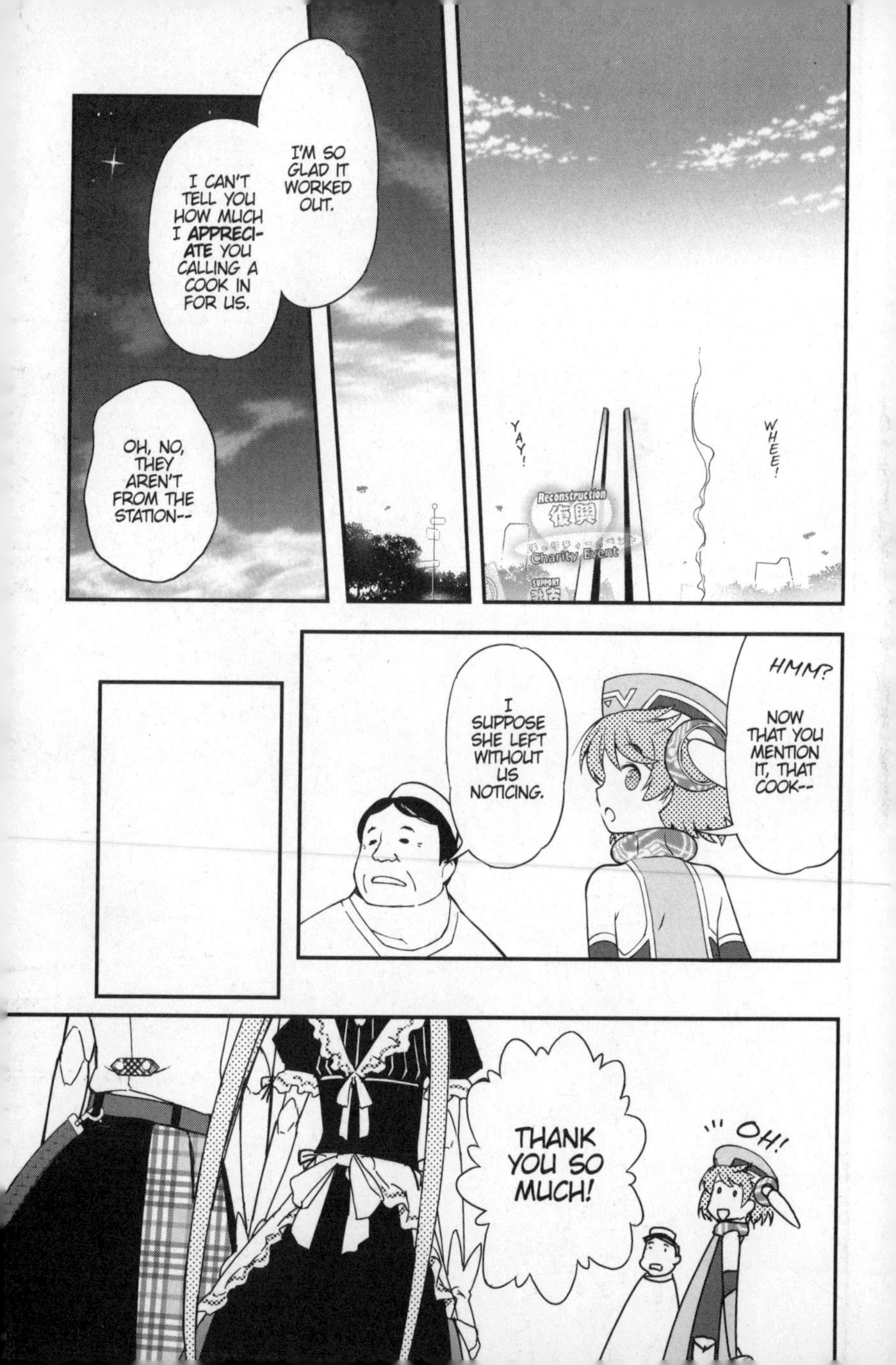
WHEE!
YAY!
Reconstruction
復興
Charity Event
SUPPORT
I'M SO GLAD IT WORKED OUT.
I CAN'T TELL YOU HOW MUCH I APPRECIATE YOU CALLING A COOK IN FOR US.
OH, NO, THEY AREN'T FROM THE STATION--
HMM?
NOW THAT YOU MENTION IT, THAT COOK--
I SUPPOSE SHE LEFT WITHOUT US NOTICING.
OH!
THANK YOU SO MUCH!

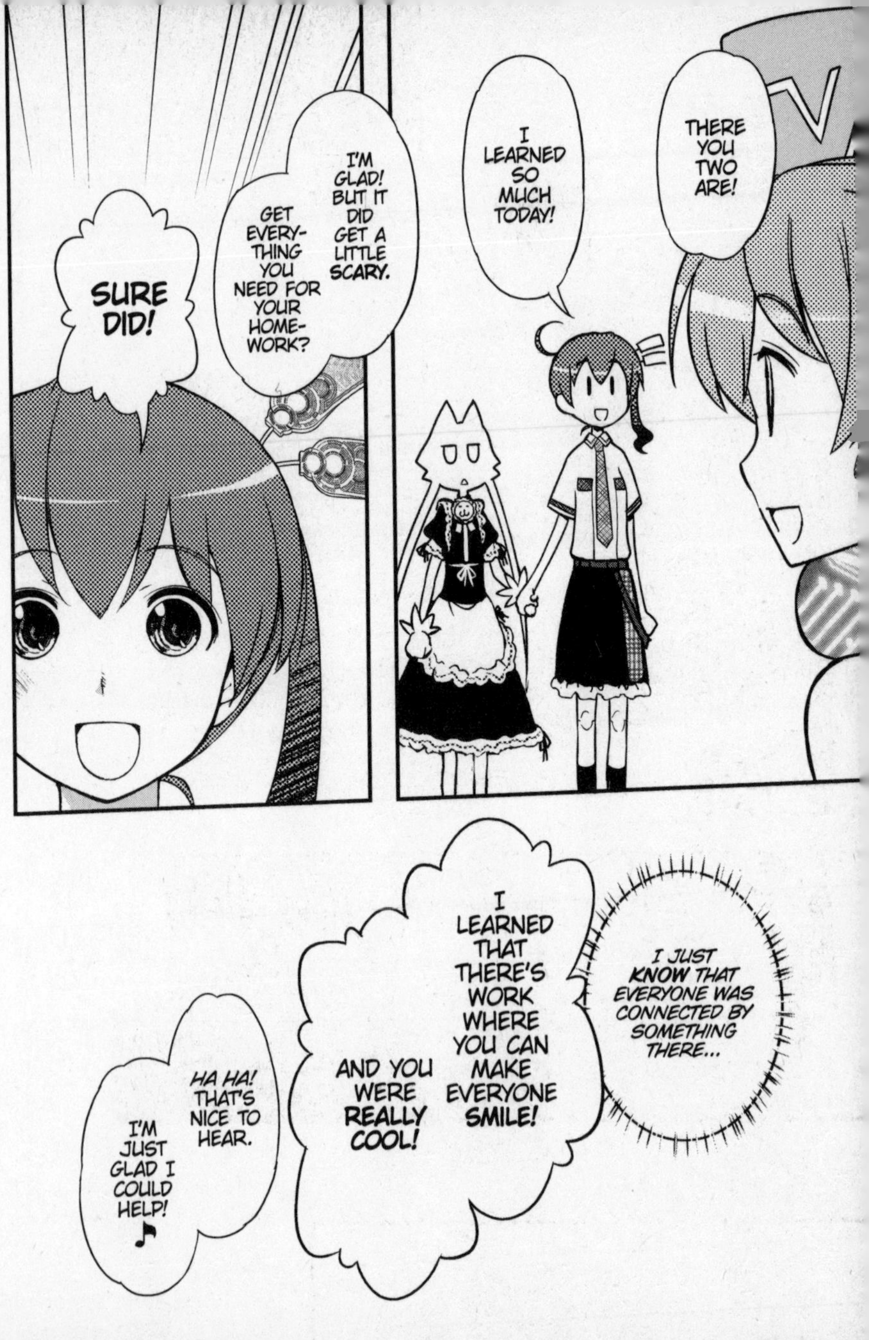
THERE YOU TWO ARE!
I LEARNED SO MUCH TODAY!
I'M GLAD! BUT IT DID GET A LITTLE SCARY.
GET EVERY-THING YOU NEED FOR YOUR HOME-WORK?
SURE DID!
I JUST KNOW THAT EVERYONE WAS CONNECTED BY SOMETHING THERE...
I LEARNED THAT THERE'S WORK WHERE YOU CAN MAKE EVERYONE SMILE!
AND YOU WERE REALLY COOL!
HA HA! THAT'S NICE TO HEAR.
I'M JUST GLAD I COULD HELP! ♪

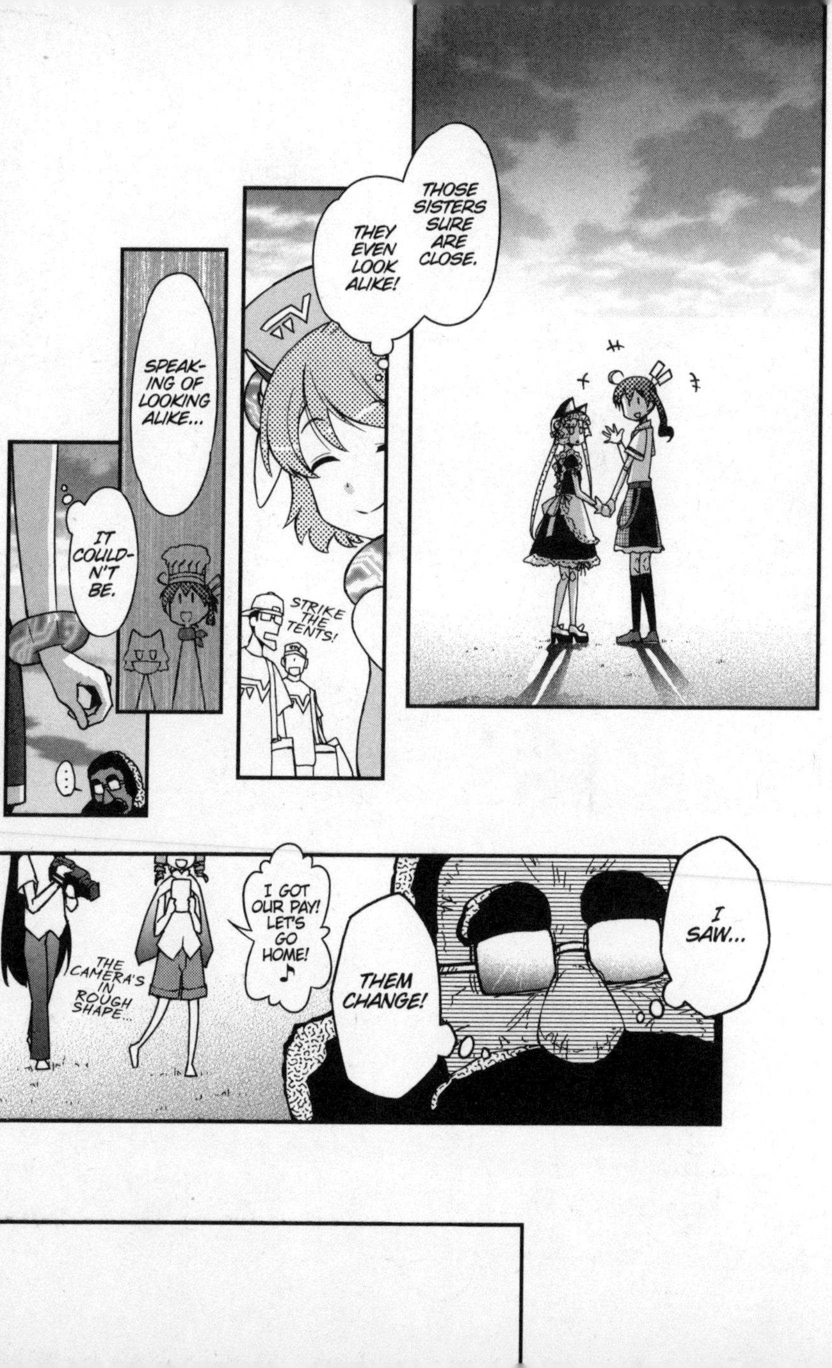
THOSE SISTERS SURE ARE CLOSE.
THEY EVEN LOOK ALIKE!
STRIKE THE TENTS!
SPEAK- ING OF LOOKING ALIKE...
IT COULD- N'T BE.
...
I SAW...
THEM CHANGE!
I GOT OUR PAY! LET'S GO HOME! ♪
THE CAMERA'S IN ROUGH SHAPE...

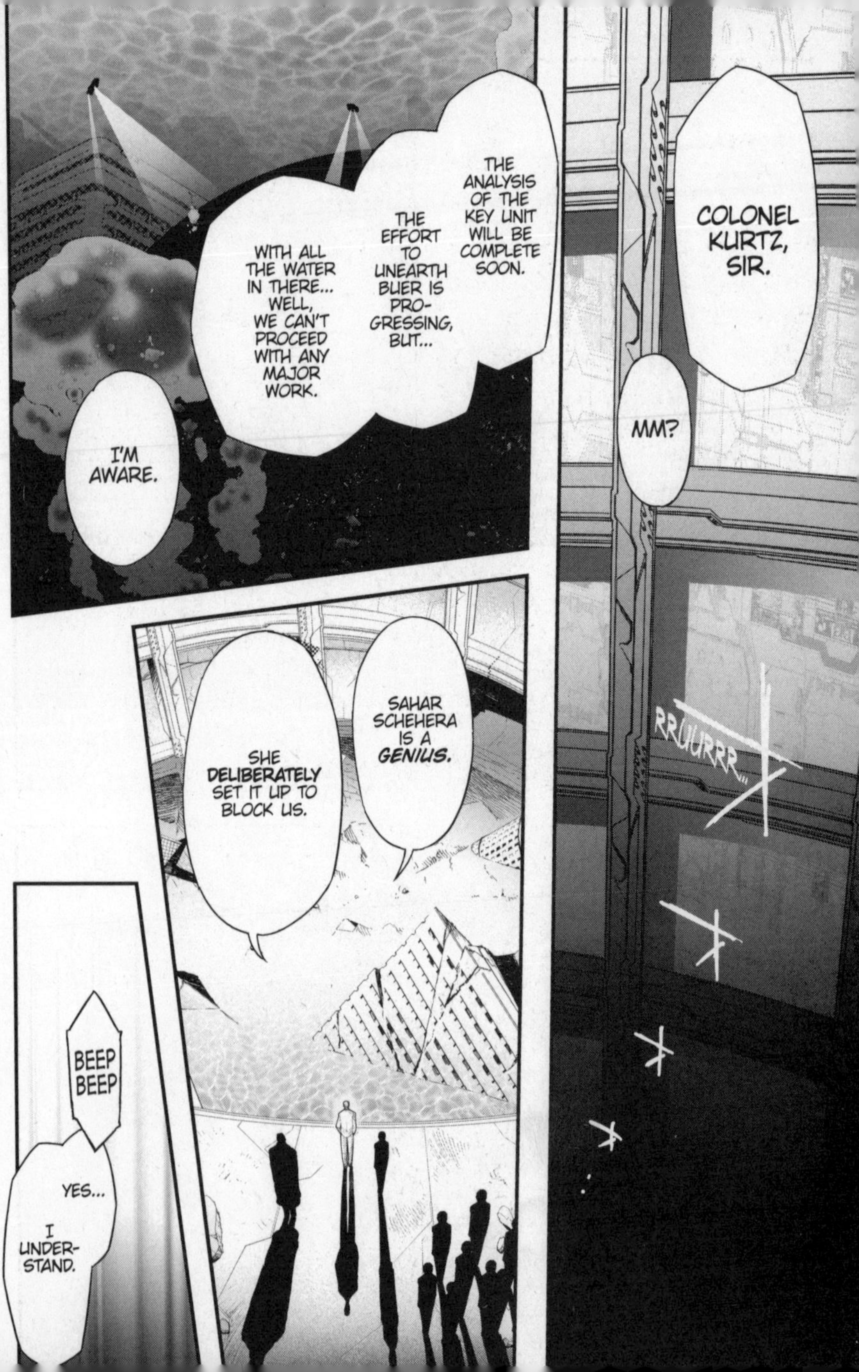
COLONEL KURTZ, SIR.
MM?
RRUURRR...
THE ANALYSIS OF THE KEY UNIT WILL BE COMPLETE SOON.
THE EFFORT TO UNEARTH BUER IS PRO-GRESSING, BUT...
WITH ALL THE WATER IN THERE... WELL, WE CAN'T PROCEED WITH ANY MAJOR WORK.
I'M AWARE.
SAHAR SCHEHERA IS A **GENIUS.**
SHE **DELIBERATELY** SET IT UP TO BLOCK US.
BEEP BEEP
YES...
I UNDER-STAND.

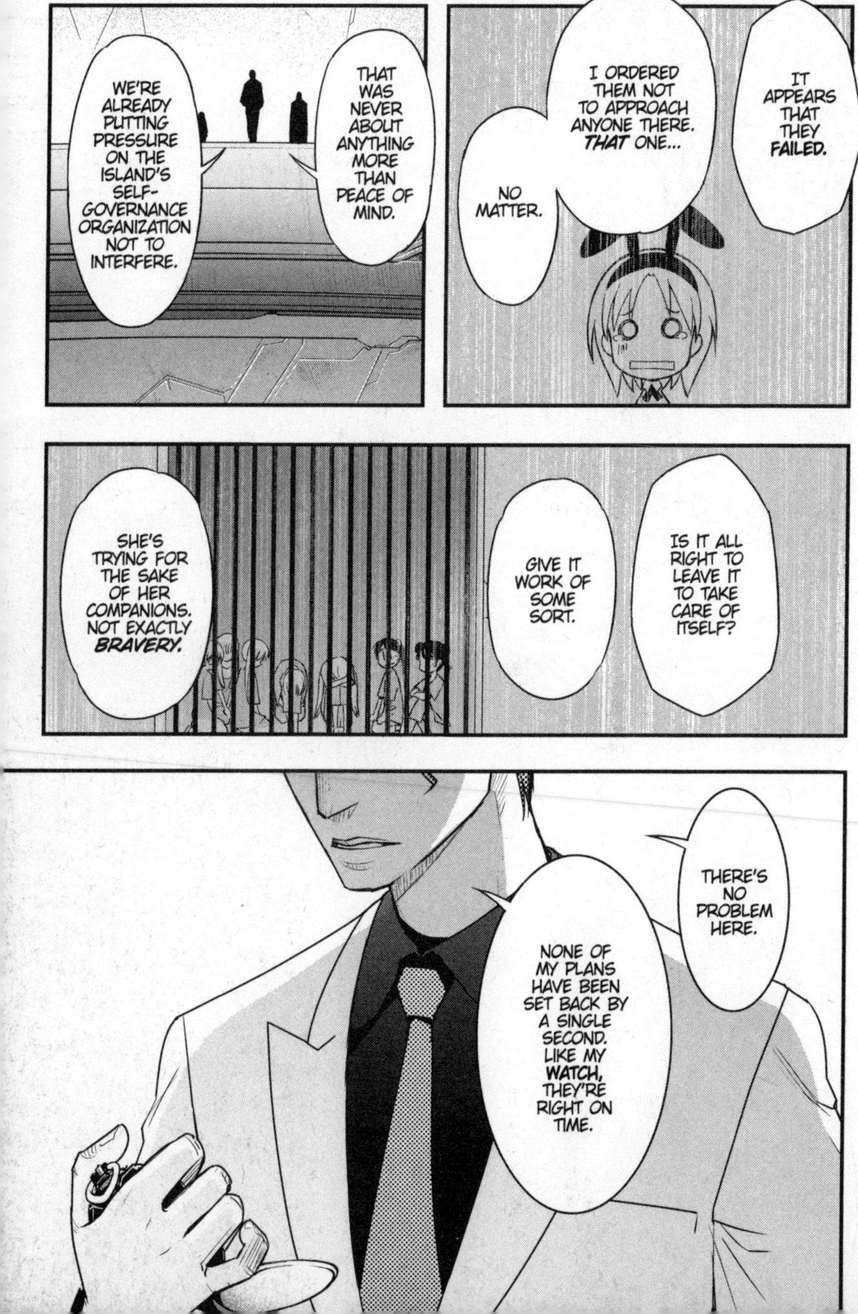
IT APPEARS THAT THEY FAILED.
I ORDERED THEM NOT TO APPROACH ANYONE THERE. THAT ONE...
NO MATTER.
THAT WAS NEVER ABOUT ANYTHING MORE THAN PEACE OF MIND.
WE'RE ALREADY PUTTING PRESSURE ON THE ISLAND'S SELF-GOVERNANCE ORGANIZATION NOT TO INTERFERE.
IS IT ALL RIGHT TO LEAVE IT TO TAKE CARE OF ITSELF?
GIVE IT WORK OF SOME SORT.
SHE'S TRYING FOR THE SAKE OF HER COMPANIONS. NOT EXACTLY BRAVERY.
THERE'S NO PROBLEM HERE.
NONE OF MY PLANS HAVE BEEN SET BACK BY A SINGLE SECOND. LIKE MY WATCH, THEY'RE RIGHT ON TIME.

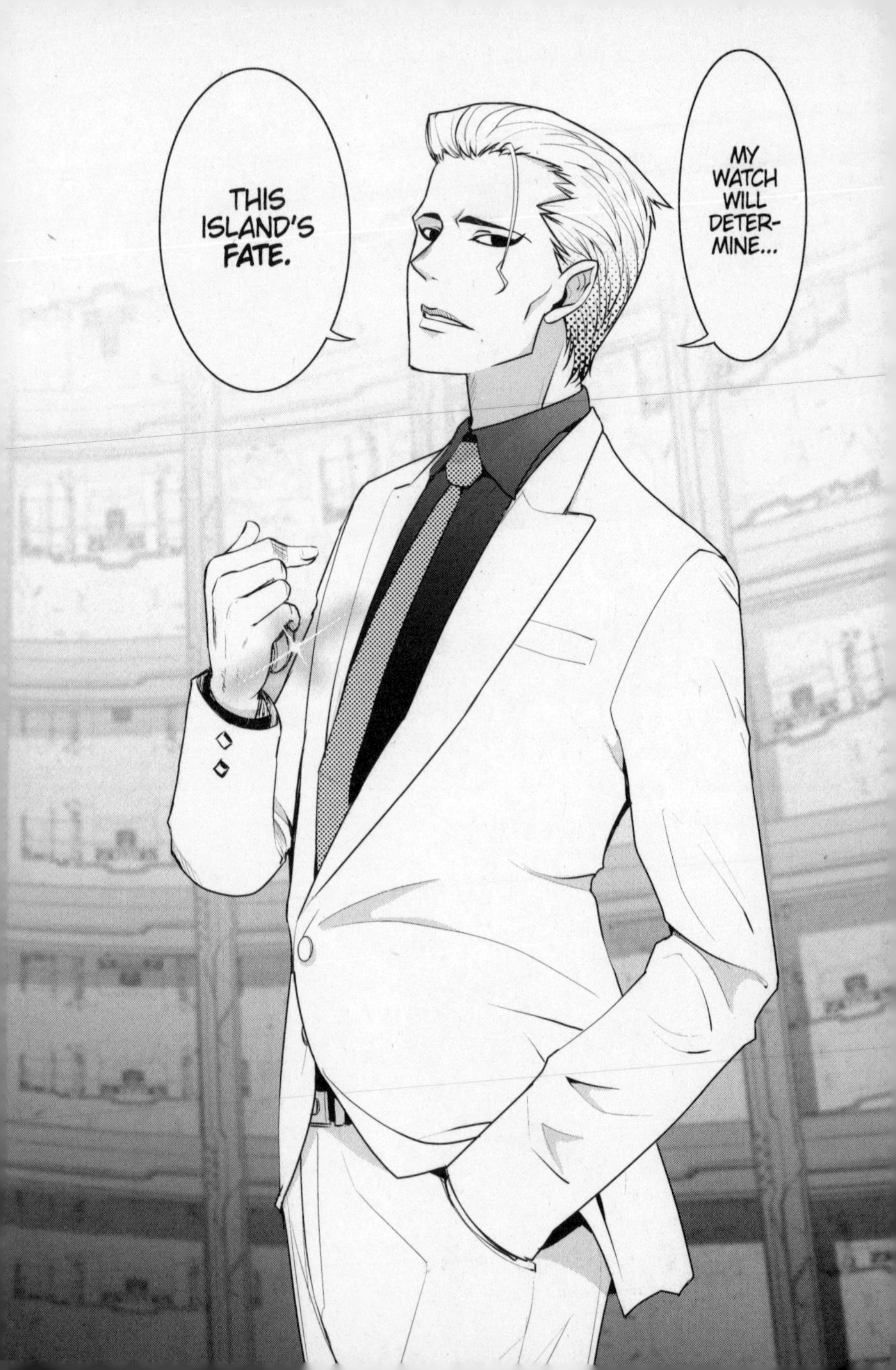
MY WATCH WILL DETERMINE...
THIS ISLAND'S FATE.

···TO BE CONTINUED

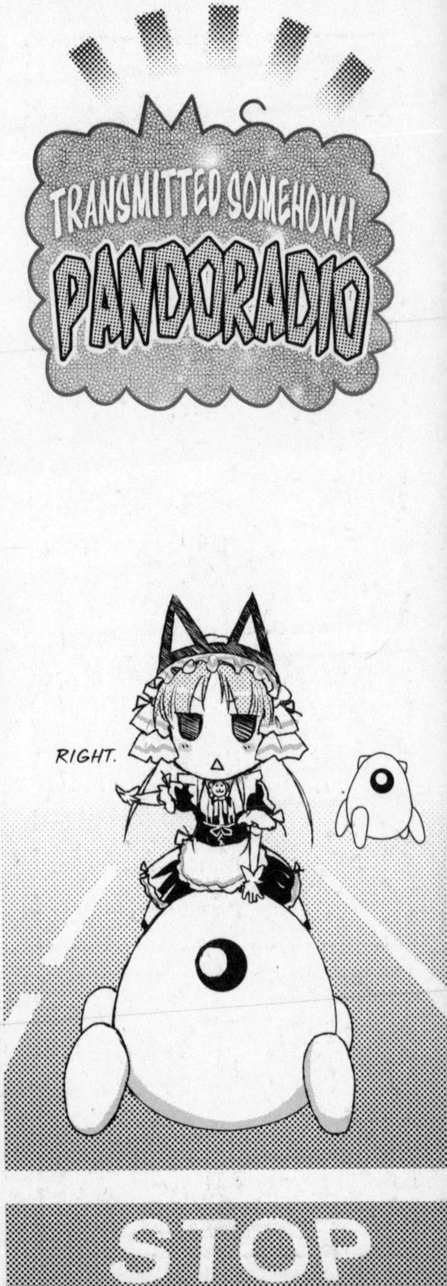
TRANSMITTED SOMEHOW!
PANDORADIO
RIGHT.
STOP

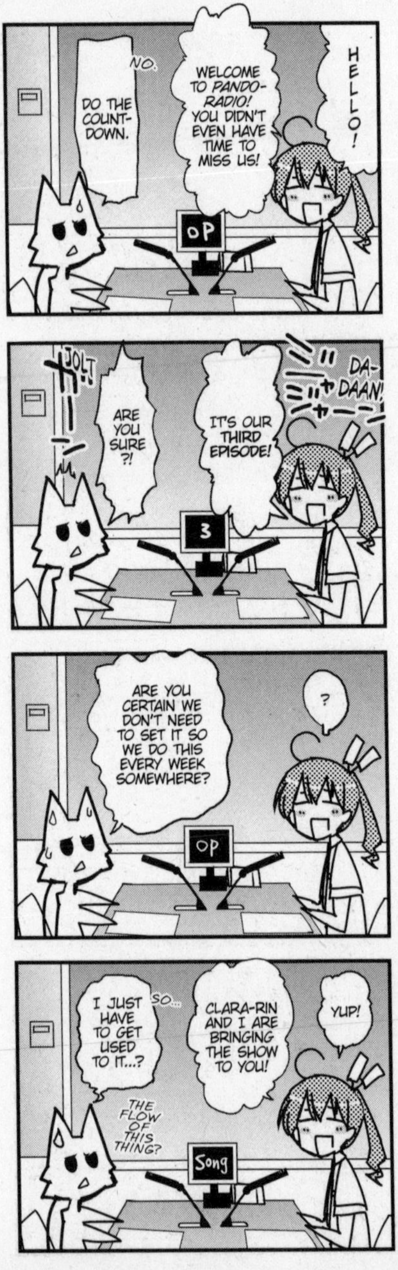
HELLO!
WELCOME TO PANDO-RADIO! YOU DIDN'T EVEN HAVE TIME TO MISS US!
NO.
DO THE COUNT-DOWN.
OP
DA-DAAN!
IT'S OUR THIRD EPISODE!
JOLT
ARE YOU SURE ?!
3
?
ARE YOU CERTAIN WE DON'T NEED TO SET IT SO WE DO THIS EVERY WEEK SOMEWHERE?
OP
YUP!
CLARA-RIN AND I ARE BRINGING THE SHOW TO YOU!
SO...
I JUST HAVE TO GET USED TO IT...?
THE FLOW OF THIS THING?
Song

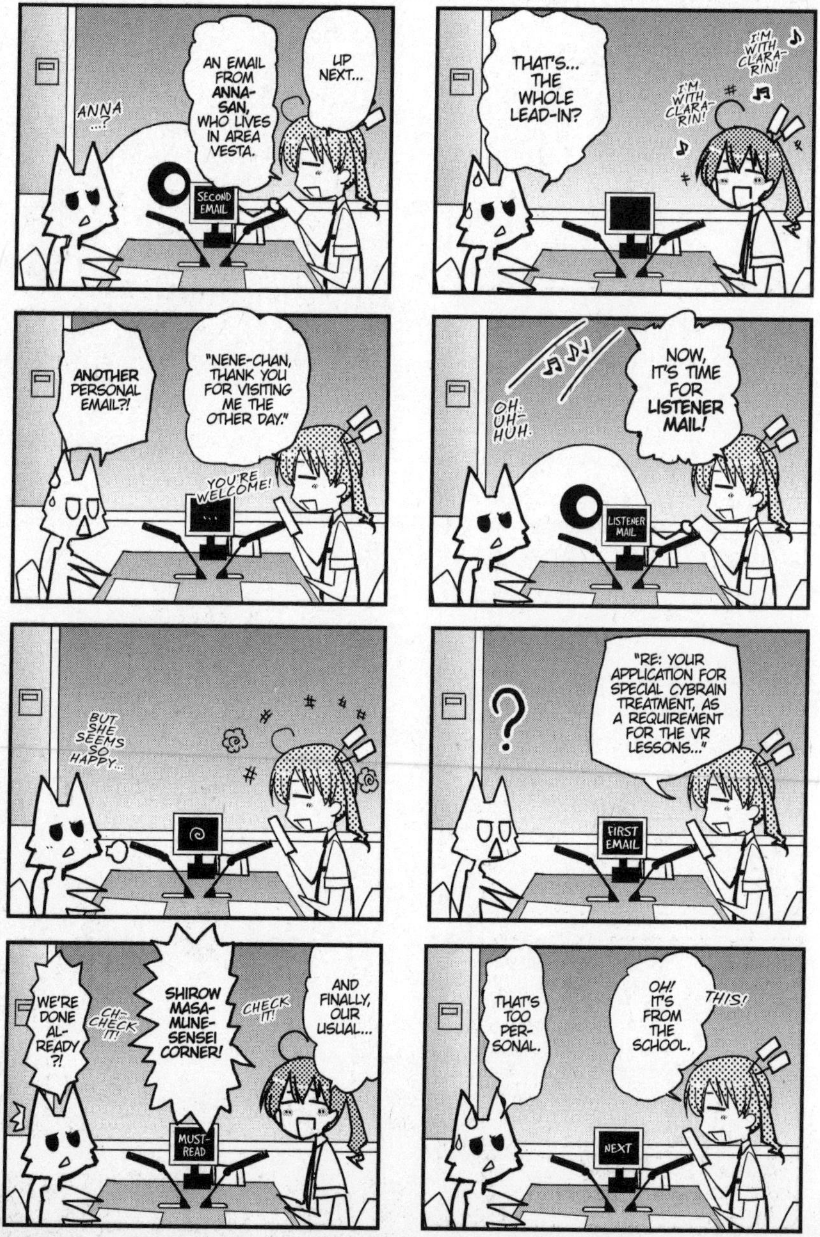
I'M WITH CLARA-RIN!
I'M WITH CLARA-RIN!
THAT'S... THE WHOLE LEAD-IN?
NOW, IT'S TIME FOR LISTENER MAIL!
OH. UH-HUH.
LISTENER MAIL
"RE: YOUR APPLICATION FOR SPECIAL CYBRAIN TREATMENT, AS A REQUIREMENT FOR THE VR LESSONS..."
?
FIRST EMAIL
OH! IT'S FROM THE SCHOOL.
THIS!
THAT'S TOO PERSONAL.
NEXT
UP NEXT...
AN EMAIL FROM ANNA-SAN, WHO LIVES IN AREA VESTA.
ANNA...?
SECOND EMAIL
"NENE-CHAN, THANK YOU FOR VISITING ME THE OTHER DAY."
ANOTHER PERSONAL EMAIL?!
YOU'RE WELCOME!
...
BUT SHE SEEMS SO HAPPY...
AND FINALLY, OUR USUAL...
CHECK IT!
SHIROW MASAMUNE-SENSEI CORNER!
CH-CHECK IT!
WE'RE DONE AL-READY?!
MUST-READ

ORIGINAL CONCEPT DESIGN NOTES

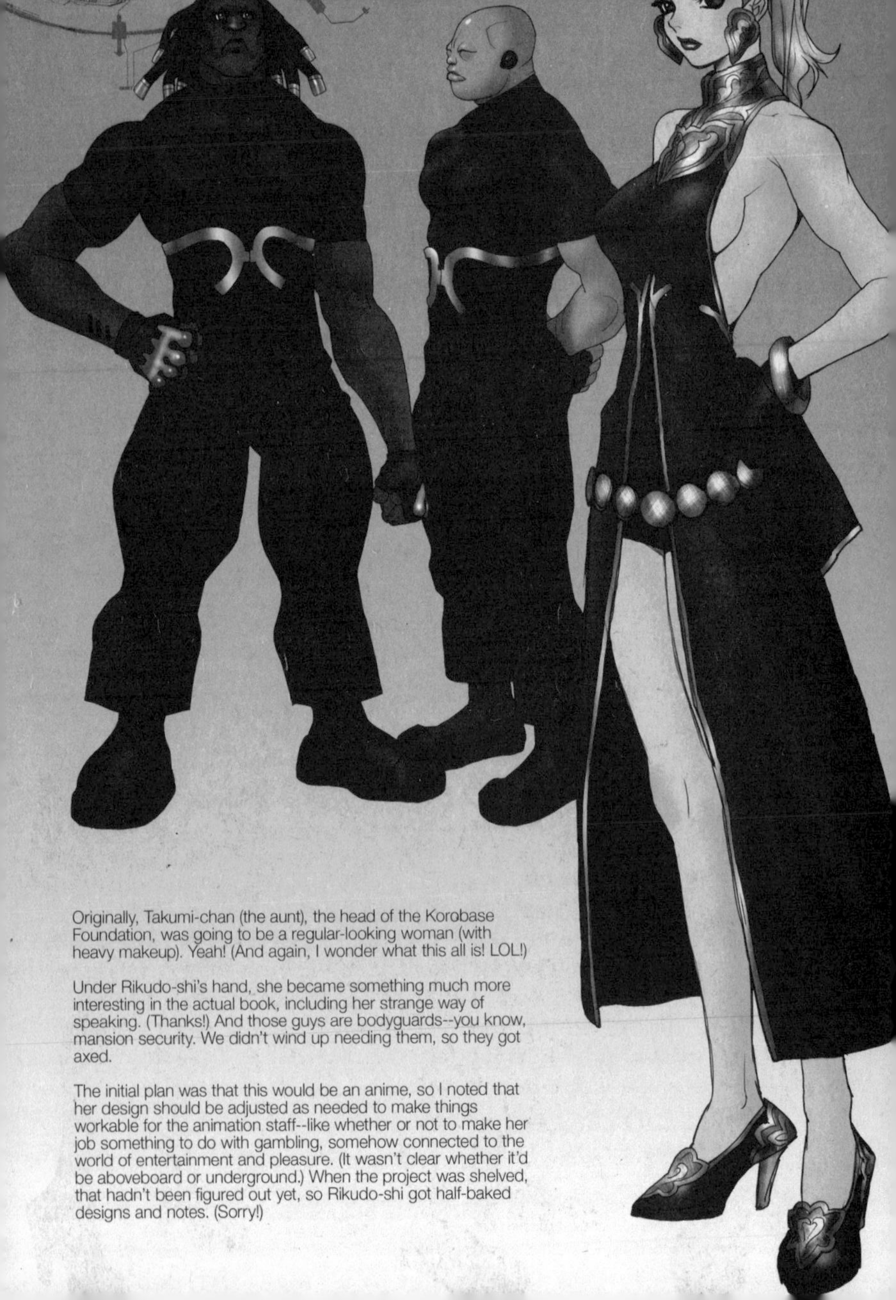

Originally, Takumi-chan (the aunt), the head of the Korobase Foundation, was going to be a regular-looking woman (with heavy makeup). Yeah! (And again, I wonder what this all is! LOL!)

Under Rikudo-shi's hand, she became something much more interesting in the actual book, including her strange way of speaking. (Thanks!) And those guys are bodyguards--you know, mansion security. We didn't wind up needing them, so they got axed.

The initial plan was that this would be an anime, so I noted that her design should be adjusted as needed to make things workable for the animation staff--like whether or not to make her job something to do with gambling, somehow connected to the world of entertainment and pleasure. (It wasn't clear whether it'd be aboveboard or underground.) When the project was shelved, that hadn't been figured out yet, so Rikudo-shi got half-baked designs and notes. (Sorry!)

ORIGINAL CHARACTER DESIGN SKETCHES

And these are character sketches that Rikudo-shi will be seeing for the very first time in this book. (What's with that?) Here's my sketch for the media idol character "Vli--(*whump!*)" from around when we were doing the initial anime plan. At the bottom, are the sketches for the cameraperson and the producer.

Vli--(*whump!*) has a proper name, of course, but since Rikudo-shi hasn't used her name in the manga so far, I'll make a point of not using it here.

If I change the names and details of these characters and make them gunners on a massive tank in another anime project (frozen to death) or include them in the project specs for *Ghost in the Shell: Arise* by changing their ages, these end up being nomadic designs. (LOL!)

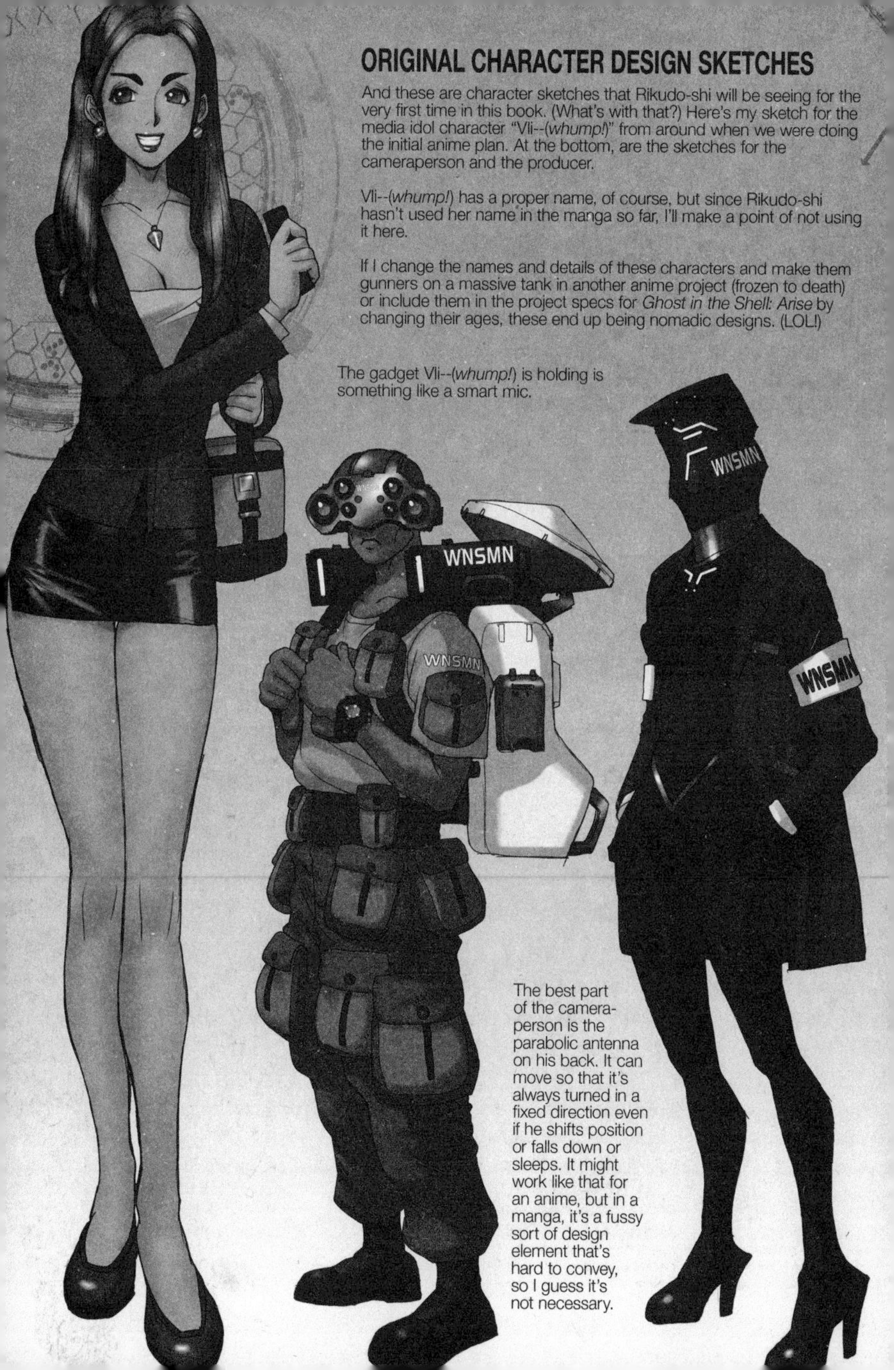
WNSMN
WNSMN
WNSMN
WNSMN

The gadget Vli--(*whump!*) is holding is something like a smart mic.

The best part of the camera-person is the parabolic antenna on his back. It can move so that it's always turned in a fixed direction even if he shifts position or falls down or sleeps. It might work like that for an anime, but in a manga, it's a fussy sort of design element that's hard to convey, so I guess it's not necessary.

Greetings! (For the third time!)

There's a note included with my original design for the aunt:
"She sacrificed everything on the altar of her own pleasure.
When you take that away, there's nothing left but laziness."

She makes her home in the top ten floors of a high-tech skyscraper (called "Penthouse Mirage") in the heart of the city. Naturally, as she's the most famous, gorgeous, bubbly, high-class millionaire in the world, she owns the place...but if you strip all that away, she's nothing but an exhausted, good-for-nothing, selfish woman who can't do anything but stuff her face and shout "what the hell?!" That was the initial design, but she actually wound up being a fairly capable person with a special genius (and way of speaking) in the book. (LOL!) She's a cheating, clever bad type, but thanks to Rikudo-shi's art and style, I think she's emerged as a charming character who's too distinctive and cute to hate. (Many thanks!)

I won't mention anything about Vli--(*whump!*) just yet. In the original plan, she had an important role in advancing the story, and she added a key element that directly related to the themes, but depending on where she pops up and what she does as the manga progresses, her role will presumably be reassessed by the people involved.

In the second chapter of *Ghost in the Shell: Arise*, another work that came into being around the same time, a "Pandora" factor appears...but the existence of these related components doesn't mean I have a grand plan or anything. Basically, I think I messed up and accidentally gave them the same name. But because I messed up, people related to *Ghost in the Shell: Arise* and people involved with *Pandora in the Crimson Shell* will probably wonder whether or not they're related somehow in the areas where there are no rights-related issues.

Anyway, it doesn't look there'll be any problems, and I don't really care if there's no movement or connection at the moment. And even if they are related, you probably won't get to see Rikudo-shi's idea of the "baked cybrain" in *Ghost in the Shell: Arise*, with its very different style.

August 30, 2013
Shirow Masamune

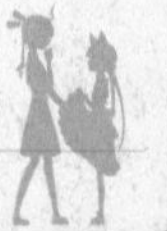

原案 》 SHIROW MASAMUNE

GHOST URN 03